The Healing of Nations

The Healing of Nations

The Promise and Limits of Political Forgiveness

Mark R. Amstutz

ROWMAN & LITTLEFIELD PUBLISHERS, INC.
Lanham • Boulder • New York • Toronto • Oxford

For DRA, as always

ROWMAN & LITTLEFIELD PUBLISHERS, INC.

Published in the United States of America
by Rowman & Littlefield Publishers, Inc.
A wholly owned subsidiary of The Rowman & Littlefield Publishing Group, Inc.
4501 Forbes Boulevard, Suite 200, Lanham, MD 20706
www.rowmanlittlefield.com

P.O. Box 317, Oxford OX2 9RU, UK

British Library Cataloguing in Publication Information Available

Library of Congress Cataloging-in-Publication Data

Amstutz, Mark R.
  The healing of nations : the promise and limits of political
forgiveness / Mark R. Amstutz.
      p. cm.
  Includes bibliographical references and index.
  ISBN 0-7425-3580-0 (cloth : alk. paper) — ISBN 0-7425-3581-9 (pbk. :
alk. paper)
  1. Reconciliation—Political aspects. 2. Truth commissions. I.
Title.
  JC571.A48 2004
  323.4'9—dc22

                            2004001064

Printed in the United States of America

♾™ The paper used in this publication meets the minimum requirements of
American National Standard for Information Sciences—Permanence of Paper
for Printed Library Materials, ANSI/NISO Z39.48-1992.

Contents

Preface

I first began to think seriously about the nature and potential role of forgiveness in domestic and international politics in 1996 after reading Donald Shriver's *An Ethic for Enemies: Forgiveness in Politics*. Prior to that time, I, like many other social scientists, had regarded forgiveness as a part of personal morality, applicable to interpersonal relationships and to religious life but not to the policies of states or the decisions of government officials. But as I began to explore this topic, I started to doubt the widespread assumption that personal and political morality were two distinct, largely unrelated moralities and that forgiveness as part of the former was irrelevant to the affairs of state. As I explored practical and conceptual dimensions of forgiveness, I became increasingly convinced that although this ethic was not easily incorporated into public life, it was nevertheless a practice that could, in principle, be applied in politics and more particularly, in confronting past collective offenses. Accordingly, I began to explore how concepts like culpability, confession, repentance, forgiveness, and reconciliation might contribute to the process of collective healing, whether at the communal, national, or international levels. In time I concluded that Desmond Tutu's claim that "without forgiveness there is no future" was as valid in political and social life as in interpersonal relationships.

While this book is rooted in multidisciplinary scholarship, it is not a study in philosophical or theological ethics or in normative political theory. Rather, as a study in applied political ethics, its goal is to identify and illuminate relevant moral norms and to demonstrate how they can be used in political life. This study focuses on one concept—forgiveness—and seeks through theoretical and empirical analysis to illuminate its nature and potential role in communal life, especially in confronting past regime offenses. In particular,

I argue that the ethic of forgiveness, when rooted in the alternative conception of restorative justice, can promote the healing and renewal of social and political life and thereby foster a more just, humane, and stable political order. The aim is not simply to clarify ideas, but to illustrate how this moral process might contribute to political healing. In assessing the limits and possibilities of forgiveness in domestic and international politics, this study explores such questions as, How can nations best reckon with widespread human rights abuses? How should an emerging regime address the injustices and criminal actions of a former government? Can governments atone for past regime crimes? If so, how? Is it morally appropriate for public officials to act on behalf of citizens in granting and receiving forgiveness? In other words, is representative or vicarious forgiveness feasible? If collective forgiveness is possible, who is entitled to reduce or eliminate perpetrators' debt or deserved punishment? Finally, how should the demand for retroactive or retributive justice be reconciled with the quest for forward-looking restoration and healing?

To ascertain the challenges, limits, and potential role of forgiveness in confronting collective offenses, I examine four case studies—Argentina, Chile, Northern Ireland, and South Africa. Although the nature and scope of injustice and wrongdoing is different in each country, all four countries had to confront the challenge of how best to address past wrongdoing while simultaneously seeking to restore political order and foster communal reconciliation. In confronting past collective offenses, emerging regimes were faced with the dilemma of reconciling legal justice with the prevention of future human rights abuses. In effect, transitional governments had to decide which strategy was most effective in fostering accountability and reconciliation, retribution and restoration.

To gain a perspective about the nature and impact of past wrongdoing, as well as to illuminate different ways by which political healing might be advanced, I interviewed scholars, decision makers, human rights workers, church leaders, and even some perpetrators and victims in each of the four countries. Although many interviewees—especially victims and perpetrators—expressed doubts about the feasibility of relying on the process of forgiveness in confronting collective offenses, it was also evident that the traditional tools of legal accountability were unlikely to promote communal healing and reconciliation. Indeed, the historical experience in these and other nations suggested that such traditional responses as revenge, retribution, amnesia, and amnesty had contributed little to the renewal and restoration of communities that had suffered from domestic political strife, regime human rights abuses, and structural injustices.

As a result of interviews with victims and perpetrators, I became increasingly convinced that neither the pursuit of strict justice nor the quest for amnesty or amnesia was likely to promote individual healing and communal reconciliation. While amnesty might facilitate short-term order and provide a forward-looking focus, absolution without accountability was unlikely to result in the renewal and restoration of a community's moral order. Similarly, even though legal retribution is the cornerstone of most criminal justice systems, such a strategy was unlikely to overcome the collective wounds of nations and to foster healing and reconciliation.

I came to doubt the efficacy of legal retribution in part because culpability for past regime collective wrongdoing is frequently so broadly dispersed throughout society that it is difficult to distinguish the guilty from the innocent, the righteous from the wicked. Additionally and more significantly, strict accountability is a challenge because antagonists' perceptions and worldviews are largely dictated by a backward-looking orientation. For both offenders and victims, political vision is generally dominated by the memory of past political conflict and suffering. For victims, memory is a means for sustaining the quest for justice—a way by which victims and their advocates can keep faith with the pursuit of truth, accountability, and legal retribution. For their part, perpetrators similarly focus on the past but use memory not as an instrument of legal accountability but as a tool of justification—as a way to rationalize past individual and collective actions, even when such actions have resulted in great human suffering.

Since neither victims nor perpetrators seem to desire accommodation or reconciliation, the quest for communal healing and restoration is likely to occur only if other political groups initiate and guide the process of national reconstruction. And if such a process is to evolve, it will necessitate not only accountability for past actions but also a moral reformation of memory—or what Pope John Paul II has termed the "purification of memory."[1] At a minimum, such reformation will be possible only if it is rooted in truth, confession (the acknowledgment of truth), remorse, and empathy. So long as antagonists' perceptions are rooted in rancor, resentment, and the quest for retribution or revenge, individual healing and communal reconciliation will be impossible.

This book would have been impossible without the assistance of numerous persons. First, I thank the many scholars and theologians who have written about forgiveness. In particular, I am grateful to the late theologian Lewis Smedes who through his compelling books first showed me that forgiveness was not some abstract, fragile practice used to avoid moral culpability but a robust ethic that could transform a past undeserved injustice into a new justice. Second, I thank my students for stimulating and challenging many of the ideas found in this book. Third, I thank Wheaton College for granting me a sabbatical leave during the spring 2000 semester that allowed me to embark on this project. Fourth, I thank the Wheaton College Alumni Association for providing financial support to travel to Chile and Argentina in 2000 and to the Aldeen Fund to travel to Northern Ireland and South Africa in 2001. Although the interviews were essential in preparing the four case studies, the opportunity to visit each country contributed to a more realistic and nuanced assessment of the possibilities and limits of applying forgiveness to serious collective offenses. Fifth, I thank my teaching assistants—Sarah Rotman, Stephanie Montgomery, and Jennifer Reynolds—as well as David Woerner, Andrea Ratzloff, and Rebecca Miller for providing invaluable assistance in research and editing. Finally, I thank my wife Donna, a clinical psychologist, for her continued encouragement in carrying out this project. Though I had periodic doubts about the efficacy and wisdom of this book, she never wavered in her conviction that forgiveness had social and political dimensions and that I had something important to say about the topic.

Introduction

There should be a place for forgiveness wherever there is confession of guilt and repentance.

—Václav Havel, former president, Czech Republic[1]

Anyone who closes his eyes to the past is blind to the present. Whoever refuses to remember the inhumanity is prone to new risks of infection.

—Richard F. von Weizsäcker,
former president, Federal Republic of Germany[2]

Whoever opts for revenge should dig two graves.

—Chinese proverb

Seeking to forget makes exile all the longer; the secret of redemption lies in remembrance.

—Jewish adage[3]

In 1976, Mario Juica, a leader of Chile's illegal Communist Party, suddenly disappeared, joining the ranks of hundreds of other radical activists who had also vanished in the aftermath of the 1973 coup d'etat. Mr. Juica's family assumed that his sudden disappearance was, as with those of many other missing persons, the work of state security agents who were seeking to eliminate all Marxist revolutionaries. After toppling the elected government of Salvador Allende, the military authorities imposed harsh political repression, leading to the imprisonment or deportation of many government officials and party leaders, the banning of all political activity, and the murder of radical leaders.

1

In March 2000—some twenty-five years after Mario had disappeared—I sat in the office of a small human rights organization in Santiago with his daughter Alicia. My goal was to learn about her human rights work and, more particularly, how she and her family had coped with the loss of a father and husband.[4] In particular, I wanted to know whether, and how, a society like Chile could be restored in the aftermath of widespread human rights offenses. Is political healing and national reconciliation possible after state agents have carried out widespread atrocities? Can national reconciliation be advanced apart from personal healing? Is interpersonal reconciliation a prerequisite for overcoming political fragmentation and social distrust?

Alicia indicated that since there has been no disclosure of truth (such as information about the fate of persons who had been abducted) and no justice (for example, trials of culpable offenders), personal and social healing had been impossible for her and other human rights victims. Alicia admitted that when her father failed to come home, her mother devoted all her energy to finding him, leaving her, as the eldest child, to assume the role of a surrogate mother to her younger siblings. For Alicia, her father's disappearance was a double tragedy given that she lost a father permanently and her mother temporarily during her adolescence.

In describing the effect of her father's disappearance, it was clear that the abduction had had a far-reaching impact on Alicia's life and that of her siblings. It was also evident that the emotional injuries from the abduction had not healed in the intervening years. Indeed, her own work for a human rights organization, which undoubtedly was rooted in her personal quest to come to terms with her father's disappearance, may have helped to keep psychological wounds fresh. And because government officials had been unwilling or unable to provide information about the fate of her father, she had experienced no emotional closure from his disappearance.[5] When I inquired how she would advance personal healing and national reconciliation, Alicia said that the prosecution and punishment of senior government leaders was the first requirement. In her view, there could be no peace or national unity until General Augusto Pinochet, the leader of the military government, had been brought to justice.

Although Alicia claimed that legal retribution was necessary for reconciliation, she did not think that trials themselves would foster either personal healing or national reconciliation. Indeed, she admitted that while truth telling and apologies might encourage victims to express compassion and forgiveness toward perpetrators, she personally was opposed to any form of forgiveness. The way forward was through truth telling and justice.

Prior to interviewing Alicia, I met with a group of retired military officers to learn about how the Chilean armed forces viewed the 1973 coup and the subsequent years of military rule.[6] I was especially interested in learning what actions they thought might help to overcome political alienation and distrust within Chilean society and foster national reconciliation. Unlike Alicia, who believed that the healing of Chilean society depended entirely on the military's taking responsibility for human rights abuses, the officers claimed that the major responsibility for the breakdown in Chilean society was the Marxist government of Allende and his radical supporters. Since the armed forces had intervened in political society to restore public order, the retired officers indicated that the military did not need to apologize for its actions. Rather, those who needed to express remorse were the Marxist activists who had fostered social fragmentation and the overpoliticization of society and brought about the collapse of the country's economy. Indeed, some officers indicated that since the military had rescued the nation from a probable slide to Communist tyranny, the Chilean people should be grateful to the armed forces for providing political and economic liberation. Gratitude, not retribution, was the appropriate response toward the armed forces.

A few officers expressed regret that the defeat and consolidation of power could not have been achieved with little or no violence. It was their belief that the political repression imposed after the coup was necessary, however, because of the threat posed by armed, well-trained revolutionary groups who were determined to defend Marxist revolutionary ideals at all costs. Some officers noted that since it had been imperative to expunge the virus of Marxism, decisive force was the only option if civil war was to be avoided and the rule of law was to be eventually restored.

When I inquired what actions might be taken to overcome political animosity and distrust, the officers responded that the healing and restoration of the country will depend in great part on the willingness of radical political groups to take responsibility for the collapse of Chile's democratic order. They acknowledged that deep political polarization existed between the military and its conservative supporters and radical, socialist groups. National reconciliation, they thought, was a worthy ideal, but the process forward could only be undertaken if Marxist groups accepted responsibility for the rupture of Chile's constitutional order and the collapse of the country's social and economic systems. According to a senior military official, if this were to occur and human rights activists were to stop demanding legal retribution, the military might be prepared to acknowledge the use of excessive or inappropriate force or both during its seventeen-year era of military rule.

According to the retired officers, the country's truth commission failed to promote reconciliation because its report was an incomplete and partisan account of the past.[7] Rather than providing an authoritative account of the collapse of Chile's political and economic institutions, officers claimed that the truth commission report offered a caricature of the truth, focusing almost exclusively on state violence but failing to explain the precipitating factors that brought about the breakdown of Chile's institutions.[8] They suggested that if truth were to contribute to national healing, it would have to be a comprehensive, dispassionate disclosure of past political conflicts and the rise of violence. In particular, such truth would have to acknowledge how radical groups, and the Allende administration in particular, polarized society; threatened property rights; ruptured the country's peaceful, democratic traditions; and undermined civic culture. According to some officers, the cause of the country's distrust and political polarization was not due to the past political role of the armed forces but rather to the activities and actions of radical political groups opposed to liberal democracy and free enterprise. Given the deep polarization, military officers said that apologies and forgiveness were unlikely to heal the country's wounds.

The radically different perceptions and experiences of Alicia and other human rights victims, on the one hand, and those of military officers, on the other hand, point to the difficulty in confronting and overcoming collective violence. For Alicia, the major obstacle to reconciliation was the legacy of violence by the armed forces; for the military, by contrast, the principal barrier was the continuing politicization and resentment by radical groups that sought to undermine the political and economic liberation accomplished by the armed forces. Although both groups held differing explanations of the political conflict that had precipitated the coup and led to political repression, they both concurred that the discovery, disclosure, and acknowledgment of truth was necessary in promoting national reconciliation. Ironically, because political antagonists interpret Chilean history from radically different worldviews, the quest for a shared truth about the past has itself remained an elusive goal.

THE NATURE OF THE PROBLEM

This book explores whether nations can overcome the legacy of gross injustice and human rights atrocities. In particular, it examines the potential role of forgiveness in reckoning with past political evil. Some of the questions that animate this book are these: Can nations that have suffered widespread injustice overcome the legacy of suffering, distrust, and enmity? Can regimes that have committed widespread atrocities carry out moral renewal and political restoration? If political healing is possible, what role should public apologies, reparations, and political forgiveness play in fostering national and international reconciliation? In pursuing the moral and political reconstruction of nations, what should be the appropriate balance between a backward-looking quest for retribution and a forward-looking emphasis on communal reconciliation and the moral and political reconstruction of nations?

There are numerous ways that states have sought to overcome the legacy of wrongdoing involving death, destruction, suffering, distrust, and enmity. These approaches have ranged from amnesia and denial, which seek to avoid reckoning with past crimes and injustices, to trials and purges, which seek to hold individuals accountable for personal wrongdoing. One potential approach—one rarely considered or applied by states—is the quest for political reconciliation through the moral reconstruction of communities. Such moral restoration will necessitate repentance, reparations, and other acts of atonement by collectives responsible for atrocities. Furthermore, groups that have suffered the offenses need to offer empathy, compassion, and even forgiveness.

This book examines the potential role of this difficult but promising road to moral reconstruction and national reconciliation. In particular, it explores the role of forgiveness in overcoming collective wrongdoing. Political forgiveness, as I will argue in this book, is not a recipe for forgetting past injuries. Rather, it is a demanding ethic that calls on political actors to confront their culpability and responsibility through the acknowledgment of truth, the expression of remorse, and a willingness to offer reparations and accept punishment. For their part, victims must refrain from vengeance, express empathy, and respond to repentance by reducing or eliminating the offenders' debts or the deserved punishment or both. To be sure, forgiveness is not the only way to promote national reconciliation. But because forgiveness focuses on the healing of victims and offenders and the restoration of communal bonds, it provides a promising, forward-looking strategy for political healing.

Political reconciliation is of course a long, difficult journey. This is especially the case after a government has perpetrated egregious, widespread atrocities, as was the case in World War II when Germany inflicted untold suffering on other nations and peoples. Thus, the transformation of enmity into friendship and distrust into partnership between West Germany and the United States exemplified the long but successful process of political reconciliation. To illustrate some of the long-term challenges involved in such reconciliation, I briefly sketch several key moral issues precipitated by President Ronald Reagan's decision to visit a West German military cemetery in May 1985 to commemorate four decades of growing U.S.-German partnership.

The Challenge of Political Reconciliation: The Bitburg Debate

In early 1985, Reagan accepted an invitation from Chancellor Helmut Kohl to visit West Germany to commemorate the defeat of Nazism and to celebrate forging a peaceful and constructive partnership between West Germany and the United States in the aftermath of World War II. In June 1984, the United States and its World War II Allies had celebrated the fortieth anniversary of the Normandy invasion. Since Germany had been excluded from this event, Kohl invited Reagan to commemorate German-American political reconciliation and to celebrate the extraordinary transformation of U.S.-German political relations from enmity into friendship. In early 1985, the White House announced that the president would be making the trip in May.

Subsequently, administration officials disclosed that Reagan would lay a wreath at the Kolmeshöhe military cemetery in Bitburg as a gesture of German-American reconciliation and would pay tribute to Jewish victims by visiting the Bergen-Belsen concentration camp. The Bitburg cemetery was selected because it was near a large U.S.-NATO Air Force base and also because it had been the location of previous joint American-French-German ceremonies honoring those who had died in World War II. Soon after the Bitburg site was disclosed, however, it was discovered that forty-nine members of the Waffen-SS, the Nazi movement's elite police force, were among the two thousand soldiers buried there.[9]

This disclosure precipitated an immediate firestorm from human rights groups, war veterans, Jewish elites, and media commentators. Fifty-three senators signed a letter urging that Reagan call off the trip, while 257 members of the House of Representatives wrote Kohl to request that the president be released from his Bitburg commitment. The most direct opposition came from Jewish groups and especially from the noted author Elie Wiesel. At a White House ceremony in which he was being honored, Wiesel spoke movingly of the need to remember the past, imploring the president to cancel his visit to the Bitburg military cemetery. "That place, Mr. President," said Wiesel, "is not your place. Your place is with the victims of the SS."[10] For Wiesel, the issue was not politics but morality—or what he termed "good and evil."[11] Since reconciliation needed to be rooted in memory, it was imperative not to dishonor Holocaust victims by carrying out a ceremony in a "tainted" burial site—a location where agents of the Holocaust were buried. Wiesel concluded his remarks as follows:

> Mr. President, I know and I understand . . . that you seek reconciliation. So do I. So do we. And I, too, wish to attain true reconciliation with the German people. I do not believe in collective guilt, nor in collective responsibility, only the killers were guilty. Their sons and daughters are not. And I believe, Mr. President, that we can and we must work together with them and with all people. And we must work to bring peace and understanding to a tormented world that, as you know, is still awaiting redemption.[12]

Since authentic reconciliation could only be based on truth and remembrance, opponents of the Bitburg trip believed the quest to commemorate international reconciliation needed to be rooted in, and consistent with, memory. And for them, laying a wreath at the Kolmeshöhe military cemetery was counterproductive to true reconciliation because the cemetery was tarnished by evil—with the burial sites of soldiers who had helped to carry out the Jewish genocide.

Reagan no doubt would have preferred to commemorate reconciliation in an untainted site. Once a decision had been made to commemorate U.S.-German political reconciliation, however, Reagan was determined to make the trip, believing that if the trip were canceled, it could potentially damage bilateral relations and harm the credibility of Germany's political leadership. Indeed, the Bitburg visit provided a means by which to communicate an important truth—namely, that political redemption is possible, even after significant atrocities have been committed. Although White House officials did not offer a moral explanation for going to Bitburg, it was clear that in confronting the dilemma of balancing memory and reconciliation Reagan favored a forward-looking orientation that gave priority to healing and restoration over remembrance of past evils.

Thus, after weighing the alternatives, Reagan decided to follow the original plan. "I think it is morally right to do what I'm doing," he said, justifying the decision largely on consequentialist logic. He emphasized that the purpose of the Bitburg ceremony was to honor the ending of World War II, to commemorate German-American reconciliation, and "to make it plain that never must we find ourselves enemies, and never again must there be anything like the Holocaust." The president then said that if these goals could be advanced by the trip, then the planned trip would be "very worthwhile."[13]

Although the decision to commemorate German liberation and German-American reconciliation at Bitburg may have been a tactical blunder, caused by poor planning, this initiative generated an illuminating debate that stimulated moral reflection on topics not ordinarily considered by either leaders or the general public. In particular, the visit encouraged the American people to explore whether political redemption in the aftermath of atrocities is possible and whether domestic or international reconciliation is possible among enemies.

In effect, the debate stimulated reflection on whether the healing of nations was possible and, if so, under what conditions. For example, is Elazar Barkan correct in suggesting that nations can bear collective guilt and responsibility?[14] Or is German president Richard von Weizsäcker correct in claiming that "there is no such thing as the guilt or innocence of an entire nation," and that guilt, like innocence, is "not collective, but personal"?[15] If guilt is only individual, how should regime offenses, such as genocide or society-wide crimes involving torture and secret killings, be addressed? Should personal accountability focus on the role of senior decision makers and state agents who may have been directly responsible for wrongdoing, or should it also focus on those who were not directly involved but contributed to the evil by supporting the regime that perpetrated the abuses? If guilt is partly collective, can nations atone for past regime atrocities through acknowledgment, remorse, and reparations? And if political atonement is possible, can such acts contribute to collective forgiveness? And if collective atonement and forgiveness are feasible, can such processes contribute to political reconciliation within and among nations?

Accountability versus Avoidance

In reckoning with past domestic or international regime offenses, governments have pursued a variety of strategies. Fundamentally, these strategies have involved two distinct approaches—engagement or denial, accountability or avoidance. The engagement approach is based on the assumption that before nations can be healed and reconciled, regime wrongdoing must be disclosed and acknowledged and then redressed through appropriate strategies of accountability. Although it may be desirable to emphasize the immediate restoration of communal relationships and the consolidation of constitutional norms, this approach assumes that healing can take place only when past atrocities have been confronted directly. Coming to terms with past collective wrongdoing is important because the failure to do so may result in latent, festering problems that impair normal interpersonal and civic relationships. Just as the failure to excise a cancer from the human body can lead to serious illnesses or even death, so too the failure to explicitly address collective offenses can result in severe social and political pathologies.

The most extreme form of accountability is vengeance, which seeks to respond to wrongdoing through private retaliation. In order to inhibit such retribution, governments pursue legal accountability by prosecuting alleged offenders in the hope that such engagement will forestall private retribution. Retribution, which is rooted in the natural human desire for vengeance, seeks to redress a victim's suffering by inflicting pain or punishment on the offender. Since a major offense results in a diminished standing of the victim vis-à-vis the offender, retribution can be viewed as a means of restoring the moral equality of people. By inflicting punishment on the perpetrator, retribution helps to restore the moral status of the victim and to erase any gains that an offender may have received through wrongdoing.

Defenders of revenge and retaliation thus view retribution as an instrument of justice—as a means by which the fundamental worth of victims can be restored. Although retribution may strengthen the political morality of a community, it may contribute little to resolving a victim's pain and suffering. Retaliation may give the victim some emotional relief from the anguish created by an offense, but it will not necessarily contribute to the restoration of a victim's well-being. More significant, however, vengeance may set in motion a series of interactions that not only perpetuate conflict but also breed greater injustices and human suffering. *Lex talionis*—legally sanctioned retaliation—is not a strategy that fosters personal healing and human reconciliation.

The foundation of any strategy of accountability is the discovery, disclosure, and acknowledgment of truth. There can be no reckoning with past regime offenses if there is no knowledge of wrongdoing. In effect, if a community is to effectively come to terms with past regime offenses, the public must have knowledge of regime atrocities and crimes and which individuals, groups, or organizations are chiefly responsible for them. While private organizations may undertake investigations of limited offenses, major human rights violations, especially those involving state organizations, need to be carried out by government-appointed commissions, such as South Africa's Truth and Reconciliation Commission (TRC) and Chile's National Commission on Truth and Reconciliation. Although disclosure and public acknowledgment of past human rights violations does not necessarily lead to justice or reconciliation, scholars regard truth as indispensable to an engagement approach and essential in carrying out a successful transition from authoritarian rule to democracy. José Zalaquett, an influential human rights scholar and a leading advisor to Chilean president Patricio Aylwin, for example, has observed that disclosure and acknowledgment of truth is an "inescapable imperative."[16]

The most widely used strategy of accountability in political communities is legal prosecution. In constitutional regimes, courts have the responsibility for determining criminal behavior and for punishing wrongdoing. Once evidence is obtained, an offender is prosecuted and then punished, if found guilty. Although punishment of legal offenses raises a number of moral, political, and legal challenges, especially when the wrongs inflicted on society are pervasive, some scholars argue that the restoration of the rule of law and the integrity of the constitutional order require that wrongdoing be publicly prosecuted. Quite apart from the long-term effects of trials on victims and offenders, the immediate impact of such initiatives is the reinforcement of the supremacy of the law. The punishment of offenders can take a variety of actions, ranging from financial reparations and community service to incarceration. Courts and political authorities can, of course, mitigate sentences through compassionate acts of mercy or legal pardons. Although mercy and pardon have similar effects in qualifying the punishment of an offender, mercy is an ethical action motivated by humanitarian considerations, whereas pardon is a legal act motivated by a political judgment about the common good for society.

Besides legal retribution, states also apply accountability through other strategies, such as official purges, restitution, reparations, public apologies, truth commissions, and even political forgiveness. Although these strategies are rooted in truth, each reckons with past wrongdoing in a different manner. Purges impose accountability by demanding that leaders, agents, and supporters of the discredited regime must be restricted from politics and even barred from government service. Restitution and reparations impose accountability by the transfer of tangible resources to victims and their families. Whereas restitution involves the return of stolen or confiscated property, reparations provide for financial resources as a symbol of a regime's culpability and as an aid to the restoration of communal relationships.

Public apologies—the expression of remorse by government leaders for past regime offenses—can also foster political healing through truth telling followed by public acknowledgment of, and contrition for, past collective offenses. The most significant innovations in the disclosure of past wrongdoing are official truth commissions, which are ordinarily established to uncover and disclose the nature and magnitude of past regime atrocities. Finally, political forgiveness—the lifting of debts or penalties for collective wrongdoing—is also a form of accountability since the mitigation of the deserved punishment is granted only after truth has been acknowledged and leaders have expressed remorse for the offenses.

The second major strategy for reckoning with past collective offenses is avoidance or denial. Governments that pursue this approach frequently do so for a number of reasons. First, since responsibility for regime wrongdoing is often pervasive throughout society, it is rarely beneficial to focus on the culpability of only a small number of perpetrators and decision makers. By limiting culpability to a few leaders and agents and absolving groups that directly or indirectly supported the regime, the quest for accountability may distort perceptions of reality, especially by giving the impression that culpability is limited and the masses are innocent. Moreover, the prosecution and punishment of leaders and agents may further polarize society. As a result, some governments assume that the best approach is to avoid trials and scapegoating altogether.

Another reason why governments may try to avoid confronting past regime offenses is the belief that accountability may inhibit national reconciliation. Since the crimes, injustices, and structural evils of the past cannot be undone, some leaders assume that the best approach is to allow the balm of time to heal the social and political wounds of the past. Confronting the unjust, evil deeds of the past will only increase resentment, distort priorities, and inhibit political healing. Thus, the best way to address past offenses is by neglecting and avoiding past wrongdoing and focusing instead on present social and political challenges and the promises and hopes of the future.

Finally, government officials pursue avoidance and denial in the belief that a forward-looking strategy is most likely to prevent the reoccurrence of past human rights crimes and atrocities. To this end, they give priority to the building and consolidation of a humane political order over claims of retributive justice. Rather than seeking to settle legal claims about past collective offenses, this approach emphasizes the institutionalization of constitutional norms and structures and the renewal of political morality. The former is indispensable in fostering a humane political order that protects human rights, while the latter is essential in fostering reconciliation.

The two most common expressions of the avoidance approach are historical amnesia and amnesties. Amnesia is the deliberate effort to deny the past or to neglect memory. Amnesties, by contrast, are public acts that relieve offenders of their individual and collective responsibility. Whether through denial or amnesties, this approach focuses on the consolidation of a new legal and political order by focusing on the restoration of peace and the pursuit of national reconciliation. Its goal is the institutionalization of a new constitutional political order by emphasizing the present and the future and by neglecting memory. In effect, it disregards the legacy of past offenses. Tádeusz Mazowiecki, Poland's first democratic prime minister, emphasized this approach when he called on his people to draw a "thick line" between the present and the past in order to focus exclusively on the building of a new democratic order.[17]

THE PROMISE OF POLITICAL FORGIVENESS

As noted earlier, regime transitions have relied on a variety of strategies to confront past collective offenses. Historically, the two most common approaches have been the extremes of denial through amnesia or amnesty and accountability through legal prosecution. Regimes have rarely pursued political forgiveness rooted in truth telling, repentance, and compassion toward offenders. But as truth commissions have become more widely accepted as a means of confronting past regime injustices, they have ironically encouraged consideration of the potential role of forgiveness in public life.

Fundamentally, forgiveness involves the healing of victims and perpetrators and the restoration of relationships, culminating in reconciliation. In forgiveness, offenders express contrition for the suffering they have inflicted, authenticating their repentance through acts of reparation and the promise not to repeat unjust and harmful behaviors. The victims, for their part, give up resentment and anger toward offenders, viewing them not as evil monsters but as human beings—morally responsible agents who are capable of change. In forgiving, victims do not condone the offense; rather, while continuing to oppose the offenders' immoral actions, they cease to resent the offenders. In effect, forgiveness, as Jean Hampton notes, involves a revised judgment of the offender, not the offense.[18]

This book investigates the potential role of collective forgiveness in reckoning with past regime wrongdoing. Since forgiveness has been regarded historically as a private ethic, appropriate for confronting personal moral wrongdoing, decision makers and scholars have been reluctant to consider the social and political merits of this ethic. Only in recent years have philosophers, theologians, and social scientists begun to explore the legitimacy of this concept as an instrument of political and social reconciliation.[19] To be sure, forgiveness is an indispensable dimension of personal morality, contributing to the lifting of offenders' moral guilt, the healing of victims' anger and their compulsion for revenge, and the restoring of harmonious relationships through reconciliation. But forgiveness, as I argue in this book, is also an appropriate dimension of domestic and international political ethics, providing resources that help political groups confront their collective responsibility while also helping to overcome and, as Hannah Arendt said, to "undo" the past.[20]

Because governments make decisions on behalf of political communities, they are moral agents for groups and nations, capable of fulfilling conditions for the granting and receiving of forgiveness. For example, senior public officials can acknowledge and apologize for past regime offenses, while also authorizing symbolic reparations as an expression of collective contrition. For their part, leaders of communities that have been victimized can refrain from retaliatory acts, express compassion and empathy toward the peoples that are responsible for offenses, and lift the penalty of deserved punishment.

Archbishop Desmond Tutu, the former chairman of South Africa's TRC, has argued that in reckoning with the crimes and injustices of past regimes, truth telling and the reformation of a people's moral and political values are indispensable to national reconciliation. In particular, Tutu argues that forgiveness can play an important role in the moral and political reconstruction of a society characterized by division, distrust, and enmity. Indeed, as the title of his widely read book on the TRC suggests, there can be "no future without forgiveness."[21] Of course, applying forgiveness to the social and political life of nations presents major challenges. To begin with, because of the widespread presumption that this ethic is applicable only to individuals and not to groups, leaders have been reluctant to regard communal restoration and political reconciliation based on forgiveness as a legitimate way of reckoning with the past. In addition, since forgiveness is often misconceived simply as a means to forget the past and to avoid accountability, leaders have been reluctant to apply such a crude and simplistic strategy as "forgive and forget."

But as I argue in this book, forgiveness is not a simplistic formula to avoid the past. Rather, it is a demanding ethic that requires full disclosure and acknowledgment of the truth and moral accountability for past wrongdoing. Indeed, a robust conception of forgiveness will impose significant moral burdens on both victims and offenders. At a minimum, offenders must be prepared to disclose and acknowledge the truth about wrongdoing, admit their own culpability, express remorse, and offer reparations; for their part, victims must avoid vengeance, express empathy toward offenders, and forgo claims of justice. When victims refuse to demand justice and instead lift the debts and deserved penalties of offenders, they are implementing the final dimension of the ethic of forgiveness. But the cancellation of debts or the absolution from retributive punishment is only one element of the ethic of forgiveness. Forgiveness, as I will argue in this study, imposes moral burdens also on offenders by calling on them to publicly acknowledge their responsibility for wrongdoing and demonstrate their remorse through appropriate public actions. Indeed, given the demanding nature of authentic forgiveness, it is not surprising that this ethic is difficult to apply to interpersonal relationships and even more challenging in public life.

To illustrate some of the ethical challenges posed by the ethic of forgiveness in communal life, especially the tension between individual action and communal responsibilities, I briefly sketch a case study about collective wrongdoing and individual remorse. Although the case study does not focus on political forgiveness per se, it illuminates moral tensions involved in confronting and overcoming past offenses.

Wiesenthal's Question

In *The Sunflower*, Simon Wiesenthal tells how he, a Jew, is asked to forgive the human rights atrocities of a dying SS soldier during World War II. Karl, the injured German soldier, had been assigned to fight along the Western front, and after committing numerous atrocities, many of them against Jewish people, he is severely injured by an artillery explosion. He is transported to a German military hospital, where Wiesenthal, an inmate in a nearby concentration camp, works on a cleanup crew. The dying soldier asks that a Jew be brought to him. A nurse orders Wiesenthal to go to Karl's bedside, whereupon the dying soldier confesses his participation in a heinous crime—the killing of innocent children and adults as they sought to escape from a house crammed with Jews that had been deliberately set on fire with hand grenades. Karl wants to confess to a Jew to relieve his guilt. He tells Wiesenthal: "I am resigned to dying soon," but before that I want to talk about an experience which is torturing me."[22] He goes on, "I want to die in peace. . . . I know that what I am asking is almost too much for you, but without your answer I cannot die in peace."[23] Karl tells Wiesenthal that he would be ready to suffer more if he could bring back the dead he killed. Although he regards Karl's confession as "true repentance," Wiesenthal walks out of the room without responding. Wiesenthal concludes his story by suggesting that the "crux of the matter" is forgiveness: "forgetting is something that time alone takes care of, but forgiveness is an act of volition, and only the sufferer is qualified to make the decision."[24] He ends his story by asking the reader what he or she would have done had they been in Wiesenthal's position.

This case involves partly personal and partly political dimensions. Although Karl personally repents for his role in committing atrocities, the offenses were not private offenses but war crimes committed as part of a Nazi war campaign. The issue of forgiveness raised by Wiesenthal is therefore a case of personal responsibility to a group, or to use Tavuchis' formulation "One to Many."[25] And since Karl is unable to express contrition to his victims, he seeks to apologize to a random representative of the people that he and his comrades had killed. Although it is unclear from the narrative, Karl's request to meet with a Jew could be viewed as a quest for absolution prior to his death, or simply as a desire to disclose moral guilt, in the hope that such disclosure would itself mitigate the burden of memory. But regardless of how Karl's motives might be regarded, a fundamental issue is whether groups or nations are legitimate moral agents. Can Wiesenthal, for example, serve as the representative of the Jewish people? Is Karl's repentance to a random representative of a group a meaningful act? Is the interaction between Karl and Simon solely interpersonal or is Karl's remorse partly individual and partly collective? And should the offenses committed by Karl and his German comrades be viewed solely as individual acts or as collective offenses? Finally, if acknowledgment, remorse, and empathy for past collective atrocities are possible, should forgiveness be considered in such a situation?

The second part of Wiesenthal's book includes a series of reflections by leading authors, theologians, lawyers, and religious and intellectual figures, a majority of them Jewish, on the subject of forgiveness. Most of the respondents support Wiesenthal's silence. Some of the justifications for this view include vicarious forgiveness is impossible because only victims are entitled to forgive offenders; full atonement must precede forgiveness; and some crimes, such as murder and genocide, are unpardonable. One of the most supportive statements of forgiveness is by Milton Konvitz, a Jewish lawyer and author. He concludes his powerful reflection as follows:

> I cannot speak for your victims. I cannot speak for the Jewish people. I cannot speak for God. But I am a man. I am a Jew. I am commanded, in my personal relations, to act with compassion. I have been taught that if I expect the Compassionate One to have compassion on me, I must act with compassion toward others. . . . It is not in my power to render to you help that could come only from victims, or from the whole of the people of Israel, or from God. But insofar as you reach out to me, and insofar as I can separate myself from fellow Jews, for whom I cannot speak, my broken heart pleads for your broken heart: Go in peace.[26]

The most negative commentary on forgiveness is by the noted Jewish author Cynthia Ozick, who is outraged to even consider the idea of forgiveness. Her condemnation of Karl is unqualified and unflinching: "Let the SS man die unshriven. Let him go to hell. Sooner the fly to God than he."[27]

Whereas most Jewish writers opposed forgiveness for atrocities, Christians were generally open to the possibility of forgiveness and reconciliation. Theodore Hesburgh, former president of the University of Notre Dame, for example, suggests that while Karl's sin is "monumental," it is still "finite and God's mercy is infinite." "If asked to be forgiven, by anyone for anything," he continues, "I would forgive because God would forgive."[28] Protestant theologian Martin Marty similarly supports the forgiveness ethic. He claims that if a perpetrator repents, even after gross offenses have been committed, there is "more value" in granting forgiveness than in withholding it.[29]

The idea of representative or collective forgiveness is morally problematic. While individual forgiveness is often personally challenging, the ethic of representative or collective forgiveness is especially difficult, posing many prudential obstacles and complex ethical issues. Is a member of a group, for example, entitled to accept the remorse of a culpable offender and to offer forgiveness? Are some actions so evil—such as those committed by Karl and his fellow SS troops—that they are beyond the possibility of moral reparation? In effect, are some human actions, whether or not committed individually or as part of a collective operation, unforgivable? If collective forgiveness is feasible, what are its essential preconditions? Is the widely accepted belief that only victims can forgive valid, or can political leaders offer forgiveness on behalf of communities—that is, vicariously? And if leaders can forgive on behalf of political communities, what are the moral reasons that might justify such action? If collective forgiveness is granted, does such forgiveness apply only to groups or also to individuals? In short, if political forgiveness is possible, who is entitled to grant it and to receive it? Most significant, since forgiveness seemingly qualifies justice, how can a state's duties to pursue public justice be reconciled with this ethic?

THE NATURE OF THE BOOK

This book in political ethics explores the potential role of forgiveness in domestic and international politics. Based on philosophical, theological, historical, and political resources, its aim is not simply to investigate the nature and merits of the idea of collective forgiveness but also to explore how an alternative discourse might contribute to the renewal and restoration of deeply polarized societies. The conventional wisdom is that regimes that have suffered from significant atrocities must confront past regime wrongdoing by prosecuting and punishing offenders. But this book, following biblical wisdom and Abraham Lincoln's restorative justice strategy,[30] suggests that social and political healing is not a natural consequence of legal retribution. Rather, I argue that restoration of communal bonds and the promotion of national reconciliation can only occur when individuals and groups are deeply committed to national solidarity and are willing to treat offenders or enemies as people entitled to human dignity.

Theologian Miroslav Volf has argued persuasively that the restoration of ruptured interpersonal and collective relationships presupposes a commitment to community—or what he terms "embrace."[31] When conflicts are defined in terms of "we" and "them" and when antagonists demand justice as a precondition for the reparation of social and political relationships, political healing and social restoration are unlikely to occur. Indeed, when victims demand justice, they may unwittingly reinforce existing alienation and divisions, thereby impairing the healing of social bonds. As a result, if ruptured relationships are to be restored, more than retribution will be required. At a minimum, antagonists must be prepared to acknowledge their shared humanity and be willing to affirm the priority of communal bonds. In this collective healing process, truth telling, acknowledgment of culpability, public apologies, and forgiveness can all contribute to the renewal and restoration of individual and collective ties.

The book has two major parts. In the first four chapters I review theoretical and conceptual issues about forgiveness and reconciliation. In the second part, chapters 5–8, I present case studies on the limits and possibilities of political forgiveness. Chapter 9, the conclusion, synthesizes major themes and arguments by presenting a preliminary theory of political forgiveness.

In chapter 1, I examine major strategies that regimes have utilized to reckon with past governmental injustices and atrocities. Since forgiveness has been historically viewed as a private, personal ethic, chapter 2 examines key elements of the concept from an interpersonal perspective, focusing on three distinct theories—the classical model, therapeutic forgiveness, and forgiveness as a virtue. Because religion has contributed significantly to the definition and promotion of this ethic, I explore some important insights about this ethic from a Judeo-Christian perspective. Chapter 3 extends the analysis of forgiveness to the political realm. In doing so, it examines different types of responsibility that arise in political communities and how forgiveness might relate to collective guilt. The chapter concludes with a brief assessment of the limits and possibilities of forgiveness in politics. In chapter 4, I examine the relationship of justice to political forgiveness, focusing on two major perspectives: Retributive justice, the prevailing approach, provides an effective strategy of pursuing individual accountability but is largely ineffective fostering reconciliation. By contrast, restorative justice—a new paradigm that focuses on the moral reconstruction of political relationships through truth telling, reparations, and forgiveness—provides a more conducive approach to the rehabilitation of broken relationships.

In chapters 5–8, I describe how Argentina, Chile, Northern Ireland, and South Africa have sought to address past collective offenses. The cases illustrate some of the major political challenges in seeking to balance accountability with the need for collective moral renewal. In the final chapter I synthesize major themes and arguments of the book in order to present a theory of political forgiveness. Since legal retribution is consistent with the rule of law, it provides an effective strategy for promoting and protecting individual rights in a context of political order. But when communities are deeply divided and resort to political violence, a communitarian perspective that emphasizes social and political goods may be necessary. Such an approach is desirable because it emphasizes not only the pursuit of the common good but also the restoration of political community. In particular, the communitarian tradition is supportive of restorative justice and the promotion of political healing through strategies of political forgiveness.

1

Confronting Human Rights Abuses: Approaches to Transitional Justice

Is there any kind of situation in which the offense is so gross and enormous that I should withhold forgiveness in the face of what appears to be true penitence? My answer would be that in every circumstance that I can picture, more value would grow out of forgiveness than out of its withholding.

—Martin Marty, Protestant church historian[1]

We are not going to be able to investigate the past. We would have to put the entire army in jail.

—Cerezo Arévalo, president of Guatemala, 1985[2]

Recognize that on the issue of "prosecute and punish vs. forgive and forget," each alternative presents grave problems, and that the least unsatisfactory course may well be: do not prosecute, do not punish, do not forgive, and, above all, do not forget.

—Samuel Huntington, noted political scientist[3]

The public's right to know is a fundamental tenet of democracy, and it should not be sacrificed to the supposedly higher interest of reconciliation.

—Juan Méndez, human rights scholar and activist[4]

In confronting the crimes and injustices of former regimes, emerging democratic governments have pursued a variety of strategies, ranging from denial to trials. The challenge of how best to reckon with regime atrocities—a process that scholars have termed "transitional justice"[5]—will depend, of

17

course, on the emerging regime's commitment to justice and human rights and on the political resources available to address the crimes and injustices of former governments. Some of the major goals that transitional regimes have sought to advance through these strategies include the restoration of the rule of law, the consolidation of democratic institutions, justice for human rights victims, political reconciliation, and national peace and unity.

Figure 1.1 lists some of the major transitional justice strategies that regimes have used to confront past wrongdoing. These approaches, which are listed along a continuum of increasing accountability, range from amnesia to full accountability and can be justified in terms of two alternative conceptions of justice: Retributive justice, which demands that offenses must be redressed, is expressed through reparations, purges, and trials. Restorative justice, the alternative theory, emphasizes the healing and restoration of community relationships through amnesty, forgiveness, and truth telling. Amnesia, which bypasses accountability altogether, disregards all claims of justice, placing all political resources in the healing of a new society without confronting the past. The truth-telling strategy is a part of both restorative and retributive theories of justice.

This chapter examines and assesses six major strategies that states have used in reckoning with past regime offenses. The aim here is to describe and evaluate each of these approaches in order to assess their potential in promoting justice and reconciliation. While each of the strategies provides advantages in confronting collective wrongdoing, none is fully effective in combining the pursuit of retroactive justice with the healing of nations and the restoration of peace. The potential role of political forgiveness in reckoning with past regime abuses derives from its balanced perspective in seeking to reconcile the demands for backward-looking justice with the quest for forward-looking healing and reconciliation. Political forgiveness, which is in figure 1.1 in between the strategies of amnesty and truth telling, is a promising alternative because it emphasizes political healing and the restoration of communal solidarity through truth telling.

In later chapters, I explore the nature and potential role of political forgiveness in confronting past regime wrongdoing. To provide a context and rationale for collective forgiveness, I explore here the dominant strategies that states have used in confronting past atrocities—namely, amnesia, amnesty, truth telling, reparations, purges, and trials.

DENIAL   ACCOUNTABILITY

| Amnesia | Amnesty | Forgiveness | Truth Telling | Reparations | Purges | Trials |

----------*Restorative Justice*----------   ===========   ----------*Retributive Justice*----------

Figure 1.1.   Transitional Justice Strategies

AMNESIA

Unlike truth telling, which is rooted in remembrance, amnesia is based on neglect and even denial. Although forgetting is seldom defended as an official government policy, nations, like individuals, can only stand so much truth. Indeed, states, like people, are not eager to acknowledge their errors, sins, and shortcomings. Thus, while truth telling is important, some periodic forgetting may also be essential if a people are to be freed from captivity of the past. This reasoning leads Michael Ignatieff to argue that the survival of nations must involve some forgetting by "forging myths of unity and identity that allow a society to forget its founding crimes, its hidden injuries and divisions, its unhealed wounds."[6]

Two major justifications have been offered for the policy of historical amnesia. First, some observers argue that forgetting is a necessary approach to cope with the demands of life. According to this argument, living involves maintaining a balance between confrontation and neglect, remembrance and forgetting. Since the emphasis on memory inevitably leads to a concern with righting past wrongs, an emphasis on remembrance can distort priorities and impede human progress. This is why Jorge Semprun, a leading Spanish intellectual, notes that "if you want to live a normal life, you must forget. Otherwise those wild snakes freed from their box will poison public life for years to come."[7]

A second and more important rationale for historical amnesia is the claim that forgetting facilitates the consolidation of democracy and the rule of law. According to this argument, transitional regimes should be forward-looking, concentrating political resources on the reformation of political culture, the institutionalization of the rule of law, and the institutionalization of democratic structures. Poland pursued this approach after the era of Communist rule ended. Tádeusz Mazowiecki, Poland's first democratically elected prime minister, argues that "witch hunts" against former government officials should be avoided and that a clear division needed to be drawn between the country's Communist past and the emerging democratic order. Thus, in his opening address to the Polish parliament in 1990, he said, "We draw a thick line between ourselves and the past."[8]

Historical amnesia can be expressed through a variety of approaches, ranging from a forward-looking orientation that neglects the past altogether to a limited historical orientation based on selective remembrance. The failure of the U.S. government to address the long-term effects of racial discrimination and the failure of Britain to address the injuries inflicted by its soldiers on the Afrikaner people in South Africa illustrate the strategy of latent neglect. Governments can also carry out much more explicit strategies of denial. Such denial generally occurs in the aftermath of war, genocide, or other major human rights violations as political groups informally disavow wrongdoing or when a government seeks to cover up serious atrocities. Bosnian Serb leaders illustrate this approach with their repeated denials that Serb security forces were committing genocide and "ethnic cleansing" against Bosnian Muslims, even in the face of significant evidence to the contrary. Argentina's military leaders also practiced this explicit denial strategy as they repeatedly disavowed knowledge of "disappearances" during the 1970s "dirty war." Only in 1983, just before transferring power to an elected government, did the military authorities begin to acknowledge some "excesses."

Historian Timothy Garton Ash observes that from a historical perspective "the advocates of forgetting are numerous and weighty."[9] For example, in the aftermath of World War II, French leaders sought to build a democratic republic not by confronting the painful legacy of the Vichy collaboration with the Nazis but by emphasizing Charles de Gaulle's unifying myth of French resistance. And while West Germany carried out numerous political acts to cleanse itself from its Nazi past, Konrad Adenauer's democratic government also deliberately suppressed the memory of this past through policies of amnesty and amnesia in order to consolidate democracy. Adenauer's major aim was not to achieve retributive justice against Nazis but rather to transform political culture, institutionalize democratic structures, and rebuild civil society in order to help Nazis become democrats. Similarly, after democracy was reestablished in Spain in 1974, the new democratic government did not establish a truth commission or prosecute General Francisco Franco's henchmen for crimes and human rights abuses. Instead, it disregarded past regime offenses, concentrating its resources on the institutionalization of the new constitutional order. Arguably, one of the longest and most sustained policies of denial is the continuing effort of Turkey to deny the 1915–1917 genocide of Armenians that resulted in the death of more than 1.5 million people.[10] This collective denial has been sustained, not by neglect or passivity, but by a deliberate eighty-year government policy of official amnesia.

Japan has been especially committed to a policy of denial about World War II. For example, Japanese people, according to journalist Ian Buruma, have continued to believe that the Pacific War was a struggle for the liberation from Western colonialism. Moreover, Japanese people continue to believe that their army did not commit widespread atrocities, as commonly alleged, and that the "Rape of Nanking" is entirely fictitious, made up by Chinese and Western writers seeking to undermine Japanese honor. On the fiftieth anniversary of the Japanese attack on Pearl Harbor, Japanese officials were invited to a ceremony in Honolulu in order to begin "a new era." The invitation, however, was conditional on an apology for the war. Japan refused to do so, however, and instead had a government spokesperson declare that "the entire world was responsible for the war."[11]

Although some political observers believe that amnesia may be prudentially necessary in some democratic transitions, most political philosophers and human rights activists claim that acknowledging past offenses is morally necessary for the renewal and restoration of political society. They argue that forgetting not only undermines the moral basis of political community but impedes the consolidation of constitutional order. If the new government is to keep faith with the victims of repression, it must hold offenders accountable. Failure to do so will undermine the transition toward constitutionalism and impede closure on the injuries and injustices inflicted by past collective action. Moreover, the failure to successfully "work through" the past—that is, to come to terms with the human rights violations of a former regime—is likely to divert attention from the lingering, unresolved claims of the past. For example, France's failure to confront the collaboration of the Vichy government with the Nazis in the aftermath of World War II has left a festering wound in the French nation that has still not healed. Crimes are thus much like a mild cancer or ulcer within the human body. So long as the cancer or ulcer is latent, it is unlikely to significantly affect a patient's health; but if the ulcer or cancer begins to grow and it is not treated medically, a patient can become gravely ill. Similarly, just as an operation may be necessary to remove a disease, so, too, prosecution and punishment may be necessary to remove the latent causes of human rights abuses.

AMNESTY

A second approach used by governments to reckon with past regime crimes is amnesty. Amnesty, like amnesia, is derived from the Greek *amnestia*, which means forgetfulness or oblivion. *Black's Law Dictionary* defines an amnesty as the "abolition and forgetfulness of the offense." Since amnesia involves nonrecognition or denial of past wrongdoing, it is completely opposed to any form of accountability or acknowledgment. Amnesty, by contrast, is based on the recognition that wrongdoing has occurred, but it offers exemption from punishment to offenders for political or moral reasons. Rather than holding perpetrators accountable for past offenses, amnesty exempts offenders from the state's criminal justice system.[12]

Historically, governments have used amnesties for a variety of purposes. One goal has been to overturn unjust or allegedly "illegal" policies or judgments of former regimes. For example, immediately after democracy returned to Czechoslovakia in 1990, the new government granted amnesty to some twenty thousand political prisoners who had committed antigovernment crimes. Another reason for granting amnesties has been to facilitate the consolidation of a new democratic order or to promote national peace. For example, President Gerald Ford pardoned former President Richard Nixon for his Watergate crimes in order to foster national reconciliation and to redirect political attention to future national concerns. Similarly, at the end of the

U.S. Civil War, President Andrew Johnson offered amnesty to all soldiers of the Confederate Army, provided they swore allegiance to the U.S. Constitution. The aim of such amnesty was to consolidate the victory of the Union forces and to transform the political sentiments of Southerners. Amnesties have also been used to help new regimes consolidate their political authority. Such was the case with Uruguay's 1986 amnesty law (*Ley de Caducidad*), enacted when the trials of military officials threatened the nascent democracy.[13] Finally, amnesties can be used to shield political leaders and state agents as well as regime opponents from prosecution. Generally, such amnesties are issued while the authoritarian rulers are still in power or as part of the transition process from authoritarian rule to democracy. One of the first self-amnesty laws to emerge in Latin America was adopted in Chile in 1978, five years after the military government had overthrown the elected government of Salvador Allende, but twelve years before democracy was reestablished in 1990.[14] The Argentine military rulers similarly enacted a self-amnesty decree shortly before giving up power in 1983.

One of the major justifications for amnesty is the belief that such action contributes to national reconciliation and peace. The peace accords formalized in Nicaragua in 1990, El Salvador in 1993, and Guatemala in 1996, for example, involved amnesties that were justified largely on the basis that they were ending civil wars. According to Nicaragua's 1990 Amnesty Law, the pursuit of "an authentic national reconciliation" requires that "the Nicaraguan family . . . pardon and forget those events that brought unrest to the nation, in order to create a climate of peace."[15] Similarly, El Salvador's 1993 Amnesty Law justifies unconditional amnesty as a means to achieve national unity and political reconciliation.

Some defenders of amnesty also argue that such action is prudentially necessary—that it is the best policy among viable alternatives. They claim, for example, that emerging democratic regimes should not use limited resources to prosecute offenders. According to legal scholar Bruce Ackerman, amnesties provide a way of dealing with the past by conserving "political capital." In his view, transitional regimes have limited political, institutional, and moral capital, and if such resources are used to prosecute past human rights abuses, fewer resources will be available for constitutional lawmaking. While Ackerman does not explicitly endorse amnesty, he strongly supports a forward-looking policy of constitutional development rather than a backward-looking policy of retributive justice. He writes: "Moral capital is better spent in educating the population in the limits of the law. There can be no hope of comprehensively correcting the wrongs done over a generation or more. A few crude, bureaucratically feasible reforms will do more justice, and prove less divisive, than a quixotic quest after the mirage of corrective justice."[16]

Amnesty supporters also defend this strategy as the most effective way of addressing widespread collective violence. Since most regime violence is a by-product of policies enacted by governmental authorities, individual prosecution is an inappropriate strategy in confronting collective violence. Contrary to common public perceptions, human rights abuses that resulted from counterinsurgency programs and political repression were not the result of "illegal" actions of rogue agents but rather the by-product of governmental policies taken to confront domestic unrest. To the extent that torture, abductions, and secret killings were used in confronting terrorism and urban insurgency, the immoral actions were chiefly a by-product of the authorized policies themselves. Thus, defenders of amnesty claim that individual agents should be absolved for offenses that resulted from official policies.

However, critics of this strategy argue that amnesty is contrary to constitutional government and an impediment to justice. Since one of the great achievements of Western civilization has been the development of constitutional government rooted in the sovereignty of law, the failure to prosecute crimes, especially egregious violations of human rights, is profoundly problematic. Amnesty—often defined by human rights activists as impunity—is problematic precisely because it disregards the fundamental constitutional norm of legal accountability based on equality and universality. Following Immanuel Kant, legal "purists" believe that an ethical legal order imposes a moral obligation to prosecute, try, and punish crimes. Retribution is important not because punishment might help to consolidate the rule of law or because it might contribute to the restoration of the moral health of victims and their families but because a constitutional order imposes on government officials a moral duty to uphold the law. According to this view, authentic national reconciliation results not from the deliberate pursuit of peace and political order but from the fulfillment of the rule of law.

The amnesty option is being increasingly contested with the growth of international human rights law and, more particularly, the claim of universal jurisdiction.[17] Indeed, a number of conventions—including the 1948 Geneva Convention on the Prevention and Punishment of the Crime of Genocide, the 1966 International Covenant on Civil and Political Rights, and the 1984 Convention against Torture—have explicitly prohibited amnesties because such actions are inconsistent with the defense of human rights.[18] Still, in the final analysis, the decision to grant amnesties is likely to depend more on considerations of domestic politics than on international humanitarian law.

TRUTH TELLING

Undoubtedly the most fundamental and widely accepted goal in confronting the offenses and injustices of a former regime is the development of a publicly acknowledged account of what happened. What groups or institutions committed crimes? Who planned and authorized the state's political repression?

Who, in effect, is responsible for past wrongdoing? What was the nature of the human rights violations? What happened to victims who are still missing? Who is entitled to reparations? José Zalaquett, a member of Chile's truth commission and key advisor to President Patricio Aylwin, argues that the first step in confronting past human rights abuses is the development of an official account of past state crimes. The truth, he writes, must be deemed an "absolute value."[19] This is especially the case where physical repression—including torture, abductions, and killings—was used by the government to counter subversion and where the truth about disappearances continues to remain hidden.

One of the accepted canons in psychotherapy is that mental health requires people to "come to terms" with the past. According to therapists, this cannot be achieved by denial, repression, or neglect but only by directly confronting past injuries so that they cease to control the present. In his "Introductory Lectures on Psychoanalysis," Sigmund Freud distinguishes between objective knowledge (knowing about something) and personal knowledge (understanding with one's heart). The former knowledge is descriptive or propositional, the latter, dispositional or interpretive. Freud believed that psychological well-being depended on both types of knowledge, and this could only be achieved if a person "worked through" the past by allowing intellectual knowledge to become dispositional, and inner personal knowledge to become propositional.[20] Thus, in confronting traumas, victims must confront the past by integrating both feelings and factual knowledge in order to be released from the grief and anger caused by the wrongdoing.

How can nations come to terms with a traumatic legacy like genocide, civil war, or political repression? Do nations have psyches like people? Can nations overcome a painful, evil past the way individuals do? Can people overcome collective trauma? If so, what are the steps to achieve national mental health? Unlike individuals, nations do not have feelings or psyches, but they do experience collective trauma and shared guilt. Such trauma and guilt are based on a composite of the moral and psychological lives of all their citizens and more particularly on the deliberate decisions and actions of governmental institutions. Thus, even though nations do not have souls or psyches, they are nonetheless collective agents whose actions bear moral consequences for them. Consequently, since the collective moral health of a nation requires that its people come to terms with past regime offenses, accountability based on truth is imperative.

Frequently, truth telling is regarded as a means to national reconciliation, peace, and justice. According to this prevalent view, truth can help restore victims and their families and contribute to the reformation of social and political structures, leading ultimately to national peace and justice. Building on the biblical admonition that "knowing the truth sets people free" (John 8:32), many transitional regimes have pursued truth telling in the belief that nations, like individuals, can overcome their painful past through the discovery and disclosure of truth. If a nation is to reckon effectively with past regime offenses, it must publicly acknowledge wrongdoing, for without truth telling there can be no accountability, and without accountability there can be no forgiveness. Indeed, the only route to individual and collective moral rehabilitation is through memory and the acceptance of responsibility. In a 1985 address on German responsibility for the Holocaust, Richard von Weizsächer, the country's president, told the West German parliament that "whoever closes his eyes to the past becomes blind to the present. Whoever does not wish to remember inhumanity becomes susceptible to the dangers of new infection." Weizsäcker then emphasized that it was important that Germany remember its wartime record since there could be "no reconciliation without memory."[21]

Discovery and Disclosure of Truth

Regimes can pursue truth telling in at least two ways. First, they can open files, disclose important historical facts, and permit a more pluralistic, tolerant political culture that is conducive to the investigation and disclosure of past crimes. This approach has been used in different degrees by former European Communist regimes. In Russia, for example, the state has opened selective files permitting investigation into programs and policies used during the era of Communist repression. The former East Germany (GDR), the Communist regime that boasted the most extensive security and spying system in Eastern and Central Europe, however, has undertaken the most significant disclosure of secret files. It was estimated that in the heyday of Communist rule, the GDR's Ministry of State Security (Stasi) had files on more than 6 million of its 17 million citizens, involving a full-time staff of nearly one hundred thousand employees and supported by some two hundred thousand collaborators (informers). In the aftermath of Germany's reunification, the new government passed legislation permitting individuals to review their personal files.[22]

A second strategy is for governments to establish truth commissions. This strategy has been a major approach of transitional societies during the 1980s and 1990s, when more than twenty countries established truth commissions to investigate regime crimes (see table 1.1).[23] Although the principal aim of such bodies was largely the same—namely, to describe the scope and the character of past human rights violations—their perceived authority and legitimacy have varied significantly, depending on their legal basis, political authority, and public support.[24]

Discovering and disclosing the truth about a former regime's crimes and abuses presents enormous obstacles. To begin with, the truth most desired by the victims and their families—the facts about detention, torture, killings,

Table 1.1. Classification of Selected Truth Commissions

Country	Name and Size	Nature and Origin	Purpose	Report
Argentina	National Commission on the Disappeared (CONADEP) (13 members)	Official; established by presidential decree, 1983	Describe the nature and scope of major human rights abuses during 1970s era of military rule	*Nunca Más—Report of the Argentine Commission on the Disappeared* (1984)
Chile	National Commission on Truth and Reconciliation (8 members)	Official; established by presidential decree, 1990	Describe the nature and scope of human rights abuses during era of military rule, 1973–1990	*Report of the Chilean National Commission on Truth and Reconciliation* (1991)
Germany	Enquete Commission (6 members)	Official; established by the German parliament, 1992	Describe the nature and scope of human rights abuses carried out by E. Germany's Communist government, 1950–1989	*Inquiry [Enquete] Commission in the Bundestag for the "Treatment of the Past and the Consequences of the SED-Dictatorship in Germany"* (1994)
El Salvador	Commission on Truth for El Salvador (3 foreign members)	Official; established as part of the 1992 UN peace process; UN sanctioned	Describe major human rights violations during 1980–1991 civil war	*From Madness to Hope: The 12-Year War in El Salvador* (1993)
Guatemala	Historical Clarification Commission (3 members, one of them a foreigner)	Official; established in 1996 as part of the UN-supervised peace accord	Describe the nature and scope of human rights abuses during the 30-year civil war, 1975–1995	*Guatemala: Memory of Silence* (1999)

Country	Commission	Status	Purpose	Report
Haiti	National Commission for Truth and Justice (7 members)	Official; appointed by the president	Describe major human rights abuses from 1991 to 1994	*If I Don't Cry Out . . .* (1996)
Honduras	National Commissioner for Protection of Human Rights (1 person)	Official; appointed by the president	Investigate disappearances during 1980–1993 period	*Honduras: The Facts Speak for Themselves* (1994)
Peru	Truth and Reconciliation Commission (12 members)	Official; established by law; began functioning in mid-2001	Investigate human rights abuses from 1980 to 2000	*Final Report of the Truth and Reconciliation Commission* (2003)
South Africa	Truth and Reconciliation Commission (TRC) (17 members)	Official; created by parliament	Discover the truth about major human rights abuses during the 1960–1994 period	*Report of the South Africa Truth and Reconciliation Commission* (1998)
Guatemala	Project to Recover Historic Memory	Unofficial; established by the Catholic bishops of Guatemala	Describe the nature and scope of human rights abuses by state and paramilitary agents	*Guatemala: Never Again* (1998)
Brazil	Study Commission	Unofficial; report prepared secretly with the support of the Catholic Church and the World Council of Churches	Describe human rights abuses, especially torture, used by the military from 1964 to 1979	*Brazil: Nunca Más*; in the U.S. the report is titled *Torture in Brazil* (1985)

and especially the status of disappearances—is likely to be the most difficult
to uncover. Military and police officials who carried out abuses are unlikely
to disclose knowledge about crimes and human rights abuses, lest the disclosure of such wrongdoing results in their own prosecution. The experiences of Chile and Argentina, which have succeeded in uncovering only limited information on the thousands of missing detainees, bear out this
conclusion. To date the most successful experiment in truth telling is South
Africa's Truth and Reconciliation Commission (TRC), which encouraged disclosure by promising amnesty to offenders who confessed their political
crimes fully.

A more fundamental obstacle to truth telling is that historical truth is not
coherent and unitary but contested. It may be possible to develop a high
level of agreement about the empirical, objective facts about the past, but
developing an authoritative interpretation of past political conflict is likely to
be elusive, since perceptions and views will depend on the worldviews of
participants. This does not mean, as some postmodern thinkers imply, that
all historical truth is subjective, rooted solely in the narratives of each observer's life. But it does suggest that historical interpretation will depend
partly on the social, political, and cultural location of those who describe and
interpret the past. Since narrative truth is likely to be disputed, Mark Osiel argues that the conclusions of a truth commission are likely to be seen as "partial"—a partiality that is likely to be expressed by the failure of truth commissions to refute the claims of perpetrators.[25]

Developing an authoritative account of a complex political conflict—such
as the Catholic-Protestant conflict in Northern Ireland, the culpability for the
1994 Rwanda genocide, or the responsibility for Argentina's "dirty war"—is
likely to be a daunting, if not impossible, task. In his study of the roots of the
Rwanda genocide, Mahmood Mamdani argues that establishing the truth
about the genocide is likely to be impossible until "a prior reconciliation with
history" occurs. Since Rwanda's history has two versions (Hutu and Tutsi),
the identification of perpetrators and survivors will depend on "one's historical perspective."[26] Accordingly, if national reconciliation is to occur, both
groups will have to develop an acceptable shared memory. Even if a commission were to succeed in developing a compelling description and explanation of past offenses, however, it is unlikely that its conclusions would alter the views and perceptions of partisans to the dispute.

In addition, since memory is likely to impede conflict resolution, the quest
for responsibility for past injustices and offenses is likely to impede conflict
resolution. According to some observers, the success of the Oslo negotiations, which ultimately resulted in an Israeli-Palestinian Peace Accord, came
about because the unofficial negotiators, supported by Norwegian government officials, made a commitment early on to avoid history lessons and to
focus solely on political negotiations.[27]

Although truth commissions may be ineffective in establishing moral truth about recent history, they nonetheless can play a vital role in disseminating factual truth about regime wrongdoing. Such truth is important because it fosters consensus about major offenses, thereby reducing, in the words of Ignatieff, the "lies that can be circulated unchallenged in public discourse."[28]

Acknowledgment and Apologies

Although the discovery of truth is important, it is not a sufficient condition for effectively reckoning with the past. Rather, the truth about the government's complicity in human rights abuses must be officially acknowledged so that a society can effectively confront and overcome its collective guilt. The aim in truth telling is therefore not simply to disclose historical facts, but to publicly acknowledge responsibility. Indeed, how senior government leaders respond to the disclosure of truth is as important as the uncovering of facts itself. When South Africa's TRC began its task of gathering data about the crimes of the apartheid regime, it did so through highly publicized open forums. And when Chilean president Aylwin made public the country's truth commission report in 1991, he did so in a televised ceremony marked by reverence and sacramental significance. In his speech, Aylwin noted that while perpetrators were chiefly state agents, all of society was partly responsible for the human rights violations of the military era. "It is Chilean society," he said, "that owes a debt to the victims of human rights violations."[29]

Official apologies are another, more demanding way of responding to the disclosure of regime crimes. Apologies—the public expression of remorse or regret for moral wrongdoing—are a speech act in which offenders express sorrow or regret toward victims in the hope that such remorse will contribute to the restoration of relationships. Apologies can foster healing because the sorrow and contrition expressed by an offender can lead victims to respond with compassion and even forgiveness toward offenders. Although apologies, like forgiveness, are thought to apply primarily to the realm of interpersonal relations, they are also applicable to the behavior of collectives— what sociologist Nicholas Tavuchis terms apologies of the "Many." According to Tavuchis, such apologies are expressed from an individual to a collective ("One to Many"), from a collective to an individual ("Many to One,") or among collectives themselves ("Many to Many").[30]

While corporate or collective apologies are rooted in the interpersonal model, they differ from personal apologies in that the emotion of sorrow plays a diminished role. This is so because official apologies tend to be formal and public and expressed vicariously by people who were not themselves involved in the commission of the offenses. Even though sorrow is normally absent from official apologies, Tavuchis does not think that this necessarily limits their effectiveness. What is important in collective apologies, he suggests, is

to publicly acknowledge the moral offense and to take responsibility for it—
that is, "to put things on record, to document as a prelude to reconciliation."[31]

Indeed, Trudy Govier and Wilhelm Verwoerd argue that the healing power
of public apologies is not found in the expression of sorrow but rather in the
significance of acknowledgment itself.[32] Since apologies are a means by which
communities can publicly admit guilt, they allow a group or community to acknowledge responsibility and to express remorse for unjustly inflicted harm.
Thus, if an apology is to contribute to the restoration of a fractured and alienated community, it must "acknowledge wrongdoing and thereby also acknowledge the human dignity and legitimate feelings of those wronged."[33]

Public apologies are a relatively recent development.[34] Fifty years ago it
would have been unusual for political leaders to express collective remorse
for injustices and crimes inflicted on other peoples. But since the 1980s, such
apologies have become an increasing part of the lexicon of conflict resolution and communal restorative justice. Following are some recent examples
of official apologies:

- After a North Korean spy submarine ran aground off South Korea's eastern coast in September 1996, its crewmen were killed in gun battles
  with South Korean troops. Four months later, North Korea apologized
  for this incident, thereby easing tensions between the two countries. In
  its declaration, the North Korean government expressed "deep regret"
  for the incident and promised not to repeat such an incident and that
  the government would "work with others for durable peace and stability on the Korean Peninsula." As a result of this apology, South Korea
  returned the bodies of the twenty-four infiltrators.[35]
- In the Catholic Church's most important apology ever, Pope John Paul II
  publicly repented for some of the Church's major institutional sins over
  the past two millennia. The Church expressed an apology in a homily
  and more formally in a carefully crafted document that had been drafted
  by an international theological commission.[36] In the statement, the
  Church repented of some of its major sins, including the Crusades and
  the Inquisition, forced evangelism, persecution of Jews, division among
  Christians, and social injustice. By issuing this apology, the Vatican
  aimed to acknowledge its historic sins and thereby create a moral basis
  for purification and restoration through forgiveness and reconciliation.
- On July 16, 2002—the thirtieth anniversary of an IRA operation in Belfast
  that killed nine people—the Irish Republican Army apologized for causing the deaths of many noncombatants in its campaign for a unified Ireland. It acknowledged that "the future would not be found in denying
  collective failures and mistakes or closing minds and hearts to the plight
  of those who have been hurt." Accordingly, the IRA statement expressed
  "sincere apologies and condolences" to the families of noncombatants.

Although apologies such as these can potentially contribute to reducing alienation and distrust, the declaration of public remorse is much more effective when supplemented by tangible actions.

REPARATIONS

A fourth way in which states can reckon with past regime offenses is to make amends for losses and injuries. Such amends can involve three types of actions: financial reparations, restitution of stolen property, and programs of personal rehabilitation. Financial reparations refer to material or financial compensation for that which cannot be returned, such as a missing person or a lost or damaged work of art. Restitution involves the return of financial assets or property that was confiscated, seized, or stolen. Rehabilitation involves deliberate programs designed to restore victims and their families to the moral and legal status that they enjoyed before regime atrocities were committed.

Reparations are a means by which states can pursue restoration of victims and their divided communities. While many personal injuries and losses cannot be relieved through monetary compensation, financial reparations provide a tangible means by which a state can assume responsibility for past crimes, express official contrition for state-inflicted suffering, and express solidarity with victims. One of the ways that Germany sought to atone for the Holocaust was to assist Jewish people in securing a homeland and to offer reparations to survivors. German leaders were aware, however, that such actions could never repair the evil that had been committed. As Chancellor Helmut Kohl observed at a ceremony marking the 40th anniversary of the liberation of the Bergen-Belsen Concentration Camp in 1985, "suffering and death, pain and tears are not susceptible to reparations. The only answer can be collective commemoration, collective mourning, and a collective resolve to live together in a peaceful world."[37]

Since money cannot bring back that which has been destroyed, financial reparations are not intended to compensate victims for their losses. Rather, they are symbolic acts of a regime's guilt and remorse.[38] Martha Minow writes that there is no method by which to determine "the value of living an ordinary life, without nightmares or survivor guilt." Moreover, assessing the losses from atrocities such as torture and secret killing "strains the moral imagination." If genocide has occurred, the challenge is to determine who should be compensated. Even if some members of a group survive, compensating them for the loss of their nation will defy computation and comprehension. As a result, Minow argues that "symbolic expressions become the only possibilities."[39]

In 1951 Konrad Adenauer, West Germany's first chancellor, called on the new democratic government to confront its collective guilt for World War II atrocities through reparations. In an address to his nation's parliament, Adenauer noted that since "unspeakable crimes" had been committed against Jews and other groups, the German state had an obligation to make "moral and material amends."[40] As a result the government initiated major reparations programs, transferring over many years some $75 billion to German citizens for financial or physical losses and an estimated $150 billion to foreign countries for destruction and harm carried out by Nazi conquest.[41]

A similar but much more modest reparations program was undertaken by the U.S. government on behalf of Japanese Americans who had been unjustly detained during World War II. From 1941 to 1945, some 120,000 people of Japanese ancestry living on the West Coast—a majority of them U.S. citizens—were removed to remote detention campuses, ostensibly to protect the country from espionage and sabotage.[42] When the war ended in 1945, no effort was made to apologize for their suffering or to assist them in returning to their communities. Thus in the 1970s, U.S. legislators began considering reparations for living detainees. One of the first steps was taken in 1976 by President Gerald Ford when he officially revoked Executive Order 9066, which had provided the basis for the internment of Japanese Americans thirty-five years earlier. After extensive negotiations, Congress enacted in 1988 the Civil Liberties Act, which provided that every living detainee would receive symbolic reparations of $20,000 plus an official letter of apology. The official apology declared in part:

> A monetary sum and words alone cannot restore lost years or erase painful memories; neither can they fully convey our Nation's resolve to rectify injustice and to uphold the rights of individuals. We can never fully right the wrongs of the past. But we can take a clear stand for justice and recognize that serious injustices were done to Japanese Americans during World War II.[43]

It has been estimated that by 1999 the U.S. government had distributed $1.6 billion to some eighty thousand detainees.[44]

A second way in which individual and collective healing can be promoted is through the restitution of property (land, art, money, and other tangible assets) that was unjustly confiscated by a prior government. Although the return of property should be a relatively simple act, in practice it can involve vexing challenges. One of these arises when significant time has elapsed from the time the property was first confiscated. Jeremy Waldron illustrates this problem by examining the moral challenges confronting New Zealand as it has sought to reckon with the mid-nineteenth-century injustices perpetrated by the British colonial authorities in appropriating lands claimed by the Maori people. Since ownership of original properties had passed along to numerous generations of innocent landowners and since most of these properties had been significantly developed, the effort to rectify past historic injustices through restitution threatened to create new injustices. Waldron therefore questions the justice of land restitution, calling into question the simple claim that "if something was wrongly taken, it must be right to give it back." It is not that he seeks to discount past injustices; rather, his argument is that "claims about justice and injustice must be responsive to changes in circumstances."[45] As a result, when restitution is likely to create new injustices, financial reparations supported through society-wide taxation may offer a more effective approach to historic property injustices.[46]

Another challenge in restitution arises from the demand for legal certification for property entitlement. For example, while German Jews had made significant deposits in Swiss banks prior to World War II, when relatives sought to withdraw money from the banks after the Holocaust, the Swiss government refused to acknowledge the legitimacy of the requests, claiming that a death certificate was necessary. Moreover, since Swiss authorities refused to disclose information about inactive accounts, the problem of financial restitution lay dormant until American business and political leaders took up the issue in the 1980s. As a result of their initiatives, the Swiss government was forced to confront the issue,[47] resulting in a historic accord in which Swiss banks agreed to provide $1.25 billion in restitution to Holocaust survivors and Jewish groups as compensation for unclaimed pre–World War II Jewish bank deposits.[48]

The restitution of private property presents even greater obstacles when the confiscated property has been radically transformed through misuse or physical changes that involve major social and structural developments. Improper confiscation was of course the case in Eastern European countries where Communist regimes confiscated most private property and instituted state enterprises and collective farms. In Czechoslovakia, for example, the Communist regime confiscated nearly all land, buildings, industries, and businesses, as well as the extensive properties of the Roman Catholic Church after it took control of the government in the late 1940s.[49] Thus, when democracy returned in 1990, the new democratic regime faced major social and economic challenges in restoring property to original owners.[50] Confiscated farmland, for example, had led to the creation of some 1,900 collective and state farms that employed about 650,000 workers. How should the privatization of these farms be undertaken, and who should care for these workers?

Finally, the restitution of property can present vexing moral problems in determining which groups should be entitled to restitution. Frequently, such decisions will necessarily involve morally ambiguous judgments in allocating the legitimacy of claims. The prudential nature of restitution was clearly evident in the Czechoslovak restitution laws that called for the return of all property seized by the Communist regime from 1948 to 1989. As a result, these laws deliberately excluded the confiscation of farms in the Sudetenland in the immediate aftermath of World War II.[51] In addition, they also deliberately excluded nearly half a million emigrants—Czechs who fled the country after Communists had come to power.

A third way of pursuing restoration is through legal, political, and personal rehabilitation of victims and their families. Legal rehabilitation occurs when transitional regimes seek to restore the legal status of victims by annulling decrees or overturning the criminal convictions of courts. In Czechoslovakia, for example, judicial rehabilitation involved the immediate annulment of all court convictions of "political crimes" during the era of Communist rule—an action that affected some two hundred thousand people and resulted in the release of numerous people from prison. More dramatically, the Czech parliament adopted legislation in 1993 that declared the Communist regime illegal.[52] The restoration of political rights is also an important dimension of rehabilitation. Since crimes and human rights abuses result in the undermining of the moral equality of people, political rehabilitation will necessarily entail uplifting and affirming those who have suffered crimes and human rights abuses while diminishing the influence and stature of those responsible for crimes. Such rehabilitation can occur as a by-product of trials and purges that diminish the influence of leaders and agents responsible for human rights abuses. But it can also occur through the public acknowledgment of wrongdoing and the expression of official apologies.

Finally, rehabilitation can involve efforts to personally assist victims and their families in overcoming mental or physical injuries that have resulted from human rights abuses. In the early 1990s, for example, the government of Chile established a medical and therapeutic assistance program to encourage psychological and medical rehabilitation. Such aid was especially important to victims and relatives who had suffered trauma in the aftermath of forced abduction and torture.[53]

Although reparations and restitution can help to compensate for physical and psychological injuries, human and property losses, and communal destruction, they can never fully recover the conditions that existed prior to the commission of the wrongdoing. The best that can be achieved is some compensatory justice through reparations and restitution and some restorative justice through rehabilitation. The first type of justice attempts to provide financial and symbolic resources to compensate for tangible and intangible losses. Restorative justice, by contrast, seeks to heal interpersonal and communal relationships by transforming subjective conditions that impair the restoration of peaceful, productive relationships. As I will argue in chapter 4, the theory of restorative justice has become more important in recent years in part because of the growing realization that retribution alone will not necessarily result in the healing of victims and the restoration of communities.

PURGES

A fifth approach that some states have used in reckoning with past regime offenses is the removal of alleged offenders from government service. Purges—sometimes defined as lustration[54]—aim to purify a political system by eliminating the power and influence of former regime officials and party supporters.[55] The major justification for purging former leaders, collaborators, and supporters from the new political order is the belief that the presence of personnel from the old political order will impede the consolidation of new moral values and a transformed political order. As French philosopher Albert Camus observed in January 1945, shortly after France had been liberated and the new democratic regime had begun prosecuting Vichy collaborators, "A country that fails in its purge is ready to fail in its restoration."[56] Indeed, in order to foster trust and confidence in the new democratic order, political cleansing from past collective injustices is imperative. Joachim Gauck, the German clergyman and human rights activist who was appointed federal commissioner for administering access to Ministry of State Security (Stasi) files in post–Cold War Germany, noted that if citizens were to trust government personnel in the new democratic regime, it was important that political and government officials be trustworthy. As a result, it was essential "to respond to the East German people's minimal demand that persons who had conspired with the regime, unbeknown to their fellow citizens, should be deemed unsuitable for public positions of trust."[57] Thus, leaders and public officials, as well as those who indirectly collaborated with the regime by serving as informers, were to be ineligible for state office. This meant that judges, lawyers, police, teachers, university professors, and other representatives of the state who had collaborated with the government of East Germany (GDR) could not serve as public sector employees.

Purges have been widely used in the past half-century to overcome the evils and sins of a former regime. Beginning in 1945, numerous European governments, including those of Belgium, Denmark, France, the Netherlands, and Norway, used screening and purges to identify regime collaborators and to rid the new government of people who had previously served the state or supported the regime. Purges were also a major element of the Allied strategy in seeking to cleanse Germany from the political and cultural effects of Nazism. Believing that the evils of the Third Reich were due in great measure to the ideology of Nazism, the Allies determined to purify German society by eliminating organizations, changing laws, and transforming cultural, educational, and social institutions that had been influenced by Nazi ideology. Since each of the four Allied powers was assigned a sector of Germany, each carried out its own denazification project. By all accounts the most thorough was the one carried out by the United States.[58]

The problematic nature of society-wide purges was illustrated in the post–Cold War era as emerging democratic regimes in Europe sought to purify themselves from the influence of former Communist government officials and collaborators. The challenge of purifying a nation of its political past without perpetrating significant procedural injustices was especially evident in Czechoslovakia. Its lustration process began in January 1991 when the Czechoslovakian parliament appointed a commission to identify former Communist agents or collaborators currently serving in government. It also charged the commission with notifying deputies who were "positively identified," giving them fifteen days to resign. If they failed to do so, the commission was authorized to disclose their names.[59] Once the lustration process began, however, the anti-Communist forces began demanding a more extensive purge.[60] The Assembly adopted a more stringent measure (the Lustration Law of October 1991) that barred from government any Communist official or security agent for a five-year period. The vetting process was to be carried out by the Ministry of Internal Affairs by reviewing the files of the former state security agency (the StB). Individuals that had formerly served as Communist leaders, secret police agents, collaborators, members of the People's Militia, or had held an administrative office in the former regime were to be barred temporarily from public service.

Predictably, the lustration process resulted in significant, acrimonious debate within the Czech and Slovak Federation. Those who supported the purges believed that former public officials and their supporters should be removed from public influence because of the untold suffering and abuses that they had inflicted on the Czech and Slovak people. Critics of lustration pointed out, however, that the purges did not target individuals who had committed crimes but instead placed blame on all those who were directly or indirectly affiliated with some aspect of the regime. Moreover, they emphasized that since the Czech Communist regime was totalitarian in character, virtually all people were partly responsible for the former regime's evil and injustice. Most troubling to critics, however, was the assumption of guilt by association. Since collaborators were people who had been in contact with an employee of the StB, critics argued that a person could be expelled from the parliament or a state job simply because he or she might have spoken to a government agent.[61]

Since purges are carried out through administrative procedures based on membership and association, they are rooted in a presumption of collective responsibility. That is, people are assumed to bear political guilt by virtue of their political association, regardless of their personal culpability. Unlike criminal trials that are used to ascertain individual guilt, governmental purges are imposed through simple screening techniques using police records, secret informants' files, political party lists, or service in governmental or political organizations. Even when efforts are made to focus on the culpability of leaders and agents most responsible for regime offenses, purges by their very nature tend to be nondiscriminatory because they are based on collective responsibility.[62] Thus, although purges may be useful in establishing a clear break with the injustices of a former regime, such a practice is morally problematic because it compromises the constitutional norm of due process at the altar of political expiation.

Still, defenders of purges claim that if former regimes are responsible for significant injustices and human rights abuses then a widespread ban on governmental service by former regime officials and agents is a small cost to pay, even if individual responsibility is not proven or legal due process cannot be fulfilled. Moreover, supporters of lustration claim that such an approach is all the more warranted if trials are not a realistic alternative. Tina Rosenberg has noted that since European Communist systems imposed a broad repression throughout society, culpability was similarly dispersed.[63] In such an environment, trials would have been nearly impossible. By contrast, in Latin America, where authoritarian regimes perpetrated more limited but more serious human rights violations, trials were a more feasible alternative in addressing past official criminality.

In seeking to cleanse a country of the values, institutions, and personnel associated with a former unjust regime, it is prudent to keep in mind the breadth and depth of responsibility for a former regime's injustices. In his inaugural address on January 1, 1990, Václav Havel, Czechoslovakia's president, observed that all society was responsible for the moral decay of the country. He explained:

> When I talk about a decayed moral environment . . . I mean all of us, because all of us became accustomed to the totalitarian system, accepted it as an unalterable fact, and thereby kept it running. . . . None of us is merely a victim of it because all of us helped to create it together. We cannot lay all the blame on those who ruled us before, not only because this would not be true but also because it could detract from the responsibility each of us now faces—the responsibility to act on our own initiative, freely, sensibly, and quickly.[64]

Because he believed that all sectors of society were partly responsible for the evils of communism, Havel tried to limit lustration in his own land. Still, if other alternatives, such as truth commissions and trials, are not politically feasible, then perhaps a limited and discriminating system of purges may be legally and morally justifiable. But the injustices associated with purges must be minimized in any effort to cleanse a country of its authoritarian or totalitarian legacy.

TRIALS

A final means by which states have reckoned with the crimes and political abuses of former regimes is legal prosecution. A large number of criminal justice scholars believe that if the rule of law is to be institutionalized, past criminal wrongdoing must be punished. According to this view, a transitional regime cannot begin by disregarding the offenses of a previous regime. Rather, it must confront the major crimes and human rights abuses of former officials and, where justified, prosecute, try, and punish those who are guilty. In calling for the prosecution of political and military leaders responsible for war crimes in the Bosnian war, U.S. Secretary of State Madeleine Albright expressed her commitment to the "first justice, then peace" approach as follows:

> Justice is essential to strengthen the rule of law, soften the bitterness of victims' families, and remove an obstacle to cooperation among the parties. It will help ensure that our forces can depart Bosnia without the fear that renewed violence threatening U.S. interests might one day return. It will establish a model for resolving ethnic differences by the force of law rather than the law of force.[65]

In short, the liberal, legalist perspective assumes that if peace and democracy are desired, justice must be pursued first.

The most widespread argument for trials is that they are necessary in order to consolidate the rule of law. If a new legal and political foundation is to be established, those who committed wrongs must be punished, thereby reinforcing the belief that all people are subject to the legal norms of society regardless of power or wealth. The rule of law is further consolidated by moral equality affirmed by courts. Whereas criminal behavior results in the dominance of offenders over victims, trials help to restore the worth of victims by reasserting the moral equality between victims and offenders. In addition, trials promote general confidence in courts and legal institutions, ensuring that no person or group is beyond the reach of the law.

Legal retributivists also claim that trials help promote reconciliation. Indeed, their motto is "first justice, then peace" or "first justice, then reconciliation." While serving as the U.S. Permanent Representative to the United Nations and later as secretary of state, Albright repeatedly emphasized this perspective, demanding that political leaders who were responsible for gross human rights abuses should be prosecuted, either in national courts or international war crimes tribunals. As a result, she was a principal advocate for the establishment of the international war crimes tribunals in The Hague in order to bring to justice leaders who had perpetrated atrocities during the Bosnian war or the Rwanda genocide. While visiting a refugee camp in Sierra Leone in October 1999, Albright declared: "The only way that reconciliation can come is if people have a sense that justice has been done and those who have perpetrated the terrible crimes are punished individually."[66]

Trial advocates also claim that war crimes trials are beneficial in rehabilitating illiberal states. Gary Jonathan Bass, for example, claims that the rehabilitation program of Germany's legal order by Western powers in the aftermath of World War II was one of the "great political successes of the century" in that it transformed a fascist regime into a democratic state.[67] This claim can similarly be made of Japan's political transformation. Advocates of legalism also argue that trials encourage the discovery and disclosure of truth. According to Jaime Malamud-Goti, a presidential advisor to Argentine president Raúl Alfonsín, trials have the advantage of disclosing specific, concrete information about past regime crimes.[68] Trials are also seen as a means to resolve claims of justice.

Unlike the prosecution of individual crimes, however, prosecuting state-sponsored offenses is a much more difficult undertaking. Such is the case for a number of reasons. First, evidence of state-sponsored crimes is often sketchy, incomplete, or altogether unavailable. It may be possible to develop a general account of regime offenses, but generating sufficient evidence to prosecute individuals is likely to be far more elusive. A related problem is the difficulty in securing evidence against decision makers responsible for the policies that resulted in collective atrocities. Since it is much easier to secure evidence for the specific actions of state agents, prosecuting low-level officials is much easier than prosecuting leaders. Thus, when Germany began prosecuting former officials and agents of the former GDR, the first trials focused on the killings by border guards. And although one Communist leader was sentenced for his part in the "shoot to kill" border policy, some senior leaders were prosecuted for crimes unrelated to the oppression of the Communist regime.[69]

A third difficulty in legal prosecution is that the state may have itself authorized policies that resulted in human rights abuses. Since Western jurisprudence is based on the principle of *nulla poena sine lege* (no punishment without a law),[70] crimes must be judged in terms of laws that were in effect at the time that the alleged violations occurred. Accordingly, prosecuting officials for actions that were sanctioned by the former authorities presents a daunting task.[71] Finally, legal accountability may not be possible if the public is not strongly in support of such action. For example, few trials have been undertaken in the former Communist regimes, where regimes were more eager to consolidate democracy and institutionalize privatization and market reforms than to confront past wrongdoing.[72] The most significant trials and truth commissions have been carried out in Latin America, where human rights violations were severe but comparatively limited in scope, especially when compared to the egregious systemic crimes carried out by totalitarian regimes.

If prosecution of former state offenses is to succeed, the domestic political environment must be conducive to trials. Favorable conditions may exist when former regimes are discredited and replaced, such as in Greece in 1974, Argentina in 1983, and the Philippines in 1986. But when a new regime comes to power through the voluntary transfer of power (for example, Brazil in the mid-1980s and Chile in 1990) or through the cooperative action of the government and opposition groups (for example, Uruguay in 1985, Poland in 1989, and South Africa in 1994), prosecution of past wrongdoing is likely to be difficult, if not impossible. This is so because such regimes are likely to have limited authority and trials could imperil the fragile democratic structures themselves. According to Samuel Huntington, emerging democratic regimes should undertake a full accounting of past human rights abuses, but should carry out trials only if a regime has been replaced by force. If transformation or transplacement has occurred, prosecution of government officials should be resisted, since "the political costs of such an effort will outweigh any moral gains."[73] In addition, Huntington argues that if trials are undertaken, they should be carried out swiftly with only the most senior decision makers being prosecuted.[74]

In sum, while each of the strategies sketched earlier can potentially contribute to overcoming the legacy of past human rights abuses, none of them alone is sufficient to ensure the restoration of relationships and the healing of political community. If societies are to fully confront and overcome past evils and injustices, they will have to come to grips with the anger, alienation, distrust, and hatred that continue to fester, even after applying some of these strategies.

In confronting past regime offenses, governments might want to consider applying another, rarely utilized approach—namely, collective or political forgiveness. As with individuals, collective forgiveness is rooted in the acknowledgment of wrongdoing, the expression of remorse through apology or repentance, the renunciation of vengeance, and the expression of empathy. Unlike other transitional justice strategies examined here, political forgiveness seeks to overcome the cycle of anger and revenge through the moral reformation of attitudes and dispositions, the "purification of memory,"[75] and the restoration of relationships through reconciliation. A major strength of this strategy is its emphasis on political healing in order to—in Abraham Lincoln's words—"bind up the nation's wounds."

The aim of this book is therefore to explore the nature and role of the extraordinary ethic of forgiveness in public life. In chapter 2, I examine the idea of forgiveness and how it is conceived and applied in interpersonal relationships, and in chapter 3 I explore its potential role in social and political life. In chapter 4, I examine alternative conceptions of justice and seek to illuminate how forgiveness and reconciliation are consistent with this concept through the tradition of restorative justice.

2

The Nature and Purpose
of Forgiveness

Forgiving . . . is the only reaction which does not merely re-act but acts anew and unexpectedly, unconditioned by the act which provoked it and therefore freeing from its consequences both the one who forgives and the one who is forgiven. The freedom contained in Jesus' teachings of forgiveness is the freedom from vengeance, which incloses both doer and sufferer in the relentless automatism of the action process, which by itself need never come to an end.

—Hannah Arendt, noted Jewish political philosopher[1]

God of forgiveness, do not forgive those who created this place. God of mercy, have no mercy on those who killed here Jewish children.

—Elie Wiesel's prayer at the
50th anniversary of the liberation of Auschwitz[2]

Forgiveness is pitiless. It forgets the victim. It negates the right of the victim to his own life. It blurs over suffering and death. It drowns the past. It cultivates sensitiveness toward the murderer at the price of insensitiveness toward the victim.

—Cynthia Ozick, contemporary Jewish author[3]

All human communities—whether families, groups, associations, nations, or the international community itself—involve human cooperation and human conflict. Because people frequently seek their own self-interest in disregard for, or at the expense of others, tensions, disputes, and conflicts are an inevitable by-product of all social and political relationships. When interpersonal conflicts become intense, individuals frequently resort to acts of violence, setting in motion a cycle of revenge that perpetuates and even escalates human suffering. Similarly, when communal conflicts within or among nations involve vital, primordial interests, groups often take up collective violence, seeking to injure or punish enemies or seeking to redress perceived wrongs through force.

To be sure, a large portion of conflicts within political society can be satisfied through claims of justice in a country's courts. While judicial institutions play a critical role in the juridical settlement of disputes, adjudication seldom contributes to reconciliation between the contesting parties. More important, however, judicial and political institutions are often incapable of resolving ethnopolitical conflicts, and the result—as the painful post–Cold War record of ethnic conflict suggests—is a breakdown of civic order and brutal and genocidal destruction.

Although the prevention and resolution of conflicts are critical political tasks, our concern here is not the management and resolution of disputes but, rather, the restoration of civic life in the aftermath of major collective violence. How should societies seek to overcome the painful legacy of human rights abuses, state terrorism, and war? Should the new constitutional regime prosecute crimes committed by officials of a previous authoritarian or totalitarian regime? Is punishment of collective wrongdoing necessary for the healing of victims and to ensure the consolidation of democratic, constitutional rule? Should individuals and groups seek restitution?

Of course, not all past wrongs can be righted, and not all broken relationships can be restored. Time and amnesia may help to relieve the suffering of past evils, but the restoration of relationships and the renewal of communal solidarity are likely to remain elusive. Denial, amnesia, and avoidance might reduce the immediate tensions about past wrongdoing, but they are unlikely to provide fundamental relief from past offenses. The criminal justice system of states may provide temporary relief to victims, but prosecution is unlikely to heal personal injuries or to restore life or lost property. Indeed, even where punishment of wrongdoing is possible, judicial settlement will be incapable of restoring the status quo ante and the effects of injuries, abuses, and destruction will continue to be felt by victims.

Moreover, criminal prosecution may not always be a viable strategy, especially if the constitutional structures are weak, the society is deeply divided over the truth of past crimes, or criminal culpability is widespread. Since no simple approach is normally available to confront and overcome past regime wrongdoing, leaders may want to consider one individual and collective practice that is rarely applied—namely, forgiveness, a faculty that in the words of Arendt "serves to undo the deeds of the past."[4]

In this chapter, I examine the nature and basis of forgiveness. I first examine its nature and its relationship to memory and forgetting. In the second section, I illuminate the Judeo-Christian roots of the idea of forgiveness, focusing on two biblical case studies—the Joseph story and the parable of the prodigal son. I then present three alternative conceptions of forgiveness—the classical or interpersonal theory, the therapeutic or unilateral approach, and forgiveness as a moral craft. In the final section, I explore the process of forgiveness, focusing on some of its preconditions and the means by which this ethic can be implemented. In the following chapter, I explore whether and how the ethic of forgiveness might be applied to groups and political communities.

THE NATURE OF FORGIVENESS

Unjust and undeserved wrongdoing may involve physical violence, psychological harm, financial crimes, destruction of property, and violation of other people's rights. Regardless of the nature of the original offenses, wrongdoing has two effects—it damages individuals physically and psychologically, and it harms relationships and ruptures the social fabric of communal trust. When wrongdoing occurs, justice requires that perpetrators must be held to account for their offenses. According to the logic of retributive justice, the basis for most criminal justice systems, offenders must accept responsibility for their unjust actions and provide some payment for the offense, through either restitution, reparation, or punishment. The logic of the retributive approach is that perpetrators must be identified and punished for their illegitimate actions.

The Concept

But there is an alternative to the retributive logic. This is the act or process of forgiving. For offenders, forgiveness occurs when victims give up their claims of justice against them, freeing them from debts incurred by the wrongdoing. Fundamentally, forgiveness involves the forgoing of retributive claims of justice, or what Nicholas Wolterstorff terms the voluntary decision "to forego possessing or experiencing some or all the goods to which one has a retributive right."[5] For victims, forgiveness entails giving up anger and resentment so that the desire to avenge the injury no longer governs the relations of victims to offenders. In his exploration of the idea of forgiveness, philosopher Avishai Margalit argues that since forgiveness entails victims' giving up anger and resentment, it necessarily entails some forgetting. This forgetting, he suggests, is a voluntary choice by the wronged person not to take into account the past offense when relating to the offender. In effect, forgiveness is "the decision that the injury is not 'admissible evidence.'"[6] Thus, when victims forgive they give up just claims against offenders and cease being controlled by the memory of past wrongdoing.

The gift of forgiveness is important because it provides a means by which victims and offenders can restore an authentic moral self-worth. Since offenders have unjustly acquired tangible or intangible resources through wrongdoing, they have established a moral inequality between themselves and their victims. Forgiveness, which calls for the diminishing of the offenders' moral stature, is a nonretributive process by which a moral equality is restored between offenders and victims. This is achieved when offenders acknowledge wrongdoing and express remorse for their unjust offenses. Although it is usually assumed that the principal beneficiary of forgiveness is the perpetrator whose debts are erased, a primary by-product of forgiveness is the moral rehabilitation of the victim. Such restoration is realized when moral equality is reestablished with the offender and when anger and resentment cease to control victims.

Another important result of forgiveness is that it provides a basis for the restoration of interpersonal relationships and for the renewal of community bonds. Wrongdoing leads to broken, alienated relationships. Forgiveness is a means by which the interpersonal enmity and social divisions can be healed. Whether or not forgiveness leads to reconciliation will depend on the extent to which victims and perpetrators carry out mutually supportive actions that are conducive to the rebuilding of trust. While forgiveness need not result in the restoration of relationships and communal bonds, it can greatly contribute to reconciliation.

Memory and Forgiveness

Memory consists of that which human beings remember. Although the past is past, memory keeps the past alive by giving it a new lease on life, albeit in a different texture and form. Memory is not an objective record of all that has happened. Rather, it is an interpreted, selective recollection of the past—one that defines individual and collective (or cultural) identities in the present. Thus, what is remembered, and how and why, will have a decisive impact in shaping personal, social, and political identities.

Memory is crucial to individual and social life because it is foundational to human identity. A person who loses his or her memory loses his or her identity. To know who we are as individuals and as members of different collectives is to know who we are (and who we are not). Since history is not a complete record of the past but an interpretive account of individual and group identity, what people remember and do not remember is a function of who they are as individuals and as a community. As theologian Miroslav Volf notes, people remember what matters to them and forget what does not, and only what is remembered can matter to them.[7]

Since memory can perform both constructive and destructive roles, the challenge in forgiveness is to cultivate accountability that fosters personal healing and the restoration of social relationships. But how should victims and offenders view past wrongdoing? If accountability and truth telling are necessary in fostering authentic forgiveness, how should "redemptive" remembering be encouraged and facilitated? Can too much memory impede forgiveness and reconciliation? Does forgiveness require some forgetting and, if so, at what point should victims and offenders shift their attention from the past to the present and future?

According to Margalit, forgiveness depends on a certain type of forgetting. Since he views forgiveness as giving up anger and vengeance, Margalit believes that forgiveness is realized only when a victim has a change of heart about past offenses—a change that will become manifest when a victim voluntarily chooses to disregard past offenses. This change can be realized either by disregarding, but not forgetting, past wrongdoing or by deliberately forgetting the offense as if it never had occurred.[8] Since Margalit conceives of forgiveness as a voluntary act to disregard, but not forget moral offenses, he favors the first model involving a combination of some remembrance and some deliberate neglect of past wrongdoing.

It is important to stress that memory is a foundational element of forgiveness. Since forgiveness is a means of confronting and overcoming past wrongdoing, reconciliation through forgiveness is possible only through the prism of memory—that is, by recalling and redeeming the past. But if memory is necessary for the healing of past injustices and the restoration of broken relationships, it can also serve, as noted earlier, as the basis for continuing resentment, anger, and vengeance. Theologian Lewis Smedes has correctly noted that "as long as our minds are captive to the memory of having been wronged they are not free to wish for reconciliation."[9] The role of memory is thus ambiguous, providing a redemptive foundation for renewal and reconciliation, as well as a basis for lingering anger, hatred, and retribution.

Since forgiveness attempts to redeem past injustices, a forgiven people will necessarily interpret the past differently than those who have not participated in forgiveness. After going through a long process of mourning that culminates in forgiveness, victims can ultimately reach what Volf calls the "stage of nonremembering,"[10] where past injustices are no longer important to victims. This does not mean that memory ceases to be important, but that people, through the healing power of forgiveness, are freed to view the past from a new vantage point. Smedes calls this transformed perspective "redemptive remembering"—one that "keeps a clear picture of the past, but it adds a new setting and shifts its focus."[11] Such remembering, he suggests, is illustrated in the Jewish Passover feast, which seeks not to memorialize the injustice suffered from Egyptian bondage but to recall the miracle of survival and renewal in the midst of great suffering. What is memorialized is not injustice and suffering but God's faithfulness.[12]

THE RELIGIOUS FOUNDATIONS OF FORGIVENESS

Judeo-Christian Roots

Although the idea of forgiveness is found in several religions and traditions, it receives its most prominent development and application within the

Jewish and Christian religions. In Judaism, divine forgiveness is available to those who acknowledge their sin, express contrition and remorse, and promise not to repeat the offense. Since the Jewish faith is rooted in law (Torah), redemption from sin is achieved through atonement, as called for by the legal structures of the Jewish faith. Such structures ensure that divine forgiveness remains rooted in God's law and justice, yet conditional on the fulfillment of demanding preconditions. Some of these structural prerequisites—such as acknowledgment of sin, remorse, desisting from sin, and repentance—help to ensure that forgiveness remains a part of communal life, not a private, individual action between God and man.

In the Jewish tradition, human forgiveness is regarded almost exclusively as an interpersonal process involving changes in people's attitudes and behaviors.[13] Although the forgiveness process presupposes intentions and dispositions that are conducive to compassion and empathy, the practice of forgiveness is ultimately expressed through words and actions. When an offense is committed, an offender incurs a debt to the victim. In Jewish thought, only a victim can rectify, modify, or annul the debt created by an offender's wrongdoing. Although God forgives sins, only victims can forgive the human offenses of perpetrators. As a result, murder, genocide, and state-sponsored killing are generally considered unforgivable offenses in the Jewish tradition because the deceased are unable to annul the claims against the perpetrators of the crimes. Moreover, since forgiveness is generally viewed only as an interpersonal process between victims and offenders, the Jewish tradition is skeptical of collective or institutional forgiveness. Thus, Judaism gives little encouragement to the idea of social or political forgiveness.

In Christianity, Jewish law is fulfilled through divine love, which is manifest through the atonement of human sins fulfilled by Jesus' sacrificial death. Forgiveness of sins is therefore unlimited and unconditional, based solely on the divine promise of God's unqualified grace expressed by the life of Jesus and fulfilled in His atonement. This doctrine, however, has been interpreted differently by Catholics and Protestants—with the latter viewing forgiveness as a process solely between the sinner and God and the former viewing it as a relationship mediated by the Church.[14] Moreover, since God's love and mercy are unlimited, divine forgiveness cannot be earned through good works. Rather, it is an unmerited gift, available to all people regardless of their offenses, provided they are truly contrite and repentant of their sin.[15]

Christians understand forgiveness as the release from bondage, guilt, and punishment arising from moral wrongdoing. As such, it involves first and foremost a transaction between people and God, in which human beings acknowledge and repent of their sins to God, who has promised to forgive all those who are contrite and penitent of their wrongdoing (1 John 1:9). But Christian forgiveness also entails transactions among human beings—between perpetrators and victims. Since human beings are called to follow their Heavenly Father in being merciful and compassionate, believers are admonished to express love and mercy toward others by forgiving those who commit offenses.[16] Indeed, the Scriptures call on believers to become reconciled with their "brother" before making offerings to God. From a biblical perspective, forgiveness is a transactional process between offender and victim (for example, Matt. 5:24). Theologian Geiko Müller-Fahrenholz has observed that

> Forgiveness can occur when the perpetrator asks for it and the victim grants it. This mutuality is basic to an understanding of the biblical concept. Both sides are changed by this encounter. A healing takes place which paves the way for a better cooperation between formerly conflicting partners. . . . A guilty and painful past is redeemed in order to establish reliable foundations for renewed fellowship in dignity and trust. Forgiveness frees the future from the haunting legacies of the past.[17]

Although some critics have suggested that Christian forgiveness is a means of bypassing culpability, authentic forgiveness is a demanding ethic that places heavy burdens on both the offender and the victim. To begin with, offenders must come to terms with their culpability and offer reparations as a way of authenticating their remorse. Similarly, forgiveness requires that victims approach past wrongdoing, not as a contest between saints and sinners, the innocent and the culpable, but as offenses among equally flawed people. Political ethicist Reinhold Niebuhr writes that forgiveness, which is the "crown of Christian ethics," is "the most difficult of moral achievements" because it presupposes love of the other and an acknowlegment of sin in the self.[18] "Forgiving love," he writes, "is a possibility only for those who know that they are not good, who feel themselves in need of divine mercy, who live in a dimension deeper and higher than that of moral idealism, feel themselves as well as their fellow men convicted of sin by a holy God and know that the differences between the good man and the bad man are insignificant in his sight."[19]

In the Jewish and Christian traditions, the aim of human forgiveness is reconciliation—the healing of broken relationships. But since forgiveness and reconciliation are two distinct moral conditions, forgiveness can occur without the restoration of human relationships. As a necessary but not sufficient condition for reconciliation, forgiveness creates a social and psychological environment that is conducive to reconciliation among antagonists. Of course, whether this happens will depend on factors other than forgiveness itself, including offenders' remorse and repentance and victims' empathy and compassion.

The Jewish tradition presents a demanding process for overcoming serious offenses and creating the possibility of restoring ruptured relationships. The process of forgiveness and reconciliation—known in the Jewish faith as *teshuvah* (the process of return)—defines the conditions by which forgiveness is to be offered. According to the *Mishneh Torah*, Maimonides'

(1140–1204) authoritative code of Jewish law, the process of return includes eight elements: 1) acknowledgment of wrongdoing, 2) public confession to God and to community, 3) public expression of remorse, 4) offender's resolve not to repeat the offense, 5) reparations to victims, accompanied by acts of charity to others, 6) offender's request for forgiveness, 7) avoidance of the conditions that caused the original offense, and 8) nonrepetition of the offense.[20] Since human forgiveness in the Jewish tradition is offered only after offenders have fulfilled requisite preconditions, there is no ready, automatic pardon of human offenses in Judaism. But when offenders express sincere repentance by acknowledging their offense, by publicly expressing contrition, and by authenticating such remorse through tangible actions, then victims are morally obligated to do what God does—namely, to pardon offenders by erasing their claims against them.

Since Christianity is a grace-based religion, overcoming moral debt is based on mercy and love and is not conditional on restitution and retribution. Such is the case because the model of divine forgiveness in Christianity—expressed in God's unlimited love through the life, death, and resurrection of Jesus Christ—provides a radical, unconditional model of forgiveness. The principle that believers must forgive others just as God in Christ has forgiven them is expressed directly and unequivocally in the Scriptures.[21] As a result, some have interpreted the Christian forgiveness as a disregard for justice. To be sure, the Christian ethic of forgiveness and reconciliation deemphasizes retribution demanded by law and justice. But the Christian strategy of restoration does not disregard or minimize the wrongdoing and culpability of offenders. Rather, it recognizes that retribution alone will not necessarily foster reconciliation.

Theologian Volf has noted that the quest for justice will necessarily involve injustices as the norms of legality, equality, impartiality, and universality are applied to disputes and human wrongdoing. "If you want justice and nothing but justice," he writes, "you will inevitably get injustice." He continues: "If you want justice without injustice, you must want love. A world of perfect justice is a world of love."[22] Punishment can of course help prevent and deter wrongdoing, but it will not necessarily build human community nor will it contribute to human reconciliation. The miracle of Christian forgiveness is its achieving of what is normally impossible among humans—the restoration of human community in the aftermath of significant wrongdoing. Such reconciliation is not achieved through private retaliation or through public retribution but rather through the miracle of forgiveness, modeled on divine love.

In short, while both Christianity and Judaism view forgiveness as a means of reconciliation, the two faiths approach the process of forgiveness differently. For Judaism, the ethic of forgiveness is a demanding, conditional process that should be limited to cases that have fulfilled the conditions of *teshuvah* and that do not involve egregious evil.[23] By contrast, since Christianity views forgiveness as a manifestation of divine grace, believers are called to follow Christ's model of unlimited forgiveness. The difference between these two perspectives can be illustrated by how remembering and forgetting are reconciled with forgiveness. For Christianity, forgiveness involves the blotting out, or erasure of, the offense, treating it as if had never occurred.[24] In Judaism, by contrast, forgiveness is not the elimination of memory but the conscious decision to disregard, but not forget, the offense. As Margalit observes, there is no magical power to undo the offense. What is possible is for people to develop a new interpretation of the past so that victims are liberated from the captivity of the past. Forgiveness therefore approaches moral wrongdoing through accountability, choosing, nevertheless, to disregard the full effects of past offenses.[25]

To further explore the nature of forgiveness and reconciliation, I examine two stories that highlight elements of biblical forgiveness. The first account concerns family jealousy and hatred, leading to betrayal and evil, and the eventual reconciliation of the family. The second story is Jesus' Parable of the Prodigal Son.

The Joseph Story

According to the biblical account (Gen. 37–50), Jacob has twelve sons, the two youngest—Joseph and Benjamin—from his wife Rachel. Joseph is Jacob's favorite, and this leads to envy and jealousy from his older brothers. This envy is compounded by Joseph's dreams in which his brothers "make obeisance" to him (37:6, 9). As a result of their growing hatred, the brothers plot to kill him, but two of them (Reuben and Judah) urge nonviolence. When a group of traveling merchants passes next to where the brothers are tending their animals, they sell Joseph for twenty pieces of silver. He is taken to Egypt where the merchants sell him to a leading government official to work as a home servant. Soon, Joseph begins to succeed professionally, and in time, gains the attention of Pharaoh, the Egyptian king, who appoints him as his deputy, making him the second most powerful person in Egypt. When the king asks Joseph to interpret a series of strange dreams, he predicts that the region will experience seven years of abundance, followed by seven years of famine. This leads Joseph to store up large quantities of grain in preparation for the coming famine. As a result, when the famine arrives, Egypt has plentiful supplies to meet its own needs as well as to sell to neighboring nations.

When Jacob hears that Egypt has grain, he asks his sons to travel there to buy food. Jacob sends his ten eldest sons, but requires that Benjamin stay with him, lest he suffer possible harm. When the brothers arrive, they bow before Joseph, the governor of the land, and although Joseph recognizes them, they are not aware of his identity. Joseph, who no doubt still resents his brothers' efforts to banish him more than twenty years ago, uses his power to manipulate and threaten them, claiming that they are spies (42:9). He tells them that they can verify their true identity by bringing their brother Benjamin to Egypt. Joseph insists that one of the brothers (Simeon) must remain jailed as security for the return of the others with Benjamin. As the brothers go home, they discover that their sacks of grain contain the money they had supposedly used to buy the grain, causing them to fear retribution from Egyptian authorities.[26]

Although at first Jacob refuses to allow Benjamin to make the trip, the threat of starvation finally forces him to relent. When the brothers and Benjamin return to Egypt, they take gifts and money to purchase more grain, as well as the money that they had discovered in their sacks. When Joseph sees his full brother Benjamin and his half brothers, he invites them to a feast at his home. Rather than bringing great joy and anticipation, the invitation causes them to fear retribution for the money found in their sacks. After releasing Simeon from prison, Joseph, who still remains unrecognized, dines with his brothers and inquires about his father.

Joseph is deeply moved by being with his brothers, especially Benjamin, and leaves them momentarily in order to weep. Joseph then orders his brothers' sacks filled with food and their money returned, as had been done previously. But Joseph also lays one final trap: he orders his silver cup placed in Benjamin's sack. Once they depart, he sends his steward to retrieve the silver cup, and after discovering it, forces the group to return to him and demands that Benjamin be placed in prison. One of the brothers (Judah) explains that Jacob, having lost one son, will be unable to cope with the loss of his youngest son (44:30–31).

The story reaches its climax when Joseph, no longer able to control his emotions, weeps openly and decides to halt his manipulation and disclose his true identity. When he reveals his true identity—that he is "Joseph your brother, whom ye sold into Egypt"—the brothers are overcome with conflicting emotions, including incredulity, fear, suspicion, and guilt. Joseph immediately tries to ease their anxiety by saying that they should not be grieved or angry with themselves for selling him. Putting a positive spin on the evil committed, Joseph says: "And God sent me before you to preserve you a posterity in the earth, and to save your lives by a great deliverance" (45:7).

Joseph, with the Pharaoh's support, encourages his entire extended family to come to settle in Egypt, where Jacob lives out his remaining years. After he dies, the brothers begin to doubt if their wrongdoing toward Joseph has been fully atoned for. Uncertain that authentic forgiveness and reconciliation have been realized, the brothers fear that Joseph might inflict retribution for their evil act perpetrated nearly four decades earlier. As a result, they decide to confess anew their wrongdoing and ask for forgiveness. Although there has been significant movement toward reconciliation since Joseph revealed his true identity, this is the first moment in the story when the concept of forgiveness is used. The brothers send this message to Joseph: "Please forgive, I beg you, the transgression of your brothers and their sin, for they did you wrong" (50:17). After hearing this, Joseph weeps, and then assures his brothers they need not be afraid. Joseph recognizes the evil his brothers intended against him, but affirms that God had a redemptive purpose in that evil and suffering: "You meant evil against me, but God meant it for good in order to bring about this present result, to preserve many people alive. So therefore, do not be afraid; I will provide for you and your little ones" (50:20–1).

The Joseph story is a powerful account of forgiveness and reconciliation, illuminating how communal solidarity can be renewed in the aftermath of betrayal. As a classic account of reconciliation, the story involves the essential elements of the forgiveness process—admission of wrongdoing, contrition and repentance by the offender, acceptance of remorse by the victim, avoidance of revenge, and reestablishment of communal solidarity. Although Joseph struggles with the impulse toward revenge, his commitment to communal/familial solidarity proves stronger.

The Parable of the Prodigal Son

As told by Jesus, this parable (Luke 15:11–32) involves a father and two sons.[27] The younger son desires to leave his family and asks for the portion of his inheritance. The father surprisingly divides the estate, giving the younger son his share of it. The son leaves, squanders his inheritance, and soon finds himself out of money and in need of food and shelter. To survive, he takes up menial work feeding pigs. But the struggle to survive is painful and difficult. In time he comes to his senses and decides to return home. The prodigal's strategy is to confess to his father and to request work as one of his laborers. He plans to say, "Father, I have sinned against heaven, and in your sight; I am no longer worthy to be called your son; make me as one of your hired men" (vv. 18, 19). As he is arriving home, the father sees his lost son and runs to embrace him. The father is overwhelmed with joy at finding his son and orders that he be clothed in the best garments and that a feast be prepared, "for this son of mine was dead, and has come to life again; he was lost, and has been found" (v. 24).

The older son, who has continued to work diligently and faithfully on the family farm, learns about the feast and refuses to attend the celebration. The older son tells the father that although he has been obedient and hardworking, his father has never recognized his faithful service but offers "the fatted calf" to his brother after he has wasted his life. We never find out whether the older son becomes reconciled to the father. All we know is that the father's love is unconditional: "My child, you have always been with me, and all that is mine is yours" (v. 31).

Unlike the Joseph story, the parable of the prodigal son offers only a partial account of human forgiveness and reconciliation. Fundamentally, the story is about the father's unqualified love for his two sons—the younger one who squanders his inheritance and undermines the family reputation and the elder son who faithfully fulfills his moral and professional responsibilities. Even though the prodigal embarrasses the father by leaving the family and living irresponsibly, the father never stops loving him. While the father is no doubt troubled by his son's past immorality and irresponsibility, he is nonetheless overwhelmed by being reunited with him, believing family ties are more basic than the behavior of his sons. Thus, when the father sees the son "far off," he runs to greet him, embracing him before he has a chance to offer his planned confession. As Volf observes, "no confession was necessary for the embrace to take place for the simple reason that the relationship did not rest on moral performance and therefore could not be destroyed by immoral acts."[28] This does not mean that moral rules, ethical behavior, and repentance are unimportant in human communities. Rather, it signifies that embrace is more fundamental than justice and that relationships take precedence over behavioral performance.

The celebration of the prodigal's return poses an ethical dilemma. When the faithful and obedient older brother finds out about the feast being given for his brother, he is angry and jealous. He is angry because his brother has wasted a part of the family estate and dishonored the family reputation, and he is jealous because he is being honored in spite of his profligate and irresponsible living. From the older son's perspective, the just, moral life lies in playing by the rules of the game of life and in fulfilling moral obligations to God and others. His worldview is legal and principled, captured by the aphorism, "you reap what you sow." Since actions have consequences, the wasteful and dishonorable life of the prodigal requires, at a minimum, remorse, punishment, and restitution. And because the prodigal has dishonored the family, the brother stops considering him as a brother, referring to him as "this son of yours." Indeed, the son not only rejects his brother, but he rejects the father as well for his unjust, unprincipled embrace of the prodigal.

A fundamental moral principle of this parable is that authentic love is unconditional.[29] While rules and principled behavior are important in sustaining communal bonds, obsession with performance can lead to legalism and judgmentalism, and impede reconciliation. Indeed, when rules are more important than communal relationships, the healing of social bonds becomes difficult, if not impossible. The prodigal story reminds us that while rules are necessary in any viable family, group, or community, commitment to communal solidarity is even more fundamental. Volf succinctly captures this important lesson as follows:

> The father's most basic commitment is not to rules and given identities but to his sons whose lives are too complex to be regulated by fixed rules and whose

identities are too dynamic to be defined once for all. Yet he does not give up the rules and the order. Guided by the indestructible love which makes space in the self for others in their alterity, which invites the others who have transgressed to return, which creates hospitable conditions for their confession, and rejoices over their presence, the father keeps re-configuring the order without destroying it so as to maintain it as an order of embrace rather than exclusion.[30]

The parable also illustrates the importance of love in overcoming alienation rooted in betrayal and injustice. While robust love does not condone wrongdoing, it provides a means by which offenders can acknowledge guilt and victims can forgive. Since forgiveness can occur only when victims are willing to recognize the humanity of offenders, the restoration of communal relationships can only occur where community members are more concerned with relationships than retributive justice. As one theologian has observed, "love makes forgiving a creative violation of all the rules for keeping score."[31]

While the Jewish and Christian religions emphasize different dimensions of forgiveness, these two biblical accounts—one from the Hebrew Bible and the other from the New Testament—show that the two faiths share a number of important beliefs about forgiveness and reconciliation. These include the following:

- Forgiveness is a priority in spiritual and human relationships.
- Forgiveness is rooted in the loving, merciful, and just character of God. Since God is loving and compassionate toward people, human beings should also be loving and compassionate toward others.
- Forgiveness requires that people hate the sin but love the sinner, that they condemn wrongdoing but affirm the dignity of people.
- Since forgiveness is a demanding ethic, it is greatly facilitated when offenders are penitent and victims renounce vengeance.
- Forgiveness is a means by which individuals and groups can restore broken relationships.

Forgiveness is thus a means by which the memory of past injuries is redeemed into hope, transforming justified anger and resentment into mercy and compassion.

THEORIES OF FORGIVENESS

Historically, philosophers, theologians, and social scientists have conceived of forgiveness in a variety of ways. Three major theories of forgiveness include the classical, unilateral, and virtue ethics perspectives. The classical perspective conceives of forgiveness as an interactive process between offenders and victims in which the two parties confront past wrongdoing and move toward the restoration of broken relationships. This theory assumes that forgiveness is an objective act by victims toward offenders that contributes to the healing of interpersonal relationships as well as communal bonds. The therapeutic perspective views forgiveness as the lifting of emotional burdens, especially anger and resentment, that have resulted from unjust and undeserved offenses. The release of anger and resentment occurs when victims inwardly forgive their offenders, thereby liberating themselves from the desire for vengeance. Finally, the third theory views forgiveness as a personal virtue or moral craft. According to this perspective, forgiveness is a practice that is learned and cultivated.

Below I briefly sketch each of these theories. While these models present alternative conceptions of the nature and process of forgiveness, they are not mutually exclusive, since elements of one theory can be integrated with another. Indeed, a comprehensive ethic of forgiveness should include elements from each of these models.

The Classical Theory

In this theory, forgiveness is an interactive process between two or more people or groups in the aftermath of wrongdoing. Unprovoked and unjust offenses create a moral inequality between offenders and victims, and forgiveness is a means by which antagonists can move toward the restoration of relationships based on moral equality. In order for forgiveness to occur, offenders must acknowledge wrongdoing and express remorse for the injuries they have unjustly inflicted on victims. They may do this through words (public acknowledgment, apologies, and repentance) and through tangible reparations. Victims, for their part, refrain from acts of vengeance, express empathy toward offenders, and release offenders from part or all of their deserved debts. The classical theory thus views forgiveness as an objective process among individuals or groups in which words and actions lead to the partial restoration of injured human relationships.

The classical theory is illustrated in Jesus' Parable of the Unforgiving Servant (Matt. 18:23–35) in which a master decides to sell one of his servants because he has failed to repay his debt. When the servant expresses penitence and promises to repay the debt, the master has compassion on him and lifts the debt. However, when he hears that the forgiven servant has been unforgiving toward others, the master cancels the forgiveness.[32] This parable highlights the interactional nature of forgiveness between an offender (servant) and victim (master), calling attention to the conditional nature of the process. In particular it emphasizes the acknowledgment of an offense, contrition, empathy, and lifting of a deserved penalty.

According to the theory, forgiveness is a voluntary, compassionate act by a victim, generally in response to an offender's repentance. If enemies are to move toward reconciliation through forgiveness, participants must thus fulfill a number of preconditions. The prerequisites ensure that forgiveness is authentic and leads to the healing of victims, the restoration of offenders, and the renewal of human relationships. Although there is no consensus on what these preconditions are, the classical theory emphasizes these elements:

1. *Consensus on Truth*: The foundation of forgiveness is an agreement about the nature, causes, and responsibility for wrongdoing. Since forgiveness is a means for healing the injuries resulting from past wrongs and injustices, it presupposes knowledge about the offenses. Theologian Donald Shriver, Jr., writes that "absent a preliminary agreement between two or more parties that there is something from the past to be forgiven, forgiveness stalls at the starting gate."[33]

2. *Repentance*: Although forgiveness is possible without repentance,[34] the restoration of relationships is unlikely without apologies and the promise to avoid future wrongdoing.

3. *Renunciation of Vengeance*: Since retaliation perpetuates the cycle of violence, victims must refrain from retaliation. A Chinese proverb captures this truth well: "Whoever opts for revenge should dig two graves."

4. *Empathy*: Empathy is the ability to view offenders as human beings. This can only occur if victims distinguish people from their evil actions and fulfill St. Augustine's admonition to hate the sin and love the sinner. This is a demanding practice because it calls all people to judge unjust behaviors while treating human beings with dignity and respect.

5. *Mitigation or Cancellation of Punishment*: To forgive a debt is to reduce or annul a deserved penalty. When victims forgive, they release offenders from justified punishment. Since forgiveness entails the forgoing of a rightful claim against someone who has committed an offense or harm, it is in tension with justice. As Smedes has noted, forgiveness involves surrendering the right to get even: "When someone forgives, he or she chooses to live with the moral scales unbalanced, the injury not avenged, the wrong not righted."[35]

Some scholars argue that reconciliation is an element of the forgiveness process. In Shriver's analysis, for example, the restoration of human relationships is the last element of a four-dimensional model of forgiveness.[36] Here we view reconciliation not as a dimension of forgiveness but as its chief by-product. Of course, whether people pursue the restoration of community will depend in particular on the extent to which offenders acknowledge wrongdoing and express remorse and victims forgive their debtors. But while these conditions are necessary for reconciliation, they are not sufficient. Only the voluntary commitment to the restoration of social bonds will ensure the healing of broken relationships.

The classical theory has one major shortcoming. By defining forgiveness as a conditional, interactive process, it makes this ethic dependent on the prior actions of antagonists. In particular by making victims' forgiveness dependent on offenders' repentance, offenders gain a double power over victims: after inflicting an original offense, a perpetrator can impede a victim's healing and restoration by simply refusing to express contrition. This limitation, however, is overcome in the therapeutic model, since it makes forgiveness a unilateral act, totally independent of the actions of offenders and in particular of their contrition and remorse. On the other hand, the classical theory provides the interactive foundation among victims and offenders that can lead to the restoration of relationships and communities.

The Therapeutic or Unilateral Theory

The distinctive characteristic of the therapeutic or unilateral theory is its concern with the healing of victims' emotional feelings and hurts. Regardless of the nature of the original harm, wrongdoing is personally damaging to people because it diminishes self-confidence, destroys self-esteem, calls into question the dignity of people (by creating a moral inequality between offenders and victims), and results in physical and emotional scars. According to this theory, since offenders' wrongdoing results in personal injuries that foster anger, resentment, and vengeance, the inward restoration of victims is necessary if they are to regain self-confidence and personal freedom. Although interactions between offenders and victims can contribute to this end, forgiveness ultimately is the responsibility of victims (and offenders) themselves as they seek to overcome the injurious effects of wrongdoing.

Wrongdoing is of course highly damaging to victims. But the suffering of victims results not only from the original injustice but from the continuing hurts derived from lingering resentment and hatred. Forgiveness is therefore necessary to release victims from their self-inflicted suffering. If people are not to drown in the misery of their own anger, they need to be released from the burden of hate. Since the past cannot be undone, the only alternative is to redeem memory through the act of self-forgiveness. In Smedes' formulation, we need forgiveness because it is "the only way we have to a better fairness in our unfair world; it is love's unexpected revolution against unfair pain and it alone offers strong hope for healing the hurts we so unfairly feel."[37]

According to the theory of therapeutic forgiveness, victims find release from being captive to past wrongdoing by personally and unilaterally releasing offenders of their debts. When victims forgive offenders, they release the offenders from their deserved punishment but the victims are, in turn, freed from their own captivity to anger and resentment and from the compulsion to inflict revenge. When departing the White House in the aftermath of the Watergate scandal, President Richard Nixon called attention to the destructive effects of lingering hatred and resentment. As he was departing his office for the last time, he told his staff: "Some people may hate you; but if you hate them in return, your hate will destroy you."

It is important to stress that therapeutic forgiveness is a subjective, personal, and solitary act. Unlike the classical model, such forgiveness does not involve the offender or the public. Rather, therapeutic forgiveness is solely a unilateral act that allows the victim to overcome past injuries by subjectively transforming a victim's memory of past wrongdoing. In this theory, the lifting of the burdens caused by offenses is not dependent on offenders' actions but on victims themselves, who decide when and how the demands for justice should be qualified or lifted altogether. Moreover, since forgiveness is not dependent on offenders' repentance, perpetrators do not determine the conditions under which forgiveness is granted. In short, self-forgiveness is a unilateral act that releases victims from anger and resentment and terminates the compulsion to get even, thereby healing and liberating them from past injustices.

In his popular, insightful book *Forgive and Forget*, theologian Smedes adopts the therapeutic perspective by viewing forgiveness as an inward, psychological process. Such a process involves, as the subtitle of his book suggests, "healing the hurts that we don't deserve." Since hate is the "instinctive backlash against anyone who wounds us wrongly,"[38] forgiveness is the means by which people reform and redeem their feelings of hate and anger. According to Smedes, forgiveness entails three elements—discovering the humanity of the person who hurt us, surrendering the right to get even, and revising our feelings toward the person we forgive.[39] As he sees it, the aim of forgiveness is to make individuals whole and to relieve them of their inner suffering, and this is accomplished by releasing offenders from guilt and releasing victims from anger and vengeance. Since human beings are caught up with their own emotional baggage of hate and doubt, Smedes suggests that the giving and receiving of forgiveness presupposes self-forgiveness. The feeling of being forgiven is so fundamental, he writes, that without it people are unable to forgive others.[40]

The therapeutic model contributes important insights about the process of forgiveness. First, it calls attention to the need to differentiate between objective wrongdoing and the subjective feelings resulting from such injuries. While a dispassionate, rational assessment of wrongdoing is important in confronting past wrongs, such hurts cannot be resolved solely through negotiations, court adjudication, or political compromise. To the extent that wrongdoing has resulted in lingering anger and hatred, such emotional baggage can only be relieved and healed by directly confronting the subjective effects of past objective injuries or crimes.

Second, the psychological perspective calls attention to the inner, long-term effects of personal hurts, especially the destructive effects of victims' unresolved anger and resentment. Since one of the strategies for coping with unjustified suffering is denial, one of the challenges in therapeutic forgiveness is to uncover latent, repressed resentment. Only when the objective cause of the suffering has been identified, can the balm of forgiveness heal the wounds resulting from past wrongdoing. Finally, the therapeutic approach, by emphasizing the independent roles of the victim and the offender in the forgiveness process, calls attention to the individual responsibility for healing personal wounds from unjustified wrongs. Whereas conventional approaches to forgiveness usually make victims' forgiveness dependent on offenders' repentance, the therapeutic model encourages victims to take responsibility for their emotional well-being by forgiving both the self and others.

Forgiveness as a Moral Virtue

Unlike the classical model, which views forgiveness as an interactive process, and unlike the therapeutic model, which views forgiveness as an individual's willingness to forgo anger toward offenders, the virtue ethics theory views forgiveness as a character trait that leads people to treat other humans with compassion. According to this model, forgiveness is not a single act that qualifies the debt or punishment of an offender, but an ongoing moral process in which offenders express contrition and victims respond with empathy and compassion. From this perspective forgiveness is not a periodic act but, in the words of Martin Luther King, Jr., "a permanent attitude."[41] Kenneth Kuanda, Zambia's president, captures this important truth when he suggests that forgiveness is not an isolated act but "a constant willingness to live in a new day without looking back and ransacking the memory for occasions of bitterness and resentment."[42]

According to the virtue ethics model, forgiveness is a desirable practice because people—who in Immanuel Kant's terminology need to be treated always as an end and never as a means—must be always regarded as having inherent worth. Moreover, forgiveness is also a morally praiseworthy (supererogatory) act because human beings, in spite of the harm that they might inflict through their crimes and injustices, are nevertheless entitled to dignity and respect.[43] In a carefully reasoned essay, philosopher Jean Hampton—who defines forgiveness as the giving up of moral hatred toward offenders[44]—argues in favor of a *qualified* duty of forgiveness. It is a moral injunction because people need to be treated as if they are decent, in spite of actions that might compromise this presumption.

Since wrongdoing is often the result of different motives, Hampton observes that as we become more familiar with the lives of offenders we may begin to view them not as "mindless, evil monsters but as human beings like ourselves, with serious problems that ignite feelings of compassion and benevolence."[45] In addition, since people tend to believe in their own decency, even after committing unjust, evil acts, Hampton thinks we should therefore be willing to treat offenders with dignity, giving them the benefit of the doubt, even as we do toward ourselves. The fact that people continue to have faith in themselves in spite of their wrongdoing provides a basis for having faith in others.

While this theory favors a presumption of forgiveness, it does not endorse an unconditional obligation to forgive. Forgiveness is a qualified moral duty because there may be circumstances—such as when people are responsible for egregious evils or are unwilling to take responsibility for their evil actions or to stop repeating wrongdoing—when moral hatred of others may be appropriate. Hampton interprets Jesus' injunction to "love one's enemies" not as a command to maintain the belief in the inherent decency of all people, regardless of their actions and motivations, but, rather, as a principle that encourages "generosity of judgment toward many." Hampton writes that while Jesus forbids malicious or spiteful hatred, he nevertheless allows people "to sustain opposition to our moral opponents, and not to reconcile ourselves with them for as long as they remain committed to their bad cause."[46]

Hampton does not tell us what wrongs are unforgivable. Her major argument is to defend the claim of forgiveness based on the inherent worth of people—a faith in human decency despite a lack of empirical evidence for it.[47] Of course, offering forgiveness based on faith in the basic decency of people provides a fragile foundation for such an ethic. But such a tenuous basis is bolstered by the fact that all human beings desire to be treated with such faith—to be given the benefit of the doubt that in spite of wrongdoing, people are worthy of respect and dignity. However, if people expect others to morally condemn their evil actions but to show them respect nonetheless—in effect "to love the sinner but hate the sin"—then they must be willing to practice this ethic toward others. Indeed, we should be willing to forgive because the universality and constancy of sin makes grace necessary for all. Alexander Solzhenitsyn writes:

> If only there were evil people somewhere insidiously committing evil deeds, and it were necessary only to separate them from the rest of us and destroy them! But the line dividing good and evil cuts through the heart of every human being. And who is willing to destroy a piece of his own heart?[48]

Thus, if people are unwilling to forgive others, they may also have difficulty forgiving themselves. As Hampton notes, the evidence and principles that people use to assess the worthiness of others will more than likely also be applied in assessing themselves.[49]

Some virtue ethics theorists also stress forgiveness as a personal self-discipline. According to this perspective, forgiveness is not a response to a particular offense, but a moral disposition and a set of learned behaviors that have been developed to cope with life's wrongs and injustices. One of the most developed accounts of forgiveness as a moral discipline is the account of Christian forgiveness by theologian L. Gregory Jones's book *Embodying Forgiveness: A Theological Analysis*. In this book Jones argues that forgiveness is a moral discipline, a craft that is rooted in a way of life. Christian forgiveness, he asserts, is not an inward emotion or an interactive process but an ongoing self-discipline. Jones writes: "The craft of forgiveness involves the ongoing and ever-deepening process of unlearning sin through forgiveness and learning, through specific habits and practices, to live in communion— with the Triune God, with one another, and with the whole Creation."[50]

For Jones, forgiveness is a "craft" of learned habits and practices that foster reconciliation. This craft is a demanding ethic that entails, among other things, accountability, responsibility, and repentance. Since Jones grounds his book in a theological analysis of Christianity, the development of moral virtues necessary for forgiveness must necessarily arise from the resources of the Christian religion itself. Jones argues that the Christian faith, rooted in the work of the Triune God (Father, Son, and Holy Spirit), establishes a demanding ethic that requires sacrificial love, forgiveness, and reconciliation.[51] Although living in accord with such norms is generally not humanly possible, Jones argues that divine resources make such a way of life possible. This is especially the case when believers cultivate holy living by developing specific habits and practices that foster communion and reconciliation.[52] The application of this ethic is also facilitated by a Christian worldview, which provides a comprehensive context for the nature of human suffering. Jones writes that "if resentment is not to ossify into hatred and desires for revenge, it must be contextualized within the larger horizon of (God's) forgiving, reconciling love."[53]

The final purpose, or telos, of forgiveness is not the healing of self, but the restoration of human relationships. Following Aristotle, who emphasized the importance of learning "crafts" for living life well, Jones argues that learning the "craft" of forgiveness "is a lifelong learning process that people are initiated into as apprentices to those who excel at the craft. Those who excel have a moral authority as teachers, and apprentices must recognize a gap between their present competencies and genuine excellence."[54] Since forgiveness is part of a way of life, the craft of forgiveness is developed not so much by reflection and by studying particular texts but by participating in specific activities under the guidance of those who are masters of the craft. Although forgiveness entails feelings, actions, and judgments, the basis for the moral discipline of forgiveness is character. Such character traits are developed through continuous reflection and practice. Just as a medical education involves the study of texts and practical training (that is, internships) by observing trained physicians dealing with specific problems, so too forgiveness requires continuous learning from study and reflective observation.[55]

These three alternative theories of forgiveness provide important insights into the practice and cultivation of this ethic. The classical theory, by calling attention to the interactive and interpersonal nature of forgiveness, stresses the importance of mutual participation by victims and offenders. It also emphasizes the need for effective interpersonal communication between antagonists if the process of forgiveness is to foster reconciliation. The unilateral or therapeutic perspective, by contrast, emphasizes the need for attitudes and dispositions that foster empathy and compassion and inhibit anger and vengeance. Although anger and resentment are natural responses to injustice and wrongdoing, the persistence of these dispositions can result in harmful attitudes and destructive behaviors. The therapeutic theory therefore gives priority to victims' unilateral forgiveness in which their justified anger and resentment are transformed and the memory of past wrongdoing is redeemed.

Finally, the moral virtue theory stresses the moral character necessary to carry out attitudes and behaviors that lead to an ongoing healing of relationships and the renewal of communal bonds. According to this perspective, forgiveness is an objective process in which victims, but also offenders, express exemplary attitudes and behaviors that permit the healing of individuals and the restoration of human relationships. Since each of these three perspectives is important to the successful implementation of this ethic, a sound approach to forgiveness will necessarily incorporate them into strategies of implementation. In the following section, I briefly explore major goals and methods in applying this ethic.

THE MEANS AND ENDS OF FORGIVENESS

Based on the insights from the three models examined earlier, forgiveness can be conceived as a process involving three essential elements—constructive interaction, attitudinal and behavioral reformation, and moral virtues necessary to implement the ethic. The first important prerequisite for forgiveness is successful interaction and communication among antagonists. From this perspective, forgiveness is a means by which fractured, alienated relationships can be repaired through reciprocal actions of victims and offenders. This will entail mutual trust-building actions, including the willingness of offenders to acknowledge moral culpability, to express remorse for their offenses, and to offer reparations to redress wrongdoing, as well as the offer by victims to forgo vengeance and express empathy and compassion toward offenders. In effect, victims must be willing and able to distinguish behaviors, which may be unjust, from people, who are entitled to respect.

Since true contrition is not based on words alone, offenders express the authenticity of their apologies through acts of atonement that seek to repair the wrong that has been committed. While many of the injuries and damages resulting from wrongdoing cannot be repaired, restitution, punishment, and financial reparations can help restore victims' dignity and communal dignity. Moreover, such actions are important in authenticating the sincerity of the offenders' repentance. What is essential in the forgiveness process, however, is not punishment or restitution per se but restoration of moral and political equality of offenders and victims. From the interactive perspective, forgiveness is simply not the cancellation of a debt but also the restoration of relationships and social community. Although the healing of offenders and the restoration of victims is important, the telos of forgiveness is reconciliation.

The role of personal dispositions is also crucial in forgiveness. For philosopher Jean Hampton, for example, forgiveness involves "a change of heart toward an offender."[56] According to conventional wisdom, if forgiveness is to occur, victims and offenders must alter their attitudes. Offenders must become contrite and repentant, accepting their own culpability, while renouncing their own self-righteousness and arrogance; victims, for their part, must forswear vengeance and accept offenders in spite of the injuries and evils that they have committed. From the therapeutic perspective, forgiveness is not so much an instrument of reconciliation as a means of overcoming anger and hate so that human beings can rediscover their true humanity.

Since latent, unresolved anger distorts the human personality and is destructive to human relationships, forgiveness is essential to personal well-being. For Kathleen Dean Moore, for example, forgiveness occurs when a victim overcomes resentment toward the person who has inflicted injury.[57] Jeffrie Murphy, following Bishop Joseph Butler, an eighteenth-century British Christian minister, similarly claims that forgiveness entails the forswearing of resentment through "the resolute overcoming of the anger and hatred that are naturally directed toward a person who has done one an unjustified and non-excused moral injury."[58] Beverly Flanigan, who integrates the attitudinal dimension with interpersonal processes, argues that forgiveness is an interactive process between victims and offenders that seeks to restore broken relationships. "Forgiving is the method by which the wounded person can readmit an outcast," she writes. "In forgiving, a wounded person reopens his heart to take in and reaccept his offender."[59] In short, if forgiveness is to occur, dispositions must change from anger to empathy, from vengeance to compassion.

The third requirement for successful forgiveness is the moral courage to carry out the arduous task of implementing this ethic. Since the natural response to human wrongdoing is the desire to avenge the offense, human beings will need significant moral resources if antagonists are to view each other as human beings entitled to dignity. For example, philosopher Robert Roberts, who views forgiveness as the willingness to give up anger,[60] claims that forgiveness presupposes personal moral virtues that enable victims to overcome anger and resentment. Susan Jacoby similarly claims that since forgiveness requires that victims release offenders from their moral debts, the capacity to forgive will depend in great measure on individual moral virtues.[61]

Since antagonists must overcome the natural inclination to continue the cycle of harm, forgiveness is a demanding ethic, placing significant demands on both the offender and victim. For offenders to acknowledge wrongdoing, express contrition, and tangibly express such remorse through restitution and the nonrepetition of wrongdoing takes humility and moral courage. Some people may be able to repent without much difficulty when the context is impersonal and general, but repentance that is specific, concrete, and personal is always a difficult act.[62] Moreover, the call to treat offenders with compassion and respect and to erase their retributive claims is even more demanding. This is so because in forgiveness victims are called to treat offenders as if they had not perpetrated the offense. Theologian Vincent Brummer observes, "one of the basic characteristics of forgiveness is . . . that the one who forgives is the one who suffers."[63]

Why should people forgive? Why should they give up claims to justice when they could receive satisfaction through offenders' prosecution and punishment? Since the topic of forgiveness and justice is explored in the next chapter, here I briefly explore why forgiveness is important in interpersonal relations.

First, forgiveness is important because it provides the sole way by which victims can be healed emotionally. According to this argument, forgiveness is necessary for victims because it is the only way by which they can ultimately overcome justified anger and the desire for revenge. While the desire to get even is a natural response to wrongdoing, the drive to retaliate not only impairs victims' healing but can itself become a new source of injury by maintaining a person's captivity to the past. Thus, if victims are to achieve liberation from the legacy of past injustices, they must regain their personal autonomy. C. J. Arnold, the noted South African antiapartheid writer, is surely correct when he writes that "there is a hard law . . . when an injury is done to us, we never recover until we forgive."[64] Retributive justice can, of course, help restore the fundamental equality among antagonists by punishing offenders. But however important prosecution and punishment may be to the maintenance of a credible and effective criminal justice system, retributive justice will not necessarily lead to the restoration of victims' self-confidence and to the renewal of forward-looking attitudes. Theologian Jürgen Moltmann notes that "the retaliating justice of penal law doesn't in itself lead to a new common future, and ultimately doesn't help the victims, or the perpetrators either."[65]

Second, people should offer forgiveness as a response to authentic contrition and repentance. As noted earlier, Christianity, and to a lesser extent Judaism, encourage victims of wrongdoing to respond compassionately to offenders by relieving them of some or all their debts. One of Jesus' central teachings about forgiveness is that we are entitled to forgiveness only in the degree that we ourselves are willing to forgive others. In the Lord's Prayer, believers are admonished to request forgiveness by promising forgiveness to others: "And forgive us our debts, as we forgive our debtors" (Matt. 6:12). Responding compassionately to offenders' remorse is morally appropriate because it grants them the opportunity, in the words of Hannah Arendt, to "undo" the evils and crimes of the past. And it is also appropriate because it allows victims and other agents the possibility of morally responding to the guilt of offenders. Of course, granting forgiveness in response to offender's repentance is problematic because there is no simple, easy way by which to authenticate repentance. How is one to evaluate offenders' expression of remorse and contrition? Are acts of restitution necessary to validate apologies? Given the subjective nature of repentance and remorse, it is perhaps unwise to place too much emphasis on repentance as a precondition for forgiveness. Perhaps the more fundamental principle is that victims need to be compassionate and ready to forgive, and that this moral responsibility increases with the rise in perceived sincerity and authenticity of offenders' repentance.

A third reason for granting forgiveness is that it facilitates reconciliation—that is, the healing of broken interpersonal relationships and the restoration of social harmony and communal solidarity. Since wrongdoing injures individual and group relationships by replacing trust with alienation and enmity, forgiveness provides a means by which antagonists can overcome their alienation, distrust, and hostility. Forgiveness facilitates the processes of repairing ruptured relationships and restoring social bonds by fostering compassion and empathy among enemies. Since the restoration of peace and harmony is greatly facilitated when offenders accept culpability for wrongdoing and express repentance, the reconciliation process is likely to be initiated and implemented only after offenders have acknowledged wrongdoing and repented of their offenses. Victims can then begin to develop an alternative view of offenders and respond to them with compassion by offering forgiveness. Only after antagonists have expressed mutual empathy can the interpersonal and intergroup processes of reconciliation get underway. The standard, common-sense view of reconciliation is that it proceeds in the following sequence: repentance, forgiveness, and reconciliation.[66]

It is important to stress that while repentance helps to restore an environment that is conducive to trust and mutual respect, contrition and remorse are not sufficient to ensure forgiveness. Since forgiveness is ultimately a gift, it cannot be demanded or expected. As Brummer notes, "forgiveness can only be freely given, and when it is forced or earned it ceases to be forgiveness."[67] Thus, while repentance creates a context that is conducive to forgiveness, it does not entitle an offender to it. In addition, note that while forgiveness will result in the lifting of some or all of offenders' debts, such an act will not necessarily lead to reconciliation. Forgiveness can of course be granted interpersonally, but reconciliation can only occur when antagonists mutually participate in the reconstruction of relationships and the restoration of communal bonds. Forgiveness can facilitate the process of overcoming alienation and estrangement, but it cannot ensure the healing of interpersonal relations and the renewal of social harmony. Only the mutual participation of antagonists can help transform alienation into trust, and division into unity.

A final reason to forgive is that there may be no better alternative to confront and overcome past wrongdoing. The natural desire to get even—whether through interpersonal vengeance or institutional retribution—may provide short-term satisfaction to victims. But such a response is unlikely to lead to individual or collective healing. Indeed, vengeance and retribution will not help retrieve human losses, heal personal injuries, repair destroyed property, or restore the original material conditions at the time of the offenses. Thus, in the final analysis, there may be no other alternative to the injustice of crimes and offenses than to acknowledge the wrongdoing and to give up claims of justice by releasing offenders from their deserved punishment.

In sum, forgiveness is an essential norm in building and sustaining harmonious, cooperative relationships. Because people knowingly and unknowingly commit offenses against others, forgiveness provides a means to undo some of the harm inflicted by others' wrongdoing. In particular, forgiveness provides a means to rehabilitate human relationships and promote peace and social well-being. In his encyclical "On the Mercy of God," Pope John Paul II observes that "a world from which forgiveness was eliminated would be nothing but a world of cold and unfeeling justice, in the name of which each person would claim his or her own rights vis-à-vis others."[68] Although the validity of forgiveness in personal relationships is widely accepted by religious and secular thinkers, many public officials have questioned the validity and feasibility of collective forgiveness. In the next chapter, I therefore explore the nature and feasibility of collective forgiveness.

3

The Possibility and Promise of Political Forgiveness

The extension of forgiveness, repentance, and reconciliation to whole nations is one of the great innovations in statecraft of our time

—Walter Wink, theologian[1]

The peace that follows from forgiveness in Christ cannot be transferred to international relations, and in particular it cannot be transferred by some doubtfully representative functionary apologizing on behalf of a reified collectivity for remote (or even proximate) historical events.

—David Martin, sociologist of religion[2]

And do not forgive, for truly it is not
within your power to forgive
In the name of those who were
betrayed at dawn.

—Zbigniew Herbert, noted Polish poet[3]

The deadly cycle of revenge must be replaced by the new-found liberty of forgiveness.

—Pope John Paul II[4]

In chapter 2, I suggested that forgiveness has been regarded historically as a personal virtue, applicable only to the spiritual realm or to individual, private relationships. Thus, when Wiesenthal raises the issue of vicarious forgiveness in *The Sunflower*, a case study that I briefly explored in the introduction, most respondents suggest that Wiesenthal, the imprisoned Jew to whom a dying

German soldier had confessed, had responded appropriately by not offering forgiveness. But the dying soldier's confession and repentance to a random representative of the Jewish people who had suffered egregious evil at the hands of German troops raises an important issue: Is forgiveness applicable to social and political groups? Are victims the sole agents entitled to forgive offenders, or may group leaders or government officials act on behalf of a group or community? If nations can grant or receive forgiveness, what types of collective crimes and institutional wrongs can be forgiven, and by whom? Moreover, are apologies and collective repentance necessary?

This chapter explores the nature and potential role of forgiveness in political life. I begin by examining the nature of collective guilt and responsibility and then explore how forgiveness can confront and overcome collective guilt and communal responsibility. I next analyze the nature of political forgiveness, identifying key dimensions of the process of political forgiveness. Since critics of collective forgiveness regard forgiveness as an aspect of interpersonal morality, I implicitly challenge this claim through an analysis of a number of conceptual and methodological issues involved in extending this ethic to groups and communities. I conclude the chapter with an assessment of the contribution that this collective ethic can make to the public life of nations.

GUILT AND RESPONSIBILITY

Ascertaining Responsibility

According to its popular usage, forgiveness involves the cancellation of debts or the forgoing of penalties or punishment. It is offered not to forget the past or to appease enemies but to promote individual healing and foster reconciliation through the restoration of social and political relationships. Since forgiveness is a response to a moral offense, this ethic is applicable only where an offender has committed a culpable offense. Although some crimes and injustices are the sole responsibility of an offender against a totally innocent victim, most individual and collective offenses involve shared culpability. Since sin is pervasive and self-interest is universal, people pursue their own interests, often in blatant disregard for, or at the expense of, the interests of others. As a result, political conflict is rarely a contest between innocent saints and culpable sinners. Rather, political conflict is a byproduct of humans pursuing individual and collective interests that they perceive as politically and morally legitimate.

Forgiveness presupposes the commission of a moral offense and consensus about the nature of, and culpability for, such wrongdoing. But since antagonists seldom agree on the causes and culpability for past offenses (individual or collective), the forgiveness ethic is especially difficult to implement.

Even when antagonists achieve consensus on the principal facts about wrongdoing, they will generally disagree on who bears primary responsibility for the offense. For example, a state's resort to war may be viewed by its own people as a purely defensive military action, whereas citizens from another state may view it solely as unprovoked aggression. As the saying goes, one group's freedom fighter may be another group's terrorist.

When governments resort to violence to resolve political disputes or to consolidate political power, how is culpability for human rights abuses to be determined? Normally, individual, small-scale crimes are defined and prosecuted within domestic political society through a state's criminal justice system using its own laws as a basis for trial. When regimes themselves resort to widespread, systemic repression, the task of defining moral and criminal culpability is much more difficult.[5] This is especially the case when a government itself authorizes actions that would normally be regarded as morally unacceptable, if not illegal. Under such circumstances, the responsibility for the government's offenses must fall not only on individual perpetrators but also on the decision makers who authorized policies and the political groups and associations that helped to sustain the regime in power.

If forgiveness is to be applicable to political life, it will only occur when conflicting groups are able to agree on the nature, causes, and responsibilities for past offenses. Establishing culpability often presents significant challenges, and it is an especially daunting task when the wrongdoing is carried out by a regime.[6] This is so not only because the social and political disputes involve greater participation but also because, as theologian Reinhold Niebuhr has argued, groups tend to distort and amplify the evil and selfishness of individuals.[7] Nevertheless, if the ethic of forgiveness is to be incorporated into the life of nations, a minimal level of consensus about past wrongdoing will be necessary.

Since truth is essential to the forgiveness process, developing a shared account of past wrongdoing is crucial. This means that antagonists must develop consensus on the nature and scope of the collective offenses and seek to identify which party or group bears chief responsibility for the wrongdoing. Although illegal, criminal actions will necessarily involve individual culpability, a major challenge in confronting social or political wrongdoing is to ascertain the nature and scope of a community's collective responsibility. Collective responsibility for wrongdoing arises when governments institute policies toward their own citizens and toward other nations that result in widespread evil. Although such responsibility is derived from criminal acts of state agents and unjust policies of government officials and is therefore rooted in the evil acts of individuals, it does not presume individual culpability. The culpability is communal, not individualistic, because the responsibility derives solely from people's citizenship or communal membership. Based on this distinction, some scholars have differentiated between collective guilt, which imputes blame without regard to actions of persons, and collective responsibility, which refers only to the liability resulting from group membership.[8]

In exploring the role of forgiveness and repentance in political life, Alexander Solzhenitsyn concludes that ascertaining culpability for past crimes and wrongdoing is a most demanding task. This is so not only because it is difficult to cross the threshold of self-love, but also because the sins of others are more visible than one's own.[9] As Mark Twain once observed, everyone believes that forgiveness is a good practice until one has to personally offer it. Not surprisingly, groups find it easy to blame others for moral wrongdoing, although they are reluctant to acknowledge their own role in fostering and sustaining it. In the words of Solzhenitzyn: "Who has no guilt? We are all guilty."[10]

Types of Guilt

At the end of World War II, the Allies began to ask whether all Germans bore some responsibility for the Nazi Holocaust. Although there was widespread agreement that leaders should bear the primary responsibility for Nazi crimes, the focus solely on top leaders tended to exonerate the citizenry.[11] On the other hand, emphasizing collective guilt seemed problematic because it imputed responsibility based on citizenship rather than on illegal actions of persons. To avoid superficial discourse about guilt and responsibility that "flattens everything out on a single plane,"[12] philosopher Karl Jaspers developed a framework for assessing guilt. His typology involves four types of guilt: criminal, political, moral, and metaphysical (table 3.1). In the first two, guilt arises from violations

Table 3.1. Types of Guilt

	Person Responsible	Nature of Wrong	Method of Atonement
Criminal	criminal offender	violation of law	trials, leading to punishment
Political	political leaders, military officers, government officials	unjust laws and policies	reparations, political reconstruction
Moral	persons who violate the moral law (one's conscience)	commission of evil, tolerating injustice	repentance; confronting pride and self-righteousness
Metaphysical	all humans	indifference, neglect; failure to oppose evil	humility and personal vulnerability; acknowledging pride

of external rules, whereas in the latter two guilt arises from subjective violations of personal morality or metaphysical obligations to others.

Criminal guilt is the objective culpability of persons for violating laws. Homicides, thefts, and the nonpayment of taxes are examples of this type of guilt, as are illegal actions by state security agents, even when a government official has ostensibly approved them. The remedy, or atonement, for such personal culpability is satisfied through legal prosecution and punishment.

The second type of guilt is political and refers to the vicarious responsibility that derives from membership in a political association. To a significant degree, *political guilt*, which derives from the collective evil attributed to the leaders and agents of a community, is communal responsibility without individual blame. Unlike criminal guilt, which is personal, political guilt is largely impersonal and involuntary, deriving chiefly from an individual's citizenship or nationality. Although all citizens bear some responsibility for the nature of the political regime where they live, government decision makers are chiefly culpable for the actions of regimes. The apartheid policies and structures enacted in South Africa by the National Party during the 1948–1990 period illustrate this type of culpability. Atonement for political crimes is normally achieved through trials, punishment, reparations, and the subsequent political restructuring of the state to ensure that radical evil is not repeated. If a regime is defeated by a foreign power, as was the case of Germany in World War II, responsibility for expiating the guilt lies with the victorious military authorities.

Moral guilt is the subjective culpability of persons for their action or inaction in light of their own moral standards. Since every action is subject to moral judgment, personal culpability is defined by each person's conscience as well as in consultation with "friends and intimates who are lovingly concerned [with one's] soul."[13] Such guilt is illustrated by the moral torture that Karl experiences on his deathbed for the evil he committed against a household of innocent Jews. Atonement of moral offenses—whether committed directly or indirectly, or by omission or commission—is achieved by humbly acknowledging guilt, by personally repenting for such acts, and by making symbolic or tangible reparations.

Scholars differ on whether repentance is sufficient to relieve moral guilt. Some argue that the only way to relieve such guilt is through punishment or tangible reparations. Philosopher Avishai Margalit, for example, calls for a rigorous standard of forgiveness, noting that remorse does not involve the "magic of an atonement offering."[14] But others argue that if retribution or reparations are prerequisites for forgiveness, then forgiveness ceases to be a gift. Thus, theologian Miroslav Volf argues that forgiveness should not depend on the prior fulfillment of justice, nor should it involve a "cheap grace" that disregards altogether claims of justice. Rather, atonement should be undertaken in a context in which community—or what he terms "embrace"— is given primacy but does not disregard the quest for justice.[15]

Finally, *metaphysical guilt* is the subjective culpability for major evil anywhere in the world. Since human beings are part of a global society, wrongdoing against any person or group results in a threat to global solidarity and communal well-being. According to Jaspers, "[t]here exists a solidarity among men as human beings that makes each co-responsible for every wrong and every injustice in the world, especially for crimes committed in his presence or with his knowledge. If I fail to do whatever I can to prevent them, I too am guilty."[16] Thus, the 1994 Rwanda genocide—a slaughter that resulted in the deaths of more than eight hundred thousand people in three months—involved a universal, metaphysical culpability for failing to halt such evil. Like moral guilt, atonement for metaphysical guilt is difficult since there is no simple way to expiate for such general, impersonal evils. At best, people need to recognize their own frailty and weaknesses, looking for guilt within themselves rather than in others. Only when individuals seek to purify their souls by voiding the pride of self-basing confession and the pride of moral victory can they move to a new level of human existence that provides the basis for rising above trivial, indifferent living.

Jaspers' schema is useful in identifying and assessing different types and levels of culpability arising from major social and political evils. It is especially helpful in structuring moral reasoning about egregious human rights violations and state-sponsored evils, such as those committed by Communist regimes and authoritarian military governments during the Cold War. Most important, the framework provides a means by which to differentiate between individual and collective responsibility and thereby assign culpability for regime offenses. Thus, such a typology helps to discriminate between the individual criminal culpability and the general, diffuse responsibility rooted solely in political association.

Although identifying responsibility and establishing legal and moral accountability is a comparatively simple task in private relationships, establishing culpability for collective offenses is a far more elusive and challenging undertaking. This is so in part because political responsibility is frequently broadly shared among state agents, government leaders, regime supporters, and the general public. Thus, in carrying out the task of accountability for past wrongdoing, Jaspers' model provides an invaluable tool for assessing different types and levels of responsibility and for establishing a framework for assigning culpability.

GUILT AND FORGIVENESS

How does forgiveness apply to the different types of guilt? Since human forgiveness is an ethical response to moral wrongdoing, it is an especially appropriate response to moral guilt—to the personal responsibility arising from the violation of one's conscience. Offenders can atone for wrongdoing by expressing contrition and authentic repentance and by demonstrating such remorse through acts of reparations and the promise of avoiding the repetition of similar wrongdoing. While such actions can help to reduce the "sting of guilt," they cannot remove the full burden of moral guilt. Indeed, Volf notes that since pursuing human forgiveness "is at the same time to admit to the deed and to accept blame," forgiveness can relieve some but not all the guilt arising from wrongdoing.[17] Thus, unlike divine forgiveness, which creates a new beginning by blotting out the past, human forgiveness establishes a new moral order rooted in memory.

Forgiveness is also an appropriate response to metaphysical guilt, which springs from indifference to, and neglect of, human suffering. Because such guilt arises from evil that is diffuse and remote, the perception of culpability is generally not as strong as with moral guilt. Nevertheless, to the extent that persons feel directly or indirectly responsible for failing to prevent atrocities and other egregious offenses, they can expiate such metaphysical guilt through spiritual restoration—what Jaspers terms "purification of the soul"—and by cultivating behaviors and moral attitudes that are conducive to a humane society. But as with moral guilt, metaphysical guilt cannot be fully relieved, since some of the residual effects, especially the memory of past wrongdoing, are likely to remain. As previously stated, human forgiveness is not a process of forgetting but a means for healing offenders and victims and restoring ruptured social relationships.

In contrast to the atonement of moral and metaphysical guilt, overcoming criminal and political guilt through forgiveness is far more problematic. Since criminal guilt involves the violation of public laws by individuals, the only legitimate response to such wrongdoing is to place it under the authority of the law. Although governments may undertake actions that mitigate the enforcement of criminal justice,[18] a constitutional regime's fundamental response to criminal behavior is to prosecute and punish offenders in light of the law. Indeed, even when victims forgive offenders, the state is bound to uphold the rule of law by prosecuting crimes to ensure the primacy of law, thereby reinforcing the principle that no person is above the law.

Political guilt arises from the direct or indirect culpability of government officials for unjust public policies that result in gross violations of human rights. Such abuses do not arise in a political vacuum but emerge from a particular social and political context where decision makers resort to excessive force to consolidate political power or to respond to domestic security threats. Since human beings are motivated by self-interest and generally seek to defend and justify their individual and collective actions, determining culpability for collective offenses is always a difficult challenge, especially when confronting state-sponsored atrocities. Thus, when collective offenses are uncovered, political leaders frequently claim that such crimes were the result of "excesses" by police and military officials, not the by-product of deliberate government policies.[19]

As noted in chapter 1, determining how best to address the criminal and political wrongdoing of former governments is one of the most significant challenges facing regimes that are consolidating a democratic political order. Given the incontestable fact of illegal and immoral use of violence, should the emerging democracies prosecute and punish former leaders and state agents responsible for the egregious abuse of human rights? Are trials the only way of responding to criminal and political guilt? Is forgiveness of crimes and political evils a possible alternative, and if so, is it a desirable one?

Later in this chapter, I argue that collective forgiveness is both possible and desirable. It is possible because forgiveness, while rooted in personal morality, is nonetheless applicable to the moral life of communities. And it is desirable because it provides a way—indeed, the only way—to overcome past wrongdoing through truth telling, remorse, and the implicit promise to not repeat the offense. Forgiveness lifts the moral burdens of past moral wrongdoing by "purifying" individual and collective memory through the deliberate moral act of viewing the past truthfully but without resentment or vengeance. The truth of the past is acknowledged, but through the morally courageous act of repentance and forgiveness, individuals and groups approach history redemptively.

Of course, some offenses may be so evil in their nature and scope that they may seem unforgivable. Indeed, some scholars claim that egregious, heinous public crimes like genocide and intentional political killings—what Kant termed "radical evil"—are so contrary to human well-being that they "transcend the realm of human affairs" and are therefore unforgivable. According to Hannah Arendt, in order for an injustice or crime to be forgivable, it must be subject to punishment. In the realm of human affairs, she writes, "men are unable to forgive what they cannot punish, and they are unable to punish what has turned out to be unforgivable."[20] Political theorist George Kateb similarly challenges the idea that forgiveness can overcome radical evil. He observes that while Jesus' teaching about love and forgiveness is normative, the Gospel does not call for forgiveness of, and reconciliation with, offenders responsible for "evil on a large scale."[21] For Kateb, therefore, egregious human rights abuses—such as the Nazi Holocaust, the Cambodian genocide, and the Rwanda genocide of 1994—are so evil that they are beyond the reach of moral redemption. Thus, while some collective offenses may be beyond the realm of forgiveness, this does not necessarily mean that forgiveness of regime offenses is impossible.

The role of collective forgiveness was powerfully illustrated in March 2000 when Pope John Paul II, in a sweeping and unprecedented act, apologized for the institutional sins of the Roman Catholic Church.[22] In his Mass of Reconciliation, the Pope declared: "I ask that in this year of mercy, the church . . .

kneels before God and begs for forgiveness for past and present sins of her sons."[23] Some of the church's major failings identified by the Vatican included religious intolerance and ecclesiastical divisions among Christians, the use of coercion in the service of truth, and injustice toward Jews, women, indigenous people, immigrants, the poor, and the unborn. In his homily, the Pope called for the "purification of memory" through repentance, declaring: "The church of today and of always feels obligated to purify the memory of those sad episodes of every sentiment of rancor or rivalry. . . . From the acceptance of divine forgiveness is born the duty to forgive one's brothers and seek reciprocal reconciliation."[24]

While numerous critics claimed that the Vatican's apology was too limited and too general, the Catholic Church's apology points to the importance of truth and vulnerability in restoring moral credibility. As Richard Neuhaus has noted, rather than undermining the church, the admission of its institutional failings—"acknowledging the truth about both the light and the shadows along the way of her earthly pilgrimage"[25]—in fact restores and renews the church's moral authority and spiritual life. The public confession, he writes, is "a sign not of the Church's weakness but of her self-confidence in an historical moment in which she is the world's singular institution of moral credibility."[26]

This historic act of institutional confession is significant not only religiously but also institutionally, for it illuminates the essential role of truth telling and confession in the renewal and restoration of collective morality of communities. More significant, by confessing publicly some of its errors and offenses, the Catholic Church was modeling a central teaching of Christianity—namely, that moral restoration is found in self-examination, confession, repentance, and forgiveness. By acknowledging that Catholics had periodically strayed from Christ's teachings through self-deception, self-righteousness, and moral insensitivity, the Pope was providing a model of collective healing. In effect, by publicly confessing the church's moral failings, the Pope was inviting individuals and collectives to undertake a comparable process of accountability, truth telling, and repentance in the hope that such actions would "purify memory" and thereby create a new foundation for the moral restoration of persons and communities.

THE POSSIBILITY OF POLITICAL FORGIVENESS

The Idea of Political Forgiveness

Can political communities repent and forgive as individuals? Whether forgiveness is applicable to political communities will depend on the capacity and willingness of groups to fulfill the requisite conditions for forgiveness. For offenders, this means that the collective must admit culpability and express contrition through apologies or reparations or both; for victims, this means that they must refuse vengeance and be prepared to treat offenders with human dignity. As noted earlier, forgiveness is a means for confronting moral wrongdoing, not a way to address strategic errors or unintended evil consequences from governmental policies. Forgiveness addresses serious moral wrongs by releasing victims from their justified anger and resentment and releasing offenders from their debt and moral guilt. Rather than imposing retributive punishment, forgiveness provides a moral nonjudicial approach to restoring individual and collective relationships.

Since forgiveness within and among political communities is rooted in interpersonal repentance and forgiveness, political forgiveness will necessarily build on the structure of individual forgiveness. This means that political forgiveness will depend on interaction between victims and offenders, attitudinal changes that contribute to empathy, and personal moral virtues that foster the healing and restoration of relationships.

Historically, legal and political philosophers have ignored the political dimensions of forgiveness. They have done so in the belief that the major moral purpose of the state is justice, conceived in terms of the protection of individual rights. Moreover, political thinkers have also neglected forgiveness because they have viewed it as a private, spiritual ethic. For them forgiveness is an aspect of personal morality to be applied among individuals in their private relationships, but it is not part of political morality. Accordingly, while individual victims can forgive, institutions must pursue justice.

Some theologians have claimed that forgiveness is chiefly a divine process,[27] while other thinkers have argued that it is solely a human process between individuals.[28] In *An Ethic for Enemies*, theologian Donald Shriver, Jr., challenges the pietistic and individualistic conceptions of forgiveness, arguing that this ethic need not be limited to religious or even private relations. Indeed, he claims that forgiveness provides a means by which communities and nations can overcome the burdens of past collective wrongdoing and international crimes and injustices.[29] Theologian Jürgen Moltmann, similarly, suggests that the church's ancient penitential ritual—one involving confession, remorse, repentance, and atonement[30]—is also relevant to public life. He writes: "I believe we can transfer basic elements of the church's practice of repentance and forgiveness into the policies whereby democracies come to term with the crimes committed under dictatorships, with the violations of human rights and the consequences."[31] How can forgiveness be incorporated into the public life of nations? How can nations repent and provide reparations for past collective wrongdoing in order to heal broken relationships? How can enmity between states be transformed into peaceful, cooperative relationships?

Arendt was one of the first theorists to explore the potential role of forgiveness in politics. She argued that forgiveness was essential to communal life because it provided a means "to undo the deeds of the past."[32] Although

she credited Jesus with the discovery of this ethic, she believed that forgiveness, despite its religious origins, should not be restricted to the spiritual
realm. More recently, Shriver has argued that forgiveness—which he defines
as an interactive process involving moral judgment of wrongdoing, the avoidance of vengeance, empathy toward offenders, and the renewal of human relationship[33]—is a legitimate ethic in domestic and international politics.

Although Shriver's study has greatly encouraged the moral reassessment of
the political role of forgiveness, his model is limited by the fact that it fails to
confront the inherent tension between justice and forgiveness, punishment
and reconciliation. Moreover, because Shriver presumes that justice and forgiveness are complementary processes, he neglects a distinctive feature of
both the popular and the scholarly conceptions of forgiveness—namely, the
cancellation of a deserved penalty.[34] Of course, Shriver omits this dimension
of forgiveness precisely because the abrogation of deserved penalties would
contravene claims of justice. Accordingly, Shriver's model emphasizes the
restoration of relationships through the avoidance of vengeance and the encouragement of empathy, not the mitigation or cancellation of debts.

P. E. Digeser offers another important model of political forgiveness.
Building on the popular conception of the term, Digeser defines forgiveness
as the releasing of financial or moral debts. He conceives of forgiveness as
an objective process that requires several preconditions, including 1) a relationship between transgressors and victims, 2) a moral or financial debt
owed by one party to the other, 3) a party with the authority to relieve an offender's deserved debt, and 4) explicit communication that an offender's
debt has been forgiven.[35] Like Shriver, Digeser does not make remorse or repentance a part of his model. He omits these and other subjective elements
because he seeks to develop a theory of political forgiveness based on individual and collective behaviors rather than on people's motivations. Although forgiveness is commonly viewed as a means to heal victims' anger
and resentment, Digeser views forgiveness solely as a purposive act that
leads to the release of debts. He argues that offenders should receive what is
their due, but claims, contrary to the conventional wisdom, that retroactive
justice is not the only, or even most important, value in public life. On some
occasions other values, such as the promotion of reconciliation and the establishment of domestic peace, may override the claims of corrective justice.
Digeser, therefore, claims that forgiveness in political life can be morally justified under some circumstances.

For Digeser, the major rationale for political forgiveness is that it can help
promote peace and reconciliation. Even though forgiveness is not a necessary
condition for political reconciliation, he claims that it can foster the restoration of communal relationships by promoting both the *process* and the *state*
of reconciliation. Forgiveness contributes to the process of reconciliation by
promoting trust and civility among, and helping to restore relationships be-

tween, transgressors and debtors. It promotes the state of reconciliation by contributing to "a settlement with the past."[36] Such a state of reconciliation does not imply a grand vision of unity and harmony of "all with all," but a state in which a new beginning is possible. For Digeser, the value of forgiveness is that "it settles the past and opens possibilities for the future."[37]

Elements of Political Forgiveness

Political forgiveness can be viewed as both an act and a process. As an act, it is the decision to relieve individuals and groups of their moral debts or deserved punishment. In the words of Digeser, collective forgiveness is "an intervention in the moral economy of rectificatory justice."[38] From a more comprehensive approach, political forgiveness can be defined as a process that fosters the healing of individuals and the restoration of communal relationships. In the analysis that follows, I focus on the process of political forgiveness, rather than the act itself.

Using Shriver's sentiment-based model and Digeser's action-based approach, as well as other theological and philosophical resources, I conceive of political forgiveness as an interactive process in which the personal and collective injuries are healed. To be successful, forgiveness depends on a number of elements, including consensus about past wrongdoing, remorse and repentance, renunciation of vengeance, empathy, and mitigation or cancellation of a deserved penalty.

1. *Consensus on Truth*: Forgiveness is possible only if actors can agree on the nature of, and culpability for, past wrongdoing. As José Zalaquette, a leading Chilean human rights scholar and member of Chile's truth commission, has observed, truth must be deemed an "absolute value."[39] A useful way of developing a shared account of the past is to pursue an official accounting of collective wrongdoing. Although trials, religious institutions, and nongovernmental organizations can contribute to the task of truth telling about former regime crimes, government-sponsored truth commissions have proven to be the most effective way to pursue this task. Consensus on truth will necessarily imply agreement about which persons or communities are chiefly culpable for past wrongdoing. Shriver argues that when individuals and groups cannot agree that some past action needs to be forgiven, "forgiveness stalls at the starting gate." This is why he suggests that forgiveness must begin with "memory suffused with moral judgment."[40] Thus, if political forgiveness is to occur, culpable individuals and groups need to acknowledge their offenses.

2. *Remorse and Repentance*: Contrition—frequently expressed through public apologies[41]—is also desirable for forgiveness.[42] Indeed, for some thinkers, remorse is a precondition for forgiveness since reconciliation is possible only when offenders acknowledge and repent of their wrongdoing.

Solzhenitsyn, for example, argues that intractable political conflicts can only be overcome through mutual repentance, since only such action "opens the path to a new relationship." He claims that the path of mutual repentance and mutual forgiveness is "one and the same."[43] To be authentic, repentance requires not only a change in attitude but also an implied promise that wrongdoing will not be repeated. Moreover, it also assumes that offenders must be prepared to provide restitution of confiscated property and to provide financial reparations for victims' injuries and losses. Although forgiveness can be undertaken without offenders' remorse, repentance greatly facilitates the process of reconciliation by helping to nurture norms and institutions conducive to a humane, harmonious society.

3. *Renunciation of Vengeance*: Persons and groups that have suffered wrongdoing have a natural inclination to retaliate, but vengeance does not lead to justice or to the healing of victims' injuries. Rather, it perpetuates hate and enmity and creates the breeding ground for even greater evil. If the cycles of violence are to be halted, victims must renounce vengeance.

4. *Empathy*: Instead, victims must follow Saint Augustine's admonition to hate the sin and love the sinner. This means that people must treat enemies and offenders with dignity and respect despite the offenses that they have committed. If forgiveness is to occur, transgressors and victims must cultivate empathy and compassion toward the "other," viewing each other as human beings worthy of respect. Since collectives tend to exacerbate selfishness and human passions, the expression of empathy is especially difficult within communities. Thus, in fostering communal rehabilitation, emphasis on the mutual responsibility for past collective offenses is important.

When he became president of Czechoslovakia in 1990, Václav Havel emphasized the shared responsibility for the injustices and evils that had been perpetrated under the Communist regime. In his first presidential address on New Year's Day, he told his fellow citizens that everyone was morally responsible for the "contaminated moral environment" of the country. "None of us is just its victim: we are all also its cocreators," he observed.[44] Thus by focusing on the mutual responsibility for past collective wrongdoing, Havel created public space for empathy to flourish among those chiefly responsible for Communist rule and those who simply accepted that rule as an inevitable political reality.

5. *Mitigation of Punishment*: Forgiveness normally entails the reduction or annulment of a deserved penalty.[45] Philosopher Nicholas Wolterstorff defines this element as the voluntary "foregoing of claims of justice."[46] The mitigation of punishment is crucial because it encourages the healing of offenders and the restoration of broken relationships. Although forgiveness does not require the full cancellation of punishment, debt-reduction is generally a by-product of the forgiveness process in which victims (or their agents) respond with compassion to offenders' repentance and remorse. It is important to stress that while human forgiveness results in the reestablish-

ment of a moral and social equality between victims and offenders, it reduces but does not eliminate offenders' moral responsibility.[47]

Although victims may initiate the process of collective forgiveness by expressing compassion toward transgressors, culpable offenders generally take the first step in the forgiveness process. This initiatory role is greatly facilitated when leaders are not themselves the guilty ones but representatives of a culpable community. West German chancellor Willy Brandt illustrated this practice during an official trip to Warsaw in December 1970 when he expressed remorse for the suffering his country had inflicted on Poland during World War II. Since Brandt had been involved in resisting Hitler's policies, he could have easily avoided the subject of collective repentance altogether. But because he was eager to foster political reconciliation among his neighboring states,[48] he knew that to do so it was important that he assume vicarious responsibility for Germany's past collective offenses. Thus, when he traveled to Poland as part of his strategy of political accommodation, he sought anew to express his nation's collective remorse. He did this in a surprising and unexpected manner when, after laying a wreath at the city's ghetto memorial, he knelt as an expression of national repentance for the suffering the Nazi regime had inflicted on the Polish people. Although many Germans viewed this act as unnecessary and inappropriate,[49] the gesture no doubt contributed to the restoration of diplomatic relations between the two countries and, more important, to the ongoing reconciliation between the peoples of two neighboring countries. By publicly conveying a nation's collective remorse, Brandt established a more liberating, compassionate politics that helped create public space for greater mutual understanding and political reconciliation.

Regardless of how political forgiveness is initiated, however, if the process is to foster healing and renewal of social and political relationships, representatives of culpable communities will have to acknowledge wrongdoing and apologize for collective wrongdoing. Victim groups, for their part, will have to renounce vengeance and pursue instead empathy toward transgressors. Only when victim groups give up their quest for retaliation and cancel part or all the deserved debt or punishment will the collective fruits of forgiveness translate into a new, forward-looking politics that makes possible a new more just political society. Although such politics is rooted in memory, past collective wrongdoing no longer governs relations between antagonists.

KEY ISSUES IN POLITICAL FORGIVENESS

Political forgiveness is a process by which individuals, groups, and communities overcome the legacy of collective wrongdoing through constructive interaction between victims and offenders. Since such a process is rooted in the interpersonal conception of forgiveness, the possibility of communal forgiveness raises a number of important methodological and substantive issues. These include whether 1) forgiveness can be extended to groups; 2) victims are the sole agents of forgiveness; 3) political communities are moral actors, responsible for the collective well-being and behaviors of its members; 4) political leaders, acting on behalf of a people, are capable of fulfilling the moral demands of forgiveness; and 5) forgiveness can be reconciled with the demands of public justice. Next I examine the first four concerns; in the following chapter, I take up the issue of justice.

Individual versus Collective Morality

As noted earlier, scholars of transitional justice commonly view forgiveness solely as a personal virtue. As a result, they regard forgiveness as applicable only to interpersonal relations, not to groups or political communities. Moreover, since forgiveness is a moral response to an offense, they similarly tend to assume that only individuals who have suffered wrongdoing have the moral right to mitigate or absolve the moral culpability of offenders. Pricilla Hayner captures the conventional wisdom on political forgiveness when she observes that forgiveness and reconciliation are "deeply personal processes."[50] According to the standard legal-political perspective, the fundamental task of the state is to uphold the law by prosecuting and punishing crimes. Governments may be able to show mercy and pardon offenders, but only victims can forgive offenders.

In exploring whether regimes can forgive and repent, it is important to differentiate between political (or public) morality and personal morality. The former—which comprises general principles (for example, liberty, equality, and impartiality), political traditions (for example, liberalism and communitarianism), and moral theories (for example, just war doctrine)—provides norms and principles for pursuing peace and justice within or among states. Private morality, by contrast, includes ethical standards such as the Ten Commandments and moral obligations such as fidelity, promise keeping, and truth telling that foster personal integrity and stable interpersonal relationships.

To a significant degree, the failure to apply forgiveness to public life is due to the widespread belief that this ethic is a personal, religious norm that is unrelated to politics. Moreover, since theorists and decision makers generally regard personal and political ethics as radically distinct,[51] they tend to be reluctant to extend personal moral values to the public realm. While personal morality and political morality are of course qualitatively different, they are nevertheless closely intertwined, with the former often providing a moral basis for the policies and actions of collectives. Indeed, the principles and doctrines of political morality are frequently derived from personal morality and more particularly, the shared ethical values and practices of individuals comprising a collective. Even though personal morality cannot be directly transposed to the public realm, individual moral values such as honor, sacrifice, promise keeping, caring, and compassion can provide an ethical basis for collective action. As a result, while confession, repentance, and forgiveness are considered elements of personal morality, such norms can also conceivably be applied within and among communities.

If collectives express apologies, offer reparations, and grant forgiveness to other groups, are such actions legitimate? Are they morally appropriate? While it is beyond the bounds of this book to define the boundaries of political morality, it is not unreasonable to suppose that the moral values and practices of individuals can be incorporated into public actions through the legitimate authority of government. Since governments use their authority to regulate human behavior and undertake actions on behalf of their members, the policies they enact will reflect the values, beliefs, and preferences of decision makers. Thus, when regimes attempt to reckon with the legacy of past collective atrocities, they may undertake such moral actions as truth telling, apologies, and forgiveness rather than legal retribution in the belief that such actions will best promote individual and political healing. Just as courts can pardon offenders and parliaments can impose taxes on citizens, so, too, public officials can undertake actions on behalf of a people that involve policies that some individuals might oppose. Since the boundaries of political morality are determined by the actions of governments, in principle there is no ethical justification for excluding forgiveness and reconciliation from political morality.

Theologian L. Gregory Jones has observed that since forgiveness aims at healing ruptured relationships, it has social and political dimensions. Indeed, he suggests that precisely because forgiveness is concerned with the restoration of human community, "we cannot neatly divide issues of forgiveness and justice into spheres of the personal and private and of the political and public."[52] As a result, just as individuals can be the victims and perpetrators of moral wrongdoing, so, too, groups and communities can also be the victims of collective evil or bear communal responsibility for perpetrating wrongdoing, especially the gross violation of human rights. Since the commission of communal offenses is partly the responsibility of regimes in authority, forgiveness provides a potential means by which human communities can overcome their evil past.

Who Can Forgive?

It is commonly assumed that only victims have a right to forgive. According to this view, since forgiveness involves the abrogation of a debt, only the individual or group that has suffered wrongdoing has the right to offer release from deserved punishment. This is why Omar Dullah, the South African minister of justice, when introducing the government's decision to establish a truth commission, observed: "We cannot forgive on behalf of victims, nor do we have the moral right to do so. It is the victims themselves who must speak."[53] Charles Villa-Vicencio, similarly, observes that forgiveness is a deeply personal process. "We can forgive harm done to us," he writes, but "it is not in our power to forgive harm done to others."[54] After Havel became president of Czechoslovakia in 1990, he was given a list of those friends who had written denunciations of him. According to him, when he learned about those who had collaborated against him, he decided to forget the names of those who had betrayed him and to forgive them. But as a state official he could not, he observed, act on behalf of others who might have also suffered human rights abuses by the secret police and their collaborators. Havel writes: "We can only offer absolution on our own behalf: to offer absolution on behalf of others is not within our power. We can try to convince people to forgive, but if they want justice, they have a right to demand it."[55]

According to the civic perspective, individuals may be able to forgive, but the task of government is to pursue justice within and among political communities. Such justice is achieved through the dispassionate, impartial application of laws to the behavior of persons and groups. Of course, government officials (executives) may, for reasons of national interest, reduce or commute the sentence of courts through acts of mercy. Although pardon and mercy share with forgiveness a mitigation or annulment of a deserved punishment, they are conceptually distinct, since the former are legal concepts used to moderate or reduce punishment, while forgiveness is a moral concept that seeks the healing of persons and the restoration of communal relationships. As Paul Lauritzen has noted, mercy and pardon are essentially palliative practices, while forgiveness is essentially a restorative ethic.[56]

Although the notion that forgiveness is a victim's prerogative is seemingly self-evident,[57] this intuitive claim needs to be qualified. To begin with, victims are not solitary, independent persons, nor do they comprise a simple, coherent group of people. Rather, victims comprise three groups: those who have suffered direct injury or violence (*primary victims*); family and friends of primary victims (*secondary victims*); and society itself (*tertiary victims*). These three types of victims correspond to three levels of suffering: first, the direct physical or psychological suffering of primary victims; second, the indirect suffering of family members who grieve the injuries or loss of a loved one; and third, the collective suffering of a community or society in response to the murder of a leader, systemic crime such as genocide, or gross human rights abuses. Such communal suffering can lead to increased collective pessimism, a loss of social trust, and the undermining of legal and constitutional norms.

Moreover, since decisions among these three levels of victims need not be complementary, conflicts may arise between victims and a government or between family and friends and the state. Thus, a family may forgive an offender while a state enforces a deserved penalty, or a government may grant amnesty to offenders, while family and friends demand justice. This means that the task of granting forgiveness must incorporate not only the primary victim's wishes but also those of family and friends, as well as society at large. Using this tridimensional classification of victims, Trudy Govier and Wilhelm Verwoerd argue that primary victims are not the only agents that are entitled to forgive. Instead, they suggest that a political community, as a tertiary victim, is also entitled to offer and receive forgiveness.[58]

A differentiated classification of victims also allows ethicists to address the moral challenge posed by crimes allegedly classified as "unforgivable." If only primary victims can forgive, then some wrongs—e.g., murder and genocide—are beyond the reach of forgiveness. But if a tridimensional conceptualization of wrongdoing is applied, the death of victims need not preclude forgiveness. This leads philosopher Piers Benn to claim that family and friends, who are themselves secondary- and tertiary-level victims, are entitled to offer some forgiveness, or what he terms "quasi-forgiveness."[59] In effect, representatives of primary victims can offer partial forgiveness.

Moral Agency of Collectives

A third important issue is whether communities are moral actors. Since collectives are not coherent, integrated persons, they do not have a mind, a conscience, a personality, or feelings, In addition, collectives do not experience sensations such as grief or pain. Groups, nevertheless, can and do make decisions and carry out actions that influence their own members' lives as well as the well-being of other groups. When groups and communities pursue actions within the society of which they are a part, their behaviors can result in a variety of intergroup relations, ranging from harmonious to conflictual ties, from trusting to suspicious dispositions, and from compassionate to vengeful behaviors. These different social conditions will foster, in turn, positive or negative attitudes that either facilitate or impede communal solidarity. For example, the continuing conflict in Northern Ireland between Protestant loyalists and Roman Catholic nationalists has resulted in intense distrust and hatred between the two groups. Similarly, the ongoing Arab-Israeli conflict has led to a high level of animosity between Palestinians and Israeli Jews, while the death and destruction carried out by Muslim terrorists against New York City's World Trade Center has caused profound distrust of Islamic radicals within the United States. On the other hand, the increasing social and economic cooperation between Germany and France through the European Union has promoted increasing understanding and trust between the two nations that were formerly enemy states. Thus, the decisions and actions of social and political groups have a profound moral impact on other groups as well as on the wider domestic or international society of which they are a part.

Although there is no such thing as a "collective will," the decisions of political communities can be viewed as possessing moral agency provided their decision-making institutions are legitimate, involve freedom of action, and are based on decision makers' moral judgments. Whether or not a group or community is capable of legitimate moral action will, of course, depend on how communities are conceived.[60] If a group or community is simply a random collection of participants, it will be incapable of independent moral action.[61] If, on the contrary, a group or community is a purposive association that seeks to advance shared interests through established decision-making structures, then such groups are likely to possess moral agency and will therefore be capable of carrying out collective moral actions, including the offering and receiving of political forgiveness. Thus, if a government leader apologizes for past wrongdoing, as President Clinton did when he expressed regret in 1998 for not halting the Rwanda genocide, such remorse can be considered legitimate moral action.

Although the actions of communities bear moral consequences, it is important not to reify groups and nations and thereby assume that they are no different from individual persons. In describing the behaviors and actions of collectives, it is therefore important to avoid the fallacy of composition—that is, believing that what is true of the parts is also true of the whole. Since a collective is not simply the sum of its parts, when individuals forgive or pursue reconciliation this does not necessarily mean that the community has itself undertaken such collective action. Moreover, it is important to avoid the fallacy of division—believing that what is true of the whole is also true of the parts. As a result, when senior government officials apologize for regime wrongdoing and express remorse through reparations, this does not necessarily mean that citizens themselves have accepted individual or collective culpability and are prepared to express individual contrition.[62] In short, collective moral action is independent of the behaviors of individuals.

Since communities are capable of collective moral action, they are also accountable for their communal policies and behaviors. This means that collectives are morally responsible for their just and unjust actions, including conquest, slavery, aggressive war, genocide, and abuse of indigenous peoples' rights.[63] Once political communities have committed egregious injustices and heinous crimes, how should they seek to atone for past collective offenses? In *The Guilt of Nations*, Elazar Barkan argues that nations, because they are collectively responsible, can make amends for past wrongdoing by the public acknowledgment of offenses and by making reparations and restitution to those who have suffered injuries and losses as a result of past offenses. According to Barkan, the increasing expression of collective remorse through tangible reparations is an important development in the international community, for it contributes to the renewal and restoration of a moral order in global society.[64]

Agents of Political Forgiveness

The fourth issue—whether representative forgiveness is possible—will depend in part on the capacity of public officials to act on behalf of a political community in the forgiveness process. When governments confront past wrongdoing, leaders frequently assume the role of vicarious agents, acting on behalf of a group of citizens (offenders or victims) or the society at large. Is such vicarious agency morally valid? Can government officials, for example, apologize for past collective offenses? Are they morally authorized to offer reparations or to forgive collective debts? Are such actions morally legitimate, especially when the government agents initiating reconciliation and forgiveness may not have been directly involved as victims or perpetrators of regime offenses? Since governments are the ultimate decision makers within the state, their actions are normally considered authoritative and binding—whether they involve taxes, diplomatic negotiations, or international reconciliation. To be sure, the extent of a government's authority will depend on its perceived legitimacy, which in turn will depend on the degree of periodic consent expressed by community members. But if government is regarded as legitimate—that is, with the presumed authority to speak and act for a collective—then a community may be said to have moral standing, capable of offering and receiving forgiveness through its public officials.

Of course, whether or not government officials can offer or receive forgiveness on behalf of a community does not necessarily answer the question of whether governments should in fact implement this ethic. Should Spain apologize, for example, for the evils perpetrated against indigenous peoples in its conquest of Latin America during the sixteenth century? Should the government of Turkey acknowledge and repent for the genocide its military forces committed against the Armenian people in the early twentieth century? Should Japan apologize for its attack on Pearl Harbor? Should the U.S. government apologize to the Guatemalan people for its support of the repressive military government in the 1980s?

This book is written in the conviction that the most expeditious and effective way of reckoning with past collective offenses is by intentionally seeking to foster political healing through reconciliation based on moral rehabilitation of antagonists. Since political forgiveness is an interactive process, political conglomerates and their duly authorized governmental agents will necessarily have to fulfill its preconditions if this ethic is to be incorporated into public life. This means that government leaders must be prepared and willing to lead a community in the forgiveness process by publicly acknowledging wrongdoing, expressing remorse for harm, renouncing vengeance, and acknowledging contrition through the willingness to cancel deserved debts or punishment.

The prospect for political forgiveness does not depend on the level of social and political development, the maturation of civil society, or the degree of democracy. Rather, it depends on the moral courage of leaders and citizens in confronting past collective wrongs through repentance, humility, and eventual reconciliation. If victims are to overcome anger and alienation and offenders are to accept responsibility for wrongdoing, they will both have to overcome their natural tendency toward pride in order to view their enemies as persons entitled to dignity. It is important to stress, however, that the declarations and actions of state agents do not themselves complete the cycle of political forgiveness. While public officials can lead the process, communal forgiveness and reconciliation are only completed when citizens of both the offended and offender communities transform their attitudes and behaviors toward the other. In short, political leaders can encourage a people in the steps of forgiveness by acknowledging and repenting of wrongdoing, avoiding vengeance, and renewing social and political relationships.

THE PROMISE OF POLITICAL FORGIVENESS

Some political crimes and communal wrongs, especially those committed in fulfillment of public policies instituted by ruling authorities, can result in systemic offenses that cannot be rectified through a state's criminal justice system. Some crimes—such as apartheid in South Africa or totalitarian rule in the former Soviet Union—may be so widespread that retributive justice would entail prosecuting a large number of state agents, placing an undue economic and administrative burden on an emerging constitutional system. Major crimes may also remain elusive, beyond the reach of the law, because of state authorities' inability to gather sufficient evidence to prosecute suspected offenders. Since many human rights abuses in military regimes were carried out covertly, gathering the necessary evidence to bring state agents to trial can be a daunting task.

In addition, while financial compensation might provide some sense of justice to victims who have lost property or loved ones, financial restitution is unlikely to provide a fully satisfactory alternative. Finally, trials might provide a legal method for prosecuting government leaders and military officials responsible for major crimes, but they are unlikely to contribute to the healing of victims and their families, the restoration of communal relationships, or the consolidation of constitutional government. In short, even if retributive justice were possible, it is unlikely that it could provide a satisfactory response to past evils.

The most convincing rationale for political forgiveness is that it provides a superior approach to the moral, legal, and political reconstruction of society. As with interpersonal forgiveness, political forgiveness provides a means by which offenders and victims can undertake mutually constructive attitudes and actions that foster the healing of persons, the renewal of social trust, and the restoration of political harmony. Next, I explore some of the positive ways that this ethic contributes to the development and sustenance of humane political communities.

First, forgiveness provides a more durable, comprehensive justice. As I argue in the next chapter, forgiveness is rooted in the alternative perspective of restorative justice. Unlike retributive justice, which focuses on the prosecution and punishment of offenders, restorative justice emphasizes the healing of persons and the restoration of interpersonal relationships and communal bonds by giving priority to what Volf terms "embrace."[65] The emphasis on restoration and renewal through forgiveness does not mean that legal accountability is unimportant. On the contrary, restorative justice demands accountability through truth telling, acknowledgment, and reparations. But whereas retributive justice seeks to restore and maintain the credibility of the constitutional legal order through prosecution and punishment, restorative justice seeks to heal the damaged social, cultural, and political fabric of society.

Critics of forgiveness argue that collective forgiveness is unfair because offenders do not receive their due. Those responsible for injustices and crimes are not made to fully pay for the wrongs that they have committed. As Lewis Smedes correctly observes, forgiveness is an outrage against "straight-line, dues-paying morality."[66] In spite of its seeming unfairness, forgiveness gives to humans something that they would not otherwise receive: victims are liberated from hate and anger and from being controlled by the memory of injustice while offenders are freed from moral and legal debts from past offenses. As Arendt has noted, forgiveness allows individuals to overcome the consequences of past wrongdoing—to be "released from the consequences of what we have done."[67] Such release is not gratis, however, but comes at a significant cost to victims because they give up their individual right to retributive claims.

Second, forgiveness is important because it provides a basis for political reconciliation. Collective offenses increase distrust and deepen alienation and division among people. The process of political forgiveness provides a means by which communities can overcome alienation and division arising from collective wrongdoing. For the offenders, forgiveness offers a process by which groups can acknowledge offenses and express remorse for their wrongdoing. To the extent that community aggression and injustice can be rectified, collective forgiveness provides a means by which groups can acknowledge and atone for past collective offenses. For peoples who have suffered wrongdoing, political forgiveness provides a means by which victims' backward-looking bitterness and anger are transformed into a forward-looking individual healing and collective renewal and restoration. Since lingering memories of wrongdoing can perpetuate bitterness and a desire for revenge, the process of forgiveness can contribute to reformation of victims' attitudes and values, resulting in greater empathy and compassion toward offenders. Forgiveness, in other words, is a means to reconciliation.

Third, political forgiveness helps people escape from the tyranny of excessive or corrosive memory. Memory is of course essential in individual and collective life, ensuring individual mental health while providing communal solidarity by sustaining distinctive cultural traditions and political ideals. Although collective memory is necessary in maintaining communal cohesion and providing a common political identity, it can also serve, paradoxically, as an instrument of exclusion or a tool of victimization. When a people defines its past through suffering and hardship, the shared memory can contribute to fear and insecurity and impede self-confidence and freedom of action.[68] Thus, while memory can foster internal cohesion, it can also impede trust and cooperation with other groups and communities.

The challenge in promoting domestic and international peace and political cooperation is especially challenging for groups and nations whose collective memory is defined by past suffering. Although collective hardship can contribute to a backward-looking memory that focuses on the violence and injustices suffered by ancestors, suffering per se need not result in a memory rooted in victimhood. The challenge for communities that have perpetrated or suffered egregious wrongdoing is to redeem memory from excessive concern with guilt or suffering through the ethic of forgiveness. As the Catholic Church's recent study on memory and reconciliation suggests, forgiveness is a means by which to "purify" a community's collective memory. According to the study, the purification of memory involves a change of heart or perspective about the past. Specifically it involves "eliminating from personal and collective conscience all forms of resentment or violence left by the inheritance of the past . . . which becomes the foundation for a renewed moral way of acting."[69]

Forgiveness can also contribute to the healing of memory by fostering a balance between a forward-looking hope and a backward-looking quest for justice. In carrying out this challenge, forgiveness can contribute to fostering equilibrium between a redemptive reflection of the past that fosters accountability and a forward-looking orientation that nurtures social renewal and institutional restoration. Amos Elon has wisely noted that although history and collective memory are inseparable elements of culture, the past "must not be allowed to become the dominant element determining the future of society and the destiny of a people."[70] He suggests that Israeli political life, which is so dependent on memory, could benefit by "a little forgetfulness." What is needed, he writes, is a shift in emphasis and proportion so that a new equilibrium between memory and hope can be achieved in Israeli political life. Forgiveness therefore contributes to the redemption of the past by providing not only a new moral perspective of the past that can facilitate reconciliation but also a more balanced orientation between memory and future hopes.

Fourth, political forgiveness is also important because, as Appleby notes, it provides a means to overcome "the vicious cycle of charges and counter-charges of political victimization."[71] Intractable political disputes—like the ethnopolitical conflicts in Bosnia and Kosovo, the civilizational conflicts between Jews and Arabs in Israel and the Occupied Territories of the West Bank and Gaza, and the politico-religious conflict in Northern Ireland and Sudan—frequently involve violence resulting in mass cruelties. Such atrocities, however, rarely encourage the political opposition to compromise its objectives.

Instead, violence encourages counterviolence, which in turn increases distrust and further exacerbates political fragmentation. Indeed, the inevitable result of a resort to violence is that it breeds a politics of victimization, where groups perceive themselves as victims of their enemy's violent actions. In Northern Ireland, for example, Protestant Unionists perceive themselves as victims of Catholic Irish Republican Army (IRA) terrorism, while Catholic Republicans view themselves as victims of Protestant paramilitary violence and economic discrimination. As Solzhenitsyn notes, however, at some point people "must stop discussing whose crimes are more recent, more serious and affect most victims." If they fail to repent and offer and receive forgiveness, he writes, "the fires will smolder forever beneath the ashes and flare up again and again, and these countries will never know stability."[72]

In the final analysis political forgiveness is desirable because there is no better alternative. Although the criminal justice system can judge and punish offenders, crimes and wrongs cannot be fully rectified. The torturing, killing, and abducting of people cannot be undone, and although seized property can be returned to its owners, the condition of land and buildings is likely to have deteriorated. Even if punishment of offenders is possible, the restoration of victims and their property may not be possible. Under such circumstances, perhaps, the only alternative for political enemies is to participate in the forgiveness process—one based on perpetrators' acknowledgment of wrongdoing and the expression of remorse followed by victims responding with compassion and empathy rather than with vengeance. In effect, antagonists attempt to heal broken human relationships by seeking to overcome what Arendt has termed "the predicament of irreversibility."[73]

Commenting on the injustice of Czechoslovakia's expulsion of Germans from their Sudeten homeland in 1945, in the aftermath of the Allied defeat of the Axis powers, Jean Bethke Elshtain writes: "Perhaps there is nothing left for the expelled and expropriated people of German descent to do but to forgive. That is the hardest thing of all to do, of course, but it may be the only way to forestall quaffing the bitter brew of injustice, suffering, and recompense sought even unto future generations."[74]

Forgiveness is an extraordinarily difficult human achievement, whether carried out individually or collectively. This is so because its preconditions involve not only humility and compassion but also moral courage. In particular, offenders must be willing to acknowledge their wrongdoing and then express remorse for their wrongdoing; victims, for their part, must be willing to accept the offenders' apology and remorse and respond with empathy, viewing perpetrators as human beings entitled to dignity. To be sure, political forgiveness is not a prevalent norm of modern politics, in great part because of its morally demanding nature. But skepticism about the public role of forgiveness is also due to the widespread belief that such an ethic undermines justice. Given the perceived tension between justice and forgiveness, I next explore the interrelationship of these norms and, more particularly, the validity of the claim that forgiveness undermines justice.

4

Justice, Reconciliation, and Political Forgiveness

Forgiveness does not negate moral accountability but it has greater transformative power than vengeance.

—John de Gruchy, South African professor of religious studies[1]

Forgiveness can be properly understood and practiced only in the context of the stance which gives primacy to reconciliation but does not give up the pursuit of justice.

—Miroslav Volf, contemporary Croat theologian[2]

To forgive those who have wronged one is an act of highest sovereignty and great inner freedom. In forgiving and reconciling, the victims are superior to the perpetrators and free themselves from compulsion to evil deeds.

—Jürgen Moltmann, German theologian[3]

In the previous chapter, I argued that communities, like individuals, have the capacity to both grant and receive forgiveness. The ethic of political forgiveness is problematic, however, not only because the concept is elusive and difficult to apply but also because it challenges individual claims to corrective justice. Since forgiveness involves freeing offenders from their debts and deserved penalties, the application of this ethic to political life is considered contrary to the accepted wisdom that collective wrongdoing must be punished. But securing individual justice through legal retribution is not the only important concern in reckoning with past regime offenses. Indeed, since justice can be pursued only in a context of social and political order, the restoration and maintenance

of a stable, peaceful, and harmonious community is also essential. Consequently, when deeply fragmented communities are confronting a legacy of past
regime atrocities and when alienation and distrust are pervasive within society,
the rehabilitation of communal bonds and the healing of collective injuries will
necessitate more than corrective justice. Indeed, if individual and collective
healing is to occur, communities will have to pursue peace and justice, reconciliation and accountability.

In this chapter, I explore the interconnection of justice, reconciliation, and
forgiveness. I begin by examining the quest for accountability. But since legal accountability alone is not an adequate response to individual and collective offenses, communities must also devote significant resources to the
restoration of communal bonds. In seeking to overcome alienation and distrust, collectives can pursue a number of strategies. One of these is political
forgiveness—an ethic that makes possible communal reconciliation. In the
chapter's second part, I therefore examine the nature and role of reconciliation. Since reconciliation, like forgiveness, is in fundamental tension with
claims of justice, I analyze and critique in the third section the prevailing belief that justice must be fulfilled before reconciliation can be pursued. I suggest that a more effective strategy is one that promotes both justice and reconciliation. In the fourth and final section, I compare and contrast two
alternative approaches to justice. Retributive justice, the dominant paradigm
in political systems, is rooted in the idea that the credibility of the rule of law
requires that wrongdoing be prosecuted and punished. Such a conception is
contrary to forgiveness and regards reconciliation as a by-product of the enforcement law. The other strategy—restorative justice—gives precedence to
reconciliation and regards forgiveness as a legitimate ethic in public life.

LEGAL AND MORAL ACCOUNTABILITY

For most liberal political theorists, the fundamental task of the state is to promote justice, which is normally defined as the securing and protecting of human rights through the rule of law. Democratic theorists argue that constitutional government, rooted in the consistent and impartial application of the
law, is the most effective way to protect individual rights and thereby ensure
political justice. According to constitutional theory, when a crime is committed the state has a responsibility to hold offenders accountable for their illegal actions. In addition, victims have a right to seek redress by pursuing civil
claims against offenders.

Vengeance

When a serious wrong is committed, a victim usually feels hurt and angry
and may seek revenge. Vengeance—defined as "the impulse to retaliate when

wrongs are done"[4]—is normally viewed pejoratively since it presumes a personal, automatic, and uncontrolled response to an offender. When carried out as an impulsive act, vengeance is problematic because it is frequently disproportional to the original offense and counterproductive because it seldom resolves the original injustice or heals the injury. More significant, however, vengeance may make injustice unappeasable and thereby foster cycles of violence. This is why Adam Michnick, the Polish human rights activist, argues that the logic of revenge is "implacable."[5] The dangers and destructiveness of vengeance are clearly evident in some societies, like Albania, Bosnia, Kosovo, and Northern Ireland, where revenge is viewed as an honorable response to personal and collective wrongdoing and where the memory of victimization continues to fuel ancient animosities.

In reckoning with past wrongdoing, the challenge for victims is how to confront past crimes and injustices without allowing their anger and desire for revenge to overwhelm their own identity and the restoration of their own well-being. Since wrongdoing results in the violation of others' rights, anger and resentment are appropriate short-term responses. The desire for vengeance—which is based on the *lex talionis* philosophy ("an eye for an eye and a tooth for a tooth") and is a "wellspring of a notion of equivalence that animates justice"[6]—is also an appropriate dimension of victims' response to egregious wrongdoing. Of course, a victim may seek to avoid anger and resentment altogether by simply disregarding or condoning past offenses. But such a response is morally problematic because it conveys a lack of respect for oneself and for others. As philosopher Jeffrie Murphy has noted, "a person who does not resent moral injuries done to him . . . is almost necessarily a person lacking in self-respect."[7] As a result, he argues that if human dignity is to be protected, resentment and anger are not only warranted but morally necessary.

In confronting past offenses, the challenge is to how to correct the harm, prevent the repetition, heal the injury, and restore broken relationships. While some anger and resentment are a natural by-product of wrongdoing, vengeance is problematic because it fails to emphasize the healing of victims, but it is also counterproductive because it perpetuates evil, exacerbating the conflict through the repetition of cycles of violence. The challenge for society in general and victims in particular is to condemn wrongdoing while also accepting offenders as human beings—or as St. Augustine counseled, to "hate the sin but not the sinner." This is a difficult, demanding task, especially since righteous indignation and moral hatred of wrongdoing are frequently corrupted, themselves becoming sources of new injustices. This occurs when hatred is personalized, leading victims to desire not only the annulment of an offense but, in the words of philosopher Jean Hampton, "a personal defeat for this enemy of morality."[8] Thus, the challenge in confronting wrongdoing is to condemn evil behavior while affirming the worth of all people, including those responsible for offenses.

Retribution

Given the dangers and problematic nature of vengeance, political systems seek to deter human wrongs by maintaining credible legal systems that ensure the prosecution and punishment of crimes. The means by which political systems seek to promote and sustain lawful behavior and to inhibit wrongdoing is through retribution, which is the means by which political systems seek to promote and sustain lawful behavior of citizens and inhibit wrongdoing toward others. Although both retribution and vengeance are similar in that they seek to punish wrongdoing, they differ in their means, goals, and motives.

In terms of means, retribution is an impersonal process carried out through the impartial institutions of the state, whereas vengeance is a personal process involving punishment by the victim or his agents. In addition, since vengeance is personal, there are no internal constraints on the violence of revenge; by contrast, a central feature of criminal justice is that it is guided by principles and constrained by rules. As Lawrence Crocker observes, the internal limits imposed on retributive punishment are "the soul of retributive justice," for they provide both a sword to punish wrongdoers and a shield to protect them from excessive or unjust punishment.[9] In terms of goals, while both retribution and vengeance impose punishment on offenders, the aim of the former is to assert the equality of people by affirming victims and punishing offenders, while the goal of the latter is to diminish the offender's standing. Finally, in terms of motives, whereas vengeance seeks to lower the offender's status below others, the aim of retribution is to affirm the worth and equality of all people. As a result, agents of revenge get pleasure by inflicting injury, whereas agents of retribution derive no personal satisfaction, save that justice has been done.

Some scholars, such as Robert Nozick,[10] regard retribution as wholly distinct from vengeance. Others, such as Martha Minow,[11] view retribution as a form of institutionalized vengeance, where prosecution and punishment are dictated by widely accepted procedures, governed by the norms of equality and impartiality, and defined by punishment that is proportional and appropriate. Bringing vengeance under institutional constraints of the state does not, of course, ensure justice, since the institutions of the state can be perverted, as totalitarian and authoritarian rules have demonstrated throughout this century.

Most legal scholars justify retribution either in terms of its inherent rightness (deontologically) or in terms of its consequences (utility). From a Kantian or deontological perspective, wrongdoing must be punished, not because such punishment deters future offenses, but because there is a moral duty to punish criminal behavior. Viewed in this light, punishment is an inherent, fitting moral response to past wrongdoing. By contrast, consequentialism justifies punishment as a necessary condition for a credible criminal justice system, which in turn is a precondition of a stable, peaceful, and just political order. According to this view, if future criminal behavior is to be deterred, the rule of law must be perceived as credible and authoritative, and this can only occur if major past offenses are prosecuted and punished. Raúl Alfonsín, the first democratic president of Argentina after the 1976–1983 era of military rule, justified the prosecution of military rulers using this approach. He argued that the main object of the trials was prevention: "To ensure that what had happened could not happen in the future, to guarantee that never again would an Argentinean be taken from his home at night to be tortured or assassinated by agents of the state."[12]

Hampton justifies retribution by claiming that it offers a way of communicating values about the fundamental worth of human beings. Following Kant, she argues that since all human beings are entitled to equal respect and since wrongdoing runs contrary to this norm by making offenders superior to victims, offenses and crimes must be punished to reaffirm the value of equal human dignity. Viewed in this light, punishment is not a means of moral education or a means to deter future crime but simply a moral response to prior wrongdoing—one that gives offenders their just deserts. As Hampton sees it, the aim of punishment is not to avenge wrongdoing or to inflict pain and injury on the offender; rather, the goal of such "communicative" retributivism is "to annul the offender's claim of superiority."[13]

Although legal retribution is important in providing justice, deterring future crime, and restoring the moral equality among offenders and victims, such an approach does not necessarily rehabilitate individuals and groups or restore fractured relationships. If the collective harm to groups and communities is to be repaired, such healing will likely result from reformation of society's moral values and the reparation of its legal and political institutions. Only through a process of moral restoration can relationships be repaired, which alone can ensure political reconciliation.

Forgiveness and Accountability

As suggested earlier, the basis for interpersonal forgiveness is empathy—that is, the willingness to identify with the offender in spite of what he or she has done. It presumes that people can hate moral wrongdoing and still love the offender. When individuals and groups forgive, they ignore the natural inclinations to get even and pursue the restoration of human relationships in spite of past wrongdoing.[14] Since forgiveness seeks to create a new beginning out of the ashes of injustice, the practice of forgiveness frequently comes into seeming conflict with the requirements of procedural or substantive justice. Not surprisingly, critics of forgiveness frequently argue that forgiveness undermines political justice by neglecting the strict enforcement of legal rules or by mitigating the appropriate penalties for criminal behavior.

Since political forgiveness allows for the possibility of reconciliation between offenders and victims without necessarily fulfilling the requirements
of strict legal justice, human rights activists generally oppose political forgiveness, believing that such a practice is contrary to a victim's basic right to
the prosecution and punishment of offenders. In addition, critics of forgiveness argue that failure to prosecute and punish offenders not only will impede justice but will undermine the rule of law. They argue that the credibility of a criminal justice system is rooted in the certainty that unlawful
behavior will be identified, prosecuted, and punished. For them, failure to
punish serious wrongdoing not only undermines the authority of judicial institutions but weakens deterrence by fostering a culture of impunity. Thus,
when government authorities disregard, condone, or absolve criminal behavior (through legal amnesty or executive pardon), the rule of law is compromised and the consolidation of democratic procedures is jeopardized.

Is forgiveness consistent with constitutional government and the rule of
law, or is forgiveness contrary to political justice? Whether political forgiveness reinforces constitutional rule will depend, of course, on how political
justice is conceived. For example, if justice requires, as the retributivist perspective claims, that all crimes be fully prosecuted and punished, then the
possibility of political forgiveness will be limited, if not impossible. However,
if political justice is conceived from a healing or restorative perspective
rooted in empathy, then forgiveness in political life becomes a feasible option. In developed democratic regimes, legal retribution is the normal
method by which individual crimes are publicly confronted. But when societies are seeking to consolidate a new democratic order in the aftermath of
war and collective crimes, they must not only rely on political and legal resources but also turn to moral and spiritual processes, including forgiveness.

Although retribution may seem to conflict with collective forgiveness,
some forms of legalism may in fact be conducive to accountability and therefore to forgiveness. For example, when retribution is conceived as a moral
obligation (a Kantian view) or as a means of preventing future crimes (a consequentialist perspective), little room exists for forgiveness. Under such conceptions, the state has a duty to prosecute and to punish individuals and
groups that have committed offenses. But if retribution is conceived as a
method to restore moral equality between offenders and victims by deflating
the former and uplifting the latter, then a retributive approach can be a
means to reconciliation.[15] Hence, if victims follow St. Augustine's admonition
of hating sinful behavior but of loving people, retribution can be viewed
both as a legally appropriate element of authentic reconciliation and as a
complement to forgiveness.

Political forgiveness not only is consistent with full accountability but can
contribute greatly to the restoration of broken, alienated relationships. Since
forgiveness gives priority to the healing of victims and to the restoration of

relationships, it can greatly contribute to political reconciliation. Collective forgiveness, as I argue later in this chapter, is a demanding ethic for both the offender and victim groups. Indeed, forgiveness may be a more demanding ethic than retribution since both offenders and victims must directly confront and overcome the legacy of wrongdoing. For offenders, this means accepting the humiliation of admitting culpability, expressing repentance, and authenticating such contrition through financial reparations and the acceptance of some penalties or punishment. For victims, forgiveness entails giving up anger and vengeance toward offenders, accepting them as people entitled to dignity, reducing or eliminating penalties, and restoring relationships.

THE QUEST FOR RECONCILIATION

In common usage, the term "reconciliation" denotes the restoration of friendship or the reestablishment of communal solidarity. From a religious, especially biblical, perspective, reconciliation implies the renewal or restoration of broken relationships—between God and people and among humans themselves. Historically, political thinkers and public officials have been reluctant to view reconciliation as a legitimate goal of politics. Because of the religious connotations of the term, they have generally regarded reconciliation as a spiritual process for restoring interpersonal relationships. As a result, theologians have tended to view reconciliation chiefly as a spiritual concept relevant to an individual's relationship to God and secondarily as a process between persons, thereby underestimating its social and political dimensions.[16]

Some scholars have suggested that reconciliation is an inappropriate political concept because it has no clear, widely accepted definition.[17] The claim that reconciliation is an inappropriate political ideal because it is conceptually elusive has little merit, however. Many core concepts in politics, including justice, liberty, human rights, and authority, are elusive and contested, yet political discourse depends on them because they define fundamental elements of a good society. And such is the case with reconciliation, an ideal concept that identifies how alienation, enmity, and distrust can be transformed into social trust and communal solidarity.

The Nature of Reconciliation

What does political reconciliation mean? Fundamentally, reconciliation involves the rebuilding of understanding and harmonious relationships. To become reconciled is to overcome alienation, division, and enmity and to restore peaceful, cooperative relationships based on a shared commitment to communal solidarity. Trudy Govier and Wilhelm Verwoerd have suggested that political reconciliation be conceived as the building or rebuilding of trust. They define trust as an attitude of "confident expectation" where people anticipate that other individuals or groups will act in a decent, competent, and acceptable manner. When people place their trust in others, they of course become vulnerable to others, but the risk of vulnerability is deemed acceptable precisely because of the relative certainty that no harm will result from such trusting attitudes and behaviors.[18]

In *Trust: The Social Virtues and the Creation of Prosperity,* Francis Fukuyama argues convincingly that social trust is indispensable to the development of orderly, creative, and prosperous societies. He shows that countries that have a high level of social capital—that is, a high degree of commitment to shared values and voluntary cooperation through civic associations—enjoy greater economic growth than countries with limited social and economic solidarity.[19] Clearly, without trust societies are incapable of developing the networks of voluntary cooperation that are indispensable to participatory, economically productive societies. Defining reconciliation in terms of trust is clearly a helpful, concrete way of conceiving this concept, especially since it calls attention to truth telling, promise keeping, and social solidarity.

Since political reconciliation involves many different levels, it is useful to conceive of the reconciliation process involving two distinct dimensions—breadth and depth, scope and intensity. The level of breadth reflects the number of people involved in reconciliation; the depth of reconciliation reflects the degree to which trust and cooperation have been restored. Such depth may range from thin conceptions, such as peaceful coexistence, to a more demanding, thick ethic, where social and political solidarity are rooted in shared goals, and widespread cooperation.

If the two dimensions are integrated, as they are in figure 4.1, we can conceive of a variety of types (macro-micro) and levels (thick-thin) of reconciliation. Since individuals can communicate their values, attitudes, and loyalties with greater ease and directness, the process of reconciliation among individuals is likely to be simpler than for collectives. But this does not mean

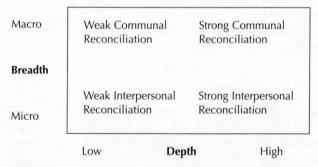

Figure 4.1. Reconciliation Based on Breadth and Depth

that groups and nations are unable to pursue modest levels of reconciliation. Indeed, as groups pursue actions and demonstrate attitudes that are conducive to the rebuilding of mutual trust and cooperation, alienation, enmity, and distrust among groups are likely to be replaced by cooperation, friendship, and trust, leading to a more peaceful and productive society.

As implied in figure 4.1, macro or political reconciliation can be conceived as involving many different levels of trust and consensus. To illuminate key differences between weak and strong communal reconciliation, I briefly describe the nature of three different ideal types or levels of political reconciliation: minimal reconciliation, maximal reconciliation, and democratic reciprocity.[20] The minimalist view, also defined as "nonlethal coexistence," is a thin, undemanding ethic that involves an end to fighting but not necessarily the resolution of the issues that led to war. Peace is achieved not through the transformation of attitudes and values or the restoration of amicable relationships among enemies but rather through the establishment of order based on a negotiated settlement or a cease-fire. The negotiated order makes communal coexistence possible through the practice of political toleration.[21] Rajeev Bhargava defends the minimalist version of reconciliation—or what he terms "a minimally decent society"—by arguing that the transition from a barbaric to a stable, decent society is a demanding, difficult journey that needs to be inspired by simple moral rules. A minimally decent society is not one that promotes a particular conception of the good life or a robust version of substantive or distributive justice; rather, it seeks a rudimentary social and political existence through the institutionalization of basic procedural norms that help to sustain and protect human life. According to Bhargava, transitional justice should not be guided by elusive goals and a vision of the common good but by "low-level ground realities" from where basic moral principles can emerge.[22]

At the opposite extreme is the maximalist view of political reconciliation—a demanding process that involves the ending of enmity and the restoration of friendship through the reformation of people's cultural values and political attitudes. According to Crocker, Archbishop Desmond Tutu's conception of political reconciliation represents this demanding ethic. He claims that Tutu's vision of a unified multiracial South Africa is grounded in the indigenous tradition of *ubuntu*, which gives primacy to social solidarity over individualism, and in the religious conversion model that permits restoration of community through confession and forgiveness. The *ubuntu* vision,[23] which is a synonym for restorative justice, is a demanding ethic because it seeks the restoration of broken relationships and the rehabilitation of both victims and offenders.

Pursuing a maximalist version of reconciliation is likely to involve two distinct strands or emphases. The first focuses on the development of shared aspirations, moral values, and social habits; the second stresses the restoration of relationships through forgiveness and the renewal of relationships based on the promise to avoid repeating injurious actions. Whereas the first strand seeks to build cohesion through shared ideological values and the imposition of the rule of law and democratic structures, the second strand is moral and spiritual, emphasizing grace and tolerance of past injustices. Since the ideological strand is normally imposed by a victorious power, its success depends on the skill and effectiveness in reforming values and institutionalizing new structures. This approach was vividly illustrated in the reconstruction policies imposed by the United States on Japan and Germany in the aftermath of World War II.[24] The second strand is obviously far rarer and much more difficult to pursue. According to Bhargava, the religious approach is an especially demanding strategy because it involves "a cancellation of enmity or estrangement via a morally grounded forgiveness"—a task that can be realized only through mutual, voluntary cooperative actions between perpetrators and beneficiaries.[25]

The third type of reconciliation is "democratic reciprocity," an intermediary form of peace that is achieved not by the pursuit of shared values but by the commitment to democratic virtues, including civility, tolerance, and respect for all people, regardless of their political beliefs and interests. Unlike social harmony, which seeks communal solidarity based on compassion, forgiveness, and the pursuit of friendship, this type of reconciliation represents a modest, undemanding approach to community order, seeking only a humane, peaceful environment where conflicts are resolved through democratic procedures and where opponents continue respecting each other's human rights.

Perhaps the most significant argument in favor of political reconciliation is the historical experience of modern domestic and international political life. Although conflict is inevitable in politics, deep, ongoing animosity is not inevitable. Peace is possible, hatred can be transformed into friendship, and distrust and enmity can evolve into harmonious, cooperative relationships. For example, the historic animosity between France and Germany, evident in both World Wars I and II, has been replaced by increasing cooperation based on shared economic interests and increasing understanding by their citizens. The creation of institutional structures of cooperation, such as the European Coal and Steel Community (ECSC) and the European Common Market, has greatly facilitated this process. Similarly, the deep animosity between Germany and the United States during World War II has also given way to a peaceful, harmonious bilateral relationship based on the former West Germany's (now Federal Republic of Germany) institutionalization of democratic norms and institutions. As noted in the introduction, President Reagan sought to acknowledge and celebrate the significant American-German reconciliation through various ceremonial visits, including a controversial visit to a German military cemetery in Bitburg.

The process of national reconciliation is also illustrated by the numerous peace accords that have ended civil wars in countries such as El Salvador,

Nicaragua, and Namibia. To be sure, the ending of domestic conflict does not imply reconciliation, but before antagonists can move toward cooperative, harmonious relationships, they must halt the fighting. The quest for political reconciliation is also evident in the successful pursuit of political accommodation among opposing groups in multilingual and multicultural nations, such as Belgium and Switzerland. More recently, the quest for reconciliation has been emphasized as a part of the transitional justice process of emerging democratic regimes. In the 1980s and 1990s, transitional regimes created truth commissions not simply to develop an official story of past regime offenses but also to promote national unity. The ostensible purpose for truth telling was the belief that the acknowledgment of truth would contribute to political healing and foster national reconciliation. Although truth may not necessarily lead to national unity, it is significant that leaders identified political reconciliation as an important objective in the healing of nations.

Democracy and Reconciliation

There can be little doubt that democratic politics is the most desirable method for addressing political conflicts. But what is a society to do if people are deeply divided, resorting to violence in order to pursue their competing and conflicting objectives? And how is a country to overcome profound political divisions in the aftermath of civil war, mass violence, and the systematic abuse of human rights? How should Rwanda confront the legacy of a three-month genocide that left more than eight hundred thousand people dead? How should Argentina address the disappearance of more than ten thousand people during the late 1970s when the military government carried out a counterinsurgency campaign involving covert abductions and killings? Is the strategy of "democratic reciprocity" appropriate to these and other cases of radical evil, or should the pursuit of transitional justice be conditioned by the historical and cultural context in which crimes were committed and in light of the domestic political resources available to pursue claims of justice?

Some democratic theorists argue that regimes should pursue only the minimalist or intermediary types of reconciliation. They claim that seeking to reform and transform the values and attitudes of people from enmity to friendship is an unrealistic expectation, especially in the aftermath of historic injustices and widespread regime wrongdoing. Rather than seeking to promote national unity, the emerging democratic regime should seek to institutionalize structures for managing conflict. Since conflict is a central feature of dynamic, creative political life, the pursuit of reconciliation and unity is likely to impede the creation and maintenance of a free, vibrant political society. In short, the pursuit of a comprehensive political reconciliation is an unrealistic, if not counterproductive goal.

Others argue that the quest for political reconciliation is harmful to political society in that it potentially threatens individual rights, especially human freedom. David Crocker, for example, suggests that the overemphasis of social harmony and communal solidarity can result in compromising legitimate rights of individuals, including the rights to withhold forgiveness, to pursue legal accountability, and to obtain reparations.[26] Timothy Garton Ash similarly has observed that the "reconciliation of all with all" is a deeply "illiberal" idea. This is so, he suggests, because a liberal society, as Isaiah Berlin and others have noted, is one that learns to live with unresolved conflicts among values and interests.[27]

Amy Gutmann and Dennis Thompson also argue that a procedural democratic framework is far more hospitable to human rights than the intentional pursuit of social harmony. According to them, the most desirable approach to transitional justice issues is through the practice of "deliberative democracy" in which citizens can freely confront ongoing conflicts and disagreements within society.[28] Excessive concern with social consensus and political agreement can threaten deliberative politics. As a result, Gutmann and Thompson argue that societies should be guided by the principle of "the economy of moral disagreement," in which citizens pursue consensus where it exists and maintain mutual respect where it does not.[29]

Given the social, psychological, and political divisions found in transitional societies, the criticisms of the maximalist version of political reconciliation seem unwarranted, especially when applied to deeply divided, wartorn societies seeking to overcome the bitter past. The challenge for South Africa, for example, where the Truth and Reconciliation Commission (TRC) was explicitly charged with promoting reconciliation and national unity, was not simply to identify the nature and scope of human rights abuses and to encourage the institutionalization of democratic structures and processes; rather, the aim was to overcome the legacy of distrust and enmity that had resulted from a long history of racial discrimination and especially from the comprehensive institutionalization of racial separation (apartheid). For the new democratic regime, the racial divisions of the past could only be replaced through a transformation in the country's moral-cultural system. Elizabeth Kiss has noted that such a task could not be achieved through legal means alone, for such transformation involves political, cultural, moral, psychological, and spiritual dimensions as well.[30]

It would be incorrect to suggest that South Africa's truth-telling process was guided solely by the maximalist version of political reconciliation. South African authorities were not interested in promoting social harmony rooted in a common ideology. Rather, they aimed to renew and transform society by consolidating democratic practices and structures and by establishing the preconditions for such a regime. To accomplish the former, the TRC assumed the society needed to confront the legacy of past injustices, undertake a moral and cultural reformation of society, and encourage individual and group accountability through repentance and forgiveness. In effect, the South African model aimed at the democratic version of reconciliation by encouraging individuals and groups to pursue maximal reconciliation through moral and behavioral reformation. In other words, the TRC was based on the belief that the intermediate level of reconciliation could not be realized without seeking to transform cultural and social values and to undertake a moral reconstruction of society that would reduce enmity and alienation among racial groups.

JUSTICE AND RECONCILIATION

Even if reconciliation is regarded as a legitimate goal of political communities, there is likely to be significant disagreement over the priority of such a goal relative to other political concerns. Should the nascent democracy pursue national unity and political reconciliation first and then seek to consolidate democratic institutions and the rule of law or should the emerging democratic order first pursue legal accountability and justice and then seek to foster national reconciliation and domestic stability? The strategy that is pursued will depend in great part on how the task of political healing is conceived.

Michael Feher distinguishes between two different approaches to national reconciliation and the restoration of political community. According to him, "purists" are those who demand full legal accountability as a precondition for political healing. They assume that criminal behavior needs to be exposed, stigmatized, and punished in order to consolidate the rule of law, without which democratic government is likely to fail. Purists, who are typically represented by human rights activists and nongovernmental organizations, thus tend to believe that before reconciliation can occur justice must be secured for victims. By contrast, "pragmatists," represented chiefly by political leaders and governmental agencies, tend to view national reconciliation as a precondition for the consolidation of democracy and the rule of law. For them, amnesty and forgiveness are morally legitimate because they provide a means for overcoming deep political cleavages and for promoting political reconciliation and national unity.[31]

Both purists and pragmatists believe that overcoming systemic injustices and deep political divisions and distrust require reconciliation. The difference between these two approaches is on how best to pursue political healing and national unity. Should a regime follow the "Nuremberg trials" model and seek to identify and punish the major offenders and then pursue communal reconciliation through the slow process of building democratic institutions? Or should a regime consolidate national unity by minimizing differences between political antagonists and focusing instead on the shared goal of pursuing, in the words of Abraham Lincoln, "a just and lasting peace among ourselves and with all nations"?[32] The major argument of this study is that the latter approach, rooted in the priority of healing and restoration, has significant advantages, especially in confronting egregious collective offenses in deeply divided societies.

As noted earlier, scholars' and decision makers' skepticism about political forgiveness and the pursuit of reconciliation derives in great part from the widespread belief that the primary moral task of the state is justice. As a result, the prevailing worldview on transitional justice is that emerging democratic regimes should first achieve justice and then pursue political reconciliation. Indeed, the "first justice, then peace" perspective—the prevailing approach in Western democratic societies—provides the foundation for most human rights initiatives by international nongovernmental organizations.[33]

But is the "first justice, then reconciliation" approach a viable alternative? Despite the importance of justice, the strategy is conceptually flawed and strategically unworkable. It is conceptually flawed because the approach assumes that the pursuit of justice and the quest for peace are in fundamental tension and that the former must be fulfilled before the latter can be undertaken. And it is an unrealistic and unworkable strategy because the conditions of strict justice—that is, the provisions that insist that punishment should be commensurate with the nature of the offenses—can never be fully fulfilled. In effect, by making reconciliation conditional on the prior fulfillment of justice, this approach relegates community healing and the promotion of national unity to a subsidiary role.

Historically, Christians have often given precedence to justice and liberation over order and reconciliation, with the result that the Christian religion has been used to justify the struggle against injustice and oppression.[34] But when Christianity is used to legitimize the struggle for liberation at the expense of the quest for social solidarity, religion becomes a tool of conflict and a means for legitimizing violence. To be sure, injustice and oppression need to be condemned while the pursuit of human liberation should be supported insofar as it affirms the dignity of people. But the biblical narrative is not one-dimensional, focusing only on liberation; rather, it also emphasizes peace, reconciliation, and the restoration of human relationships. Indeed, since the Scriptures condemn oppression while also calling for reconciliation, biblical ethics requires that the restoration of political life in the aftermath of regime wrongdoing should involve both justice and reconciliation. Indeed, Miroslav Volf argues that the quest for communal reconstruction is best undertaken when the quest for peace—or what he terms "embrace"—is viewed as more fundamental than the search for justice.[35]

In addition to its conceptual limitations, the "first justice, then peace" strategy is also unrealistic, consigning the political quest for national unity and domestic tranquillity to oblivion. Since justice is an ongoing quest, the demand that justice must be fulfilled before the public authorities can pursue reconciliation means that no political action will be undertaken on behalf of reconciliation. It is impossible to develop a fully just policy or program, since all conceptions of justice—all judgments, policies, and programs designed and carried out on behalf of justice—are themselves distant approximations of the ideal of justice. And since all accounts of justice are conditioned by the specific contexts and particular circumstances in which they are designed and implemented, policies and programs that are developed to advance justice will necessarily involve partiality and ambiguity, resulting in some injustice.[36]

The "first justice, then peace" approach is also problematic because reconciliation is not an automatic or even inevitable by-product of justice. It may be possible to rectify some past offenses and to restore some moral equality between victims and victimizers, but justice per se does not necessarily foster the preconditions for community. While the prosecution and punishment of some offenders may help to restore the credibility of criminal justice institutions and may contribute to legal accountability, the imposition of some justice will not necessarily create community. The establishment of a minimal order, defined as the absence of war, is not the same as the creation of a harmonious ordering of society—or what George Weigel has called *tranquillitas ordinis*.[37] The latter can only be created by developing harmonious relationships based on a shared commitment to the common good based on human dignity. More particularly, the restoration of communion will occur only when antagonists demonstrate empathy and compassion toward each other and carry out mutual actions that help to rebuild collective social and political ties. Thus, political healing is likely to occur only when antagonists confront and overcome past offenses and pursue actions based on shared moral ideals.

In the final analysis, the "first justice, then peace" approach is problematic because it may impair forgiveness and thereby impede reconciliation. To begin with, if justice is a precondition for forgiveness, its fulfillment will make forgiveness unnecessary. Forgiveness, it will be recalled, is a way of coming to terms with past wrongdoing: offenders acknowledge wrongdoing and express contrition, victims release offenders from some or all their debts, and both parties express empathy toward each other in spite of the alienation caused by the original offense. But if forgiveness is conditional on justice, forgiveness becomes superfluous, for justice rectifies the wrongdoing that forgiveness is intended to heal. In addition, if justice is a prerequisite to forgiveness, then the fulfillment of justice makes forgiveness a victim's moral duty rather than an unearned gift. But since forgiveness is a nonjudicial action that lifts the debts of offenders for moral reasons, it cannot be merited through a perpetrator's actions, nor can it be earned by the pursuit of justice. Forgiveness is a gift that lifts offenders' debts with the hope that such action will provide healing to victims and perpetrators and foster healing of broken relationships.

ALTERNATIVE THEORIES OF JUSTICE

The prevailing method used by governments to confront criminal offenses is legal retribution. This approach aims to protect individual rights through the rule of law and more particularly through punishment of wrongdoing. The retributive justice tradition, rooted in both deontological and utilitarian reasoning, demands that offenders be held accountable for their wrongdoing through prosecution and punishment. In recent years, criminal justice scholars have developed an alternative tradition known as restorative justice that emphasizes healing and restoration rather than punishment. Unlike retributive justice, which places a premium on individual rights and the prosecution and punishment of offenders, restorative justice emphasizes the restoration of communal bonds through social and political reconciliation. Its aim is not to right wrongs, but to restore a stable social and political order.

Retributive Justice

Retributive justice, or strict justice, calls for holding offenders accountable for their criminal deeds. When public officials refuse to hold criminals accountable for their crimes, they commit impunity, and thereby destroy the moral and social fabric necessary to sustain civil society. From an interpersonal perspective, retributivism assumes that evil must be identified and punished before human relationships can be renewed and restored. According to retributive justice theory, when perpetrators commit an offense against other people, they destroy the fundamental moral and legal equality among human beings. To repair ruptured relationships between victims and victimizers and restore their moral equality, offenders must be diminished through public condemnation, and victims must regain the former moral status. Retribution is the process by which this fundamental equality is restored. The retributive justice paradigm is thus based on the belief that a humane political community can be sustained only if wrongdoing is prosecuted and punished, for only if past offenses are held to account can a community confidently pursue and advance its future collective well-being.

Diane Orentlicher, an international human rights scholar, argues that states have a legal and moral duty to prosecute egregious human rights crimes. Because the international legal order is based in part on international human rights law, states must prosecute individuals who are responsible for serious human rights violations. She argues that when states fail to fulfill this obligation, the international community should take action against them.[38] The distinguished legal scholar Carlos Nino, by contrast, argues that there is no duty to prosecute since such state action will depend on the environmental constraints faced by the new regime. Indeed, Nino claims that criminal prosecution may risk provoking further violence and a return to undemocratic rule.

As a result, rather than viewing prosecution as a duty, he argues that "we should think of a duty to safeguard human rights and to prevent future violations by state officers or other parties."[39]

Retributivists offer several reasons for prosecuting and punishing serious human rights crimes. First, they claim that justice demands that perpetrators should pay for their offenses. Second, they argue that all criminal offenses, but especially those involving gross human rights abuses, should be brought under the subjection of the law. Only by prosecuting crimes can the rule of law be maintained and consolidated. Third, retributivists claim that trials reduce the possibility of revenge. Since trials establish an official accounting of past wrongdoing, it is thought that they inhibit individuals from taking the law into their own hands. Fourth, trials are desirable because they lead to an official account of the past. Moreover, since trials impose rules of evidence and cross-examination on the disclosure of facts, retributivists claim that trials provide a more authoritative account of the past wrongdoing than truth commissions, which are generally based on comprehensive investigations and testimony from victims. Finally, trials are an effective way to settle legal claims—in part because they are presumed to be based on the impartial application of the law and also because court verdicts establish finality to conflicts.

Although the retributive justice model provides a legitimate and effective way of addressing individual crimes in a robust constitutional environment, the model is not well equipped to address past collective violence and systemic injustice. Indeed, the model suffers from a number of limitations. First, legal retribution focuses on backward-looking accountability rather than on the forward-looking moral reconstruction of society. Its emphasis is on the restoration of the rule of law through the punishment of offenders. Since transitional regimes are frequently constitutionally weak and politically fragile, the emphasis on rectifying past wrongs diminishes the limited resources available to confront the pressing social, political, and economic needs of society. Indeed, one of the advantages ascribed to the restorative justice model is that it provides societies with an orientation that focuses on the moral rehabilitation of people and restoration of communal relationships.

A second limitation of legal retribution is that it is not an effective approach for confronting systemic injustices and collective offenses. For example, when a regime carries out genocide, such as the Hutus in Rwanda or the Serbs in Bosnia, or a people establish discriminatory policies, such as the apartheid laws of South Africa, how should an emerging democratic government pursue legal culpability? If responsibility for criminal wrongdoing is widespread, such as for the gross human rights abuses perpetrated by the military forces of Argentina in the 1970s and Guatemala in the 1980s, how should transitional regimes pursue legal retribution? Since trials are designed to assess individual culpability, they cannot be used to assess widespread societal and institutional culpability. Most important, trials tend to oversimplify truth by focusing solely on the guilt of a few people. Thus, while legal retribution is appropriate in dealing with individual criminal behavior, such an approach is ineffective in addressing the responsibility of collectives.

A third limitation of retribution is that trials are often unfair, focusing on the offenses of low-level agents rather than on senior leaders. This anomalous condition, evident in some of the trials of East German agents after the fall of Communism, often results because the absence of evidence may inhibit the prosecution of senior decision makers while an abundance of evidence may make possible the prosecution of low-level agents. Thus, senior officials who authorized policies are spared accountability while soldiers and agents who committed acts are prosecuted and punished.

A further shortcoming of legal retribution is that it can threaten and destabilize fragile regimes, especially when societies remain politically divided. When regimes attempt to prosecute people who remain influential in society, political stability can be threatened, and the regime itself can be imperiled. This shortcoming was demonstrated in Argentina when the continuing prosecutions of military and police officials led to numerous military disturbances that brought to a halt all trials and eventually resulted in the freeing of all officials previously sentenced.

Finally, some critics argue that legal retribution is a morally inappropriate strategy in confronting gross human rights abuses committed under a prior regime. While retribution no doubt helps to rebalance the moral scales between offenders and victims, the effort to right wrongs through retaliatory punishment can be problematic, especially when the offenses were widespread and committed long ago. Thus, when the democratic government of Czechoslovakia took power in 1990, the new regime wisely refrained from prosecuting and punishing Communist leaders and agents who may have been responsible for the widespread killings that took place in 1948–1949 when Communists consolidated their power.[40] Instead, the government pursued a limited effort to temporarily prohibit government service to those who had been directly or indirectly involved with the former Communist regime.[41]

Applying retributive justice to international human rights crimes—especially to the two dominant categories of offenses, war crimes and crimes against humanity—also presents significant challenges. Ascertaining when international human rights abuses occur and how best to prevent such collective offenses is a daunting challenge, particularly when these norms are applied to war-torn areas, such as Bosnia, Chechnya, Congo, Kosovo, and Liberia. For example, how should El Salvador's 1980s leftist insurgency be judged? Was the state justified in carrying out a vigorous antisubversion campaign against the revolutionary guerillas[42] that resulted in widespread human rights violations? By what legal and moral norms should the 1970s urban terror perpetrated by Argentina's Montonero guerrillas and the contemporary terrorism of Hamas radicals in Israel be judged? More specifically, was the widespread violence and repression used in toppling the Allende government and in subsequently consolidating power legally and morally justified? Was the violence and terror used by the African National Congress (ANC), the guerrilla movement seeking to topple the apartheid regime, morally warranted? While it is beyond the scope of this study to address these questions, these legal and moral issues are raised to illuminate the complexity and ambiguity in domestic political violence involving state and antigovernment forces.

Domestic political violence can be especially brutal, posing serious challenges to the international legal norms that have been devised to regulate and constrain warfare. This is so because domestic civil strife frequently involves covert operations that rely on terror and indiscriminate killing. As a result, when revolutionary violence threatened regimes with urban insurgency and terrorism in the 1960s and 1970s, some Latin American governments responded with counterinsurgency strategies that did not conform to the codified laws of war. To be sure, international war and urban insurgency are radically different. Wartime violence is not identical with government force designed to eliminate a threat to its power or to consolidate political power. Nor is such internal state violence legally and morally equivalent to domestic law enforcement. Such police action, which is designed to regulate a stable, orderly society, involves limited, carefully targeted force and is governed by a state's criminal justice system. By contrast, a state's domestic antiinsurgency campaign, which is in an intermediary zone between international war and domestic law enforcement, must be assessed by the nature of the threat that the state is seeking to contain. Clearly, domestic law enforcement, domestic counterinsurgency, and international wars present radically different contexts and legal and moral justifications for the use of force. In short, regime violence should not be conflated with either international wars or domestic law enforcement.

If prosecution of past wrongs is deemed essential to the consolidation of the emerging democratic regime, perhaps the best that can be achieved is the trial of senior government officials responsible for the decisions that resulted in crimes. But such a strategy poses enormous obstacles since the evidence for criminal culpability of government officials and senior military leaders is likely to be difficult to obtain. Not surprisingly, Germany found it easier to prosecute soldiers who killed citizens trying to flee East Berlin than the leaders who established the evil regime of totalitarian communism. And while Argentina was successful in prosecuting the junta leaders responsible for widespread killing and disappearances, the top leaders that were found guilty were subsequently pardoned because of the political instability caused by the trials. In pardoning the five senior leaders, Carlos Menem said that his action was designed to "create conditions that permit the definitive reconciliation among Argentineans."[43]

Restorative Justice

   Given the inherent limits of retribution in transitional societies, a growing
number of scholars and public officials have emphasized an alternative approach known as restorative justice. Unlike legal retribution, which is concerned with punishment and the maintenance of a credible justice system,
the aim of restorative justice is to repair broken relationships and to heal the
wounds of victims and offenders alike. Whereas retribution focuses chiefly
on objective wrongdoing, restorative justice emphasizes the transformation
of subjective factors that impair community, such as anger, resentment, and
desire for vengeance. According to Kiss, restorative justice is an approach
based on four principles: 1) restoration of human dignity to those whose
human rights have been violated; 2) legal accountability for offenders, ensuring that they are aware of the harm that that they have committed; 3) establishing preconditions for the protection of human rights; and 4) promoting reconciliation.[44] Since the first three norms are common to both
retributive and restorative justice, the distinctive feature of the latter is reconciliation—a condition that is realized when the anger and enmity among
individuals and groups is transformed, first, into tolerance and acceptance
and then gradually into harmonious, cooperative relationships. The telos of
restorative justice is thus reconciliation.

   Some have suggested that restorative justice is simply a strategy of easy reconciliation—seeking to create a new beginning without coming to terms with
the past. But restorative justice does not disregard past wrongdoing. Rather, it
seeks to describe comprehensively and fully the truth about past offenses,
recognizing that antagonists may have widely divergent perspectives about
the nature, causes, and culpability for past offenses. To the extent that the parties can agree on the awful truth about past crimes and injustices, the restorative justice perspective encourages individuals, groups, and institutions to admit culpability, to express repentance, and to authenticate remorse through
acts of reparation and restitution. At the same time restorative justice de-
emphasizes the division of society into perpetrators and victims, preferring instead to view most or all of society as victims or survivors.

   Restorative justice is the approach taken by President Abraham Lincoln as
he pursued the political healing of the United States from the injustices of
slavery and the bitter, destructive Civil War. Rather than seeking legal retribution against political and military leaders of the Confederacy, Lincoln's
strategy called for reconciliation among all peoples.[45] Mahmood Mamdani
similarly assumes that in the aftermath of deadly political violence, such as
Rwanda's 1994 genocide, a restorative approach offers the most promising
hope for healing and peacekeeping. He suggests that communal healing—
what he terms "survivor's justice"—must be based on changes in the underlying political institutions that have permitted ongoing political violence.

Thus, rather than focusing on the culpability of individual perpetrators, Mamdani suggests that the fundamental blame for the genocide should be placed on the underlying rules and practices of the political regime.[46] Accordingly, he suggests that victims, but not offenders, should be identified and acknowledged, since identifying perpetrators would lead to excessive focus on their culpability and thereby detract from the needed cultural and political reforms necessary for promoting reconciliation.

It is important to stress that restorative justice is not an attempt to bypass the rule of law. Although the restorative approach does not demand adherence to strict legalism, it nevertheless demands truth telling coupled with contrition as the way to heal individual and collective injuries. Since offenses have resulted in a moral inequality between perpetrators and victims, restorative justice seeks to restore the moral equality of citizens not through the law but through the moral reformation of people. This is achieved when offenders acknowledge their responsibility and victims refrain from vengeance and acknowledge empathy toward their former enemies. Although morally demanding, such behaviors have the effect of liberating victims from being captive to anger and resentment. In effect, such attitudinal and behavioral changes result in moral autonomy for both offenders and victims.

If the preconditions of restorative justice are fulfilled, individuals and communities may grant individual and collective forgiveness. Such forgiveness, which is likely to occur only after victims perceive offenders' contrition as authentic, would be expressed by the recognition of the offenders' humanity and by the modification of legitimate claims of restitution and retribution. Although individual forgiveness is essential in the moral rehabilitation of victims as well as the restoration of communal bonds, such forgiveness will not necessarily abrogate legal claims for punishment and reparations. Indeed, offenders should be prepared, as an expression of the authenticity of their remorse, to accept a state's legal punishment. In effect, political forgiveness may modify and reduce, but not abrogate, the claims of legal retribution. Moreover, forgiveness increases the possibility of reconciliation. But whether the renewal and restoration of relationships results in reconciliation is up to the individuals and collectivities. Restorative justice creates the environmental context in which communal bonds can be restored, but whether such restoration occurs will depend on the voluntary actions of individuals and political groups.

In the aftermath of significant collective atrocities, the only effective way of confronting systemic human rights abuses and preventing their repetition is through a comprehensive strategy of moral reconstruction and political renewal. Only through a multidimensional strategy that seeks the restoration of legal, social, cultural, political, and spiritual life are peace and justice likely to be realized. Legal retribution can of course contribute to regime accountability for egregious state crimes and injustices, but legalism alone cannot achieve the moral reconstruction that is necessary to restore a broken and divided society.

Ernesto Sábato, the distinguished head of Argentina's truth commission, observed in his prologue to the commission's report *Nunca Más* ("Never Again") that the commissioners were not in search of "vindictiveness or vengeance" but "truth and justice." In his view, courts should pursue their "transcendent mission" based on a strategy of truth and justice because national reconciliation is possible only if the guilty repent and justice is based on truth.[47]

One of the most important efforts to apply the restorative justice paradigm to collective crimes is the South African TRC, a body established by the South African Parliament to investigate gross human rights violations of the apartheid era. The government's establishment of the TRC was based partly on pragmatic political realities and a principled belief that the public acknowledgment of past crimes and injustices would contribute more to the consolidation of democracy than trials. As viewed by leaders, traditional legal and political strategies rooted in retributive justice were unlikely to contribute to unity and national reconciliation. What was needed was a demanding, multidimensional strategy—one rooted in restorative justice—that emphasized legal accountability yet called for political reconciliation based on the restoration of society's moral-cultural system.

In his book on the TRC, Tutu, the Commission's chairman, claims that it would have been unwise, indeed impossible, to impose retribution, or what he terms "the Nuremberg trial paradigm,"[48] on South Africa. Due to South Africa's limited political and economic resources, it was imperative that it use them with care in the consolidation of new democratic structures by balancing different claims, including "justice, accountability, stability, peace, and reconciliation."[49] In Tutu's view, applying retributive justice would have placed an undue burden on the nation's courts and would have given little emphasis to the restoration of victims and the promotion of political reconciliation. Tutu instead advocated the strategy of restorative justice, believing that such an approach would best pursue political healing and justice. For him, restorative justice was the preferred strategy because it promoted communal solidarity and social harmony by seeking to restore broken relationships, to heal victims, and to rehabilitate perpetrators. Most important for Tutu, restorative justice was consistent with the African social tradition of *ubuntu* that placed a premium on harmony, friendliness, and community.[50]

In sum, the healing of political communities in the aftermath of egregious human rights violations is a difficult, challenging political task. According to the conventional wisdom, the most effective way of consolidating democracy and restoring the rule of law is through retributive justice. Although the effort to identify, prosecute, and punish culpable individuals for illegal acts is entirely appropriate in developed political systems, the application of strict legalism is problematic when confronting systemic political violence, especially in states with frail political and legal institutions. In such circumstances—where political violence is widespread, society is deeply fragmented, and distrust and enmity are pervasive—the principal challenge may be not to capture and punish offenders but to foster rudimentary cooperation and political order rooted in a renewal of civic values. If such is the case, relying on the restorative justice paradigm may be desirable since it conceives of justice not only in terms of individual rights but also in terms of peaceful, harmonious communal ties. Moreover, since the restorative model calls for individual healing based on truth telling, repentance, and forgiveness, the quest for justice is not inimical to individual and collective forgiveness but complementary to it.

5

Retributive Justice and the Limits of Forgiveness in Argentina

We don't forget. We don't forgive. We don't seek reconciliation.

—The motto of HIJOS, an Argentine human rights organization[1]

In a war it is incorrect to speak of the violation of rights. This terminology is applicable only to times of peace. What nation during war—at any time in human history—can say that it respected human rights totally and absolutely?

—General Robert Viola, former president of Argentina[2]

Disappearances, then, are a "continuing offense" and not only or strictly in legal terms. For as long as the uncertainty remains, they are an open wound in the fabric of society that is not healed by amnesty laws or clemency decrees and much less by lofty calls to "reconciliation" lamely uttered from time to time by political and religious leaders. Without public acknowledgment, reconciliation is an empty gesture, or worse, another name for impunity.

—Juan Méndez, General Counsel, Human Rights Watch[3]

On the night of July 14, 1976—some four months after Argentina's military forces had carried out a coup d'etat against the government of Isabel Perón—state security personnel kidnapped Hugo and Blanca Tarnopolsky and two of their three children. Hugo was part owner of a chemical plant, while Blanca served as an educational psychologist. Although both identified with leftist intellectual causes, neither was formally a part of any political movement or group. Their eldest son, who was also abducted, was fulfilling his military service at the Navy's School of Mechanics (Escuela Superior de Mecánica de la Armada, ESMA) in Buenos Aires. Their daughter, a high school student, was taken from her grandmother's house, where she was spending the night. Only the middle son avoided capture because he was away from home with several of his friends. Since the night of their kidnapping, the Tarnopolskys have never been seen again.[4] They, like more than ten thousand other people who disappeared during the country's "dirty war" from 1976 to 1979, are presumed to have been killed by state security agents as part of the government's antisubversion campaign. Since military and police authorities have refused to disclose information about the fate of those kidnapped, family members of the "disappeared" have never received official notification about the fate of their loved ones.

How should a society reckon with widespread regime violence, such as that perpetrated by the Argentine military and police authorities in the late 1970s? Should a government first prosecute and punish the people responsible for human rights crimes and then seek to consolidate democratic institutions and promote national unity? Or should a transitional regime concentrate its scarce political resources on the promotion of national unity and the consolidation of the rule of law, de-emphasizing legal accountability? How should a government seek to heal the wounds of past regime crimes and injustices? Since the pursuit of justice and reconciliation are frequently in conflict, how should a country honor the demands for legal accountability while simultaneously promoting unity and national healing?

In this chapter, I describe and assess Argentina's effort to reckon with the widespread human rights abuses committed during the 1970s dirty war. In the first part, I examine Argentina's political, economic, and social decline in the 1960s that culminated in the early 1970s with the outbreak of widespread political violence. I then sketch how the government attempted to contain and defeat rampant terrorism through a covert antisubversion campaign. In the second part, I describe how the democratic government of Raúl Alfonsín sought to reckon with the abuses and crimes of the past, focusing on truth and legal accountability. In the third section, I offer a preliminary assessment of the government's "truth plus trials" strategy. Finally, in the fourth section, I explore some of the factors that have impeded the renewal of civil society and the promotion of political forgiveness and national reconciliation.

Perhaps the only alternative for reckoning with gross human rights violations, such as those committed by Argentine government agents, is to prosecute offenders and allow the balm of time to heal individual and collective political and social wounds. But since this study assumes that political healing is likely to occur only when sufficient resources are devoted to this end, I argue that the Argentine approach of "truth and trials" favored retribution over restoration, justice over reconciliation. By giving precedence to legal accountability and by neglecting the moral rehabilitation of the nation's political culture and the promotion of national reconciliation, the government failed to devote sufficient resources to the reformation of the country's moral-cultural system and the promotion of national unity. In effect, the Argentine strategy overemphasized backward-looking justice and thereby neglected to give sufficient emphasis to forward-looking reforms needed to promote healing and reconciliation.

THE DECLINE OF CIVIL SOCIETY

In 1930 Argentina was considered one of the most developed countries in the world, with a standard of living comparable to European nations. From the early 1930s through the late 1980s, however, Argentina's economy vacillated between periods of growth and decline. Although multiple factors contributed to Argentina's postwar economic stagnation and political instability, the radical restructuring of Argentine society by Juan Domingo Perón is commonly regarded as a major cause of the country's political malaise and economic woes. Perón, a populist military dictator from 1945 to 1955, gained enormous political power by organizing and mobilizing urban workers, and then used this power to create social and economic policies on labor's behalf. During his ten-year rule he concentrated power in the state, expanded governmental control over the economy, and redistributed resources to the labor class.

While Perón's nationalization of foreign industries and redistribution of income resulted in strong political support from the working class, the restructuring of Argentina's social and economic institutions and policies had disastrous economic consequences that resulted in increased political polarization. Perón's demise came in 1955 when he challenged the power of the Catholic Church, a cherished pillar of traditional Argentine society, by legalizing divorce and placing parochial schools under state control. These developments not only angered the church but also business groups and the armed forces. By 1955 the military had grown weary of Perón's politics and had given him an ultimatum: resign voluntarily or be removed by force. Rather than marshalling support from his followers, he resigned and fled the country. Soon thereafter, the military outlawed the Peronist Party and halted many of the pro-labor social and economic programs initiated by Perón.

Despite the ban on the Peronist political party, the labor unions continued to exert significant influence over the country. As a result, the country remained deeply polarized politically—a condition that impeded not only the governing of the nation but the restoration of confidence in the economy as well. Because of continued economic stagnation and rising civil strife, the military authorities decided to restore the legality of the Peronist Party in 1973.

The Rise of Militancy

In the late 1960s antigovernment political groups began to carry out protests and periodic armed raids to dramatize opposition to public policies and the increasing authoritarian measures of the military government. In mid-1969 university students and union workers carried out massive demonstrations and riots, with the most severe disturbances occurring in the northwestern city of Córdoba. Rather than seeking to appease rebels, the government instituted even harsher political and economic measures, such as the curtailment of social spending, the freezing of wages, and the forceful breakup of strikes. Such actions only exacerbated domestic political tensions.

By the early 1970s the antigovernment movement involved two major armed groups: the Montoneros,[5] a leftist spin-off of the Peronista youth faction, and the Marxist People's Revolutionary Army (ERP), a small, militant organization deeply committed to revolutionary change.[6] Whereas the Montoneros were inspired by the ideals of corporatism, nationalism, and workers' rights that Perón had emphasized during his dictatorship in the late 1940s and early 1950s, the ERP was based on the anticapitalist, Communist rhetoric rooted in Maoist and Trotskyite political ideas. Moreover, although the Montoneros were willing to pursue reforms within the structure of the Peronist Party, the ERP was committed to the revolutionary destruction of the existing regime.

The strategy of the Montonero and ERP revolutionaries was to use urban terror to undermine the government. Unlike most modern terrorism, which relies on random violence on civilians to induce fear in society, the Montoneros and allied revolutionary groups targeted political, military, and business leaders and their respective institutions. Their acts of terror included kidnappings and killings of state agents and business leaders, bombings, and other acts of sabotage against banks and major industries. One of the first dramatic acts of terror involved the kidnapping and murder of former president General Pedro Aramburu.[7] To finance their campaign of terror, the Montoneros attacked banks and demanded large ransoms for the kidnapping of industrial leaders. In 1974, for example, revolutionaries kidnapped the director of a major Argentine corporation and succeeded in extorting a ransom of $60 million, as well as in securing a promise to provide large sums of food and clothing for slum dwellers.

By 1972 urban guerrillas were carrying out an average of two acts of armed political violence per day. In response to this rising terror and the nation's rising economic stagnation, the government decided to legalize the Peronist Party (formally known as the Justicialist Party) and to allow it to compete in the March 1973 presidential elections. The military authorities carried out these actions because they assumed that the Peronists were not strong enough to win politically but that their reintegration into the country's political life would help to restore public order. After the Peronist Party was legalized, the Montoneros temporarily gave up their revolutionary campaign and devoted their energies to electoral politics.

Since Perón's return from Spain was predicated on the condition that he not run for president, the Peronists selected Héctor Cámpora as their presidential candidate, with the tacit understanding that Perón himself was the real power behind Cámpora's candidacy.[8] Not surprisingly, the Peronists won the election, and Cámpora, after holding office for only a few months, resigned, thereby paving the way for another election, which Perón and his wife Isabel won as president and vice president, respectively. Although some political groups—especially the business-industrial class and the military—had been apprehensive about Perón's return to power, the rampant violence throughout society had led numerous middle-class groups to support the charismatic leader. Their hope was that the former dictator might restore public order, foster economic growth, and promote confidence in public institutions.

The Restoration of Perón

Although the Peronista electoral victory had been possible because different factions had worked together, the coalition of union workers and students masked deep political cleavages within the movement—divisions that became more evident and pronounced after Cámpora had assumed the presidency. For example, when a large number of terrorists and subversives were released from prison, as had been promised during the election campaign, conservative union leaders felt betrayed. When Perón permanently returned from Spanish exile in June 1973, the welcoming ceremony at Buenos Aires' airport turned into a gun battle between Peronist right-wing union workers and radical left-wing student groups who were competing for control of this important political event.[9]

Thus, when Perón took office in September 1973, he faced growing political divisions among his followers, especially between right-wing union workers and left-wing students and middle-class workers. During his earlier dictatorship Perón's ideology had been strongly identified with the fascist norms of corporatism, anti-imperialism, and nationalism. But in the late 1960s, as the economic plight of workers had declined, Perón had begun to express support for leftist student and labor groups that advocated a radical restructuring of society. Consequently, once Peronists regained power, deep political cleavages began to emerge between conservative workers and radical students groups (collectively known as the Revolutionary Tendency of the Peronist Party).[10] The former identified with authoritarian, conservative politics and longed for a return to labor-oriented programs of the former Perón government, while the latter were committed to socialism and the revolutionary restructuring of society. For the former, the existing state was legitimate and violence against the country was unacceptable; for the latter, by contrast, the existing state was illegitimate and had to be radically transformed, if not destroyed.

Although the bombings, kidnappings, and killings had a deep social and economic impact on society, the most profound effect of the terror campaign against the state was psychological. To seek to alleviate this fear and insecurity, Perón himself harshly condemned revolutionaries on his return to the country and sought to reduce the Montoneros' political influence within the government and major institutions in society, especially universities.[11] Once he had assumed the presidency, he made it clear that he would pursue the traditional aspirations of labor unions, not the radical demands of students. As a result, he immediately began to purge the Montoneros from positions of influence within the labor movement and from government positions and to endorse state actions against rebel groups.

In June 1974, about nine months after Perón assumed office, he died, propelling his ill-equipped wife Isabel into the presidency. Soon thereafter the Montoneros announced a resumption of their war against the state, declaring that the government was "neither popular nor Peronist." In response to rising leftist terrorism, Isabel's government instituted more stringent anti-insurgency measures. At the same time, right-wing political groups, especially the so-called Argentine Anticommunist Alliance (Triple A), began to establish paramilitary death squads.[12] Some of these paramilitary groups were allegedly organized and directed by José Lopéz Rega, the government's social welfare minister and one of the most influential presidential advisors. Because Isabel was regarded as a weak and politically ineffective leader, the country's political and economic conditions deteriorated further. Domestic political violence increased to its highest levels. For example, whereas 200 political deaths had been reported in 1974, the number of deaths in 1975 had increased to more than 860.[13] Moreover, whereas guerrillas were carrying out an average of about two terrorist acts per day in 1972, by 1976 the level of violence had increased to nearly eight violent acts per day.[14] Economic conditions also deteriorated significantly under Isabel's tutelage, with inflation rising to nearly 30 percent per month.

Given the growing economic stagnation and the rampant political violence, professional and business groups began to call for a new government—one that could restore public order and foster economic growth. Rather than waiting until the elections scheduled for 1977, the military carried out a coup d'etat in March 1976, an unconstitutional act that was nevertheless supported by numerous sectors of society, including business and professional groups, the middle class, elements of the media, and even the Catholic Church. As one observer has noted, "the coup was not simply a case of the military imposing its will on a reluctant civil society but the result of a civic-military alliance, which found support in the international community."[15]

The Dirty War

After the military took control of the government, it immediately embarked on a campaign to restore domestic order by eliminating the terrorist, revolutionary threat—which observers estimated at from one thousand to fifteen thousand revolutionaries.[16] This goal had the backing not only of business, professional, and religious elites but also of significant segments of the middle class that had grown weary of violence. The government devised an anti-subversion campaign—dubbed the "Process for National Reorganization"—ostensibly aimed at restoring domestic order and protecting "Western, Christian civilization" from Marxist, secular revolution. What most citizens did not realize, however, was that this anti-terrorist campaign would itself resort to terror tactics to defeat the threat of terrorism.

Instead of using limited, discriminating force to deter revolutionary aggression and to protect citizens' rights, the state embarked on an antisubversion campaign that involved torture, kidnapping, and secret killings. Since such actions have been historically considered inconsistent with wartime legal conventions and with international morality, the pursuit of domestic order—a legitimate moral objective—was compromised by the adoption of methods that were themselves immoral. Thus, instead of restoring order through legitimate means, state security and military forces resorted to an unconventional war that involved the abduction, torture, and killing of more than ten thousand people. The war even involved the forced, secret adoption of infants born to detained mothers.

In 1983 the military decided to return power to civilian authorities, in great part because of the regime's diminished moral authority and political credibility.[17] Prior to transferring authority to the new civilian regime, military rulers took three actions to limit legal accountability for its human rights violations during the dirty war. First, the government issued an official report on the antisubversion campaign. The report admitted that human rights violations had occurred but claimed that such actions had been the unavoidable by-product of revolutionary insurgency. The military authorities also declared that persons who had "disappeared" and who were not in exile or in hiding should be considered dead. Second, the military government enacted the "Law of National Pacification," which granted immunity from prosecution to all alleged terrorists and all state personnel for crimes committed from May 25, 1973, to May 25, 1982. Third, the government issued a decree calling for the destruction of all public documents relating to the state's antisubversion campaign. These actions are significant because they served to undermine subsequent efforts to uncover the truth about the dirty war.

CONFRONTING THE DIRTY WAR

In the 1983 presidential elections, Radical Party candidate Raúl Alfonsín repeatedly stressed human rights and a full legal accounting of past regime crimes. Throughout the campaign he frequently promised that if elected, he would prosecute military and police officials responsible for the crimes of the dirty war, denouncing his Peronist Party opponent for the labor movement's accommodation to the military.[18] Alfonsín won the election—in great part because of his call for truth and trials.

Once in power, the new government, confident that the military no longer posed a major threat to civilian authority, adopted a selective retributive strategy to reckon with past regime crimes. It was a selective approach in that it focused only on the most serious criminal offenses. In particular, the government decided to prosecute only senior leaders responsible for policies involving illegal acts and subordinate officers who had "exceeded" their orders.[19] The aim of this limited retributive strategy was to restore the rule of law, to further weaken the institutional power of the armed forces, to prevent the reoccurrence of state crimes, and to pursue justice for those who had lost loved ones in the covert war.

Prior to embarking on the retributive strategy, Alfonsín made a number of important institutional changes in order to further weaken the political power of the military and give the new government increased constitutional authority. One of the first acts of the new government was the purging of the military's top leadership, forcing fifty-nine generals and admirals to retire.[20] Political strategists hoped that by replacing top military leaders the new government would restore civilian authority over the armed forces and transform the dominant political and moral values within the military services. In addition, Alfonsín undertook actions to consolidate civilian authority, foster the rule of law, and promote human rights. Some of the forward-looking initiatives included repeal of all antisubversion laws enacted by the military, abolition of military jurisdiction over civilians, ratification of human rights treaties, and reform of military code in order to limit the armed forces' jurisdiction over common crimes committed by soldiers. The government also undertook a number of backward-looking initiatives. These included the nullification of the military's self-amnesty law, changing the Military Code so that federal appeals courts could review the judgments of military courts, and issuing decrees in order to initiate legal prosecution of guerrilla leaders and senior military leaders who were allegedly responsible for human rights crimes.[21]

The government's strategy of selective retribution was based on two values—truth telling and legal accountability. In the following, I examine how the government pursued each of these norms.

Truth

If a society is to effectively confront past regime crimes and injustices, it will need to develop a shared account of what happened and why. As noted earlier, the quest for truth will involve two types of knowledge—objective or factual truth and interpretive or moral truth. The first type is based on objective data that can be verified empirically. In the Argentine context, the quest for such narrative truth involved the gathering of historical facts, such as the number and nature of terrorist attacks, the frequency and intensity of bombings, the names of people killed or kidnapped, and the methods for torturing detainees. Ordinarily, governmental truth commissions are well equipped to discover and disclose factual truth provided they are given adequate resources and sufficient time in which to carry out a dispassionate and thorough investigation. Gathering data that is subject to empirical verification is both possible and necessary. Moral or interpretive truth, by contrast, involves the interpretation of facts, and is much more elusive. This is so because human memory is conditioned by a person's identity. As Michael Ignatieff has observed, "what you believe to be true depends, in some measure, on who you believe yourself to be."[22] As a result, developing an interpretive account of the causes, consequences, and responsibilities for Argentina's dirty war presented a much more daunting challenge, especially since antagonists have continued to view and justify their actions through the prism of their particular worldviews.

Although objective truth has an important role in moral and institutional reconstruction, the promotion of peace and reconciliation is advanced most effectively through the generation of moral truth. As Ignatieff has noted, the truth that matters the most to people is not narrative or factual truth but interpretive truth, which is the truth that is most difficult to generate.[23] Since opposing narratives of the past are rooted in conflicting worldviews, an official commission is unlikely to reconcile radically divergent perspectives. Commissions can of course increase the prospects for interpretive consensus. They can do this through the discovery and public disclosure of factual knowledge, which can, in turn, encourage antagonists to reassess their ideological convictions and political ideals. In effect, the disclosure of factual data can foster moral truth by decreasing the misperceptions about political conflict and violence and thereby creating sufficient public space for antagonists to reassess their own ideals and ideological presuppositions.

Officials of the Alfonsín administration believed that truth could best be pursued through a commission that investigated regime offenses and uncovered state crimes. Since the discovery and disclosure of truth was assumed to be an absolute value, President Alfonsín began his administration by creating a truth commission. The fundamental aim of the thirteen-member National Commission on Disappeared People (CONADEP) was to identify the fate of missing persons and to provide an official accounting of the nature and role of the state's antisubversion campaign.

After collecting thousands of statements and testimonies about missing persons, as well as investigating the role of military and police repression, the CONADEP presented its findings to Alfonsín in September 1984, publishing a summary of its report two months later under the title *Nunca Más* ("Never Again"). The report, which Ronald Dworkin called "a report from hell,"[24] describes the nature and scope of the government's covert anti-insurgency strategy, focusing on the military institutions that participated in the abduction, torture, and murder of citizens. Some of the report's key findings were 1) more than 4,000 people were killed and an estimated 8,960 people who had been kidnapped or arrested were still missing; 2) kidnappings and torture were a major part of the state's "architecture of repression;"[25] and 3) the state imposed repression not only on revolutionaries but also on those who were never involved in political action.[26]

Although the report uncovered and disclosed much factual information about victims, the study's most important contribution was to document the nature and scope of the state's criminality in carrying out its antisubversion campaign. As Ernesto Sábato, the noted Argentine author and chairman of the CONADEP, observed in the report's prologue, the military dictatorship established a campaign of repression that "brought about the greatest and most savage tragedy in this history of Argentina."[27]

The publication of *Nunca Más* had an electrifying impact on Argentine society. For the first time, citizens had credible evidence about the nature and scope of state crimes perpetrated during the dirty war. Although many Argentineans had surmised that military and police officials had embarked on a covert campaign to exterminate political opponents, the publication of the CONADEP report provided empirical confirmation of what many had assumed—namely, that the government was responsible for massive and systematic human rights abuses. Since the task of the commission was simply to investigate and disclose factual truth about the disappearances during the dirty war, it made no judgments about individual culpability. Nevertheless, by discovering and disclosing the names of persons who had been abducted and killed and by identifying those organizations and centers that had been involved in torture and other abuses, the report implicitly confirmed the regime's collective culpability for widespread human rights violations.

Legal Accountability

The second major norm guiding the Alfonsín administration's transitional justice strategy was legal accountability. Senior government officials believed that if the rule of law were to be restored, leaders and police and military officials would need to be held responsible for the decisions and actions that had resulted in widespread abuse of human rights. In addition, they also believed that legal accountability was indispensable to the consolidation of democracy and the renewal of Argentine civic culture.

Urban terrorism and the resulting dirty war had not only exacerbated political cleavages but had also greatly weakened legitimate public authority and undermined the moral values and social trust on which political authority ultimately rests. As a result, the state's participation in a covert, unconventional war had weakened the moral fabric of Argentine society, undermining its civic institutions and political morality, especially its social capital (trust, social solidarity, and voluntary cooperation). If confidence in constitutional structures were to be restored, according to Argentine human rights leaders, it would be essential to hold the principal decision makers legally accountable.

According to Carlos Nino, one of Alfonsín's key legal advisors, the goal of prosecuting top leaders responsible for human rights abuses was deterrence, not punishment—that is, to prevent the repetition of gross human rights violations. Whereas the pursuit of comprehensive retributive justice would have involved prosecuting an untold number of state agents directly responsible for human rights crimes, the government strategy sought to restrict trials to those senior leaders most responsible for the systematic violations of human rights.[28] In early 1984, Alfonsín ordered the trial of nine members of the three former military juntas. After the Armed Forces Supreme Council, the senior military court, found "nothing objectionable" about the junta members' actions, the case was transferred to a civilian appeals court, which began a trial in April 1985.[29] Since state security officials were potential accomplices in the antisubversion crimes, the government's case against former leaders was based largely on the testimony of victims. Using individual survivors' accounts of abductions, killings, illegal detentions, torture, and even robbery by state security officials and agents, government prosecutors sought to demonstrate patterns of criminal activity instigated by government leaders.[30] The survivors' riveting accounts of torture and killing by police and military officials were widely reported by the media, even by those newspapers that had been supportive of the dictatorship, and had a profound psychological impact on Argentine society.

On December 9, 1985, the federal court handed down its verdict: five of the defendants, including the two top military officers, General Jorge Videla and Admiral Emilio Massera, were convicted, while the four military leaders that had served in juntas after 1980 were acquitted. Videla and Massera were given life sentences for their role in killings, kidnappings, other illegal deprivations of liberty, and robberies as part of the government's antisubversion campaign.[31] The three other junta members, General Robert Viola, Admiral Armando Lambruschini, and Air Force Chief Orlando Agosti, were sentenced to seventeen, eight, and four-and-a-half years, respectively. A year later the country's Supreme Court reaffirmed the five convictions and four acquittals, but reduced the sentences of Viola and Agosti.

The Unraveling of the Retributive Strategy

Although Alfonsín's criminal justice strategy had been to prosecute only a small number of top leaders, once the truth commission report had been published and trials of senior officials had commenced, the demands for retribution became self-escalating. As Mark Osiel notes, "once the Pandora's box of *Nunca Más* (Argentina's official report) had been opened, events took on a dynamic of their own. To squelch that dynamic is to stifle, at the very outset, a significant expression of democratic process."[32] Thus, once prosecutions had begun, judges began to pursue cases independently against midlevel officials in the belief that their duty was to bring to justice all people culpable of major crimes during the dirty war.[33] These trials exceeded the government's original strategy and greatly complicated its plan of pursuing other objectives, especially the consolidation of constitutional structures and the promotion of national reconciliation. In view of the growing polarization and instability resulting from these subsequent trials, the government decided to halt the criminal prosecution process. Therefore, it proposed a law (the Full Stop Law of December 1986) that would halt all criminal prosecutions. According to the measure, prosecutors were given sixty days from the passage of this measure to file criminal charges against police and military officers. Although the goal of the law was to curb and then halt criminal prosecutions, this measure ironically had a boomerang effect, resulting in an outburst of judicial activism as prosecutors rushed to meet the "full stop" deadline. It is estimated that during the first two months of 1987 some four hundred new criminal cases were filed.

In addition, while the state was pursuing criminal cases, a growing number of individuals, groups, and organizations initiated civil law claims against the state for the human rights violations of state agents.[34] In response to criminal court proceedings against midlevel military officials, elements of the armed forces became increasingly restless in 1987 and 1988, culminating in several military uprisings. The most important of these occurred during Easter Week of 1987 when soldiers took over military bases in suburban Buenos Aires, Córdoba, and Salta.[35] This action led to large demonstrations in support of the Alfonsín government. These included a massive public demonstration in Buenos Aires' Plaza de Mayo and protests by many civilians who surrounded the three rebel-occupied military compounds.

To contain the growing political turmoil in the nation, the Alfonsín government enacted the Due Obedience Law of July 1987, which created a presumption that low- and middle-ranking officers who had committed acts of violence had done so under orders from superiors. The aim of the law was to focus blame on senior decision makers in order to limit the responsibility of agents who had implemented the decisions. Despite the legal protection that this measure afforded low- and midlevel military officers, a number of state courts continued to prosecute midlevel officers. This action resulted in growing tensions between the state and the armed forces and led to two additional army uprisings in 1988.

In response to continued political unrest and economic hyperinflation, Alfonsín resigned in June 1989, five months before his term officially ended, thereby thrusting Carlos Menem, the newly elected president into office. Menem, the Peronist Party candidate, had won office in part with his promise to restore confidence in the economy and to care for the needs of the labor class. Soon after assuming office, Menem issued a decree halting all trials and pardoned some 277 people: 39 senior and midlevel military officers awaiting trials for human rights crimes, 174 military officers involved in the uprisings, and some 65 Montonero guerrillas.[36] In issuing his presidential pardon that freed most imprisoned military officials and guerrilla leaders, Menem declared: "a permanent reconciliation among all Argentineans . . . is the only possible solution for the wounds that still remain to be healed."[37] A year later Menem issued another pardon in order to "create conditions that permit the definitive reconciliation among Argentineans." As a result of the December 29, 1990, decree, the five convicted senior military leaders, as well as Mario Firmenich, the former Montonero guerrilla leader, were freed. Both of these actions were unpopular in Argentina, especially among human rights groups, and represented a dramatic shift away from the strategy of accountability and retribution.

Although the Alfonsín administration had hoped that its truth and trials strategy would help consolidate the democratic transition and the rule of law, promote national unity, and facilitate the moral reconstruction of the nation's moral-cultural order, the strategy failed to do this. Indeed, the strategy had the paradoxical effect of undermining some of these goals. For example, by focusing on the culpability of military and police personnel, the government reinforced an "us-them" division, not only impeding national reconciliation but further intensifying political cleavages. In addition, by focusing on the criminal culpability of senior military officials, the government failed to give sufficient attention to the restoration of civil society and the rehabilitation of a human rights culture.

Thus, when Menem pardoned convicted military leaders soon after assuming office, some observers regarded this action as evidence of the moral bankruptcy of the government's truth and trials strategy. Not only had the quest for legal accountability undermined the consolidation of constitutional government, but the trials themselves had done little to disclose specific information about the fate of missing persons. Indeed, some commentators have suggested that the very processes undertaken by the Alfonsín government inhibited political accommodation, exacerbated political divisions, and provided a new source of polarization within society.[38]

Restoring the Quest for Truth

In the 1990s, two developments were especially significant in rekindling public concern with the atrocities of the dirty war. The first development emerged in 1995 with the revelation by Horacio Verbitsky, a leading Buenos Aires journalist, that the military had killed prisoners during the dirty war by dumping them into the Atlantic Ocean from airplanes. This story, based on the confession of Adolfo Scilingo, a retired naval officer, confirmed that the military had been involved in weekly flights disposing of captives. Scilingo claimed that Admiral Luis María Mendía had ordered this action in order to prevent bodies from being exhumed at a later date. As Admiral Mendía put it, "The subversives will be transported by plane, and not all will reach their destinations."[39] According to Scilingo, between fifteen hundred and two thousand captives were killed in "death flights" in 1977 and 1978, and he personally took responsibility for the murder of some thirty people. This riveting story, which was first disclosed on one of the most popular television programs in the country, was published in a series of newspaper articles and then as a best selling book titled *The Flight*.[40]

The second issue that helped to reawaken interest in the military's criminality was the search for kidnapped children. During the dirty war, detained pregnant mothers were allowed, indeed, encouraged, to give birth to babies. These children were then given up for adoption after their mothers had been killed. The establishment of the Grandmothers of the Plaza de Mayo—a sister organization to the Mothers of the Plaza de Mayo[41]—was created to help locate abducted grandchildren and to reunite them with their true families. In 1992 the search for kidnapped children was strengthened with the creation of the National Commission for the Right to Identity, which established a coordinating center for missing children. As of 2002, more than 240 cases of "stolen babies" have been documented, with genetic testing providing positive family identification for about one-third of them.[42] Since the crimes of "baby trafficking" and falsification of public documents were expressly excluded from the amnesty laws passed in the 1980s, courts have been able to pursue legal prosecution for officials who may have been involved in either planning or carrying out the kidnapping of infants.[43]

Although Alfonsín's amnesty laws and Menem's pardons greatly diminished the demand for trials, the horrifying disclosures about dumping prisoners into the ocean and the heightened concern with identifying the true identity of abducted children ironically led to increased demands for truth, especially for knowledge about the fate of family members. Unlike some of the early demands for trials and punishment by human rights groups, relatives of missing detainees and children have insisted on truth telling, not punishment. For them, the paramount purpose for judicial investigations is to provide an opportunity to determine information about the fate of their missing loved ones. As a result of these and other related political developments, the quest for truth, especially the search for the fate of the missing, was rekindled in the mid-1990s. The success of the truth-telling movement was evident in the 1995 disclosure of the names of 545 people who had been killed ("forced to disappear") during the dirty war.

In November 2001 the Federal Court of Appeals of Buenos Aires issued a historic ruling by nullifying the "full stop" and "due obedience" amnesty laws. The three-judge court unanimously upheld the earlier decision that ruled those laws were unconstitutional and contrary to international human rights law. This watershed ruling allowed trials of military officials charged with torture and kidnapping to continue and provided an opening for others to commence. In 2002 more than twenty-five federal courts were conducting criminal investigations. Unlike earlier prosecutions, which focused on the guilt of individuals, the major aim of these "truth trials" is to use the subpoena power of the courts to compel testimony in order to uncover information about missing persons.[44]

ASSESSING THE TRUTH AND TRIALS STRATEGY

In his prologue to the truth commission report *Nunca Más*, Sábato, the commission's chairman, writes that the commissioners did not pursue their work with feelings of "vindictiveness or vengeance." Rather, he suggests, they were guided by the belief that the only basis for true reconciliation was a strategy of "truth and justice," since "there [could] be no true reconciliation until the guilty repent and we have justice based on truth."[45] Although leaders assumed that the punishment of major offenses was essential in establishing and sustaining a stable constitutional regime, the healing of victims and the restoration of society could not be fulfilled solely through trials.

Perhaps the major achievement of Argentina's truth and justice process was the disclosure of information about the criminal nature of the government's antisubversion campaign. Through the truth commission's investigations and the public testimony of witnesses at trials, the government succeeded in discovering and disseminating factual information about regime atrocities. During the 1985 trials of the junta leaders more than eight hundred witnesses testified, giving dramatic testimony about torture, abductions, and other human rights crimes. The government was also partially successful in translating factual (propositional) truth into moral (dispositional) truth.

The wide dissemination of *Nunca Más* and the continuing media coverage of the human rights atrocities greatly contributed to the public's awareness of the government's systematic abuse of human rights. This was achieved in great part through the broad media reporting about the truth commission report and especially the extensive media coverage of the eight-month trial of the top military leadership. Throughout the trial, television stations broadcast highlights of the trial, focusing on the dramatic testimony of witnesses. Newspapers similarly gave extensive daily coverage to the trial, devoting one or two pages to witness testimony.

But if Argentina's truth and justice strategy contributed to the discovery and acknowledgment of truth, it was largely unsuccessful in promoting other legitimate political and social goals, including the restoration of victims, the consolidation of democratic institutions, and the promotion of national unity. In particular, the retributive strategy failed to encourage the development of cultural and moral norms that might have contributed to reconciliation through forgiveness. Indeed, the truth and trials strategy itself undermined other values, such as the quest for mutual political accountability, the institutionalization of toleration and civic respect, and the promotion of political reconciliation. In great part this was due to the oversimplification of responsibility for regime crimes, the neglect of the context in which violence occurred, and the failure to emphasize healing and moral restoration. The lack of concern with national reconciliation in Argentine society is captured by the motto of HIJOS, a human rights organization for children of the disappeared. Its motto is "we don't forget, we don't forgive, and we do not become reconciled."[46]

Samuel Huntington argues that the failure to bring military leaders to justice was due not to a flaw in the government's truth and trials strategy but to a failure in timing. "Alfonsín's failure to move quickly and decisively in 1984, when public opinion supported action," writes Huntington, "made human rights prosecutions the victim of changes in power relationships and public attitudes."[47] Mark Osiel—who claims that the government's approach of "cautious gradualism" was misconceived—similarly believes that Alfonsín would have been more successful had he adopted "an intransigent posture" toward military crimes at the outset of his administration when his influence was strongest. Osiel argues that the president should have challenged the military directly by dismantling its intelligence services, cutting its budgets, and adopting a hard-line approach to human rights abuses. Even if such actions had risked the stability of democracy, Osiel thinks that this challenge needed to be undertaken if the rule of law was to be restored.[48] Still others claim that the government's failure in securing justice was due to the failure of implementation. Some human rights groups claim that the retributive justice strategy failed because the government did not carry out a vigorous and determined campaign to prosecute and punish all major human rights offenders. Because of the government's lack of resolve, when political turmoil surfaced in 1986 and 1987, Alfonsín halted all trials; and when political instability persisted in 1989 and 1990, Menem pardoned all guerrillas and state agents who were in prison or were under investigation.

The most persuasive explanation for the failure of Argentina's retributive strategy is offered by Jaime Malamud-Goti, a senior legal adviser to Alfonsín. He argues that trials, rather than strengthening democratic institutions and the rule of law, had the ironic effect of further polarizing society and eroding the authority of democratic institutions.[49] According to Malamud-Goti, the government's strategy of "corrective justice" was flawed in several respects. First, the state's prosecution of military leaders focused excessively on the offenses of perpetrators rather than on the restoration of victims and the creation of a rights-based democracy. While supporting punishment of offenders, Malamud-Goti claims that punishment should be pursued only when trials result in the formation of stronger democratic values and institutions. Although he favored trials while a presidential advisor, in the 1990s he began to question that policy, arguing that "the advantages of corrective justice may be overridden by the drawbacks inherent to prosecution and conviction of human rights violators."[50]

Second, Malamud-Goti claims that Argentina's retributive strategy was flawed not only because it failed to foster a rights-based civic society but also because it further undermined the authority of the courts. By placing the courts at the center of the transitional justice process, courts had to adjudicate a deeply political issue, one that divided Argentine society.[51] Military institutions accused the courts of being political, while human rights groups demanded the expansion of the number and scope of trials. Thus, while military officials claimed that they were scapegoats, human rights groups protested that too few people were being prosecuted and that sentences were too lenient.

Third, Malamud-Goti argues that trials reinforced division and fragmentation rather than the consolidation of national unity. Since prosecutions sought to determine the guilt or innocence of people, trials fostered a bipolar "us versus them" perspective that perpetuated an ongoing conflict between groups perceived as innocent and those considered guilty. As a result, he suggests that political antagonists "were trapped in a game without end."[52] Moreover, political polarization contributed to the illusion that those not prosecuted and found guilty were innocent. By defining culpability in narrow, legal terms, trials reinforced the belief that culpability was limited to those state officials who were prosecuted. But as Malamud-Goti notes, responsibility for Argentina's collective violence was shared throughout society, and the belief that there was only one group (the military) that had perpetrated and supported the dirty war was a gross distortion of the truth.

It is significant that the 1976 military coup that toppled the government of Isabel Perón received widespread political support from many sectors of Argentine society. The Catholic Church, the media, the middle and upper classes all approved of regime change in the hope that violence and political instability would end. Thus, the prosecution of state agents not only oversimplified culpability and thereby undermined the truth about regime offenses but further polarized society.

The Argentine case illuminates the difficulties of seeking to consolidate the rule of law through selective trials. As this case suggests, the pursuit of limited retribution reinforced political cleavages within the Argentine polity and further compromised the challenge of promoting national unity and reconciliation. Moreover, rather than facilitating truth telling, the quest for legal accountability had the ironic effect of inhibiting discovery of the fate of the missing. It did so because those with knowledge about human rights crimes (for example, torture, kidnappings, and secret killings) refused to provide relevant information, fearing that such knowledge would inevitably be used to prosecute agents rather than as a means toward the healing of victims' families.

To be sure, Argentine leaders hoped to discover truth about the missing detainees while also pursuing justice to the greatest possible extent. In the final analysis the retributive strategy provided only partial, temporary justice and only some factual truth—primarily general knowledge about the military's role in abducting, torturing, and killing people but little specific information about the fate of the missing. It is, of course, impossible to know how the restoration and reconstruction of civil society would have fared had Argentina pursued a restorative justice strategy.

Moreover, it is impossible to know the outcome of the government's retributive strategy had the Alfonsín administration been able to fully implement its strategy of few trials. But once the government began the process of legal accountability, the retributive strategy expanded rapidly as federal courts, independent of the wishes of the executive, began to investigate and prosecute midlevel military and police officials. In addition, judges began to hear cases in civil trials, where state officials were sued for violating people's civil rights.[53] The political instability created by the armed forces in the late 1980s was a by-product not of the trials of the junta leaders but of greatly expanding prosecutions by federal courts throughout Argentina.

In retrospect, had Argentina made truth an absolute value and relegated trials to a secondary role, the state may have been more successful in establishing a more robust moral foundation on which to carry out the renewal of the nation's political culture and the restoration of political society. Luis Moreno Ocampo, the legal assistant to Julio Strassera, Argentina's chief prosecutor in the 1985 junta trial, observes that the disclosure of truth from the truth commission's report and the trials was "the most powerful healing tool."[54] But if truth telling was the most important element in the government's transitional justice strategy, greater effort could have been made to discover detailed factual truth as well as moral truth about political violence. The former could have contributed to the healing of victim families, while the latter could have facilitated political accommodation and reconciliation. Although numerous factors impeded the development of truth about the state's dirty war, the subordination of truth telling to trials inhibited the quest for a comprehensive, authoritative truth.

THE CHALLENGE OF POLITICAL FORGIVENESS AND NATIONAL RECONCILIATION

Although truth and legal accountability are essential in maintaining a credible constitutional order, these norms alone are not sufficient to overcome regime wrongdoing, rehabilitate civic culture, and foster national reconciliation. Indeed, the Argentine case suggests that the very pursuit of accountability may imperil the disclosure and acknowledgment of factual and interpretive truth about past political violence and may exacerbate political divisions within the nation. Clearly, if a deeply fragmented society that has suffered widespread violence is to overcome the legacy of widespread human rights crimes, perpetrators and victims must participate in a process of moral rehabilitation. At a minimum, such a process will depend on culpable organizations and groups acknowledging their wrongdoing and expressing remorse for it. For their part, victims' groups will be encouraged to respond with empathy toward offenders in the hope that the admission of culpability and the expression of remorse may facilitate some rehabilitation among individuals and groups. The state can also facilitate the process of communal restoration by providing symbolic or tangible reparations or both as expressions of collective repentance for a former regime's offenses.

Individual versus Collective Responsibility

Earlier I noted that an overemphasis on collective responsibility can result in a neglect of individual culpability, while an exclusive focus on personal accountability can oversimplify culpability. Criminal guilt, of course, has the advantage that it is objective and personal, whereas political guilt is diffuse and vicarious, deriving from mere association or from indirect support for policies that may have contributed to governmental offenses. In the Argentine case there can be little doubt of the criminal guilt of government leaders and state agents who carried out the dirty war, but it is also clear that the antisubversion campaign would have been impossible without the tacit and even overt support of major sectors of society. While a significant portion of the Argentine citizenry may have been unaware of the government's covert operations, numerous groups—business elites, middle-income professionals, the media, the Catholic Church—nevertheless provided essential support to the military regime in its war against urban terrorism. Thus, the exclusive focus on the individual guilt of top military leaders and the neglect of the collective responsibility of religious, business, media, and professional groups that indirectly supported the military's authoritarianism reinforced the myth that the armed forces were exclusively responsible for the systemic abuse of human rights.

Argentina's transitional justice strategy would have been greatly strengthened had its concern with criminal culpability been supplemented by a concern with political and moral responsibility. In effect, it would have been politically prudent to use Jaspers' framework of guilt, discussed in chapter 3, to illuminate the criminal, political, and moral dimensions of guilt. Since criminal responsibility is personal and direct, it is comparatively easy to ascertain. In the context of the dirty war, urban guerrillas who carried out bombings, abductions, and bank robberies as well as state agents who participated in abductions, secret killings, and torture were criminally responsible. Public officials who instituted state terrorism were of course politically responsible for the collective offenses of the nation.[55] While criminal responsibility was limited to a relatively small number of leaders and state security agents, political responsibility involved a much larger number of people, especially when pro-military political groups are included.

Moral culpability for Argentina's gross human rights violations was even more extensive. Moral guilt, it will be recalled, involves the violation of a person's own moral values. To be morally guilty is to violate one's own conscience by directly committing unjust, evil acts or by indirectly failing to confront such actions by others. In the Argentine context, this meant that agents who carried out torture, abductions, and secret killings—acts that are universally considered immoral—were responsible for violating foundational personal and political morality. It also meant that citizens who were aware of secret killings, abductions, and forceful adoption of infants also bore some moral culpability in failing to protest, condemn, or halt such actions.

Perhaps the most dramatic illustration, mentioned earlier, of the role of moral guilt in confronting the offenses of the dirty war is retired Navy Captain Adolfo Scilingo's confession that the navy had disposed of captives by dumping them into the sea. Although Scilingo claimed that his confession was prompted by a desire to illuminate the culpability of senior military leaders and not necessarily to clear his conscience, it is evident from his horrendous story that his participation in these operations had troubled him deeply. Indeed, after his first flight, Scilingo became so distraught that he had confessed his criminal actions to a military priest. Although the priest absolved him, saying that killings "had to be done to separate the wheat from the chaff,"[56] he remained psychologically tormented by the memory of his past actions. Indeed, his willingness to talk was inspired by his desire to confront his own moral guilt and to encourage others to provide information about the fate of the missing.

A month after Scilingo had disclosed the use of death flights, Victor Ibañez, an army sergeant, revealed in a newspaper interview that the army had also dumped prisoners into the sea. According to Ibañez, who had served as a guard at an army detention center near Buenos Aires, some two thousand men and women were dumped into the sea after injecting them with a strong sedative. A day after a leading Buenos Aires daily published this account, Argentina's army chief of staff, General Martín Balza, publicly acknowledged that the armed forces had made mistakes in fighting urban guerrillas. In particular, he admitted that the military had used "illegitimate means of obtaining information, including the suppression of life."[57] In his carefully worded statement he declared: "I assume our part of the responsibility for the errors of this conflict between Argentines that today moves us again."[58] Two months later the navy chief of staff, Admiral Enrique Molina Pico, issued a similar statement of qualified remorse. He admitted that in seeking to defeat terrorism the armed forces had failed to respect domestic law or to abide by the laws of war. After admitting that the navy had used "wrong methods" that allowed "unacceptable violence," he pledged that such strategies would never be used again.[59]

With the exception of Balza's apology, and to a lesser extent, Molina Pico's qualified admission, Scilingo's dramatic confession had limited impact on the behavior of the armed forces, which continued to pursue a policy of silence and denial. Even Menem, who had been imprisoned by the military, continued to defend the armed forces for having defeated urban terrorism. Since the government had been trying to put the evils of repression behind by focusing on economic growth and job creation, Menem viewed Scilingo's confession as a major distraction to his strategy of social and economic renewal. He publicly expressed anger at his disclosures, declaring that "those who have a bad conscience should confess to a priest."[60] Soon thereafter, Scilingo was imprisoned for alleged financial crimes and then stripped of his rank.[61]

Although Scilingo's confession generated little additional truth from the armed forces, it had a profound effect on Argentine society, prompting groups and organizations to reflect on their direct and indirect complicity in the widespread human rights abuses of the anti-insurgency campaign and to express remorse for institutional indifference. For example, up to this point the hierarchy of the Roman Catholic Church had refused to admit its complicity in the dirty war. Church leaders had not only remained silent during the conflict but had failed to confront the state about known atrocities. As Emilio Mignone has shown, Catholic bishops, military chaplains, and especially the Papal Nuncio Pio Laghi all helped to morally legitimate the covert war of repression through their teaching and actions and also through their silence.[62]

The lack of remorse for the violence inflicted during the dirty war is illustrated graphically by Alfredo Astiz, a retired naval captain and one of the most flamboyant agents of the dirty war. Astiz, who earned the nickname of "blond angel of death" because of his golden hair and baby face, was assigned to ESMA, which the navy used as a detention-torture center, from where he worked to infiltrate human rights groups and to carry out covert operations. He was allegedly involved in several secret kidnappings and killings, including the murder of two French nuns and a Swedish-Argentine teenager.[63] In 1996 he was forced to retire from the navy because, as an unrepentant military agent who had committed egregious crimes, he continued defending the military's dirty war. Moreover, when Astiz admitted in an interview two years later that he was proud of his role in the military's covert war against guerrillas, the government viewed his widely published comments as provocative and inflammatory and sentenced him to sixty days' detention.

Qualified Repentance

When CONADEP began its investigations into gross human rights violations, military and police officials not only refused to acknowledge wrongdoing but opposed all cooperation with the investigation. As the truth commission report notes, far from expressing any repentance, military leaders justified their covert, anti-insurgency campaign because of the virulent threat posed by urban guerrillas and the political demand that they restore public order. Although junta leaders believed that they had been called to "save the nation and its Western, Christian values," in reality they were responsible "for dragging these values inside the bloody walls of the dungeons of repression."[64]

With the return of democracy in 1983, the armed forces adopted a policy of noncooperation and silence in regard to the search for truth and accountability. While some state agents and military officials have admitted that the dirty war resulted in a disregard for the laws of war as well as domestic constitutional protections, they have claimed that the search for truth has been one-sided, placing responsibility for wrongdoing chiefly on the armed forces rather than on the urban guerrillas that initiated the violence. Since the Argentine citizenry expected the police and armed forces to respond to the threat of terrorism, the appropriate response for the nation, in the view of a senior official of the "Círculo Militar," Argentina's Army Officers' Club, was gratitude, not apologies.[65] Not surprisingly, some elites continued to defend the armed forces, while other groups remained ambivalent about the responsibility for past regime abuses. Even after it was disclosed that the armed forces had carried out "death flights," Menem continued to defend the armed forces.

Although Scilingo's confession prompted some individuals and institutions to disclose indirect responsibility for past wrongdoing, generally individuals and groups that participated in the dirty war have been reluctant to admit moral culpability or to express public apologies. Political groups have remained fundamentally divided over the nature and causes of the dirty war. As a result, militants who initiated urban terrorism and military officers who planned and executed covert violence have refused to repent. Some leaders have admitted that excesses were committed in prosecuting the secret military campaign, but most apologies have been general and qualified. For example, after Scilingo admitted that a military priest had condoned "death flights," senior bishops immediately confessed their guilt for not having done more to prevent human rights crimes. They declared: "We will surely carry on our consciences for the rest of our lives our repentance for not having done more to prevent young people who belonged to our church from choosing guerrilla violence, and to prevent the repressors from committing such aberrations against human rights."[66]

The military has similarly been reluctant to admit human rights abuses. Even after Balza had publicly confessed that the armed forces had used inappropriate strategies in confronting urban insurgency, the army refused to admit collective responsibility for regime crimes or to modify its policy of silence and noncooperation. The other branches of the armed forces along with the police also continued to practice silence and noncooperation.

Scilingo's disclosures and Balza's confession are significant because they led other people and groups to issue mea culpas. The Argentine Episcopal Conference of the Catholic Church, for example, issued a thirty-nine-point statement of repentance in which it expressed remorse for its institutional failures in preventing crimes. As with other institutions, the bishops expressed a general apology without specifically admitting institutional guilt. "We are profoundly sorry to have been unable to ease more the pain produced in such a great drama," the bishops declared, and then asked for a pardon for "all who, deforming Christ's teachings, encouraged guerrilla violence or immoral repression."[67] Even Firmenich, the former leader of the Montoneros, admitted in a television program in 1995 that his group's use of clandestine violence had been a mistake. At the same time, while expressing remorse for not following the Christian ethic of loving enemies, he refused to repent for the suffering inflicted by the Montoneros. Thus, Scilingo's confession not only prompted further disclosures about past human rights atrocities but also encouraged some individuals and groups to publicly confront their individual and collective guilt.

Institutional Responsibility and the Possibility of Forgiveness

During the 1990s the Menem government began a program of financial reparations to the families of the missing as well as to those who had been detained. The aim of the program was to allow the nation to atone publicly for its past collective crimes through financial reparations. In addition, the government hoped that by making restitution it could put to rest the continuing demands of human rights groups. Menem decreed the "law of indemnification" as a means of containing the potential liability of the state in a growing number of civil suits—one of them resulting in a judgment of one million dollars. Under the indemnification program, the state limited the governmental liability to about $220,000 for each murdered person—a sum to be paid in government bonds over time.[68] In addition, the government enacted legislation authorizing compensation to people who had been "wrongly imprisoned." People detained during the dirty war by the police or the military were eligible for about $75 for each day of detention. By the mid-1990s, the state had paid out more than $36 million to roughly six thousand claimants.[69]

Some human rights groups, especially the Mothers of the Plaza de Mayo, have been highly critical of the reparations program, believing that the injustices and crimes of the past can only be atoned for through truth and legal accountability. Accordingly, when Hagelin accepted financial reparations of $700,000 as final settlement for his daughter's "disappearance,"[70] human rights groups were highly critical. Hebe de Bonafini, the head of the Association of the Mothers of the Plaza de Mayo claimed that Hagelin's decision to accept money was disgraceful because it replaced justice with a monetary settlement. Bonafini taunted Hagelin by asking him, "what are you going to buy with the money?"[71]

Despite some truth telling, selective apologies, and state financial reparations, there has been little opportunity for political forgiveness. Fundamentally, the major antagonists have failed to reach a consensus about the truth concerning Argentina's 1970s political conflict. The armed forces, fearing prosecution, have maintained a policy of silence and refused to disclose information on the fate of the missing. As of 2003, most of the nine thousand missing persons remain unaccounted for. Moreover, antagonists have also failed to develop agreement on the moral truth of the conflict—that is, finding consensus about which groups and individuals are chiefly responsible for the dirty war. Antagonists have refused to acknowledge individual and collective responsibility, and because acceptance of responsibility is the foundation for political forgiveness, the national quest for restoration and renewal has remained stalled.

Argentine political forgiveness is of course impossible when offenders refuse to acknowledge guilt. The political conflict in Argentina that gave rise to the dirty war has not been resolved, and antagonists have continued to remain silent about the abuses of the dirty war or to justify their strategies and tactics. The leaders of the armed forces have, with few exceptions, continued to justify their covert anti-insurgency campaign as a necessary, albeit last resort, strategy. Given the continuing political divisions within society as well as the opposing perspectives on the country's past, it is unlikely that distrust and political cleavages will be significantly reduced in the near future.

Perhaps the collective healing of Argentina's "radical evil" can only be realized with the passage of time. This chapter suggests, however, that deeply divided societies like Argentina have much to gain by confronting their collective offenses through a forward-looking restorative justice strategy that emphasizes the moral and political reconstruction of society. Like individual forgiveness, collective forgiveness is possible when political actors pursue truth, admit culpability, and practice empathy and compassion.

In late 2001 Argentina's economy collapsed under the weight of its external financial debt. But the country's financial troubles, which are rooted in the continuing divisions among major political groups, are not unrelated to the failure of the country to pursue a forward-looking strategy of national unity and political reconciliation. Thus, if the nation's economic confidence is to be restored, the existing distrust, animosity, and political fragmentation in Argentine society will have to be transformed into greater social harmony and political consensus. Such change is possible and can be greatly facilitated through a revived effort in the moral and political reconstruction of society based on truth telling, repentance, compassion, and forgiveness.

6

The Quest for Reconciliation through Truth Telling in Chile

We should not waste all our efforts digging into wounds that are irreparable. . . . We cannot progress by digging deeper into divisions. It is time for pardon and reconciliation.

—Patricio Aylwin, president of Chile, 1991[1]

The [Chilean] Army, as an institution, will never ask for forgiveness. Forgiveness is a personal expression.

—Mario Fernandez, minister of defense of Chile, 2000[2]

It is best to remain silent and to forget. It is the only thing to do: we must forget. And forgetting does not occur by opening cases, putting people in jail.

—General Augusto Pinochet, September 13, 1995[3]

Justice is necessary here so we can have some peace. Without it, there will never be reconciliation. We will always be a divided people with much pain, and the pain will be passed down within families from generation to generation.

—Paula Garcia, Chilean human rights activist[4]

On September 11, 1973, Chile's armed forces toppled the Marxist government of Salvador Allende. During the 1970 election, Allende had promised to bring about radical social and economic changes if elected, and despite his narrow electoral mandate, he nonetheless instituted major public policy reforms, greatly expanding governmental control over social and economic life. Although some of these policies led to short-term improvement of workers' standard of living, they also undermined the national economy by fostering recession, inflation, and unemployment. Most important, the effort to institute socialist policies led to deep political cleavages and intensified social fragmentation. By 1973 ideological divisions had become so intense that the country was on the verge of civil war. Thus, many Chileans were relieved when the armed forces carried out a coup d'etat that brought down the Allende government.

However, most coup supporters assumed that the military authorities would hold power only for a short span of time in order to restore confidence in the economy and the country's democratic institutions. Instead, military authorities, led by General Augusto Pinochet, kept power for nearly seventeen years through harsh authoritarian rule that involved widespread human rights violations. These human rights abuses were most serious in the immediate aftermath of the coup, but continued throughout the era of military rule.

In March 1990 democracy was restored in Chile. To help consolidate the rule of law and to foster social and political reconciliation, the newly elected government of Patricio Aylwin sought to directly confront the atrocities and human rights abuses perpetrated by the military regime through truth telling. As conceptualized by Aylwin administration officials, political healing and national reconciliation could occur only if the nature and scope of the government's human rights violations were first identified and disclosed. Aylwin was thus committed to the public disclosure of truth, after which the state officials could acknowledge and accept responsibility for the previous regime's wrongdoing. Although it was impossible to provide full satisfaction to victims, symbolic reparations would offer a means by which official contrition would be expressed.

In this chapter, I describe and assess Aylwin's "truth and reparations" strategy. In the first part of the chapter, I sketch some developments that contributed to the breakdown of Chile's constitutional order under the government of Allende. In the second section, I briefly sketch the nature and policies of the military regime of Pinochet, from the coup in September 1973 until the restoration of democracy in March 1990. In this section, I call attention to the widespread violations of human rights resulting from the imposition of political repression. In the third section, I examine some of the principal elements of the Aylwin administration's strategy to consolidate democracy while also confronting past regime violence. Since truth was regarded as a precondition for national reconciliation, discovering the truth about past regime violence was considered a central goal of the democratic transition. In the fourth section, I provide a preliminary assessment of Chile's "truth and reparations" strategy. Although the truth commission report led to increasing public awareness of the scope and effects of state violence during the era of military rule, truth telling did not lead to national reconciliation—the ostensible aim of the truth and reparations process. In the fifth and final section, I explore the limited role of forgiveness in Chile's democratic transition.

While the Aylwin truth and reparations strategy did not directly incorporate political forgiveness as a precondition for national healing and political reconciliation, it nonetheless emphasized components of the forgiveness model—namely, truth telling, official acknowledgment, and symbolic reparations. The Chilean strategy of transition did not call on individuals, groups, or institutions to acknowledge wrongdoing, nor did it encourage repentance. Rather, the plan emphasized accountability through the disclosure and acknowledgment of truth, in the hope that accountability would contribute to the psychological healing of victims and to the restoration of broken social and political relationships.

THE BREAKDOWN OF CONSTITUTIONAL ORDER

Salvador Allende, the Popular Union (*Unidad Popular* [UP]) candidate, was elected president in September 1970. He won with a slim plurality, receiving only 36 percent of the vote. Since this was less than the constitutional requirement of an absolute majority, Allende's election was confirmed by a congressional vote a month later.[5] Given the slim plurality of the popular vote, Allende's election provided a weak, uncertain mandate.

Notwithstanding the deeply divided electorate and the tenuous political mandate, Allende was determined to bring about radical social and economic changes. He was committed to reducing Chile's foreign economic dependence and to increasing the government's control over, and ownership of, major sectors of the economy. Allende admired Fidel Castro and was determined to replace capitalist structures with state socialism, which he believed would greatly improve living conditions of the poor, foster a more egalitarian society, and reduce Chile's dependence on the United States. In effect, Allende was committed to "socialism in democracy, pluralism, and liberty" or what he termed the "Chilean way" (*vía Chilena*).[6]

Soon after assuming power, Allende began carrying out major structural and policy reforms. On the diplomatic front, he reoriented Chile's foreign policy toward Communist and nonaligned nations, reducing his ties with the West while strengthening relations with the East. He immediately reestablished diplomatic relations with Cuba, formalized ties with China, and strengthened his relationship with the Soviet Union. On the domestic front, he expropriated foreign companies, expanded agrarian reform, and nationalized basic industries. Since copper was Chile's major export commodity, providing nearly 80 percent of the country's export revenues, gaining control of this resource was deemed a key goal of the Allende government. During the previous administration of Eduardo Frei the Chilean government had passed the 1967 Chileanization of Copper Law that gave the state authority to gain partial ownership of foreign-owned copper mines. As a result, the government was able to establish partial control of the two major U.S. copper companies in Chile (Kennecott and Anaconda). Thus, when Allende took office, he simply extended a process that had begun earlier by demanding the full expropriation of foreign copper mines. Accordingly, Chile took full control of the mines in 1971.[7]

Allende's UP government was also committed to transforming Chile's traditional land tenure system. During the Frei administration some 1,408 farms with 3.5 million hectares of land had been expropriated by the state, in accordance with a provision of the Agrarian Reform Law of 1967. The breakup of these farms had resulted in a transfer of land to some 20,000 peasants. Allende, however, increased the pace of land reform by expanding the number of farm expropriations and by tolerating peasant groups that had taken over farms. By the end of 1972, nearly 4,690 farms with 9 million hectares of farmland had been taken over by the state or by peasant groups. And by early 1973 virtually all agricultural land eligible for nationalization under the 1967 land reform law had been expropriated by the state.[8]

As suggested earlier, a primary aim of the UP government was to improve workers' living conditions. The Allende administration pursued this goal by stimulating economic demand through wage increases while simultaneously freezing prices, especially for food and other essential commodities. Although these policies led to modest improvements in workers' incomes in the first year, by late 1971 major imbalances between supply and demand had begun to develop in the economy, leading to significant production declines in various economic sectors. Economic contraction was first evident in the agricultural sector, where production first stagnated and then declined precipitously.

The fall in agricultural output was precipitated by agrarian reform, newly instituted policies governing agricultural production, and the growing political and economic uncertainties resulting from the imposition of state socialism. It has been estimated that agricultural output declined 3.6 percent in 1972 and more than 16 percent in 1973. The shortfall in agricultural production resulted in rising food imports, which nearly quadrupled from $168 million in 1970 to $619 million in 1973.[9] When food scarcity first became evident, women protested by marching in Santiago with their pots and pans. The demonstration, dubbed the "march of the empty pots," was an important political development that helped galvanize political opposition to Allende's radical reforms.

In addition to economic recession, Chile began to suffer from inflation—caused in great part from an excessive money supply and an economic demand that far outstripped the supply of commodities. Whereas inflation was about 8 percent in 1971, by 1973 it had increased to more than 1,000 percent, the highest of any Latin American country up to that time.[10]

The most polarizing governmental initiatives were those designed to promote socialism by increasing state ownership of key sectors of the economy. By mid-1972, the government claimed that the state owned ninety-eight major enterprises and had significant control over eighty-three others.[11] To expedite the transformation of economic life and to express solidarity with the government's socialist programs, militant workers had begun to take over various industries without legal authority. By 1973 these illegal seizures were estimated to have affected nearly three hundred enterprises. And when the head of the Central Workers Confederation (CUT), Chile's major labor union, called on workers to show support for the embattled Allende government in mid-1973, they responded by occupying factories and agricultural centers, taking over more than 240 companies in a single day.[12] Although these nongovernmental actions were popular with workers, they led to deep social and political polarization, calling into question Allende's plan to bring about socialism through constitutional, democratic processes.

Although peasants, workers, and many academics and intellectuals strongly supported the social and economic transformations underway, the radical structural changes being carried out in society also generated significant political opposition. Those that opposed socialist reforms included some nonunion workers, small-scale businessmen, professional associations, nongovernmental groups, the Catholic Church, and evangelical groups. Fundamentally, the poor and labor classes, which had been historically identified with the Socialist, Communist, and Radical parties, supported Allende, while the middle and upper classes, which were identified with the National Party and the Christian Democratic Party (*Partido Demócrata Cristiano* [PDC]) were strongly opposed to him. Since the National Congress was controlled by an anti-Allende political coalition, known as the Democratic Confederation (CODE),[13] executive-legislative cooperation had all but stopped in 1971, greatly intensifying political fragmentation. As a result, by mid-1972, the armed forces had begun to consider the possibility of intervening in the constitutional process to resolve the political stalemate between Allende and his congressional political opposition.

The governmental executive-legislative stalemate reflected the growing political polarization in the country. Beginning in the late 1950s, electoral power was distributed in roughly three equal sectors between the political left, center, and right. Although large ideological differences existed among political parties, democratic government had thrived in Chile because of its strong middle class and a political center that served to mediate political conflict between the two extremes. This equilibrium collapsed under the Allende government as polarization increased, making political compromise virtually impossible. The absence of a centrist sector was evident in the March 1973 congressional election, when government forces (UP) received 43.5 percent of the vote and the anti-Allende political coalition (CODE) received 56.5 percent. Despite the growing polarization, Allende refused to compromise on his goals. Shortly after the congressional election, he further antagonized the opposition forces by decreeing a reorganization of elementary and secondary education. The initiative, known as the National Unified Educational System (*Educación Nacional Unificada* [ENU]) immediately intensified political conflict, in part because it was viewed as a means to pursue ideological indoctrination. Although the program included some useful reforms, the initiative unnecessarily antagonized large sectors of the society, especially the Catholic Church, long a major institution involved in primary and secondary education in Chile.[14]

The deep political fissures in the Chilean political system first became apparent in October 1971 when truckers began a nationwide strike. The strike began when Allende sought to set up a public trucking firm in a remote province of southern Chile. Chilean truckers, believing that their industry would be taken over by the government, as had occurred in a variety of industries already, called for an indefinite strike. The strike paralyzed the transport of goods throughout the central region of the nation and had a devastating economic impact on the country. Its social and economic consequences were even more influential because thousands of small business associations (*gremios*) joined in the strike, fearing that they, too, would eventually be taken over by the government. The truckers' strike ended in early November, but only after Allende had appointed the military chiefs of the army, navy, and air force to his cabinet. Less than a year later, the truckers began a second strike that was even more destructive than the first. The truckers not only refused to transport goods but used their vehicles to block major highways.

By August 1973 Chile was on the verge of civil war. The economy had stopped functioning, inflation was rampant, unemployment was rising, lawlessness and violence were increasing, and governmental institutions were fast losing authority as political groups took matters increasingly into their own hands. Still, peasants and workers continued to strongly support Allende, as evidenced by the significant support UP candidates received in the March congressional elections. But given the deep political divisions between the supporters and opponents of Allende's radical restructuring of society, constitutional government was becoming increasingly precarious. To cope with growing political instability and violence, Allende requested temporary "state of siege" authority from the National Congress, but was refused. More significant, the Chamber of Deputies, the Lower House of the Congress, declared that the government had engaged in unconstitutional actions and called on the military to "place an immediate end" to the state of affairs.[15]

Not surprisingly, on September 11, 1973, the armed forces carried out a coup d'etat that ended Chile's long-standing record of constitutional government. When military forces began taking control of the country, Allende rushed to La Moneda, the presidential palace, in an effort to rally his supporters. By the time Allende tried to rally political support, the armed forces were in full control of communication and transportation networks. When he refused to surrender, the air force bombed the palace. Allende then killed himself to avoid being taken prisoner. By early afternoon, the military had eliminated all major opposition and was in full control of the country.

There was substantial public support for the coup. As noted earlier in this chapter, professional and business groups were eager for an end to the chaos that had resulted from the experiment in socialist political economy. According to the leader of the association of Chile's retail businessmen, most businessmen were "satisfied with the coup."[16] Political parties and groups from the center and right supported the overthrow of Allende. The PDC, for example, viewed the coup as a necessary result of the "economic disaster, institutional chaos, armed violence, and moral crisis" that the Allende government had produced. The National Party similarly expressed its support for the coup, noting with gratitude that the nation had been freed from the yoke of Communist oppression. Religious leaders also voiced support for the coup as a means of restoring public order. Cardinal Silva, the head of Chile's Roman Catholic Church, offered his services to the Pinochet government in order "to give the good news to the bishops of the world about what had happened in Chile, to say that this wasn't the putsch of some soldier."[17]

Of course the widespread support for the coup was based on the belief that the military would return power to constitutional authorities as soon as public order had been restored and the radical, revolutionary elements within society had been weakened or destroyed. PDC leaders, for example, supported the coup because they believed that once the military had eliminated the totalitarian threat they would return authority to elected officials.[18] Indeed, the PDC cooperation with the military junta was predicated on the assumption that military rule would be short-lived. Few political or professional leaders ever expected that the effects of the coup would last seventeen years.

MILITARY RULE AND THE ABUSE OF HUMAN RIGHTS

In carrying out the coup, military authorities imposed swift and total control over all major geographical and economic sectors of society. In taking control of the state, the military used force whenever they met resistance. In a number of locations in Santiago, some militants engaged in brief gun battles, but by the end of the first day, armed resistance had virtually ceased. To prevent popular uprisings by armed revolutionary groups,[19] the military *junta* (the leaders of the army, navy, air force, and police) instituted a two-day curfew and imposed martial law. The lifting of constitutional constraints gave security officials the right to search, detain, and imprison people suspected of supporting revolutionary causes. Accordingly, security personnel rounded up potential opponents, including leftist activists, union militants, and members of revolutionary groups. Hundreds of government officials and radical political leaders were immediately imprisoned or killed and many simply disappeared. To gather information about radical groups, alleged troublemakers were tortured and then secretly killed to avoid accountability. It has been estimated that within the first days of the coup, several hundred people were killed and more than 10,000 detained, most of them in Santiago's national stadium. By the end of the first year of military rule, more than 1,200 people had disappeared or been killed. Of the more than 3,000 people who were killed during the era of military rule, more than 1,000 were classified as disappeared detainees (*detenidos desaparecidos*).[20]

Since Marxism was viewed as the cancer that had destroyed Chile's democratic values and traditions, military authorities determined that the only effective solution to this political disease was to eliminate groups committed to the Marxist ideology. As Edgardo Boeninger, a former president of the University of Chile, has pointed out, "from the outset, the military government interpreted its mission as a war against Marxism."[21] Accordingly, the government banned the Communist Party and other leftist parties of Allende's UP coalition and sought to eradicate all radical organizations and movements through political repression, including widespread intelligence gathering, censorship of the media, and imprisonment, exile, or killings of leaders and militants. Subsequently, all political parties were suspended and the National Congress dissolved.

In announcing the transfer of political authority from elected officials to the military, Pinochet indicated that the military chiefs—the Junta—would serve as "the Supreme Command of the Nation with the patriotic duty to restore *chilenidad*, justice, and the institutions, which have broken down."[22] Only the courts were left intact, and even the decision to honor judicial authority was quickly compromised by the imposition of martial law, which effectively gave military tribunals final judicial authority. In sum, the Pinochet government decided that the Chilean political system must be purified of its Marxist, revolutionary virus, and that to carry out this task, it was necessary to depoliticize the country altogether.

In 1974 Pinochet established a secret police force, Directorate for National Intelligence (DINA), to direct the gathering of intelligence and to carry out clandestine operations as a means to depoliticize society. In its first year of operation, DINA focused on the destruction of the MIR, an urban guerrilla organization, and in 1975 and 1976 it focused on the elimination of Socialist and Communist militants.[23] In 1976 Orlando Letelier, Allende's foreign minister and ambassador to the United States, was killed in a Washington, D.C., car bombing. When U.S. law enforcement agents traced the crime to DINA agents, relations between the two countries deteriorated to the point where all U.S. military aid to Chile was suspended. In response to domestic and international criticisms of DINA, Pinochet abolished the covert operations organization in 1977, replacing it with the National Information Center (CNI).[24]

One of the few institutions to assist victims of political repression was the Catholic Church. Soon after the coup, Cardinal Raúl Silva established an ecumenical Committee for Peace (COPACHI) to provide legal assistance to victims of human rights abuses and their families. When Pinochet forced the closure of the Committee, Cardinal Silva replaced it with Vicariate of Solidarity (*Vicaría*), located within the Santiago archdiocese.[25] Although the Committee and the Vicariate were rarely successful in winning their legal battles on behalf of human rights victims,[26] both organizations played a key political role in highlighting the moral priority of human rights during the period of greatest repression. Moreover, when a truth commission was established in 1990 to investigate human rights violations of the Pinochet era, the Vicariate's human rights records provided an indispensable data source.

By the late 1970s the Chilean economy had begun to thrive under market-based policies. These policies encouraged job creation through free enterprise and free trade and through public policies that encouraged investment (domestic and foreign), monetary stability, and privatization of public enterprises. In 1982, however, the Chilean economy collapsed, largely in response to a global recession sparked by high petroleum prices. The economic downturn led to bankruptcies, massive unemployment, widespread political opposition, and the proliferation of grassroots opposition groups. As public unrest grew, the Pinochet government responded by declaring a state of siege in August 1983 and by arresting more than twelve hundred people. Three years later public protests and demonstrations escalated again. After Pinochet's motorcade was attacked in September 1986, military authorities responded by declaring a new state of siege, leading to the arrest of some fifteen thousand people. Pinochet and his military regime were widely opposed in the Western world, and the adoption of repressive measures only served to increase Chile's international isolation.

Public demonstrations and protests represented an important step in the restoration of democracy because they encouraged anti-Pinochet political groups to coordinate their efforts. In 1985 opposition groups established an informal political alliance, or National Accord, and two years later created the *Concertación para la Democracia* (Alliance for Democracy)—a fourteen-party coalition whose goal was to restore democracy to Chile. As required by the 1980 Constitution, a referendum was held in October 1988 to determine whether the electorate supported eight more years of military rule or whether they wished to end Pinochet's tenure and elect a new president. The referendum, which Pinochet was convinced he would win, resulted in a surprising but resounding victory for the pro-democracy political coalition, with the Concertación (the "No" vote) receiving nearly 55 percent of the vote and the pro-Pinochet coalition (the "Yes" vote) 43 percent.[27]

Because of these results, presidential elections took place a year later. In the elections, Patricio Aylwin, the leader of the PDC and the candidate of the Concertación, won a resounding victory with 55 percent of the vote. When Aylwin assumed office in March 1990, democracy was once again restored.

PROMOTING RECONCILIATION THROUGH THE DISCLOSURE AND ACKNOWLEDGMENT OF TRUTH

Although military repression had greatly reduced political conflict, Chile remained a deeply divided country politically at the time of the democratic transition. Although political polarization had greatly declined, significant cleavages remained, manifested in particular between conflicting views and attitudes of supporters and critics of Pinochet. A large portion of the citizenry remained deeply divided over such issues as the justification for the coup, the legitimacy of the authoritarian policies used to maintain public order, and the diverse policies and programs advocated by party leaders. Thus, as the country embarked on its democratic transition, political divisions once again became more pronounced and visible.

Given conflicting worldviews and divergent interpretations of recent history, how should a re-emerging democracy reckon with past regime wrongdoing? Should it use scarce political resources primarily toward the consolidation of democracy and the promotion of job creation, or should it first seek to consolidate the rule of law by prosecuting past crimes and human rights abuses?

Potential Strategies for Confronting Regime Crimes

In confronting the legacy of past human rights abuses, three fundamental strategies were available to Aylwin as president: legal accountability, benign neglect, and truth telling. The first called for the prosecution and punishment of state officials who were chiefly responsible for criminal acts committed during the era of military rule. Advocates of this approach believed that the only way to recover the credibility of Chile's constitutional/democratic order was to restore the rule of law, a goal some believed could only be realized if perpetrators were brought to justice. As noted earlier, governments normally confront wrongdoing by prosecuting and punishing criminals. While such a strategy may be appropriate when confronting private illegal acts, criminal prosecution of state wrongdoing presents enormous challenges, especially when the crimes are a direct by-product of a covert, unconventional war strategy. More significant, retributive justice is problematic because it seeks to maintain the credibility of the rule of law by punishing wrongdoing rather than by seeking the restoration of communal bonds and the renewal of the moral-cultural political order. As a result, the pursuit of retributive justice may be not only an unrealistic strategy but an impediment to the consolidation of a democratic order.

The second strategy that Aylwin could have pursued was to simply disregard past wrongdoing and to focus all his attention on the consolidation of a new constitutional political order. Advocates of the "benign neglect" strategy argued that although trials and punishment would no doubt contribute to the consolidation of a constitutional order, the prosecution of human rights violations could lead to further political conflict and threaten the restoration and consolidation of democracy. Accordingly, the new government should devote its energies and resources to economic growth and development, the restoration of the country's moral order, and the consolidation of the democratic transition, minimizing, if not disregarding, the crimes, violence, and injustices of the past. In short, this second strategy justifies impunity in the name of future economic prosperity and political reconciliation.

The third alternative, truth telling, was essentially a compromise between the other two approaches. Whereas the trials approach tends to focus too much on the past and the benign neglect approach completely disregards it, the truth telling strategy falls in the middle. It does so by pursuing partial accountability through the discovery and disclosure of truth and the promotion of national reconciliation through reparations, the consolidation of democratic structures, and the renewal of civic life. In essence, this approach seeks to balance victims' backward-looking demands for truth and justice with the forward-looking quest for democratic consolidation and reconciliation.

Aylwin chose the third alternative. His approach was guided by two values—to repair and heal the damage that had been inflicted on individual victims as well as on collective life by the military regime and to prevent the reoccurrence of such wrongdoing. To foster the healing of victims and the reparation of civic life, Aylwin made truth telling an absolute value. Once the truth had been discovered and disclosed about past regime wrongdoing, then the state could acknowledge wrongdoing and offer reparations to victims and their families as a sign of collective remorse.

A number of factors led the government to pursue this strategy. First, it was politically realistic. Although Pinochet had lost the 1988 referendum, he remained an influential political actor in the Chilean political landscape in 1991. As former president, he was constitutionally entitled to membership in the country's Senate and to serve as the army's chief until 1998. As leader of the army, Pinochet exerted enormous influence. In 1989, Pinochet had declared: "No one touches anyone. The day they touch one of my men, the rule of law ends. This I say once and will not say again." Pinochet also retained widespread public support, especially from business and professional groups, the middle class, and even some working poor. For many, he was a national hero who had rescued Chile from communism and had instituted policies that had resulted in unprecedented economic expansion. Most important, since Pinochet had not been forced from office but had voluntarily relinquished power, the armed forces remained an influential political actor—as evidenced by the fact that 43 percent of the electorate had expressed support in the plebiscite for eight more years of Pinochet rule.

A related reason for pursuing a truth and reparations strategy was that any effort to prosecute and punish human rights offenders would have come into conflict with existing law. In 1978 the Pinochet government had decreed an Amnesty Law (Decree Law 2,191) that exempted from prosecution all politically motivated crimes committed during the 1973–1978 period.[28] Since the majority of human rights violations occurred in the first three years after the coup, a retributive strategy would be significantly constrained by the Amnesty Law. And since the *Concertación* did not have the legislative power in the National Congress to override the amnesty law, pursuing a retributive strategy would entail significant political capital and would be unlikely to succeed in the short term.

Third, Aylwin selected the truth telling strategy because it combined backward-looking accountability through truth-telling with a forward-looking emphasis on reconciliation. In effect, the Chilean strategy sought to promote renewal and reconciliation while also providing some symbolic justice and reparations to victims. Since knowledge of regime wrongdoing was thought to be indispensable to the restoration of the Chilean political community, truth would be regarded as an "absolute, unrenounceable value."[29] The need for an official account of past regime wrongdoing was based on the belief that the restoration of the political community could occur only if a shared account of the past existed. Since national identity presupposes a shared memory, the reduction in lies and in conflicting interpretations of the past is indispensable. Although truth telling would not necessarily lead to criminal prosecution, the disclosure of regime wrongdoing would itself be a form of punishment, since the reputation of former regime officials would be tarnished by the knowledge that the military regime had perpetrated human rights crimes. In effect, truth would serve both punitive and restorative purposes.

Finally, the government settled on the truth strategy because it was feasible. Advisors thought that it was more important to succeed in carrying out modest measures than to fail in implementing a just, comprehensive strategy. As José Zalaquett, a leading human rights lawyer and member of Chile's truth commission, points out, Aylwin was guided by the Weberian ethic of responsibility, which demands that the pursuit of moral goals should be judged in terms of consequences. "Political leaders ought not be moved only by their convictions, unmindful of real-life constraints," writes Zalaquett, "lest in the end the very ethical principles they wish to fulfill suffer because of a political or military backlash."[30] Chilean officials were aware that Argentina's pursuit of truth and justice had been problematic. Indeed, they had concluded that an important lesson of that transitional justice process was that

Chile should "stake out a policy it could sustain."[31] Accordingly, Aylwin was determined to pursue "truth and as much justice as possible" without impeding the restoration of democracy.

Aylwin's policy would be guided by two goals: the government would first seek to repair the damage inflicted by the military on Chilean society, and then it would establish measures to prevent the repetition of human rights abuses. The first goal would be pursued through truth telling, followed by official acknowledgment of regime abuses and symbolic reparations to victims. Legal accountability—defined as the quest for "as much justice as possible"—would be guided by prudential considerations. The goal of preventing future human rights abuses would be carried out through the consolidation of a democratic order and the cultivation of moral and cultural norms consistent with a humane, tolerant society.

The Search for Truth

A day after assuming office, Aylwin gave an inaugural address at Santiago's National Stadium—a location with much symbolic significance, since thousands of people had been detained there in the wake of the coup. Although he did not immediately announce a plan to reckon with past human rights violations, the president indicated that his government would seek to balance the quest for truth and justice with the need for forgiveness and reconciliation. Accordingly, he called for an ethic of responsibility that incorporated both the virtues of morality and the need for prudence.[32]

Two months into his presidency, Aylwin appointed an eight-member truth commission to investigate the nature and scope of the gross human rights violations of the former government. Headed by Raúl Rettig, a noted lawyer, the National Commission on Truth and Reconciliation was given nine months to issue a report describing the nature and scope of major human rights abuses perpetrated during the Pinochet era—that is, from September 11, 1973 until March 11, 1990. In carrying out its mission, the commission was restricted to investigating flagrant human rights violations, including kidnapping and arbitrary detention that had resulted in death or disappearance. Even though torture was assumed to be a widely used intelligence-gathering practice, the commission did not have authority to investigate torture itself, except as it had resulted in the death of victims. The sole mandate was to disclose killings and disappearances, not suffering and injustice. Moreover, since the commission had been created by presidential decree, it had no subpoena power to compel testimony or to cross-examine witnesses. As a result, the commission's investigation depended chiefly on the voluntary testimony of witnesses and data disclosed by human rights organizations.[33]

The commission delivered its report to Aylwin on February 9, 1991, and a month later he presented its major findings in a major televised address. He also sent a copy of the report to all victims' families with a personal letter. Aylwin knew that if healing and reconciliation were to result from truth telling, it was important to emphasize the report's "sacramental value." Accordingly, in presenting its key findings, the president acknowledged that the military government was responsible for gross human rights violations and that he, as head of state, was prepared to accept the culpability of the state and to seek to foster healing and restoration. Zalaquett, a member of the truth commission, observed that the president's symbolic actions in disclosing the commission report "went farther to promote healing in Chile than practically anything else."[34]

The nine hundred–page report sets forth four types of knowledge relating to the systemic abuses of human rights from the coup in 1973 until the restoration of democracy in March 1990. First, it describes the political context that gave rise to the military regime and the changing political environment in which crimes occurred. Second, it explains the nature and scope of the military regime's abuse of human rights. Third, it identifies the names and circumstances of persons who were killed or missing. Fourth, it describes and assesses the role of war tribunals and the behavior of civilian courts in responding to human rights crimes. Finally, it provides recommendations for repairing and preventing future human rights violations. One of the most informative elements of the report is the examination of how different sectors of society—such as the church, political parties, professional associations, the media, and the international community—responded to violations of gross human rights. The report also examines the significant personal, social, and psychological damage that torture, abduction, death, and disappearance inflicted on the families of victims.

The truth commission's most basic finding was that the military regime was responsible for carrying out a systematic campaign of political repression that relied on widespread atrocities. The report disclosed that 2,279 persons had been killed or had disappeared during the era of military rule.[35] Moreover, more than half (1,261) of the deaths and kidnappings occurred in 1973—that is, during the coup and its immediate aftermath—with the number of atrocities declining rapidly after this date. The commission report also identified another 641 potential victims of human rights crimes, but because of insufficient evidence was unable to make a final judgment about them.

Finally, the commission report offers two types of recommendations— those designed to repair the damage from human rights abuses and those designed to prevent the reoccurrence of these violations. To foster renewal and reparations, the truth commission called on the state and the entire Chilean populace to acknowledge and accept responsibility for the military regime's offenses and to offer moral and material reparations to help restore the human dignity of those who had been victimized by violence. Since state agents had perpetrated many human rights crimes, the report implies that the government should initiate the renewal and reconstruction of social and political relationships and contribute to the moral restoration of victims and their families. While material reparations are important, the truth commission report gives even greater priority to the moral reconstruction of society through the pursuit of truth, justice, forgiveness, and reconciliation. It observes that "the reparation process means having the courage to face the truth and achieve justice: it requires the generosity to acknowledge one's faults and a forgiving spirit so that Chileans may draw together."[36]

In January 1992, the Chilean government created the National Corporation for Reparation and Reconciliation in order to implement some of the commission's recommendations. Among other things, the corporation was charged with giving legal and financial assistance to victims' families and investigating cases of disappeared persons that the truth commission had been unable to solve.[37] Its other major task was to administer financial reparations to eligible beneficiaries.[38] Although reparations included fixed-sum payments as well as health and education benefits, the major compensation was a monthly pension of about $375, or roughly the median monthly wage in Chile, which was to be distributed according to provisions specified in the corporation's charter.[39] Interestingly, no medical or financial assistance was made available to the thousands of people who had been tortured.[40]

Aylwin's televised presentation of the commission report was arguably the most important address of his presidency. In the speech he acknowledged the commission's central finding that the State was responsible for widespread human rights violations and then went on to accept collective responsibility for the military regime's abuses. While noting that truth could not be imposed on society, the president nevertheless called on citizens to accept the truth commission's major finding that military authorities had committed gross human rights abuses in taking, consolidating, and sustaining political control. And even though many Chileans had surmised that the government had used significant force to combat political militants and revolutionary groups, the report offered convincing evidence of the widespread abuse of human rights. As Jorge Correa, the commission's executive secretary, noted, the release of the report resulted in a shift in the political discourse about Chile's past, since Chileans could no longer deny that the military regime had committed atrocities in the eradication of radical politics and in the maintenance of political order.[41]

In his address the president also stressed the moral unacceptability of human rights abuses perpetrated by state agents. To begin with, a humane, democratic society can never violate human rights in order to correct "the errors, excesses, or crimes that may have been committed previously."[42] In a democratic, constitutional order, state agents may never avenge injustices through illegal acts. And since war is itself subject to laws and moral rules, combating internal terror would not have justified torture, abduction, or the killing of prisoners. Of course, self-defense is permissible when domestic society is threatened from either internal terror or external aggression, provided it does not itself violate the moral norms that the state is sanctioned to uphold. In short, the state may never use illegal or immoral methods to advance legitimate goals.

Aylwin also stressed the importance of focusing on the future, especially on the moral reconstruction of society and the consolidation of democratic institutions. The president noted that if Chileans are to successfully rebuild their broken society, they will need to promote accommodation and reconciliation. Rather than digging deeper into the past and seeking to find blame, Chileans should focus on the restoration of their society. "It is time for pardon and reconciliation,"[43] declared the president in his address from the presidential palace—a truth visually reinforced by a tapestry hanging in the background depicting Jacob's reconciliation with Esau. More than symbolism, however, would be needed to overcome the deep alienation between political antagonists.

If political antagonists were to become reconciled, it was important to identify offenders and victims—to know those who were culpable and in need of pardon and those who were victims of injustice and called to forgive. Although I have suggested earlier that collective forgiveness is possible, Aylwin suggested that a collective pardon would not be decreed by the state. Instead, forgiveness needed to be viewed as a transaction between offenders and victims in which the former repented and the latter responded with empathy and generosity.[44]

Finally and most significant, the president emphasized the important role of the state in dealing with the past. In particular, he called for the acknowledgment of regime wrongdoing, the expression of public contrition, and for public atonement through reparations. Since public officials had carried out crimes, the state itself needed to assume collective responsibility. Accordingly, Aylwin claimed that he, as head of state, was authorized to call on the military to admit culpability, to express collective remorse, and to call for national healing. In addition, he asked the military and security forces that were involved in criminal wrongdoing to "recognize the pain they have caused and cooperate in healing the wounds."[45] The president's declarations were widely discussed in the media and were followed by similar expressions of contrition by leaders of conservative and moderate political parties. As the head of the commission's staff has noted, Aylwin's speech represented a major "sign of reconciliation."[46]

In sum, the Aylwin administration sought a middle ground between victims' demands for justice and the military regime's demand for amnesty. Fundamentally, the strategy for reckoning with past regime wrongdoing bypassed punishment in favor of political reconstruction and moral renewal based on a multidimensional process that included truth telling, public acknowledgment, and reparations to victims. Although public officials hoped for "as much justice as possible," they pinned their hopes on the restoration of victims and the political reconstruction of society's moral-cultural order through the acknowledgment of truth, contrition, and symbolic reparations to those who had been victimized by regime wrongdoing. They hoped that such moral-cultural initiatives would lead to the restoration of victims and to the moral renewal of political society. In short, the renewal of the political order was thought to depend not on trials and punishment but on the restoration of the nation's democratic traditions and political morality.

ASSESSING AYLWIN'S TRUTH AND REPARATIONS STRATEGY

Unlike Argentina's reckoning with its collective wrongdoing through trials, Chile pursued a transitional justice strategy that emphasized restoration and healing through truth telling. Rather than relying on a retribution strategy, Chile sought to confront past crimes and injustices through the disclosure and public acknowledgment of state wrongdoing, supplemented by symbolic reparations for victims.

The disclosure of the truth commission report was an important occasion, for it marked the moment when it was no longer possible to deny the military government's responsibility for widespread use of violence, torture, and kidnapping. Soon after the report was published, the National Congress passed a resolution unanimously commending the report. Subsequently, major political parties and leading institutions similarly acknowledged the truth about the military regime's crimes. The air force and police also officially acknowledged the report's general conclusions, while the army and navy condemned the findings as biased and incomplete. They did not deny the facts of widespread killings and disappearances but contested the report's interpretation of the conditions that had given rise to intense conflicts that threatened the stability of the political order. In particular, Pinochet challenged the report's interpretation of historical events preceding the coup and contemptuously dismissed the report's call for a total prohibition of repressive measures involving human rights violations. Rather than renouncing military force, Pinochet said that the report's plea for *nunca más* ("never again") should apply to the illegitimate policies of the Popular Unity government, not to the military authorities that had reluctantly intervened in Chile's political life. The armed forces, he suggested, had intervened only to restore public trust and political order after UP radicalism had led to political chaos.[47]

Did the discovery and disclosure of truth contribute to national reconciliation, as the Aylwin government had hoped? While most Chileans were widely in favor of the truth commission's work and praised Aylwin for his sensitive and symbolically important address on the report's findings, there were widely different perceptions about the effect truth telling had on reconciliation. For example, in one public opinion poll, taken soon after the report was distributed, nearly the same percentage of people believed that the report's findings did not contribute to national reconciliation as those that did.[48] Although it is very difficult to estimate the impact of the commission's findings and conclusions on the healing of the nation's political wounds, the disclosure and acknowledgment of the truth by Aylwin undoubtedly contributed to the restoration of public trust and to the renewal of a democratic political culture. By providing convincing evidence that the military and police had committed human rights crimes, the report contributed to the moral restoration of victims' families and to the undermining of the moral authority of the armed forces and police.

Although the commission did not provide a final, authoritative account of collective violence, it disclosed sufficient regime wrongdoing that called into question the moral standing of military authorities. Many Chileans had, of course, been grateful for the military's intervention in 1973, believing that such action had helped to avert civil war. But they were also appalled to learn that the military authorities had used excessive violence and morally inappropriate tactics to consolidate and maintain power.

Even though the truth disclosed by the commission was deemed useful by a large majority of Chilean political moderates, political partisans of the left and right were critical of the report, questioning either the fairness and adequacy of the historical interpretation or the completeness of the findings about killings and disappearances. As noted earlier, Chile became deeply polarized in the early 1970s under the Allende administration. Although the intervening years had greatly undermined the power of leftist political movements and had thereby greatly reduced political polarization, a major impediment to the political healing of the nation was the continuing antagonism and distrust between the radical right and the radical left.

Because their political goals and perceptions of the past remained virtually irreconcilable, their perceptions of the commission report were bound to reflect conflicting worldviews and opposing interpretations of the past. For example, leftist political groups and human rights associations, which sought to weaken the armed forces' political influence, have remained committed to bringing military leaders to justice. Conservative political groups, by contrast, believed that the armed forces not only saved the country from revolutionary communism but also carried out vital reforms, making Chile the most successful experiment in democratic capitalism in Latin America.

Thus, rather than fostering accommodation, the commission's truth telling tended to reinforce, at least in the short term, the political antagonism between political groups of the right and the left, especially between the armed forces and radical human rights groups. Victims' groups were disappointed that the truth commission had not been more successful in identifying per-

petrators and in disclosing the remains of missing detainees. Military authorities, for their part, felt that the commission had not fully appreciated the
chaotic conditions that existed in mid-1973—conditions that had forced
them to topple the Allende regime. As the consolidation of democracy continued under Aylwin and subsequent administrations of Eduardo Frei
(1994–2000) and Ricardo Lagos (2000–present), the antagonism between the
armed forces and leftist political groups persisted as well. These tensions
have been especially evident in the ongoing conflict over the prosecution of
Pinochet and other state officials culpable for human rights crimes.

In the early 1990s, as the composition of courts began to change, criminal
prosecution for past crimes became more feasible. A major victory for human rights activists occurred in 1993 when General Contreras and Brigadier
Espinoza, former leaders of Chile's DINA, were tried and found guilty. This
judgment was appealed to the Supreme Court, which upheld the guilty verdict for both officials. Another pivotal ruling by the High Court was its decision in 1999 that abductions and disappearances were not covered by the
amnesty law since such crimes were unresolved and therefore open cases.
This judgment meant that the courts could continue to investigate and prosecute the people allegedly responsible for kidnappings and secret killings if
the death of victims had not been certified.

The most dramatic development in the Chilean political saga on human
rights was the unprecedented detention in London of former President
Pinochet. Since democracy was restored in 1990, no political development
has rekindled the political antagonism between the left and right as the
Pinochet extradition request and subsequent efforts by Chilean judge Juan
Guzmán to bring him to trial. These judicial proceedings have forced Chilean
society to once again contend with the seventeen-year legacy of authoritarian military government. The Pinochet saga began in October 1998 when
Scotland Yard arrested the former president, who was recuperating from
back surgery in a London clinic. British law enforcement authorities issued
the warrant for his arrest in response to an extradition request by Spanish
magistrate Baltasar Garzón. The judge charged that since Pinochet was responsible for masterminding the torture and death of Spanish nationals, he
should be held criminally liable. After an eighteen-month detention involving many legal challenges and court judgments,[49] Pinochet was allowed to
return to Chile on medical grounds.

After returning to Chile in March 2000, however, Pinochet was pursued by
Judge Guzmán. He was first stripped of senatorial immunity by the country's
Supreme Court and then indicted by Guzmán—an action that was overruled
by the Supreme Court because he had not been deposed, as required by
Chilean law. After being properly deposed and given medical tests, Judge
Guzmán indicted Pinochet a second time, placing him under house arrest. This
time Santiago's Appeals Court confirmed the indictment but reduced the

charges from kidnapping and murder to concealment of the crimes. The quest for a trial finally came to an end in July 2001, when the Appeals Court ruled, based on medical tests, that Pinochet was too infirm to stand trial.

When Aylwin disclosed the commission report's findings in 1991, he indicated that the time had come to stop looking backward. "We should not waste all our efforts digging into wounds that are irreparable,"[50] he said. Yet in the aftermath of Pinochet's arrest, the wounds of the past, especially those related to missing victims, appeared to be more evident at the beginning of the new millennium than in 1990 when democracy resumed in Chile. Even with the closure of the Pinochet case, a growing number of court actions are underway as families seek information about, and retribution for, the death of loved ones. Clearly, for many Chileans the past is not past.

One of the most important initiatives to foster truth telling and political accommodation was the government's creation in 1999 of a negotiating forum among leading human rights attorneys, civic and religious leaders, and representatives of the armed forces to help uncover the fate of disappeared victims. Known as the Table of Dialogue (*Mesa de Diálogo*), this group carried out eight rounds of talks that culminated in an agreement on how to gather information about missing victims. Under the agreement, military and police personnel were encouraged to disclose information on the fate of more than one thousand known missing detainees, with the promise that the informers' identities would be kept secret to eliminate the fear of self-incrimination. As a result of this initiative, President Lagos announced in early 2001 that the government had obtained information on some 180 additional missing persons, considerably fewer than had been expected. Most important, since the bodies of many of these victims had been thrown into rivers or the ocean, the president indicated that it would be impossible to locate their remains. Thus, despite significant efforts to gather additional information on the disappeared in order to bring closure to the past, cooperative initiatives have generated little knowledge for victims' families.

FORGIVENESS IN CHILE?

As this overview of recent Chilean political history suggests, the restoration of democracy has resulted in some public disclosure and acknowledgment of the truth about the military regime's abuse of human rights. The state has expressed official remorse through public pronouncements and provided reparations to victims' families through financial, medical, and educational assistance. In addition, the moral standing of victims has been enhanced through deliberate state actions, including public recognition of victims, the reburial of some victims, and the establishment of memorials.[51] These symbolic acts by democratic authorities have been undertaken in order to encourage the restoration of communal bonds and the promotion of national reconciliation. While such measures have contributed to the moral restoration of victims and their families and to the restoration of democratic government, they have not succeeded in overcoming Chile's deep political fragmentation. Indeed, the truth and reparations process, ostensibly carried out to foster reconciliation, has resulted in little reconciliation and virtually no collective forgiveness. There are several reasons for this.

To begin with, Chilean people remain deeply divided over the meaning of their country's recent history. Despite the work of the truth commission, there is no shared memory about the era of military rule. Chileans remain deeply polarized over Allende's rule, the 1973 military coup, and the subsequent political repression imposed by the armed forces. At the end of the era of military dictatorship, two long-time observers of Latin American politics characterized Chile as a "nation of enemies."[52] And despite Pinochet's efforts to eliminate radicals from the Chilean political system, the nation remained deeply polarized as dictatorship gave way to democracy. Moreover, rather than reducing polarization, the government's effort to reckon with the past human rights violations only fueled political conflicts over the content and meaning of the past. Alexander Wilde, a Ford Foundation official in South America, has observed that "Chile remains haunted by divided memories of a recent history that includes the dictatorship and the sharp polarization that preceded it."

With the return of democracy, these competing and conflicting perspectives have become especially evident when important symbolic events occur, such as the London detention of Pinochet, the discovery of the remains of disappeared persons, or the trial of military officials for human rights crimes. Wilde, who terms these sporadic debates "irruptions of memory," argues that these conflicting collective representations of the past reveal mutually exclusive worldviews that result in a public discourse that is deeply fractured.[53]

Of course, one of the aims of creating an official truth commission was to discover and acknowledge the truth about the political violence of the Pinochet regime. The commission report did succeed in discovering and disclosing information about the state's abuse of human rights and, in particular, in identifying more than two thousand victims who were killed by military or police personnel. It was much less successful, however, in providing a comprehensive narrative about the nature, causes, and responsibility for the kidnappings, terror, torture, and secret killings. Thus, while the truth commission report may have achieved significant agreement about factual truth, it was much less effective in generating consensus about interpretive or moral truth. Indeed, despite the acceptance of many of the report's factual findings, the political left and political right have continued to hold different perceptions of the causes, justifications, and effects of the military's violence and repression. Since these different interpretive accounts are rooted in competing worldviews, a more comprehensive political accountability for past offenses is unlikely to emerge until a more integrated narrative of the past can be developed.

And the emergence of such a narrative is implausible without greater empathy and collective vulnerability—the second major reason for the absence of political forgiveness and reconciliation. If broken relationships are to be healed and fractured communal bonds are to be restored, political enemies must be willing to accept the humanity of their antagonists. For those who have committed offenses, this means that they must be willing to acknowledge culpability and express remorse. For those who have suffered from the offenses, they must be willing to view offenders as people. Following St. Augustine's dictum, they must hate sin but be prepared to accept sinners as human beings worthy of dignity in spite of their unjust behaviors. But Chilean antagonists have preferred righteous indignation to empathy.

Alexander Solzhlenitsyn once noted that if nations are to overcome their divisions and hatreds, they will have to collectively pursue a strategy of mutual repentance that can alone end "the cycle of self-righteousness and self-justification."[54] But Chilean groups have been unwilling to acknowledge collective offenses or to express remorse for the injustices and violence of the past. Human rights activists and leftist partisans, for example, have continued to hold the military and their conservative supporters solely responsible for the fall of a just, democratic, and humane regime under Allende and for subsequent political violence. On the other hand, military officials and their supporters have continued to believe that the coup, while regrettable, was a necessary action to save the nation from the evils of Marxism. Pinochet, who has said that the army should not ask for a pardon "for having fulfilled its patriotic duty,"[55] has indicated that Chileans should be grateful for the military's preventive action. Since major political antagonists remain committed to contradictory political worldviews and collective memories, they similarly remain divided over accountability and responsibility for past collective violence.

Another obstacle to accountability and forgiveness is the unwillingness of the military to acknowledge using unjust and immoral tactics, including covert abductions, secret killings, and torture. In combating leftist insurgency, the armed forces of major South American countries, influenced by Cold War counterinsurgency strategies, adopted a national security strategy that relied on covert unconventional operations. Dubbed "the national security doctrine," the counterinsurgency strategy relied on secrecy, intelligence gathering, and covert operations, which unlike conventional wars, were not accountable to the law.[56] Torture was used widely to gather information from detainees. To a significant degree, the tactics of this strategy reflected those used by the French security forces against the Front de Libération Nationale (FLN), the Algerian nationalist revolutionary movement demanding political independence. Although the national security doctrine was clearly inconsistent with the international laws on war, military leaders relied on it because they considered it an effective way of combating revolutionary terror and leftist urban insurgency. Most significant, the use of secret operations enabled state security agents to avoid accountability.[57]

A fourth reason for the limited level of forgiveness is the government's 1978 self-amnesty law. Forgiveness, as I have noted earlier in this chapter, involves the mitigation or cancellation of a deserved debt or punishment. To be morally valid, however, the forgiveness of debts must be offered by victims or their legitimate agents. A self-amnesty action, such as Chile's 1978 Amnesty Law, is not an authentic expression of forgiveness since the release from potential punishment is not related to guilt. Rather, the amnesty is granted to prevent accountability altogether.[58] Indeed, amnesty is granted before the truth is discovered and disclosed. Most important, such action has the effect of impeding authentic forgiveness since individual and collective offenders are not constrained to disclose knowledge about their own wrongdoing or to accept responsibility for their actions. Unlike the South African truth commission process, which made amnesty conditional on truth telling, Chile's self-amnesty law provides protection from prosecution and punishment even if perpetrators refuse to confess or to disclose information about missing victims.

Fifth, there has been little collective forgiveness because the Aylwin government and subsequent administrations have failed to make truth telling and reconciliation major priorities for Chilean society. The democratic government assumed that the disclosure and acknowledgment of truth based on the work of an official commission, coupled with modest symbolic reparations for victims and their families, would foster reconciliation. But unlike the South African model, which made the quest for truth a long (more than three years), public, and highly publicized process, the Chilean approach to truth telling was relatively short term and secret, never capturing the imagination of Chilean society. Thus, while the Aylwin administration acknowledged past collective offenses of the military regime, the public was not given an opportunity to confront and respond to the truth about collective crimes.

Finally and most important, the state's truth and reparations strategy failed to emphasize the need for mutual repentance and collective forgiveness as a means of restoring Chilean political morality. To a large extent the failure to emphasize these moral actions stems from the ambivalence of Chilean public officials about the pursuit of national unity and reconciliation through truth telling rather than through retributive justice. Since a significant portion of Chilean society continues to demand individual legal accountability for actions and policies taken during the era of military rule, government leaders have been reluctant to call for actions that limit legal retribution. As a result, rather than explicitly pursuing reconciliation through truth, reparations, and forgiveness, many Chilean public officials continue to hope for an unrealistic and impossible goal—namely, the restoration of national unity, political reconciliation, full accountability, and retributive justice.

Since the 1978 amnesty decree had pardoned all political violence between 1973 and 1978, the government recognized that honoring the existing statute was essential to the consolidation of democracy. Moreover, Aylwin recognized that a forward-looking strategy rooted in pardon for past offenses was crucial to the renewal of a political community. In his nationally televised speech on the commission report, he accordingly called on victims and their families to forgive offenders and to put the past behind them in order to focus on the moral, political, and social reconstruction of Chilean society. He said: "We should not waste all our efforts digging into wounds that are irreparable. . . . We cannot progress by digging deeper into divisions. It is time for pardon and reconciliation."[59] But rather than calling for political groups and state institutions to acknowledge their guilt for past collective offenses, Aylwin noted that forgiveness could not be imposed collectively since it could only arise from "repentance from one party and generosity from the other."[60]

Despite Aylwin's call for forgiveness, however, Chilean society has experienced little political or individual forgiveness or national reconciliation. While the president has acknowledged official wrongdoing and expressed contrition for the abuse of human rights, individual and collective offenders have not themselves accepted responsibility for offenses, nor have they publicly expressed repentance for their actions. Military and police officials have been unwilling to acknowledge that the violence against Allende partisans was contrary to moral and legal norms. Leftist political groups, for their part, have been unwilling to accept responsibility for the polarization and instability caused by Allende's radicalism or for the violence perpetrated by urban guerrilla groups. Given the lack of agreement on truth and the absence of contrition and empathy, antagonists have been reluctant to pursue reconciliation through forgiveness. Thus, rather than fostering accommodation and creating the preconditions for reconciliation, the government's public pursuit of truth telling has yielded little reconciliation and may have even led to increased polarization between the military and human rights militants.

More than a decade after the restoration of democracy, Chile remains a polarized society. The absence of political healing was especially evident in the aftermath of the Pinochet detention in London in 1998, when human rights groups became more vocal and persistent in their political demands for trials. To be sure, Chile's truth and reparations strategy has helped citizens to reckon with the effects of past regime violence and repression. But significant work still remains to be carried out in the healing of political wounds, the quest for national reconciliation, and the consolidation of a humane moral order. The continuing efforts to renew and restore Chile's civic society will of course involve participation by major political antagonists, including political parties and military institutions. But its success will also depend on other mediating institutions, especially the church, professional associations, educational institutions, labor organizations, and human rights and students' groups. Only when a humane, tolerant, and peaceful moral order is fully institutionalized will Chile's democratic transition be fully complete.

In the final analysis, the Chilean case illustrates the necessity but insufficiency of truth telling in overcoming the violence of a repressive regime. Although truth is a necessary condition in confronting the legacy of collective wrongdoing and in particular for encouraging individual and collective forgiveness, it is not a sufficient condition for reconciliation. The healing of individuals' psychological wounds and the restoration of social relationships and political bonds will of course depend on truth, but the disclosure of facts about past regime violence (objective truth) is not enough. If truth is to lead to healing, antagonists must themselves accept and acknowledge that a shared interpretation of the past will also be necessary. Only when antagonists have developed a shared narrative of the past can truth telling become a redemptive force in public life. Indeed, if moral truth cannot be developed, the disclosure of facts is likely to serve as much for healing as for the renewal and intensification of political conflict.

7

Intractable Politics without Truth or Forgiveness: The Case of Northern Ireland

My conclusion from reading the reports of twenty-five years of violence, from mass murder to petty arson to casual threats, is that both peoples have one thing in common and that is their dislike of each other.

—Steve Bruce, scholar of Irish politics[1]

One of the main reasons why violence was not much greater over the past twenty-five years has been the way that Christians and their Churches have chosen consistently to seek to cut cycles of vengeance by calling for, and practicing, non-retaliation and forgiveness.

—The Faith and Politics Group, a group of leading Irish Christians[2]

I submit that statements of remorse and pleas for pardon and expressions of forgiveness are necessary preludes to and essential concomitants of conflict resolution, but they are not sufficient; they are not effective without cessation of the wrongs and the hurts of conflict, without, in short, the change of behavior and the full purpose of amendment which Christian tradition has always held to be the defining condition of genuine repentance, and without the just changes of structures and institutions which are necessary for true reconciliation.

—Cardinal Cahal B. Daly, noted Irish Catholic clergyman[3]

A prevalent Western assumption is that the expansion of modernization will foster rationality, economic prosperity, and a more humane political system. Scholars have assumed that as societies become better educated and more self-sufficient, their need for God and religion will decline. According to conventional wisdom, what matters in political systems is prosperity and improving living conditions; core beliefs and identity are of secondary importance. But the experience of the post–Cold War era, marked by the conflicts in Bosnia, Kosovo, Chechnya, Kashmir, sub–Saharan Africa, and the Middle East, suggests that this belief is untenable. Indeed, rather than displacing culture and religion, the expansion of modernization and globalization has itself reinforced the longing for communal bonds rooted in shared moral values and cultural norms. Ironically, the growth of secularism has itself increased its opposite—namely, a longing for transcendent religion.

The contemporary political conflict in Northern Ireland illustrates the priority of the politics of identity over the politics of prosperity. Although Irish citizens have experienced significant economic and social change in the past half-century, the dominant political issue for the people of Northern Ireland continues to be the question of national identity. This issue—frequently defined as "The Irish Question"—is basically this: To whom does Northern Ireland belong, Britain or Ireland? Or stated in a more personal way, are the people of Northern Ireland Irish or British? The issue is politically intractable because national identity, unlike most other political problems, cannot be resolved through compromise, since one is a citizen of either one country or another, but not both.[4]

Like the conflicts in Argentina, Chile, and South Africa, the dispute in Northern Ireland has resulted in great human suffering. It has been estimated that since the resurgence of political violence in 1969, the conflict has resulted in more than 3,200 deaths and more than thirty thousand injured victims. But unlike the political conflicts in Chile and Argentina, which were precipitated by ideological disputes over the nature and role of government, the conflict in Northern Ireland, much like the apartheid conflict in South Africa, has concerned the nature of the political regime itself. The dominant issues focus on citizenship, political participation, and the structure of government. But whereas the South African dispute concerned a domestic issue—namely, the dismantling of apartheid and the establishment of a nonracial, democratic order—the Northern Ireland conflict centers on a transnational dispute involving the political identity of its 1.5 million residents. The so-called Irish Question is essentially a transnational political dispute: should Northern Ireland be a part of Ireland or a part of the United Kingdom? Since the conflict centers on political identity and religion, and since both identity and religion are rooted in historical antecedents and primordial affinities, the dispute is not easily amenable to compromise.

Given the complexity and intractability of the Northern Ireland conflict, the pursuit of peace has been difficult, and the achievement of a final political settlement has remained elusive. Despite significant accomplishments in the peace process, especially the signing and subsequent ratification of the Good Friday Agreement (GFA) of 1998, political order in Northern Ireland remains precarious. Little cooperation exists between Catholic nationalists and

Protestant loyalists, and modest progress has been made in reducing the political animosity and distrust between them. The challenge therefore remains how to reduce hatred and distrust between nationalists and loyalists and how to achieve a *modus vivendi* that is mutually acceptable to the antagonists. If a political settlement is to be realized, some accountability for past injustices and violence will be necessary. Nevertheless, while the official disclosure and acknowledgment of truth can contribute to public accountability and the restoration of trust, such measures will not alone heal the individual and collective wounds of past political conflict. If a permanent peace is to be established in Northern Ireland and trust is to be restored, some forgiveness and reconciliation will be necessary to overcome past wrongdoing. Of course, if antagonists are unable to devise and implement a power-sharing government, no amount of retributive or restorative justice will lead to community building.

In this chapter, I explore the limits and possibilities of political forgiveness in fostering a more peaceful and harmonious Northern Ireland. In the first part, I describe the nature of the conflict and provide a historical overview of some of the major events that have shaped the political conflict in Northern Ireland. In the second section, I sketch the rise and effect of political violence on the people of Northern Ireland, focusing on the conflict during "the troubles" from 1969 until 1998, when the GFA was signed. Given the persistent animosity between Catholic unionists and Protestant loyalists, I offer several alternative explanations for the intractability of this dispute. In the third section, I highlight some of the major developments in the peace process that culminated with the GFA. Although the multilateral accord was hailed as a major breakthrough in the peace process, the GFA framework provides at best a fragile structure for preventing violence and little impetus to political reconciliation. In the final section, I explore how the ideas of repentance and forgiveness might contribute to the transformation of Northern Ireland's moral-cultural system. Given the intractability of the political issues in Northern Ireland, political negotiations alone are unlikely to establish a durable political order between Catholic nationalists and Protestant unionists. What is needed is a reformation of values and attitudes so that vindictiveness, discrimination, and exclusion are replaced with forgiveness, fairness, and inclusion. Since forgiveness, remorse, and compassion are likely to be important dimensions of a reformed culture, Christians can play an important role in the remolding of contemporary culture.

NATURE OF THE CONFLICT

The seeds of the contemporary political conflict in Northern Ireland were sown in the early seventeenth century, when Britain, after trying to conquer

Ireland for centuries, succeeded in establishing a small agricultural settlement, or plantation, in the northern section of the island known as Ulster. The local natives resented being displaced from their land by British and Scottish settlers and carried out numerous unsuccessful rebellions to drive them away. The last great rebellion occurred in 1688, when the Ulster-Scots settlers, fearing an attack by Catholics, closed the gates of the city of Derry. Subsequently, King James I, Britain's Catholic king, sought entry into the city. When he was refused, he imposed a siege that lasted for nearly a year.

The siege was not broken until July 28, 1689, when the ships of William of Orange, Britain's new Protestant monarch, broke through to the besieged city, saving the defenders from imminent starvation and defeat. A year later the Ulster conflict between the Catholic natives and the Protestant settlers was decisively settled when the forces of William of Orange defeated those of King James II in the Battle of the Boyne on July 12, 1690. Given the historical significance of the siege of Derry and the Battle of the Boyne, both events have remained powerful historical symbols for Ulster Protestants. Annually, the Orange Order, the largest Ulster political movement in Northern Ireland, organizes parades on July 12 to celebrate their deliverance from Catholic rule.

The modern roots of Northern Ireland's political conflict date from the late nineteenth century when Irish nationalists began to demand greater political autonomy. In response to growing rebellions in the second half of the nineteenth century, Prime Minister William Gladstone declared that it was his government's intention to "pacify" Ireland by granting "home rule"—political autonomy in domestic affairs. Since Ulster Protestants were a political minority in Ireland, they strongly opposed home rule, which they feared would become a tool of religious and political oppression. Their strong desire was to remain a part of the United Kingdom—a desire symbolized by the signing of the so-called Ulster Covenant of 1912.[5] According to this declaration, its signatories pledged to use "all means which may be found necessary to defeat the present conspiracy to set up a Home Rule Parliament in Ireland." The Covenant was thus a religious-political pledge by Protestants of Ulster to oppose political self-determination.

The Partition of Ireland

The prospect for home rule led political forces in both the north and south of Ireland to become more politicized. Indeed, the campaign for home rule transformed Irish politics by causing Protestants to become a stronger, more unified, and more determined political movement while also encouraging the aspirations of revolutionary groups in the south. As the conflict between Protestants and Catholics expanded, violence increased in frequency and intensity. In the early twentieth century, civil war between northern Protestants and southern Catholics was only averted because of two developments—the outbreak of World War I that distracted antagonists from their own political conflicts and the British government's partitioning of the country in 1920.

The partitioning of Ireland was instituted by the British parliament with the passage of the Government of Ireland Act. According to this law, local and regional affairs were to be administrated by two distinct governments. A parliament in Dublin was to be responsible for the administration of local and regional affairs in the twenty-six predominantly Catholic counties in the south; a second parliament in Northern Ireland (at Stormont Castle, near Belfast) was to be responsible for the administrative affairs of six Ulster Protestant counties.[6] In addition, a Council of Ireland was to be established to coordinate the work of both governmental bodies. Finally, since both Ireland and Northern Ireland remained a formal part of the United Kingdom, each was to have elected representatives in the Westminster Parliament.

It is important to stress that the aim of the Government of Ireland Act was not to divide Ireland but to respond to conflicting political demands of Catholics and Protestants. The aim was to offer a temporary compromise in the hope that a permanent, peaceful resolution could be found at a later date. Partitioning was thus viewed as a temporary, stopgap measure: Catholics, who were demanding self-rule over the whole of Ireland, would receive limited political authority over most of the country, while Protestants, who opposed home rule and wished to remain within the British Empire, would receive qualified authority over Ulster.

The decision to partition Ireland was especially troubling to Irish nationalists. They believed not only that Ireland was entitled to full political independence but that the country should remain unified as a single state. While many Irish citizens were content with the new political arrangement of qualified sovereignty over most of the Irish territory, nationalists, led by the Irish Republican Army (IRA), were deeply opposed to this development. As a result they embarked on a campaign of political violence in order to place further pressure on the British government to modify its actions. In response to the continuing and intensifying political violence in the south, Britain signed a treaty with Sinn Fein, the political wing of the Irish Republican Army (IRA), granting political independence to the Irish Free State in 1921.

The Government of Ireland Act also troubled Ulster Protestants because they believed that partitioning would inevitably lead to the weakening of their historic ties with the British Crown. Nevertheless, Unionists, who had originally opposed home rule, eventually recognized that given the creation of a quasi-autonomous political community in Ireland's northern counties, they had no alternative except to accept responsibility for those administrative affairs that the British parliament had devolved to them. As a result, Unionists reluctantly began carrying out local responsibilities such as policing, education, and social services, but they resisted any measures that might strengthen their ties to the Irish Free State. Indeed, the growing demand by

Irish nationalists for a unified state only deepened their suspicions and resolve to remain a part of the United Kingdom.

Some observers have argued that the source of Northern Ireland's late-twentieth-century political conflict was the territorial partition of the island, but such a view is simply not compelling since the political, cultural, and economic tensions between Protestants and Catholics predate the division of Northern Ireland. Historian A. T. Q. Stewart has written that "whatever the 'Ulster Question' is in Irish history, it is not the question of partition."[7] Indeed, he suggests that partition, rather than causing and exacerbating a political conflict between religious "sects," may have helped to prevent a civil war. Partition came about because a minority in Ireland (the Protestants in Northern Ireland) asserted their right to dissent from the majority (the Catholics in the Irish Republic) by demanding continued union with the United Kingdom. In effect, the Protestants of Ulster have opposed becoming a part of a united Ireland because they fear the consequences of minority status in a united Catholic Ireland. At the same time, the Protestant majority in Northern Ireland, fearful of being absorbed by a united Irish Republic, has sought to maintain political control over public and private affairs in the north—a quest that has resulted in discriminatory policies against the Catholic minority. Thus, the Ulster problem is rooted in the fears of two political groups—the Protestant minority in a united Irish Republic and the Catholic minority in a Protestant-controlled Northern Ireland.

The Stormont Government

Although Catholics comprised only about one-third of Northern Ireland's population of 1.2 million in the 1930s and 1940s, Unionists established policies and institutions that ensured continuing Protestant control over the political, social, and economic life of the country. They achieved this control in part by maintaining electoral dominance over local and regional politics through the single-member district electoral system used in parliamentary elections as well as gerrymandering.[8] Since Catholics were dispersed throughout the six counties of Ulster, Protestants had a natural advantage in regularly electing a disproportionate number of members to Westminster.[9] Moreover, Protestants historically received a disproportionate share of the public-service jobs. For example, even though Catholics comprised more than one-third of Northern Ireland's population, in 1969 only 12 percent of the police force, the Royal Ulster Constabulary (RUC), was Catholic.[10]

The inequalities and discrimination that were practiced in private and public life in Northern Ireland did not derive from a deficient character or immoral values. Rather, discrimination and injustice were a by-product of the political antagonism and deep psychological distrust existing between the two groups. Thus, when Protestant Ulstermen gained control of local or regional governmental agencies they gave preferential treatment to their fellow believers, and when Catholic Republicans gained power, they, too, discriminated in favor of their coreligionists.[11] Protestant favoritism in public and private life was much more pervasive than Roman Catholic favoritism, not because Catholics were more moral but because Protestants had more political power and therefore more opportunities to exploit it.

In view of the continuing political and economic inequalities, a growing number of Catholics began challenging the Protestant monopoly of power and the discriminatory practices in housing, employment, and education. In 1964, a political movement, known as the Campaign for Social Justice, emerged that began to demand greater equality and fairness in housing and social services for Catholics. Three years later, the Northern Ireland Civil Rights Association (NICRA) was established to spearhead further human rights reforms. This initiative, modeled after the United States civil rights movement, led to widespread protests and marches. Some of the major changes demanded included "one man, one vote" in local elections, an end to gerrymandering, an end to discrimination in local government, prohibition of police detention without trial, and the disbanding of the "B-Specials," the part-time Protestant police force. While these initiatives resulted in a number of important reforms,[12] the success in bringing about some reforms only intensified the demands for greater social change. Most significant, the civil rights movement led to the undermining of the alliance between the British state and the political demands of the Unionists.

THE RISE OF VIOLENT CONFLICT

In August 1969, a riot broke out in Derry when a group of parading Protestants was attacked. This resulted in an immediate police crackdown that fueled rampant demonstrations and violence in other urban areas. The civil strife had its most destructive effect in Belfast, where major riots left seven people dead and destroyed many homes. As violence intensified, the United Kingdom government sent British troops to restore order.[13] Even though the presence of British troops provided the potential for increased security for Catholics, many Nationalists interpreted the introduction of armed forces as a further manifestation of continuing British imperialism and political oppression.

The Troubles (1969–1998)

Despite the growing presence of British military forces in Northern Ireland, the Stormont government was unable to quell the rising violence, especially the attacks by paramilitary groups. In 1972 alone, some 470 people were killed and 4,876 were wounded from these acts of terror. Because of the growing instability and violence, the United Kingdom suspended the Northern Ireland Parliament and imposed direct rule, governing through the secretary of state for Northern Ireland (a position in the UK cabinet). The aim of direct rule from Westminster was not to take over the governmental affairs of Northern Ireland permanently but only to restore public order and confidence in regional political institutions. Given the growing fears and distrust, direct rule became the only viable strategy for containing political violence.

A year after direct rule was imposed, Irish and British authorities developed a new political framework in Sunningdale, England, to facilitate power sharing among Catholics and Protestants. According to the so-called 1973 Sunningdale Agreement, a devolved parliament was to be elected, a power-sharing executive was to be established based on the distribution of parliamentary membership, and cooperation between the north and south of Ireland was to be encouraged. Although the accord ensured that changes in the constitutional status of Northern Ireland could be brought about only with the consent of its citizens, many Unionists nevertheless opposed the agreement. They did so partly because they resented the deliberate fostering of functional cooperation between Northern Ireland and the Irish Republic. Not surprisingly, the first experiment in power sharing collapsed after only five months, resulting in the resumption of direct rule by the Westminster Parliament. Predictably, this action further intensified the IRA's campaign against "British imperialism" and exacerbated the distrust and political antagonism between Unionists and Nationalists.

The governments of Ireland and the United Kingdom made repeated efforts during the 1975–1995 period to develop initiatives to facilitate the Northern Ireland peace process. None of these initiatives, however, succeeded in resolving the deep animosity and distrust existing between the Unionists and Nationalists or in developing structures that effectively reduced political violence. Indeed, Nationalists intensified their opposition to British forces, whose presence they viewed as a major impediment to the unification of Ireland. To dramatize their political demands, IRA combatants intensified their low-intensity war against the British, carrying out more deadly bombings.[14] Some of the spectacular IRA attacks included the 1979 killing of Lord Mountbatten, the Queen's cousin, and the bombing of the Conservative Party Conference at Brighton in 1984—an attack that nearly killed Prime Minister Margaret Thatcher and many of her cabinet members. At the same time, IRA prisoners staged hunger strikes in order to dramatize their political demands.[15]

It has been estimated that from 1969 to 1994 paramilitary forces killed 3,173 people (2,228 civilians and 945 security forces).[16] Most of this violence was perpetrated by the IRA, which was responsible for more than 1,700 deaths, a majority of whom were civilians.[17] According to Paul Arthur, since the late 1970s 2 percent of the population of Northern Ireland has been killed or injured by political violence. Given the small size of Northern Ireland, the pervasive terror and killings has had an impact on most Protestant and Catholic families.[18]

Despite the high level of violence, Northern Ireland's urban violence is not unique. Akenson, for example, notes that the crime rate in several major U.S. cities in the early 1970s was similar to the level of political violence in Northern Ireland.[19] What makes the Northern Ireland case noteworthy, however, is not the level of killings but rather the use of terrorism to advance change. The IRA's terror campaign has been extraordinary in its impact. Domestically, the random bombings and killings have had a devastating domestic social and psychological impact, and internationally, the media coverage of the terror has helped to gain sympathy for the political grievances of the antagonists, especially the demands of Sinn Fein.

Theories of Political Violence

What explains the relentless pursuit of a united Ireland by Catholic Republicans in Northern Ireland? And why have Protestant Unionists been equally committed to remaining in Britain? While numerous theories have been developed to account for the political animosity between Republicans and Unionists, four explanations are especially important: the nationalist thesis, the socioeconomic argument, political liberalism, and the ethnonationalist thesis.[20] While not one of the explanations is fully adequate to explain the persistence and intensity of the conflict, together they illuminate important facets of a complex, intractable dispute.

According to the nationalist thesis, political conflict in Northern Ireland is rooted in the colonial relationship between Britain and Ireland and can only be resolved when Britain withdraws fully from Ireland. Britain conquered and colonized Ireland and thereby compromised Irish identity. Emerging at the onset of the twentieth century, Irish nationalism demanded a separate Gaelic nation-state. The establishment of the Irish Republic in 1921 was a partial fulfillment of this vision, but Britain's partition of Ireland and its continued governmental involvement in Northern Ireland are evidence that the United Kingdom has not fully overcome its imperial past. This theory essentially explains the perspective of Sinn Fein.

The socioeconomic explanation views political conflict as a by-product of economic exploitation of Catholics by Ulster Protestants. As noted earlier, after home rule was granted to Northern Ireland in 1921, the Protestant majority created policies and practices that ensured their political and economic domination over the Roman Catholic minority. As a result of the discriminatory practices established by Protestants, a civil rights movement emerged in the late 1960s that led to increasing violence and, in turn, to the resumption of direct rule by Britain.[21] Although Irish Catholics have repeatedly condemned discriminatory policies and structured inequalities, the establishment of a more equitable social and political order, while desirable, is unlikely to satisfy Catholics. As Bruce notes, the core complaint is that Protestants "are in the wrong country," and this complaint is unlikely to change with increased social and economic justice.[22]

The third explanation, political liberalism, views the dispute over Northern Ireland as a result of passionate sectarianism. According to this theory, the intractable nature of the conflict derives from the priority given to group identity over the shared dignity of all people. Since Nationalists and Loyalists are influenced by their own communal and religious values to the neglect of universal, rational norms, the liberal perspective assumes that the development of a humane, peaceful society can only occur when antagonists' ideals are reformed. In particular, this means that the Nationalists' and Loyalists' political goals need to be more inclusive in scope and moderate in intensity, with politics becoming more like a hobby than a controlling ideology. Steve Bruce writes that the liberal solution to sectarian conflict is to persuade the protagonists to redefine their concerns so that "the ugly caterpillar of sectarianism is transformed into the beautiful and inoffensive butterfly of tradition."[23] But the idea that the conflict in Northern Ireland is due chiefly to misperceptions and the irrational pursuit of group politics is not persuasive, since the conflict over sovereignty is real, not illusory.

The fourth major explanation, the ethnonationalist perspective, regards the dispute as a conflict between two competing ethnic groups[24]—Ulster Unionists, who are British, and Irish Nationalists, who are Irish. These groups also differ in religious and linguistic preferences, cultural traditions, and political ideals: Unionists prefer British culture, view English as their primary language, desire to be a part of the United Kingdom, and are Protestant; Irish Nationalists, by contrast, prefer Irish culture, regard Gaelic as their national language, desire to be a part of a united Ireland, and are Roman Catholics. While the rise of ethnonationalism as a dominant force in Ulster politics is beyond the scope of this chapter to explain, it is sufficient for our purposes to note that religious affiliation has helped to sustain conflicting identities. Indeed, some scholars argue that religion has served as the fundamental cause of the conflict. According to Bruce, while economic and social differences have played an important role in Ulster politics, the defining element in the conflict has been religion, giving the dispute "its enduring and intractable quality."[25]

Since each of these theories illuminates important factors that have contributed to the persistence of political violence in Northern Ireland, no single explanation alone will suffice.[26] As John Hickey has wisely observed, "there is no single-causal explanation of the troubles which plague the society encompassed in the State of Northern Ireland."[27] Nevertheless, if one must select among the alternative theories, the most compelling explanation for the persistence of Northern Ireland's conflict is the priority given to political identity. The dominant issue is who belongs to the group and who does not—that is, who is "us" and who is "them." Unlike modern democratic politics, which emphasize individual human rights and personal economic prosperity, the politics of ethnonationalist societies give priority to cultural and religious fault lines, which, in turn, encourage fragmentation and disintegration rather than unity and integration. Thus, if Northern Ireland is to become a more harmonious and peaceful community, the sectarian moral-cultural system will have to be replaced by a more universalistic democratic political order that emphasizes human rights and personal responsibilities rather than communal identity.

PROMOTING CONFLICT RESOLUTION

The Peace Process

Beginning in 1980 the prime ministers of the United Kingdom and Ireland began holding periodic Anglo-Irish summits in order to promote cooperation between the two states and in particular to assist in the resolution of the Northern Ireland conflict. These bilateral negotiations culminated in the 1985 Anglo–Irish Agreement, which confirmed the willingness of both states to help resolve the "Ulster problem." According to the accord, the two governments committed themselves to foster North–South cooperation and to seek to undermine the paramilitary threat. Although the agreement reaffirmed the principle that the status of Northern Ireland could only be changed with the consent of the people of Northern Ireland, Unionists, nevertheless, were adamantly opposed to the accord. They opposed the agreement because negotiations had been undertaken without their participation and also because the Irish government had been given a role in some domestic affairs of Northern Ireland. For their part, Nationalists were divided in their response. Moderate constitutionalists, led by John Hume and his Social Democratic and Labour Party (SDLP), supported the accord because they believed that cooperation between the two governments was essential to a peaceful resolution to the conflict. Republicans, those who supported Sinn Fein[28] and its outlawed military wing, the Provisional IRA, opposed the accord because they believed that Anglo–Irish cooperation could weaken the Irish government's resolve to unify the island.

In the early 1990s, SDLP leader John Hume and Gerry Adams, the head of Sinn Fein, began secret talks in order to reconcile differences among Republicans. They announced their unprecedented dialog in 1993, declaring that "the exercise of self-determination is a matter for agreement between the people of Ireland." At roughly the same time Irish Taoiseach (prime minister) Albert Reynolds and British prime minister John Major began holding important secret negotiations on the fate of the Northern Ireland conflict.

These talks culminated in an Anglo–Irish accord in December 1993 that reaffirmed the centrality of self-determination and consent in seeking a peaceful resolution to the conflict in Northern Ireland. According to the Downing Street Joint Declaration, the principle of self-determination implied that the Irish people had a right to self-government, while the principle of consent implied that self-determination could be exercised only with the expressed approval of a majority of the people of Northern Ireland.

Earlier the British secretary of state for Northern Ireland, Peter Brooke, declared that the British government "had no selfish economic or strategic interest in Northern Ireland." This was an important statement designed to pacify Republicans, who claimed that British involvement in Northern Ireland represented a continuation of past imperial policies. In effect, the admission was designed to remind all the people of Ireland, but especially Northern Ireland, that the future constitutional status of Ulster would not be determined by British designs but by the desires of the people of Northern Ireland. At the same time, the statement was an astonishing admission, for Northern Ireland had been, and continued to be, a part of the United Kingdom.[29]

One of the most important developments in the peace process occurred in August 1994 when the Provisional IRA announced a cease-fire.[30] In response to this development, the Ulster Defense Association (UDA), a Protestant paramilitary group, announced that it was suspending its paramilitary operations. These cease-fires contributed significantly to an improved negotiating climate, and culminated in December 1994 when representatives of Sinn Fein and the British government met officially for the first time. Soon thereafter, British officials also carried out discussions with Unionist political representatives. As a result of these talks, Britain ended routine army patrols and began to reduce the size of its military force in Northern Ireland. In addition, the British government announced that it would pardon a number of Catholic and Protestant prisoners who had only served half of their sentence.

Another important development in the peace process occurred in February 1995, when the British and Irish governments set forth two "framework documents" designed to guide future negotiations. One was a joint governmental declaration that established guidelines for structuring Anglo–Irish negotiations and for promoting cooperation between the north and south of Ireland and also between the Republic of Ireland and the United Kingdom. The second statement outlined devolution principles for carrying out negotiations between Nationalists and Unionists. In addition, the documents called for a Northern Ireland Assembly, elected by proportional representation; an end to the Irish constitutional claim to Northern Ireland; increased cooperation between the British and Irish governments; and a reaffirmation that changes in the constitutional status of Northern Ireland would require the consent of Northern Ireland's political parties, the people of Northern Ireland, and the UK Parliament.

Using the "framework documents" as a foundation, the British government attempted to get negotiations underway in mid-1995. Since Britain demanded that the IRA begin surrendering (decommissioning) its weapons as
a precondition for participation in the peace negotiations, Sinn Fein was not
a part of the emerging peace process.[31] According to Major, Sinn Fein would
be invited to participate in the multiparty talks only after the IRA made a
commitment to "progressive disarmament" and embarked on a "verifiable
process of decommissioning." To help resolve this stalemate, Britain and Ireland established an international commission, headed by U.S. Senator
George Mitchell, that would explore the feasibility of achieving a verifiable
decommissioning and advise whether paramilitaries were committed to this
goal. The Mitchell Commission concluded that rather than making disarmament a precondition for participation in the peace process, negotiations
should be based on a commitment to democratic principles and nonviolence.[32]

The Irish government welcomed the Mitchell report. Major, however, rejected the proposal, indicating that the simultaneous pursuit of decommissioning and talks was unacceptable. To dramatize its dissatisfaction with the
British government's intransigence on decommissioning, the IRA ended its
cease-fire with a large bomb explosion in east London—a terrorist act that
killed two people and destroyed property worth some $140 million. In spite
of the IRA's terrorist acts, the British and Irish governments were determined
to move the peace process forward. They established new ground rules for
all-party negotiations, including a three-part structure for the negotiations,[33]
and selected Mitchell as the overall chairman of the talks. The all-party negotiations began in June 1996 with representatives from nine political parties
not including Sinn Fein, which had refused to restore an IRA cease-fire. After a slow start, the negotiations languished until mid-1997, when the new
Labour Party government of Tony Blair made the peace process a high priority. With the increased commitment of Prime Minister Blair and the periodic support of U.S. president Bill Clinton, the talks intensified in late 1997,
culminating in a successful peace settlement in April 1998.

The Good Friday Agreement

Mitchell, the conference chairman, established a deadline (April 9, 1998)
for concluding the peace negotiations. Of the eight major political groups involved, Sein Fein, led by Adams, and the Ulster Unionist Party (UUP), headed
by David Trimble, proved to be the most implacable opponents. Two days
before the April deadline, the UUP rejected the sixty-five-page draft accord.
When the negotiations were about to collapse, Blair flew to Belfast to rescue
the conference. For his part, Clinton called the Irish Taoiseach and the British
prime minister to offer his assistance and later pleaded with Trimble and

Adams, the leaders of the two major opposing political groups, to seek accommodation. After being ensured that their respective concerns would not be ignored, the two antagonists agreed to accept the accord. The historic GFA involved a number of major elements. Constitutionally, it affirmed that Northern Ireland remained a part of the United Kingdom, while calling on the British and Irish governments to disavow claims to Northern Ireland (by repealing, respectively, the Government of Ireland Act and Articles 2 and 3 of the Irish constitution). Institutionally, a North–South Ministerial Council was to be established to promote socioeconomic cooperation between the Irish Republic and Northern Ireland, and periodic British–Irish Intergovernmental Conferences were to be held in order to promote bilateral cooperation between Britain and Ireland in such areas as transport, agriculture, environment, culture, health, and education. In addition, the GFA called for the early release of prisoners from groups fulfilling their cease-fire pledge and for the establishment of an independent commission on decommissioning to ensure the disarmament of all paramilitary groups. According to the agreement, the GFA was to become effective after citizens had approved it. Thus, after people overwhelmingly approved the accord in separate referenda,[34] the power-sharing government was formed in mid-1998.

Assessing the GFA

The GFA did not resolve the political animosity between Protestants and Catholics because little effort was given to resolve historic differences between the two political antagonists. Rather, the aim was to establish a new political framework that would inhibit violence and lead to the establishment of a constitutional order to protect the rights of all people. The goal was not to achieve justice but to create peace through the creation of a governmental structure that allowed Nationalists and Unionists, Republicans and Loyalists, to pursue their respective political objectives without violence. In effect, the aim was to encourage antagonists to learn to live "in disagreement but in dialog with each other."[35]

While acknowledging that violence had left a legacy of great suffering, the GFA suggested that the best way to honor victims of political violence was to make a "fresh start." Such a beginning should be based on a commitment to democratic decision making and the pursuit of reconciliation, tolerance, trust, and the defense of human rights without necessarily apportioning blame for past crimes. In short, while recognizing that substantial differences continued to exist between "equally legitimate political aspirations," the accord established a framework by which the antagonists could pursue conflict resolution through peaceful, democratic procedures.

The GFA is a significant development in the annals of modern Northern Irish history because it establishes a multiparty government among antagonists who have renounced violence and accepted democratic principles as authoritative. Of course, whether the antagonists can reform their cultural traditions and moral values in order to create and sustain a humane, participatory decision-making process will be determined in time. What is clear is that the GFA alone is not sufficient to ensure trust and social solidarity. The legacy of victimhood is too deeply entrenched in the social and cultural patterns to be transformed overnight by the establishment of a new peace accord. But the establishment of a power-sharing structure provides the basis by which the process of cultural and social transformation can begin. Political scientist Arthur has noted that the GFA provides an opportunity to test whether antagonists can learn to cooperate and whether "the Western political tradition can reshape its myths and produce a process of reconciliation, forgiveness, and healing sufficient to transcend the villainy of its past."[36]

In previous chapters, I have emphasized the need for truth telling and accountability in pursuing authentic political reconciliation and the restoration of social trust. But when distrust and enmity are deep and pervasive, the pursuit of truth not only may be impossible but may impede the process of political healing. Accordingly, the Northern Ireland peace process seeks to create a political foundation without necessarily resolving conflicting memories. Indeed, the GFA avoids history and memory altogether. Negotiators could have followed the South Africa model by establishing an official truth commission that would have offered amnesty to people who fully disclosed wrongdoing. Reconciling different historical interpretations of four centuries of Anglo–Irish history would have been a difficult, if not insurmountable, task. Indeed, the quest for an authoritative resolution of conflicting historical memories would have undoubtedly exacerbated the conflict, since such a quest would have intensified political rivalries and disputes. In short, since memory has itself been a source of Northern Ireland's political problem, the negotiators decided to emphasize peacemaking without regard to past crimes and injustices.

It is also significant that the GFA did not seek to address accountability and retribution for past wrongdoing. Rather, it released most paramilitary prisoners in order to strengthen communal solidarity and foster reconciliation.[37] Although this decision was strenuously opposed by some, especially those who had been direct or indirect victims of violence and raised genuine moral concerns about the seeming disregard for justice, political actors and peace organizations justified this action as a necessary step in creating a new, forward-looking peace process. For example, the Faith and Politics Group, an interdisciplinary task force of religious leaders, argued that overcoming a bitter, violent past required balancing "the claims of punitive justice, of mercy and forbearance, of truth," with the requirements for promoting "the common good and peaceful democracy."[38]

One of the major barriers to the GFA agreement was the issue of decommissioning. The agreement was signed with the understanding that Sinn Fein would become part of a new government, provided the IRA continued its cease-fire and proceeded to put its formidable weapons arsenal "beyond use," with an international inspection body certifying such decommissioning. When the IRA refused to comply with its decommissioning promise, Northern Ireland's First Minister David Trimble threatened to resign and bring about a collapse of the power-sharing government. The resignation became unnecessary, however, when the British government reimposed direct rule after learning in October 2002 that Sinn Fein government officials had shared government intelligence with the IRA.

Peace without Forgiveness or Reconciliation

The peace process that culminated in the GFA was based on a quest for a political framework that would allow opposing political groups to share governmental authority without necessarily resolving the fundamental question of the constitutional status of Northern Ireland. The aim was not to settle constitutional issues or to confront past wrongdoing by determining culpability for past violence; rather, the GFA was simply a prudential agreement to create a power-sharing government so that political antagonists could live together while holding radically different worldviews and espousing mutually exclusive political goals. Nevertheless, since the accord established a *modus vivendi* among political enemies, it provided a basis for the promotion of civic order and social trust. Terence McCaughey writes: "[W]hat was achieved by the Good Friday Agreement of 10 April 1998 was not forgiveness, much less reconciliation. What was achieved was an agreement to disagree. . . . Forgiveness will take longer, and reconciliation longer still."[39]

Unlike Argentina, Chile, and South Africa, where truth commissions provided the basis for the reconstruction of political community, the Northern Ireland peace process has avoided truth telling altogether.[40] Undoubtedly, the reason for the absence of truth telling was the continuing enmity and distrust among major political groups. Indeed, given the lack of consensus over the future constitutional fate of Northern Ireland, the major goal has not been political healing or communal reconstruction, as was the case in the three other cases. Rather, the aim has been to construct a decision-making structure that is acceptable to all major political actors and that fosters public order.

IS POLITICAL FORGIVENESS POSSIBLE?

I have argued that forgiveness provides a means of confronting and overcoming past regime wrongdoing and politically motivated crimes. I have suggested that when political conflicts are intractable, negotiations are unlikely to lead to peaceful resolution. Indeed, such conflicts tend to fuel deep animosity and distrust that frequently exacerbate political violence. When such conditions exist, the normal processes of participatory conflict resolution are broken down and are replaced by violence fueled by vengeance. Cardinal Cahal Daly has observed that when confronting intractable conflicts, like Northern Ireland's, "anger can be countered only by a genuine offering of forgiveness."[41] While political forgiveness is a rare and difficult act, especially when individual and collective offenders are unwilling to confront their culpability or to express empathy toward enemies, it is nonetheless an option worthy of consideration. Clearly, forgiveness is a last step in the conflict resolution process.

Politics is the normal process by which participatory regimes resolve major systemic disputes. When society is deeply fractured, however, as is the case in Northern Ireland, majoritarian decision-making procedures are unlikely to be sufficient to resolve disputes. While the GFA is a significant achievement in that it establishes a fragile power-sharing framework, the hard work of communal development has yet to be realized. Such a task will require overcoming entrenched hatred and pervasive distrust and promoting communal solidarity between groups. If such an undertaking is to ultimately succeed, it will necessitate radical behavioral and attitudinal changes. In effect, the values and norms of civil society must be reformed. Although government can contribute to the cultural and moral reformation of society, the renewal of civic life will ultimately depend on mediating, nongovernmental institutions, such as schools and universities, professional associations, neighborhoods, religious groups, and churches. Such nongovernmental organizations can play an important role in reforming moral values, attitudes, and practices that are conducive to the protection of human rights and the promotion of public justice.

Churches and Forgiveness

The moral language of repentance, forgiveness, and reconciliation is especially appropriate in Northern Ireland since a large number of its people are identified as Christians—a people who believe that divine forgiveness of sins is the basis for moral rehabilitation. Because God forgives individuals freely and unconditionally, believers are called to express compassion, mercy, and forgiveness by following the model set by the Heavenly Father. In effect, Christianity is a religion that gives priority to individual and communal forgiveness. Although forgiveness and reconciliation are not uniquely Christian concepts, Christianity's emphasis on compassion and forgiveness gives believers a unique opportunity to apply these moral virtues in public affairs. Justice is also an important biblical theme that needs to be nurtured, but when communities are unstable and violent, the challenge is not only to pursue justice but also to restore public order.

Generating a more peaceful and humane society will require important changes in people's attitudes and behaviors as well as the cultural and social norms that sustain existing patterns of behavior. In particular, the development of a more coherent, trusting society will necessitate a transformation in the exclusionary cultural norms that characterize Northern Ireland's "identity politics." Developing cultural norms that are more universal and inclusive will necessitate greater emphasis on human rights and individual responsibilities. If the moral-cultural order is to be reformed, churches can play an important role in teaching and modeling values and practices conducive to a humane civil society. In particular, churches can contribute to the moral reformation of culture by encouraging confession, repentance, and forgiveness. In addition, Christians can contribute to this task as individuals by modeling values that are conducive to social peace and communal harmony.

If churches are to contribute to the peace process, ecclesiastical leaders must use their authority as moral teachers to challenge and guide their members as to how they should carry out their civic responsibilities. The task of church leaders is not to provide solutions to political and social problems but to help structure moral debate about public affairs—that is, to bring relevant moral norms to bear on political and economic life. If churches were to carry out this task more faithfully, they would no doubt meet significant resistance from their members, but they would also increase the prospects for the reformation of cultural and social norms.

Christians can play an important role in this transformational task by calling attention to the nonexclusionary nature of the Christian religion and by practicing empathy and compassion. Most important, they can encourage an attitude of contrition and promote acts of repentance. At the same time, Christians can and should apologize for past collective wrongdoing. In 1994, the Archbishop of Canterbury, George Carey, powerfully illustrated the important role of Church leaders' remorse. In a sermon in Dublin he said: "As an English Churchman, I am aware of just how much we English need to ask forgiveness for our often brutal domination and crass insensitivity in the eight hundred years of history of our relationships with Ireland."[42] A year later, Cardinal Daly of Northern Ireland responded to the important and courageous words of Archbishop Carey with a similar expression of public apology. In a homily in Canterbury Cathedral on January 22, 1995, Daly said:

On this occasion of the visit of an Irish Roman Catholic Primate to Canterbury Cathedral, I wish to ask forgiveness from the people of this land for the wrongs and hurts inflicted by Irish people on the people of this country on many occasions during our shared history, and particularly in the past 25 years. I believe that this reciprocal recognition of the need to forgive and to be forgiven is a necessary condition for proper Christian and human and indeed political relationships between our two islands in the future.[43]

Although church leaders' apologies appear to have had a limited effect on the political process itself, their declarations have been important to the ongoing peace process by encouraging other leaders and groups to take public responsibility for wrongdoing. Soon after Archbishop Carey issued his apology in Dublin, for example, Gusty Spence, a former Loyalist paramilitary leader, apologized for the killing of innocent victims when announcing a Loyalist cease-fire in October 1994. Speaking on behalf of the Combined Loyalist Military Command, Spence offered "the loved ones of all innocent victims over the past 25 years abject and true remorse."[44] In mid-2002, the IRA issued an unprecedented public apology for killing "noncombatants" as part of its military strategy. In its apology, issued on the thirtieth anniversary of the "Bloody Friday" terror attack in Belfast that left nine people dead and many others seriously wounded, the IRA declared that while it had not intended to injure or kill noncombatants, many civilians had been killed or injured nonetheless. Accordingly, the IRA offered its "sincere apologies and condolences" to victims' families. The IRA declaration also noted that "the future will not be found in denying collective failures and mistakes or closing minds and hearts to the plight of those who have been hurt." Instead, calling attention to the need for "equal acknowledgment of the grief and loss of others," the statement observed, "on this anniversary, we are endeavoring to fulfill this responsibility to those we have hurt."[45]

Although some leaders have responded cynically to such apologies, the public expression of contrition is a vital precondition to political forgiveness. Without an acknowledgment of individual and collective wrongdoing or a public admission of remorse, victims are unlikely to express empathy toward offenders or to seek a reduction or absolution of offenders' justified punishment. Even though repentance is not a necessary precondition for divine forgiveness, contrition is crucial in overcoming the harmful effects of serious crime and violence. It is essential because it facilitates the development of an alternative moral discourse rooted in mutual respect and empathy that can help renew and restore social trust. Still, it is important to emphasize that contrition and apologies are only the beginning of a long and difficult journey in reconstructing the moral fabric of a broken society.

Christians can also give witness to biblical norms of mercy, reconciliation, and forgiveness. Such is the example of Gordon Wilson, a Methodist, who lost his twenty-year-old daughter, Marie, to a craven terrorist act by the IRA in 1987. The bombing at Ennskillen, a country town seventy miles west of Belfast, was carried out during a Veterans' Day memorial, leaving eleven dead and sixty-three others injured.[47] Instead of calling for vengeance, from his hospital room, Wilson called for reconciliation and forgiveness. On the day that Marie died, Wilson told a reporter, "I have lost my daughter, but I bear no ill will. I bear no grudge." He also said that he would pray for those responsible for his daughter's death. Because of Wilson's call for healing in the aftermath of the bombing, Protestant paramilitaries were dissuaded from carrying out retaliatory acts. After he was released from the hospital, Wilson embarked on a personal campaign for Protestant–Catholic reconciliation. As a public recognition of his important work, Irish Taoiseach Reynolds made Wilson an honorary member of the Irish Senate in February 1993. When he died several months later, tributes and commendations poured forth throughout Ireland for his courageous moral witness.

Obstacles to Forgiveness and Reconciliation

Despite the prevalence of Christian values in Ireland, political groups have been reluctant to apply Christian virtues such as compassion, contrition, repentance, forgiveness, and reconciliation to the political process. Several factors account for this: To begin with, churches have historically been part of the problem in Northern Ireland. It is important to stress that while the Christian religion provides important moral resources to sustain community and to overcome wrongdoing, churches have also exacerbated social and political divisions within society. To be sure, Roman Catholics and Protestants share many core religious beliefs on such theological topics as salvation, redemption, human sin, and divine forgiveness. Nevertheless, significant social, cultural, political, and institutional differences have helped to sustain deep distrust between the two religious groups. Since Protestants and Catholics have tended to live in segregated, self-contained communities, each with its own schools, churches, and political organizations, sectarianism has thrived and intensified social differences and distrust. As a result, religious beliefs about grace, compassion, forgiveness, and reconciliation are rarely incorporated into social and political discourse. Indeed, the animosity and distrust between political antagonists have been so deep and pervasive that the potentially healing balm of religious beliefs has been neglected if not undermined by sectarian political dogma. In short, rather than fostering shared beliefs and practices, religion has been used to divide people. Such separation has in turn reinforced conflicting political goals.

A second impediment to empathy and forgiveness in Northern Ireland has been the problematic role of memory. Since memory is an essential requirement in sustaining individual and collective identity, maintaining a humane civic society will depend in part on historical myths and shared ideals. The challenge in building and sustaining a civil society is to foster a memory that is inclusive and adaptable to conflicting perceptions. In Northern Ireland, history has been used as a tool of conflict by helping to ossify memory and to sustain opposing worldviews. Although the major source of political conflict concerns the constitutional fate of Northern Ireland, the Nationalist-Unionist dispute has been sustained by perceptions of injustice and in particular by memories of victimhood. For Republicans, Catholics have been victims of oppression and exploitation by the British government and Loyalist paramilitaries; for Loyalists, by contrast, Protestants have been victims of terrorism and unjust killings by the IRA. Indeed, the deep animosity and distrust between political antagonists is rooted in the conflicting memories of injustice.

The problematic nature of memory is especially evident when groups hold radically different perceptions of past events and parties are unable to achieve consensus about the nature and responsibility for past wrongdoing. Such is the case with "Bloody Sunday," January 30, 1972, when British troops killed fourteen Roman Catholic civil rights protestors in Londonderry. Although an investigation carried out by Britain's chief justice, Lord Widgery, exonerated the troops and placed the blame on the civilian protestors, Catholics have never accepted the commission's findings. When new information became available about the 1972 incident, prime minister Tony Blair reopened the case in 2000 by establishing a new commission of inquiry, headed by Lord Saville. Since this limited investigation is likely to take three to four years and cost up to $200 million, a truth commission over all political violence during the troubles would likely be a never-ending task. Clearly, the quest for an official account of past wrongdoing is not a realistic strategy. But even if it were feasible, it is unlikely that a commission could develop an official account of past wrongdoing that would be deemed authoritative by both Unionists and Republicans.

Perhaps the only way forward is to seek to de-emphasize the record of past crimes and injustices and to focus on the present challenges of generating consensus about political goals and procedures and cultivating moral norms that are conducive to a humane communal life. To some extent, this is the approach taken in the GFA model. But this approach is clearly a second-best strategy. Although it provides a framework for public order, by neglecting accountability for past political offenses both victims and offenders are deprived of the possibility of working toward authentic reconciliation. Political offenders are deprived of the opportunity to confront their culpability and express remorse, while victims are deprived of the opportunity to express compassion and forgiveness. In effect, by establishing a peacekeeping structure, the GFA fosters a negative peace, but by failing to address culpability and injustice the accord impedes the development of a positive peace rooted in the restoration of humane communal ties.

A third, related reason for the lack of forgiveness is the prevalence of victimhood—that is, the exclusive concern with the suffering and oppression of one's own group at the hands of political antagonists. There can be little doubt that the political violence during the troubles had widespread effect on the entire population of Northern Ireland. In 1997 the British government appointed a Victims Commissioner, Sir Kenneth Bloomfield, to examine the nature and suffering of victims in Northern Ireland. In his report, titled "We Will Remember Them," he found "some substance in the argument that no one living in Northern Ireland through this most unhappy period will have escaped some degree of damage."[48]

The celebration of victimhood is problematic in political society, however, because it leads groups to focus solely on their own historical traumas and to disregard the suffering of others. And when groups become totally self-absorbed by their own hurts and injustices, they are likely to lose perspective about the suffering of others. Victimology is therefore harmful because it leads to an "egoism of victimization" that leads people to become callous and indifferent toward others. As John Mack has noted, "ethno-nationalist groups that have been traumatized by repeated sufferings at the hands of other groups seem to have little capacity to grieve for the hurts of other peoples, or to take responsibility for the new victims created by their own war-like actions."[49] Given the prevalence of victim-centered political discourse, Arthur observes that Northern Ireland is a society without empathy.[50]

Finally, applying norms of repentance and forgiveness has been difficult because the dispute is not easily amenable to moral decision making. Since the conflict centers on the constitutional fate of the land and people in the north of Ireland, the issue is not subject to compromise. And while the moral attributes of compassion, remorse, repentance, and forgiveness have an important role in healing political communities in the aftermath of moral offenses, such virtues have little role in the resolution of zero-sum conflicts like the territorial issues of Northern Ireland. The fundamental issue remains unchanged: will Northern Ireland continue as part of the United Kingdom (as Unionists demand) or will it become part of a united Ireland (as Nationalists demand)? Not one of the major political organizations has been willing to acknowledge wrongdoing. Indeed, rather than viewing themselves as partially responsible for the intractability of the conflict, antagonists have perceived themselves purely as victims of each other's offenses. Since antagonists have regarded past behaviors as morally justified, neither party has seriously considered formal apologies or expression of institutional remorse, or explored the need for granting or receiving forgiveness. To the extent that terror and killings have been used against enemies, paramilitary groups have regarded such actions as necessary, either to advance goals or to inflict retribution. Accordingly, political groups have been reluctant to acknowledge culpability for wrongdoing.

To be sure, some Christians, as individuals and members of churches and social groups, have regularly condemned political violence and called for the promotion of a just and peaceful political order. For example, a group of Irish Christians concerned with the relationship of faith and politics has noted that churches have played an important role in inhibiting political violence. In their study of reconciliation and political healing in Northern Ireland, the Irish Faith and Politics Group observes that Christians have helped to reduce the incidence of violence because believers have chosen "to cut cycles of vengeance by calling for, and practicing, nonretaliation and forgiveness."[51] At the same time, the group acknowledges that churches have contributed to the political fragmentation and division of Northern Ireland and are therefore partially responsible for the suffering and injustice. It notes that Christians have fed sectarianism by defining denominational identity primarily in opposition to different religious traditions. As a result, the group avers that believers must acknowledge "the substantial contribution" that churches have made to the conflict.[52]

As I noted earlier, political forgiveness requires a number of preconditions, including consensus about wrongdoing, the admission of culpability by offenders followed by the expression of remorse and the expression of compassion and empathy by victims. Regrettably, political antagonists in Northern Ireland have failed to fulfill these requisite conditions. Not only have Unionists and Nationalists remained committed to conflicting political goals, but they have made little progress in developing a humane culture. Because each major group has regarded its cause as morally just, they have refused to compromise their objectives or to acknowledge moral shortcomings in their goals and strategies. But until they do, it is unlikely that a just and secure peace will be established in Northern Ireland.

In sum, coming to terms with past collective violence has not been possible in Northern Ireland because the more basic issues of the nature and boundaries of political community remain unresolved. Fundamentally, the conflict in Northern Ireland centers on the constitutional fate of the six counties of Ulster, with Irish Roman Catholics demanding those counties become part of a united Irish Republic and Ulster Protestants demanding that land remain a distinct, independent territory of the United Kingdom. Since sovereignty is indivisible, the conflict is not subject to compromise. This explains the persistence, intractability, and destructiveness of the dispute. The Good Friday Agreement of 1998 was of course an important achievement in that it established a peace framework based on a willingness to renounce violence and to participate in a power-sharing government. But political opponents' irreconcilable goals remain, and until the question of political identity is resolved, the pursuit of moral politics based on truth, repentance, empathy, and forgiveness will be difficult, if not impossible. In the meantime, the people of Northern Ireland have achieved an important goal. They have agreed to renounce violence and to work peacefully and harmoniously in governing Northern Ireland in the hope that at some future time they will be able to settle the constitutional question.

8

The Promise of Reconciliation through Truth and Some Forgiveness in South Africa

If we are going to move on and build a new kind of world community there must be a way in which we can deal with a sordid past. The most effective way would be for the perpetrators or their descendants to acknowledge the awfulness of what happened and the descendants of the victims to respond by granting forgiveness, providing something can be done, even symbolically, to compensate for the anguish experienced, whose consequences are still being lived through today.

—Desmond Tutu, leading South African church leader[1]

Telling the truth about the past alone does not heal; it might lead, in fact, to acts of violent vengeance. Remembering then becomes a fanning of the embers of a dying fire so that it bursts into flame again and devours us. The only way to redeem the past, to break the cycle of violence is not to take revenge, but to have the moral courage to forgive.

—John de Gruchy, professor of religious studies, South Africa[2]

This thing called reconciliation . . . if it means this perpetrator, this man who has killed Christopher Piet, if it means he becomes human again, this man, so that I, so that all of us, get our humanity back . . . then I agree, then I support it all.

—Cynthia Ngewu, mother who lost her son to the apartheid struggle[3]

Undoubtedly, the most innovative post–Cold War approach for confronting the crimes and injustices of former regimes is South Africa's "truth and reconciliation" initiative. This effort, begun in 1995 with the creation of the Truth and Reconciliation Commission (TRC), involved the promotion of peace, political reconciliation, and the reconstruction of South Africa's moral-cultural system through truth telling.

The South African model is based on three core beliefs. First, it assumes that the healing and reconciliation of a people is only possible if the past is known and acknowledged. Since truth is an essential precondition for justice and for reconciliation, public authorities have a responsibility to discover and disclose as much knowledge as possible about the past collective wrongdoing. Without an accounting of individual and collective crimes and injustices, especially those committed by the state itself, there can be no justice and no collective healing. Second, the TRC is based on the belief that the prosecution and punishment of regime crimes may be institutionally impossible or, at worst, counterproductive, to the development of a democratic order. Given the absolute value of truth, coupled with the potential threat to domestic order by retributive actions of the state, the TRC model provides amnesty to offenders who disclose the truth. In effect, the TRC gives moral precedence to truth telling over retribution.

Finally, the model assumes that truth telling will help promote national peace and reconciliation. According to the TRC model, reconciliation cannot be realized alone through political negotiations and legal actions but will necessarily entail the reformation of dominant values, cultural norms, and social and political structures. This means that individuals and groups, especially those responsible for past wrongdoing, must adopt a more humane moral-cultural system that is conducive to human rights. What is significant about the "truth plus amnesty" experiment is not that it de-emphasizes punishment but that it focuses on the reformation of communal bonds by encouraging moral reflection based on truth telling, confession, forgiveness, and reconciliation.

Although the South African approach is rooted in political morality, the framework itself does not make moral demands on individuals and groups. The process calls for truth telling with the promise that those who confess their politically motivated crimes will be given amnesty. Offenders need not express remorse for their crimes; apologies are not required for amnesty. Moreover, victims are not required or even expected to forgive contrite offenders; the framework does, however, establish a moral context and encourage a moral discourse that facilitates the process of individual and collective renewal. The process gives priority not only to confession but also to the need to restore relationships and renew community life. It makes space not only for apologies and repentance but also for forgiveness and reconciliation.

South Africa's bold experiment in transitional justice is significant because it challenges the conventional wisdom that presumes that the consolidation of constitutional government requires the prosecution of criminal wrongdoing. Rather than demanding legal retribution, the South African paradigm calls for healing and restoration. Although some South African leaders believed that the crimes of apartheid should be punished, most political leaders assumed that prosecution would not necessarily promote victims' healing and the consolidation of national unity. As a result, they were opposed to a retributive justice perspective not only because they thought it failed to advance reconciliation but, more important, because they believed that such an approach focused on the punishment of offenders and neglected the rehabilitation and healing of victims. As a result, South African negotiators adopted an innovative approach: victims would be given an opportunity to describe their suffering and to receive reparations from the state, while perpetrators who confessed their wrongdoing fully and truthfully would be exempt from criminal and civil prosecution.

Some South African critics have argued that the TRC strategy was a second-best alternative, based on expediency and political calculations. This judgment, however, cannot be sustained. The South African model of transitional justice was developed not as a pragmatic response to existing political forces but in part as a moral framework for coming to terms simultaneously with the history of past crimes and injustices and the promise of a more peaceful, democratic society. To be sure, the political settlement reached by South African negotiators in 1993 paving the way for multiracial democracy was the result of difficult bargaining between those who demanded trials and punishment and those who did not. But the negotiated settlement was not guided only by political realities but also by conflicting moral demands between the need to confront and account for past crimes and injustices and the expectation to build a just, peaceful, and productive new society, between backward-looking retributive justice and forward-looking restorative justice. Thus, while South Africa's approach was grounded in political realities, it was not based on political expediency but on a political morality concerned with how to confront past injustices and how to promote the common good in the future.

In this chapter, I explore and assess this bold strategy in truth telling, with the aim of uncovering the extent to which national reconciliation is advanced through truth, reparations, and forgiveness. In the first part of the chapter, I describe major features of the apartheid society that existed from 1948 to 1990 and sketch some of the processes by which South African political leaders forged a democratic transition that culminated in the adoption of an Interim Constitution in 1993. Second, I examine the nature of the TRC model as an instrument of truth telling, exploring, and assessing the arguments for pursuing truth through the promise of conditional amnesty. Third, I describe and evaluate the logic of South Africa's TRC model by contrasting the strategies of retributive justice and restorative justice. I argue that while the latter approach is not a morally legitimate conception of political justice, it provides advantages in the moral reconstruction of society over a purely legal/retributive approach. Fourth, I explore how the TRC's emphasis on the moral reconstruction of society has promoted national reconciliation through individual and collective forgiveness. The chapter concludes with a preliminary assessment of the TRC model and the commission's effectiveness in pursuing the model's stated goals.

COMING TO TERMS WITH THE PAST

The Apartheid Regime

In 1948, the National Party (NP), the political party of the Afrikaner (Boer) people, gained control of parliament. For the next forty-four years they would govern the South African state. Although racial discrimination and segregation had characterized South Africa since colonization in the mid-seventeenth century, the Afrikaners sought to institutionalize segregation through a systematic program of social engineering. This program—known as apartheid, or separate development—was the most extreme form of segregation practiced by any modern state. According to historian Leonard Thompson, the apartheid system was based on four ideas:

First, the population of South Africa comprised four "racial groups"— White, Coloured, Indian, and African—each with its own inherent culture. Second, whites, as the civilized race, were entitled to have control over the state. Third, white interests should prevail over black interests; the state was obliged to provide equal facilities for the subordinate races. Fourth, the white racial group formed a single nation, with Afrikaans- and English-speaking components, while Africans belonged to several (eventually ten) distinct nations or potential nations—a formula that made the white nation the largest in the country.[4]

These ideas were institutionalized through a large body of legal statutes, including:

- Mixed Marriages Act (1949), which made interracial marriage illegal;
- Population Registration Act (1950), which required that all people be classified by race;
- Group Areas Act (1950), which specified where members of each race could live;
- Reservation of Separate Amenities Act (1953), which required that public facilities be racially segregated;
- Black Authorities Act (1951), which together with subsequent legislation, established black homelands;
- Immorality Act (1957), which prohibited sex between people of different race groups;
- Prohibition of Political Interference Act (1968), which prevented members of different ethnic groups from belonging to the same political party.

It is important to stress that racial discrimination did not begin with the government of the Afrikaners. Throughout the nineteenth and early twentieth centuries, white rulers had established legal and de facto segregation that encouraged racial discrimination. Africans, for example, were denied the right to own land and to vote and significant restrictions were placed on where they could live and work. Some of the most dehumanizing statutes were applied to African miners, who were forced to live apart from their families in proximity to mines.[5]

After the NP gained control of the South African Parliament in 1948, it proceeded to further institutionalize racial segregation through the theory of apartheid, under which the development of distinct ethnic groups would best be realized through comprehensive racial segregation. Indeed, to advance apartheid, the Afrikaner government imposed the most extreme form of racial engineering ever practiced in the modern world. For example, the government imposed more stringent racial segregation by forcing the relocation of more than 3.5 million people between 1960 and 1983. These forced removals further intensified the problem of overpopulation in the already crowded all-black Bantu homelands, increasing their proportion of the country's total population from 40 percent in 1950 to 53 percent in 1980. Thus, by 1980 the population density in the homelands had increased to nearly twenty-four people per square kilometer, compared with nine people per square kilometer in white areas.[6]

As a result of the growing social, economic, and political inequalities in South African society, black political opposition to the apartheid regime increased. At first, the political opposition was limited chiefly to the actions of labor groups and the two major African opposition groups—the African National Congress (ANC) and the Pan-African Congress (PAC). But in the 1970s, political opposition efforts intensified both domestically and internationally. In 1973, the UN General Assembly declared apartheid "a crime against humanity," and four years later the Security Council imposed trade sanctions (an arms embargo) on South Africa as a way to foment political reform. As domestic and international condemnation of apartheid increased, the South African regime began to carry out modest structural reforms in the early 1980s.[7] Rather than mollifying public opinion, reforms only intensified the opposition's political demands. In response to growing violence, the government imposed a state of emergency that gave security forces increased authority to detain political opponents and to use force against those threatening public order. The intensification of the liberation campaign is demonstrated by the growth in political violence: from 1960 to 1989 about seven thousand people were killed in political conflicts, whereas in the four years preceding the establishment of multiracial democracy (1990 to 1994) more than fourteen thousand died as a result of political violence.[8]

Reckoning with the Past

In February 1990, President F. W. de Klerk set in motion a reform process that would culminate four years later in the election of Nelson Mandela as president of a new multiracial democratic regime. The transition began with the lifting of the ban on the ANC and other opposition political groups, the release of Mandela and other political prisoners, and the partial lifting of the state of emergency. Following two years of intense negotiations among the country's political elites, especially the governing NP and the ANC, delegates to the Convention for a Democratic South Africa (CODESA) signed an Interim Constitution in November 1993 that established the basis for a transitional government. According to the Interim Constitution, the transitional Government of National Unity was tasked with establishing a permanent constitution and creating the preconditions for national unity.

Fundamentally, South Africa could have pursued one of three strategies in confronting past crimes and injustices: amnesia, punishment, and truth telling. The first strategy, based on forgetting and denial, would seek to draw a line between the present and the past and would concentrate all political and economic resources on the consolidation of constitutional democracy. The second strategy, legal retribution, would demand full legal accountability for past offenses, believing that the consolidation of democracy and the rule of law were impossible without the prosecution and punishment of offenders. The third strategy, the one adopted by South Africa, represented an intermediary approach between the extremes of impunity and comprehensive trials, between denial and retribution.

Following the psychoanalytic model of mental health, this strategy assumed that acknowledging the truth about the past was indispensable to the healing of society and to the consolidation of constitutional government. As a result it placed retributive justice at the service of truth, and to maximize its discovery and disclosure conditional amnesty was offered to offenders who confessed their culpability fully. Fundamentally, South Africa's "third way" strategy combined a backward-looking focus on truth telling and accountability with a forward-looking emphasis on the moral restoration of society and the promotion of national unity.[9]

South African leaders selected the third strategy in great part because it reflected a political compromise among the major political forces in the country but also because they believed that neither historical amnesia nor trials provided options conducive to national healing. Indeed, based on the experiences of previous truth commissions, they assumed that it was most likely to foster the consolidation of a democratic order, contribute to the restoration and healing of victims, and encourage national reconciliation.

As viewed by leaders, traditional legal and political strategies rooted in retributive justice were unlikely to foster unity and national reconciliation. What was needed was an alternative strategy that gave priority to the healing of victims, the public acknowledgment of past crimes and injustices, and the restoration of communal bonds. Such an approach would provide a demanding multidimensional strategy that emphasized legal accountability yet called for political accommodation, social reconciliation, and the moral reconstruction of society. The 1993 Interim Constitution's postamble captured the spirit of this strategy when it declared "a need for understanding but not for vengeance, a need for reparation but not for retaliation, a need for *ubuntu*[10] but not for victimization."

THE TRUTH AND RECONCILIATION COMMISSION

In mid-1995, the South African Parliament passed the Promotion of National Unity and Reconciliation Act that called for the establishment of the TRC. As conceived by this parliamentary act, the major purpose for creating the commission was to discover and disclose truth about past crimes and injustices in the belief that public acknowledgment of such truth would contribute to the consolidation of democratic society and promote national unity and reconciliation. Fundamentally, the goal of the TRC was to uncover and disclose information about gross human rights abuses during the apartheid era.[11]

The truth that the TRC sought was of two sorts—factual and moral.[12] Factual truth consisted of empirical, objective evidence about past crimes and abuses that was gathered and corroborated through voluntary disclosure and investigation. Moral truth, by contrast, was based on subjective awareness and individual and collective acknowledgment of past wrongdoing. Whereas factual truth is objective and detached, moral truth requires that individuals personally appropriate the objective information and personally respond to the effects that those facts have had on people's lives. "What is critical," observes the TRC report, "is that these facts be fully and publicly acknowledged. Acknowledgment is an affirmation that a person's pain is real and worthy of attention. It is thus central to the restoration of the dignity of victims."[13]

President Nelson Mandela appointed the seventeen members of the TRC from a list of nominees, and made Archbishop Desmond Tutu, the 1994 recipient of the Nobel Peace Prize, its head.[14] Not only did Tutu bring international stature to the commission's work, but he also provided moral leadership and even spiritual inspiration when the commission was faced with internal dissent or external criticism. Antjie Krog, a leading South African writer and poet who covered the commission's hearings for the South African Broadcasting Company radio, has written the following of Tutu's TRC leadership:

The [TRC] process is unthinkable without Tutu. Impossible. Whatever role others might play, it is Tutu who is the compass. He guides us in several ways, the most important of which is language. It is he who finds language for what is happening. And it is not the language of statements, news reports, and submissions. It is language that shoots up like fire—wrought from a vision of where we must go and from a grip of where we are now. And it is this language that drags people along with the process.[15]

The TRC's responsibilities were divided into three areas, each directed by a committee: The first and most important committee, composed of nine commissioners including Tutu and deputy chairman Alex Boraine, focused on human rights violations. The committee's primary responsibility was to gather information from victims and organizations about gross human rights abuses and to determine who should be officially classified as a victim. Given the heavy responsibilities of this committee, especially in the early phases of its work, the commission appointed ten additional members to assist in its work. The second committee focused on amnesty and was led by three judges appointed by Mandela and was supported by two commissioners. It was responsible for determining which applicants would receive amnesty. The third committee, composed of five commissioners, focused on reparation and rehabilitation. Its responsibility was to make recommendations to the state on how to assist victims of gross human rights violations and to offer policy recommendations that would promote national healing.

Compared with other truth commissions, the TRC is undoubtedly the most expansive and elaborate truth commission ever established. To begin with, it functioned much longer than most other commissions.[16] Because it was the product of parliamentary action and not a decision of the executive, the TRC had far more domestic political support, especially from political leaders, than other truth commissions. Moreover, the TRC could subpoena witnesses, compel disclosure of information from governmental agencies, and requisition documents from organizations. And unlike most other commissions, which have carried out their work in secrecy, the TRC carried out its work with transparency and openness. In addition, the TRC had the authority to disclose the names of alleged perpetrators.[17] Finally, the TRC had the authority to grant amnesty to offenders who confessed their politically motivated crimes, provided their disclosure was complete.

Truth Telling

The human rights committee pursued factual truth by gathering evidence about gross human rights violations that were perpetrated during the apartheid era by state security officials as well as by members of the liberation movement. More than 22,000 victim statements were completed and some 160 victims' hearings were held throughout the country, involving more than 1,200 victims and their families. The media widely publicized these hearings and left an indelible impact on South African society. A major innovation of the TRC was its inclusion of institutional and group hearings. Institutional representation was thought to be especially important since apartheid crimes and injustices had been perpetrated with the tacit, if not explicit, support of a significant number of groups and institutions of civil society.

Since the commission had refused to consider collective responsibility, the inclusion of institutional hearings—which covered such organizations as political parties, the media, business and labor groups, the legal community, the armed forces, religious communities, prisons, and the health sector—provided perspectives that greatly enriched the TRC's analysis.[18] Based on the evidence accumulated through investigations, victim statements, and institutional hearings, the TRC published its findings and recommendations in a five-volume report, released in October 1998.[19]

Although the disclosure of factual findings was an important step in South Africa's democratic transition, the quest for moral truth through open hearings, public testimony, and the personal and collective acknowledgment of wrongdoing was even more significant. TRC activities—especially its victim and institutional hearings, amnesty decisions, and the participation or nonparticipation of former leaders—contributed significantly to media commentary and public debates that encouraged a society-wide acknowledgment of collective injustices and wrongdoing. While victims and their families were generally eager to publicly share their accounts of suffering and injustice, getting leaders and offenders to acknowledge their personal and institutional role in crimes proved a far more elusive task. Few leaders of the former apartheid regime testified or requested amnesty. Some, such as former president P. W. Botha, were contemptuous of the commission's work. Despite the relatively small number of officials who were willing to openly acknowledge personal and collective responsibility for past human rights crimes, the TRC established an environment in which a significant measure of moral truth was achieved.

Amnesty

One of the most significant, yet problematic, elements of the TRC process was the provision of conditional amnesty to offenders. The logic for the amnesty was set forth in the Interim Constitution's postamble, which declared that "[i]n order to advance such reconciliation and reconstruction [of society], amnesty should be granted in respect of acts, omissions and offences with political objectives and committed in the course of the conflicts of the past." Unlike self-amnesties, commonly enacted by authoritarian regimes to pre-empt future trials, the South African amnesty is not a blanket, unconditional expression of impunity. Rather, the TRC policy makes amnesty conditional on full disclosure of offenders' crimes.

Since truth was considered essential to individual and collective healing, political leaders believed the investigation and the disclosure of past injustices and gross human rights were indispensable to the moral reconstruction of society. To encourage the perpetrators' confessions, the TRC promised amnesty to those who fully confessed politically motivated crimes.[20] Offenders were not required to apologize or to express remorse but only to disclose their offenses. Although repentance was considered desirable, the TRC did not make remorse a condition for amnesty since such a requirement would have demanded that public officials judge offenders' motivations. Of the more than seven thousand people who applied for amnesty, only about twelve hundred were granted amnesty.[21]

Reparations

Undoubtedly the major institutional shortcoming of the TRC process was reparations. Although the Reparation and Rehabilitation (R & R) Committee was responsible for recommending reparations, it had no statutory authority to promise monetary compensation or rehabilitative measures. As a result, a large gulf developed between the committee's recommendations and the government's actions. More significant, a glaring contradiction emerged between the authority to grant amnesty and the inability to deliver monetary compensation. Offenders who received amnesty were immediately set free, while victims who testified about their suffering and loss received nothing.[22] Part of the delay in providing reparations was that the R & R Committee did not present its recommendations until October 1997. As a result, the earliest interim reparations (about 2,000 Rands, or roughly $330) were not made until July 1998, more than two years after the victims' hearings had commenced.

The committee's principal recommendation was that the government should grant all victims monetary reparations. The committee had considered offering victims support services rather than money and had also considered allocating reparations based on the severity of the suffering. In the end, the committee decided to recommend equal financial compensation for all qualified victims,[23] regardless of need or level of suffering. Since the committee recommended that victims be given roughly $20,000 over six years,[24] the total cost for reparations was estimated at nearly $400 million. Given the enormous social and economic needs of the masses, as well as the high level of national unemployment (over 35 percent), the South African government was reluctant to fulfill this commitment immediately. However, the failure to provide reparations led to widespread criticism of the government, calling into question the implicit promise of reparations to those who participated in the truth-telling process.

According to one South African human rights activist, "victims were asked to sacrifice justice in return for reparations. The fact that the Government now appears to be turning away from individual reparations . . . is a betrayal of the promises made to victims."[25] Fortunately, the Thabo Mbeki government announced in April 2003—shortly after the TRC formally terminated its work with the delivery of its final findings and recommendations—that the state would provide about $3,900 to each of the victims' families.[26] While this sum is about one-fifth of what the TRC had originally recommended, the decision to compensate victims and their families is an important development that will help bring closure to the truth and reconciliation process begun in 1996.

THE LOGIC OF THE TRC

In his book on the TRC, Tutu claims that it would have been unwise, indeed impossible, to impose retribution—what he terms "the Nuremberg trial paradigm"[27]—on South Africa. Due to the country's limited political and economic resources, it was imperative that it use them with care in the consolidation of new democratic structures by balancing different claims, including "justice, accountability, stability, peace, and reconciliation."[28] In Tutu's view, applying retributive justice would have placed an undue burden on the nation's courts and would have given little emphasis to the restoration of victims and the promotion of political reconciliation.

An alternative strategy that confronted past injustices while focusing on the reconciliation and the renewal of society was needed. For Tutu, this alternative strategy was restorative justice, which he defined as "the healing of breaches, the redressing of imbalances, the restoration of broken relationships, a seeking to rehabilitate both the victim and the perpetrator, who should be given the opportunity to be reintegrated into the community he has injured by his offense."[29] While retributive justice is an impersonal, punitive process that advances human rights through legal prosecution of individual claims, restorative justice emphasizes the maintenance of communal solidarity by emphasizing social harmony and reconciliation. Most important for Tutu, restorative justice is consistent with the African tradition of *ubuntu* that places a premium on harmony, friendliness, and community.

The Theory of Restorative Justice

In his foreword to the commission's report, Tutu observes that reconciliation can only be pursued through full disclosure. He suggests that the "Esau option"—seeking a short-term gain at the cost of a longer term but greater benefit—is a tempting but shortsighted approach.[30] Since reconciliation demands that offenders admit their culpability and express sorrow for their offenses, the only sound strategy for building a human rights culture and consolidating democratic structures is through truth telling. The paradigm of restorative justice provides the rationale by which the acknowledgment of truth becomes an instrument of reconciliation. Such a paradigm assumes that overcoming past crimes and injuries will necessitate, at a minimum, the perpetrators' disclosure of the fate of persons who were killed or abducted, the acknowledgment and remorse for such actions, and the promise to never repeat such human rights crimes again. In effect, the restorative justice model is rooted in the religious "conversion model" that assumes that salvation depends in part on confession, repentance, and the promise to "sin no more." This is why theologian Gregory Jones has observed that the "miracle of reconciliation" can be realized only when antagonists pursue restorative justice through truthfulness, forgiveness, and repentance.[31]

As conceptualized by the TRC, the restorative justice approach involves several distinct steps in the healing and restoration of communal solidarity. First, it calls for a redefinition of crime that focuses on personal injuries and human suffering rather than on impersonal rule breaking. Second, it emphasizes reparations for victims in order to facilitate their restoration into the fabric of communal life while simultaneously encouraging the rehabilitation of perpetrators based on full accountability for past offenses. Third, it encourages direct conflict resolution among victims, offenders, and the community. Finally, it calls for "a spirit of understanding" between victims and offenders, without mitigating or undermining offenders' accountability for wrongdoing. Such accountability is not only legal and political but also moral.[32] Indeed, at the heart of the restorative justice approach is the conviction that in the aftermath of serious crimes the promotion of reconciliation can be advanced only through the renewal of individual and collective morality.

One of the noteworthy features of the TRC process was the absence of vengeance. Indeed, many victims were eager to forgive offenders who acknowledged their culpability and to bring some closure to past injuries. In the TRC report, Tutu observes that "on the whole we have been exhilarated by the magnanimity of those who should by rights be consumed by bitterness and lust for revenge; who instead have time after time shown an astonishing magnanimity and willingness to forgive." At the same time, he makes a plea to white South Africans, "please try to bring yourselves to respond with a like generosity and magnanimity," he notes. "When one confesses, one confesses only one's own sins, not those of another. . . . That is why I still hope that there will be a white leader who will say, 'We had an evil system with awful consequences. Please forgive us.' If that were to happen, we would all be amazed at the response."[33]

Some commissioners and observers were dissatisfied with the TRC's use of moral/biblical language. According to some critics, the use of religious/moral discourse compromised the quest for justice and the consolidation of a constitutional, democratic order. TRC commissioner Wynand Malan, for example, questioned the appropriateness of public institutions using a religious conversion model based on confession, repentance, and forgiveness. He argued that the use of a "religious paradigm" had encouraged leaders "to stand up and apologize in order to experience the level and extent of black readiness to forgive."[34] But Malan doubted that such apologies would contribute to national healing. Tutu and his supporters, however, were not cowed by those who opposed the use of religious language and sought to de-emphasize moral reasoning.

Replying to his critics, Tutu repeatedly stressed that legal and political instruments alone were insufficient to overcome the alienation and distrust that had resulted from institutionalized racial discrimination. Indeed, after visiting Rwanda in the aftermath of its 1994 genocide, Tutu called attention to the inadequacy of trials to rehabilitate a broken, alienated society. He observed that the only way to break the "spiral of reprisal and counterreprisal" was not through trials but through "confession, forgiveness, and reconciliation." These practices, he noted, are not "just airy-fairy religious and spiritual things, nebulous and unrealistic" but rather, "the stuff of practical politics."[35]

Since the TRC legislation provided only rudimentary guidelines and structures for pursuing national unity and reconciliation, the commission had to devise its own theory of political healing. In particular, it had to develop a moral justification for giving precedence to reconciliation over punishment, communal justice over individual rights. Most significant, it had to carry out its tasks in the belief that confession of wrongdoing justified the granting of amnesty from civil and criminal prosecution. The commission wisely did not seek to provide a comprehensive moral theory by which to justify its work. Rather, it encouraged a moral debate about the reconstruction of society using religious concepts associated with conversion—namely, confession, contrition, repentance, forgiveness, and reconciliation. In addition, the commission relied on indigenous social concepts, especially the idea of *ubuntu*, that gave precedence to communal solidarity over individual rights. The TRC did not seek to impose values or to create a new ideology, but rather opened a moral debate about South Africa's past. John de Gruchy, a leading South African scholar, has written:

> The critical question is how we are to take the debate further and process the memory of our corporate past that the TRC has set before us. What we do with these memories will, in large measure, shape the moral contours of the future of South Africa. Our past will either be redeemed, or our future will be cursed, depending on our response. In other words, we do not only have the task of remembering, but of remembering rightly. And remembering rightly is a moral act, which builds the foundations for a moral culture.[36]

The Quest for Reconciliation

When South Africa established its truth commission, it specified "national unity, the well-being of South African citizens and peace" as major goals that were to be achieved through reconciliation. As conceived by the TRC, national reconciliation was viewed as a goal, a process, and a condition. As a process, reconciliation involved procedures and methods that were conducive to the end of peaceful, harmonious relationships and communal solidarity. As a goal, reconciliation specified the desired outcome—a unified, peaceful, harmonious society. To achieve this end, reconciliation had to be pursued at a variety of levels, including spiritual, psychological, social, and political.[37] National reconciliation, in short, was conceived as a multidimensional concept that specified goals, methods, and dimensions that were relevant to the restoration of interpersonal relationships and communal solidarity.

Although South Africa's opposition leaders were strongly committed to the institutionalization of comprehensive constitutional norms, they also knew that the pursuit of justice needed to be balanced by the quest for national reconciliation and a peaceful transition to full democracy. As a result, government leaders adopted a strategy of restorative justice that emphasized reconciliation over trials, truth telling over punishment. This strategy, while aiming toward democratic deliberation, recognized that the historical context and the political and social realities did not permit retributive justice without undermining other important moral values.

In light of the political dynamics in South Africa in the mid-1990s, South African leaders adopted a modest strategy—one that pursued truth through the promise of amnesty based on a political compromise that facilitated the transition and consolidation of universal, multiracial democracy. Richard Goldstone, a leading international judge and member of South Africa's Constitutional Court, observed that if the liberation movement had insisted on prosecuting former leaders, "there would have been no peaceful transition to democracy, and if the former government had insisted on blanket amnesty then, similarly, the negotiations would have broken down. A bloody revolution sooner rather than later would have been inevitable."[38] Thus, the decision to pursue national reconciliation based on a restorative justice model was a deliberate policy, based on an assessment of existing political conditions.

Since the TRC model was based on the belief that truth was the basis for individual healing and collective reconciliation, the challenge for the commission was how to ensure that truth would, in fact, promote restoration and harmony as opposed to division and revenge. In effect, a fundamental moral task of the commission was to ensure that the discovery and disclosure of truth contributed to collective healing and not to increased distrust and hatred. Since the truth about past crimes and injustices could potentially foster division, conflict, and even vengeance, the challenge for the TRC was to create a moral framework by which the quest for truth and the promotion of national reconciliation could be bridged. The TRC pursued this goal by providing a moral vocabulary by which to structure moral reflection and by fostering a discourse focused on core moral issues of "transitional justice." Such issues included concerns about the legitimacy of amnesty, the effect of amnesty on reconciliation, the role of apologies and forgiveness in promoting reconciliation, the relationship of truth telling to national unity, and the impact of amnesty on the rule of law.

Some democratic theorists argue that emerging constitutional regimes should not pursue reconciliation directly.[39] They claim that seeking to transform the people's values and attitudes from enmity to friendship is an unrealistic expectation, especially in the aftermath of historic injustices and widespread regime wrongdoing. Rather than seeking to transform the values and attitudes of enemies and to heal the injuries of victims through therapeutic rehabilitation programs, transitional regimes should use their scarce political resources in consolidating democratic structures and restoring the rule of law. Thus, democratic theorists assume that the pursuit of a comprehensive political reconciliation is an unrealistic, if not inappropriate, national goal.

A second and more serious criticism of the pursuit of political reconciliation is that it is inconsistent with democratic theory because it is potentially threatening to individual rights, especially to human freedom. David Crocker, for example, argues that an overemphasis on peace and communal solidarity can threaten individual rights, including the rights to withhold forgiveness, to pursue legal accountability, and to obtain reparations.[40] A similar critique is offered by historian Timothy Garton Ash who claims that the idea of reconciliation is deeply "illiberal," since a liberal society is one that learns to live with unresolved conflicts among values and interests.[41] But surely the aim of the TRC was not to advance an ideology that restricted freedom. Rather, the aim was to promote the building of a multiracial, democratic nation, and to do this, it was necessary to confront and overcome deep social and economic disparities and significant political and cultural cleavages that had been exacerbated, if not caused, by apartheid. Thus, the TRC's aim was not to advance ideological monism but to promote a unified society rooted in a pluralistic and tolerant moral-cultural system.

Given South Africa's deep social, psychological, and political divisions during the country's democratic transition, the criticisms of political reconciliation seem unwarranted. The challenge for South Africa was not simply to identify the nature and scope of human rights abuses and encourage the institutionalization of democratic structures and processes but to overcome the legacy of distrust and enmity that had resulted from a long history of racial discrimination. For the ruling authorities, social, political, and economic divisions could only be healed through the moral reconstruction of society. And as Elizabeth Kiss has noted, such a task could not be achieved only through judicial means but had to include political, legal, cultural, moral, psychological, and spiritual dimensions as well.[42]

Forgiveness

Collective forgiveness was not an explicit element of the TRC model. Whereas truth, reparations, and reconciliation were viewed as indispensable to individual and collective reckoning with past wrongs, forgiveness was considered a personal, discretionary act. Nevertheless, the TRC made room for, if not directly encouraged, individual and collective forgiveness through its emphasis on the restoration of relationships through confession, empathy, and amnesty. It will be recalled that the founding legislation for the TRC determined that individual and collective healing presupposed the full disclosure of gross human rights violations supported by some reparations and rehabilitation initiatives. It was assumed that truth telling would set in motion moral processes that would contribute to individual healing and collective reconciliation. Of course if truth were to foster reconciliation, antagonists would have to transform their pain and anger into trust and cooperation through the development of compassionate attitudes.

Since truth telling is the fundamental requirement of forgiveness, the TRC's emphasis on the disclosure and acknowledgment of truth helped to create a context in which the ethic of forgiveness could be expressed. Moreover, since forgiveness is an interactive process, the TRC model presumed that the balm of confession and remorse would foster empathy and possibly even individual forgiveness, and thereby create space for victims' healing and the restoration of social and political bonds. As conceived by the TRC, the granting of amnesty, like the process of forgiveness, was not a solitary, isolated event but the culmination of an interactive process among antagonists rooted in truth.

Tutu's repeated use of spiritual language had a powerful impact on the TRC process. His repeated emphasis on personal healing and social rehabilitation through the acknowledgment of suffering, confession of wrongdoing, remorse, and empathy contributed significantly to making room for the ethic of individual and collective forgiveness. By calling for the disclosure and acknowledgment of truth and by celebrating the empathy and compassion of victims, the TRC helped to create moral conditions that facilitated the healing of victims and the restoration of relationships. There can be little doubt that the numerous expressions of offenders' remorse and victims' forgiveness in TRC hearings were a direct result of the moral discourse cultivated by Tutu and his fellow commissioners. Moreover, there can be little doubt that such actions contributed to an environment that encouraged individual healing and promoted communal reconciliation. In short, the repeated use of moral language to foster healing and restoration was not accidental but derived from a belief that overcoming the injustices of apartheid required the moral restoration of human relationships.

It is important to stress that the amnesty made available to perpetrators who confessed their offenses was only a partial, incomplete expression of forgiveness. Perpetrators who disclosed and acknowledged their guilt were of course promised redemption from future legal prosecution. But the TRC program of conditional amnesty neglected important elements of a comprehensive ethic of forgiveness. In particular, the amnesty for truth process did not depend on offenders' repentance, victims' renunciation of vengeance, or empathy between antagonists. Nevertheless, the promise of absolution from legal retribution to those who confessed their crimes is significant because it highlights the moral imperative of truth telling, the basis of the forgiveness process. What is lacking in this incomplete model of forgiveness is the cultivation of attitudinal and behavioral changes between offenders and victims that contribute to the healing of victims and the restoration of social and political bonds.

Critics of forgiveness generally emphasize that forgiveness negates justice because offenders are not forced to pay their deserved debts. But authentic forgiveness is not a cheap way of avoiding culpability. On the contrary, it is a rare, demanding ethic based on a thoroughgoing moral accountability—one that presupposes the offenders' voluntary and public confession of wrongdoing. If confronting moral culpability were easy, forgiveness would be far more common in both private and public life than is normally the case. More particularly, if confession were not a demanding ethic, the number of whites applying for amnesty would have undoubtedly been much higher. In practice, few state security agents and government leaders applied for amnesty.[43] Both former presidents Botha and de Klerk declined to apply for amnesty, and Botha even refused to testify in the TRC hearings altogether.[44] In addition, many Afrikaner business, professional, and church leaders similarly refused to confront their own individual and collective responsibility.

JUDGING THE TRC

Although it is premature to offer a comprehensive assessment of the TRC's effectiveness in fostering democratization and promoting national reconciliation, it is still possible to offer some preliminary judgments about the South African experiment in pursuing reconciliation through truth telling. I first examine the merits of the TRC model and the restorative justice approach on which it is based and then offer some assessment of the TRC process itself.

Evaluating the Model

Although the formal powers and institutional authority of the TRC were noteworthy, the distinct features of the TRC were not its structures and powers but rather its theory—the logic and assumptions that informed the commission's work. Since the founding legislation had not established a developed rationale or logic for the commission's work, the TRC commissioners and staff had to devise a social theory that explained and justified the alleged healing powers of truth telling in overcoming the crimes and injustices perpetrated in a prior era. Moreover, since the discovery and disclosure of truth were not necessarily conducive to peace and harmony, the challenge was to devise a credible rationale for the TRC's work. Such a theory emerged through an intense discussion and debate within the TRC as well as society at large. The shared discourse involved TRC commissioners and staff, but it also profited from public debate involving political and civic leaders and cultural and social elites (for example, scholars, media analysts, religious leaders, and officials from nongovernmental organizations).

The theory that emerged from the TRC's analysis provided a general justification and explanation for the redemptive powers of truth telling. In particular, the theory, rooted in a restorative justice paradigm, emphasized the need for the healing and renewal of interpersonal and communal relationships and the possibility of social and political reconciliation. In addition, the emerging TRC theory was influenced profoundly by the idea of spiritual conversion, whereby wrongdoing is redeemed through confession, remorse, reparations, and forgiveness, coupled with traditional African values that give precedence to communal obligations and social solidarity. Some of the key elements of the TRC model included the following:

- Truth is essential for accountability, for public justice, and for individual and collective healing.
- To encourage the disclosure of truth, perpetrators are granted amnesty, provided their testimony about criminal wrongdoing is complete.
- Although retribution is an important element in maintaining the rule of law, punishment does not necessarily heal victims or restore communal trust.
- In coming to terms with past wrongdoing, official initiatives should focus on the healing of victims and the restoration of relationships.
- Both justice and reconciliation are important values in re-establishing a political society based on the sanctity of human rights.
- In confronting past wrongdoing, perpetrators can find healing through confession, apologies, and reparations, while victims can find healing through the renunciation of vengeance and the granting of forgiveness.
- Although truth, repentance, and forgiveness may be necessary for reconciliation, they are not sufficient to ensure its fulfillment.
- Reconciliation requires the deliberate efforts of antagonists to promote mutual trust and interdependence and to oppose vengeance.

As noted earlier, remorse and forgiveness were not a formal part of the TRC model. Nevertheless, commissioners, especially chairman Tutu, repeatedly urged offenders and organizations to apologize for injustices and injuries that had resulted from apartheid-related conflicts, regardless of intentions. Moreover, while victims were not called to forgive offenders, amnesty and victims' hearings provided an opportunity for victims and their families to respond with compassion. Tutu repeatedly pleaded with white political, professional, and business leaders to express remorse for their individual and collective participation in a discriminatory, repressive political system, arguing that if genuine apologies were conveyed, black Africans would respond with magnanimity and even forgiveness.

Scholars and activists have raised a number of concerns about the TRC model. For example, some TRC critics have questioned the legitimacy of the restorative justice paradigm because they think the model undermines values, such as accountability, blame, and punishment, that are essential to building a stable, humane society. They claim that if societies fail to identify and condemn evil, the consolidation of human rights will be thwarted. Other critics claim that fidelity to the law requires not only the prosecution of crimes, but also the condemnation of immoral laws and unjust structures and the prosecution of leaders who were responsible for their enactment. John Dugard, for example, critiques the TRC for minimizing the "memory of apartheid" by failing to hold leaders accountable for the establishment of the immoral rules of apartheid.[45] Tutu claims, however, that trials would have been expensive and diverted political attention from the pressing needs to consolidate constitutionalism and foster job creation. In his view, the forward-looking restorative justice paradigm offered the advantage of diverting scarce resources to the consolidation of democratic institutions and the promotion of national unity by balancing the claims of justice, accountability, stability, peace, and reconciliation.[46]

Critics have also challenged the legitimacy of reconciliation as a public policy goal. As noted earlier, a number of scholars have called into question the need to deliberately promote national unity and political reconciliation. Rajeev Bhargava, for example, writes that rather than promoting reconciliation through public policies, societies should promote a limited public order—or what he terms "a minimally decent society." He claims that reconciliation is an excessively demanding political goal.[47] Crocker similarly argues that reconciliation is a potentially dangerous and undemocratic doctrine since it could threaten individual rights. For Crocker, as well as for other scholars deeply committed to political liberalism, the only legitimate way to reckon with past atrocities is through "democratic reciprocity."[48]

But democratic procedures do not necessarily or automatically foster community. Indeed, electoral democracy may, as Fareed Zakaria has noted, exacerbate political tensions and weaken community.[49] As a result, rather than enhancing individual freedom, democratic procedures might in fact threaten human rights. Thus, since democratic decision making presupposes a stable, unified community,[50] the consolidation of democracy is likely to occur only if communal solidarity is strengthened through the cultivation of shared values and the development of strong institutions.

Is the multidimensional process of reconciliation, as conceived by the TRC, morally and politically misguided? Given the fragmented nature of

South African society and the long history of racial discrimination, the potential for major war among different ethnic and political groups was not insignificant in the early 1990s. Moreover, given the lack of democratic practice among coloured and black peoples and the large economic inequalities between racial groups, the development of constitutional, democratic institutions was not an inevitable by-product of political change. Therefore, a major task of the transitional regime of South Africa was to promote reforms that contributed simultaneously to justice, accountability, and reconciliation. And if these multiple, and at times conflicting, goals were to be advanced, an all-encompassing strategy had to be devised—one involving legal and political reforms coupled with social, cultural, moral, and spiritual changes. Kiss argues that the pursuit of reconciliation through restorative justice involved nothing less than the "moral reconstruction" of political institutions and human relationships. Given the demanding nature of this task, Kiss claims that the TRC model depends on "a leap of faith, a belief in the possiblity of moral transformation of both persons and institutions."[51]

TRC critics have also expressed concerns about the presumed healing properties of truth. Truth commissions are based on the premise that knowledge of the past, coupled with the acknowledgment of the truth, will contribute to the healing of victims, the promotion of peace, and the restoration of communal relationships. Building on the biblical admonition that if we know the truth, it will set us free (John 8:32), truth commissions, including Argentina's and South Africa's, have pursued truth in the hope that such knowledge would foster individual and collective healing. The TRC, for example, is based on the belief that truth and reconciliation are inextricably linked—that the disclosure of past wrongs contributes to personal healing and communal reconciliation. If truth is to foster reconciliation, both factual and interpretive knowledge will be needed. Indeed, knowledge of the past can contribute to political healing only when it is widely known and shared and, most important, when victims and offenders individually and collectively confront the painful past by "working through" the legacy of suffering, anger, and guilt.[52] Of course, while truth telling may not be a sufficient condition for reconciliation, it most surely is a necessary element insofar as knowledge of the past permits individuals and collectives to confront their responsibility for past injustices.

TRC critics have also alleged that the model failed to distinguish between the atrocities committed by the state and those committed by the liberation movement. Although the military conflict between the state security forces and the ANC guerrillas, Umkhonto we Sizwe (MK),[53] was a covert, unconventional war, the TRC believed that rules of war were nonetheless applicable to such a conflict. In particular, it believed that terror, civilian killings, abductions, and torture were not only gross human rights violations but also violations of the laws of war.[54] Accordingly, it believed that it was morally obligated to investigate all major human rights abuses, regardless of who had perpetrated the crimes. As TRC vice chairman Boraine observed, "the goal of the TRC was to hold up a mirror to reflect the complete picture. In particular, its objective was to identify all victims in the conflict and to confront all perpetrators of gross human rights violations."[55]

TRC officials claimed that if truth telling was foundational to reconciliation, then the commission needed to carry out its investigations dispassionately, treating crimes by all sides similarly. Without assuming the moral equivalence of the violence by state and revolutionary forces, the commission stressed the need to investigate all killings, abductions, torture, and other egregious abuses of human rights as fully as possible and to make the findings public. This perspective was strongly challenged by liberation movement activists and in particular ANC leaders. It was also addressed powerfully by ANC leaders Kader Asmal, Louise Asmal, and Ronald Suresh Roberts in their book *Reconciliation through Truth*. The authors argue that the TRC will not be able to fulfill its implicit mandate of creating a new moral order if no distinction is made between those who opposed apartheid and those who supported it.[56] Krog paraphrases the book's core argument as follows: "It is not a question of bad apples on both sides . . . [but] a question of a bad tree, a weed, on the one hand, and an apple tree on the other. . . . If the Truth Commission cannot distinguish between right and wrong, how can it weave a moral fabric?"[57]

The ANC leaders took strong exception to the TRC approach of treating all political violence alike. Instead, they claimed that it was imperative to distinguish between the crimes and injustices of an evil, discriminatory system and the military operations of a liberation movement. Not only was the idea of moral equivalence morally problematic, but it was counterproductive to the healing and restoration of South Africa. Accordingly, the ANC, led by deputy president Mbeki, sought to influence the TRC's report and when that strategy failed, it unsuccessfully sought a court injunction to halt the publication of the TRC final report. The ANC's fundamental charge was that the TRC, by calling attention to the crimes and abuses of the MK, was attempting to criminalize the liberation struggle. According to Mbeki, the TRC's emphasis on the MK's crimes and abuses gave the impression that "the struggle for liberation was itself a gross violation of human rights."[58] After the TRC report had been released, he repeated this charge by stating:

One of the central matters at issue was and remains the erroneous determination of various actions of our liberation movements as gross violations of human rights, including the general implication that any and all military activity which results in the loss of civilian lives constitutes a gross violation of human rights. . . . The net effect of these findings is to delegitimise or criminalise a significant part of the struggle of our people for liberation and to detract from the commitment made in our Constitution to honour those who suffered for justice and freedom in our land.[59]

Another contentious element of the TRC theory was the offer of conditional amnesty to offenders who confessed. Since many victims' families were eager to bring to trial political leaders and security agents who were responsible for killings and abductions, the offer of conditional amnesty was deeply offensive to some human rights activists and victims. As a result, the amnesty provision (Section 20-7 of the TRC Act) was challenged before the country's Constitutional Court, but the court unanimously upheld the provision.[60]

Finally, some TRC critics opposed the repeated use of moral language in reckoning with the past. They believed that the frequent reference to apologies, repentance, forgiveness, and reconciliation was not conducive to the quest for justice and the consolidation of democracy. Although some analysts were critical of Tutu's use of spiritual terminology, the antipathy toward the moral and religious concepts was not to their alleged religious bases but rather, to the failure of the state to prosecute and punish criminal offenders. For them, the TRC theory was flawed because it gave precedence to reconciliation and social solidarity over individual rights.

Assessing the Commission

In October 1998, the TRC delivered its principal findings and recommendations in a five-volume *Final Report*. Since the amnesty committee still had a substantial number of amnesty applications to process at the time, the TRC continued to function after this date but with a significantly reduced staff. In March 2003, the TRC issued the sixth and last volume of its *Final Report*.[61] The last volume includes a report by the amnesty and reparations and rehabilitation committees as well as a discussion of the responsibility by major political groups for the gross violations of human rights.

While it is hazardous to offer judgments about the impact of the TRC at such an early date, some preliminary observations about its role in South African society are in order. First, the TRC was successful in discovering and disclosing truth about gross human rights crimes perpetrated during the apartheid era. It succeeded in this task largely because of broad participation of citizens in the TRC's investigations.

Another major achievement of the TRC was its effectiveness in engaging South African society. Several factors contributed to the commission's success, including 1) its nature, longevity, and public support; 2) the strong political backing for its work; 3) its significant statutory authority; and 4) the broad media coverage it garnered. Unlike most truth commissions, which are secret, short-lived, and underfinanced, the TRC was an open, lengthy, and well-staffed operation. Moreover, whereas executives have appointed most truth commissions, the TRC was established by the country's parliament, thereby enjoying significant political credibility. In addition, the TRC had significant statutory powers, including the authority to issue subpoenas and to offer amnesty to offenders. Finally, since the TRC hearings were widely publicized in the media, South African people were confronted repeatedly with the truth of past regime atrocities, leading to a widespread collective acknowledgment of the pain and suffering inflicted by apartheid.

A third TRC achievement was its success in framing the moral discourse about transitional justice and in fostering attitudinal changes that contributed to the nation's political healing. To a significant degree the TRC's success was due to its chairman, Desmond Tutu, who undertook his work not as a political leader or jurist but as a clergyman. Because Tutu approached the TRC's task of healing and reconciliation in spiritual and moral terms, he wore his Anglican vestments throughout the hearings and regularly prayed before public hearings. Moreover, he repeatedly emphasized throughout the TRC hearings the important role of compassion, truth telling, acknowledgment of wrongdoing, and forgiveness in fostering political healing.[62]

Finally, the TRC helped foster a foundation on which national unity and reconciliation could be promoted. It did so by emphasizing, among other things, truth telling, legal and moral accountability for past wrongdoing, empathy for perpetrators who acknowledged crimes, and the need for reparations for victims.[63] Given the deep political, economic, and racial cleavages institutionalized by the apartheid regime, the promotion of national unity would necessitate significant institutional reforms. Most important, reconciliation would require a significant transformation in the country's dominant moral values and cultural patterns.

Perhaps Tutu's most important contribution as TRC chairman was his continued emphasis on the reformation of South Africa's moral order. He repeatedly reminded the nation that there could be no future without reconciliation and that this was possible only through moral reformation based on confession, mercy, and forgiveness. Some observers have criticized the TRC for not bringing about more change. One leading journalist claimed, for example, that the TRC had contributed to truth but not to reconciliation.[64] Thus, while South Africa may not have achieved its aim of becoming a unified, integrated ("rainbow") nation, it has nonetheless carried out a process that has greatly improved the prospects for communal solidarity.

In summary, South Africa's truth and reconciliation experiment represents the most successful governmental initiative to promote peace and harmony through the discovery and acknowledgment of truth. Perhaps South Africa could have pursued the consolidation of multiracial democracy through amnesia and pardon or through trials of former regime leaders. But either strategy would have no doubt compromised essential goals—amnesia, because it would have neglected truth as the basis for the moral reconstruction of society, and retribution, because it would have compromised the quest for national unity and political reconciliation. Since the foundation for authentic reconciliation is truth telling, the TRC's focus on the disclosure and acknowledgment of truth helped nurture a moral basis for pursuing the consolidation of communal solidarity. Of course, truth telling could not ensure peace, but without it, long-term communal unity and peace would have been impossible. As Boraine, the deputy vice chairman of the TRC, has noted, "while truth may not always lead to reconciliation, there can be no genuine, lasting reconciliation without truth."[65] This point was reinforced by a *New York Times* editorial that lauded the commission's work as the most "comprehensive and unsparing examination of a nation's ugly past" that any truth commission has produced thus far. "No commission can transform a society as twisted as South Africa's was," the editorial goes on, "but the Truth Commission is the best effort the world has seen and South Africa is the better for it."[66]

The South African TRC process did not call for either individual or political forgiveness. Individuals could—and did—forgive perpetrators, but this act was entirely personal. Moreover, the TRC did not call on Afrikaner organizations to repent. Rather, the TRC established a process that focused on the disclosure of individual and collective offenses in the hope that such confession would create a psychologically and political safe environment that might foster empathy, compassion, and reconciliation among antagonists. To be sure, whether individual victims chose to forgive was entirely a personal decision. The TRC, however, did offer conditional amnesty (limited institutional forgiveness) to perpetrators who confessed their wrongdoing. While this partial forgiveness depended solely on truth telling and not on repentance, it nonetheless helped foster a public discourse where healing, restoration, and reconciliation were emphasized.

In the final analysis, the significance of the South African experiment in transitional justice is not measured solely by the extent of truth, national unity, and political reconciliation achieved within the country. Rather, it also depends on the extent to which the moral discourse of restorative justice is accepted as an effective strategy of confronting and overcoming past regime offenses. Judged by that standard, the TRC model provides one of the most promising innovations in moral politics in modern times.

9

Conclusion: Toward a Theory of Political Forgiveness

The fact is that forgiving is the only way for any fairness to rise from the ashes of unfairness.

—Lewis Smedes, theologian[1]

Nations may cling to the angry past or embrace the hopeful future. But the path to peace and prosperity for all nations today lies through the gate of forgiveness.

—Patrick Glynn, political scientist[2]

A duty to prosecute all human rights violations committed under a previous regime is too blunt an instrument to help successor governments which must struggle with the subtle complexities of reestablishing democracy. . . . Rather than a duty to prosecute, we should think of a duty to safeguard human rights and to prevent future violations by state officers or other parties.

—Carlos Santiago Nino, Argentine legal scholar[3]

Traditionally, political communities have relied on judicial institutions and processes to prosecute and punish collective crimes. Courts, however, have frequently proven inadequate in confronting regime offenses, especially when domestic and international political conflicts involve widespread human rights abuses and political violence. Even when they have succeeded in punishing some individuals, legal retribution, as the experience in Argentina suggests, may not contribute to national reconciliation or the consolidation of communal harmony. If a just communal order is to be restored, public officials must

211

give as much attention to reconciliation and the restoration of public trust as to the reparation and punishment of offenses. In pursuing both rehabilitation and accountability, political forgiveness provides a legitimate strategy for fostering social justice and political healing.

In this concluding chapter, I seek to formulate a preliminary theory of political forgiveness. The aim is to identify core elements of such a theory and to sketch the potential and limits of such an ethic in political life. Since the appropriateness of political forgiveness will depend partly on how political communities are conceived, I begin by describing the distinctive features of the two major views of political society—political liberalism and communitarianism. I next contrast liberalism's tradition of retributive justice, which emphasizes the promotion and protection of human rights through the rule of law, with the communitarian tradition of restorative justice, which emphasizes the healing of victims and the renewal of social and political relationships.

I argue that in confronting collective offenses the restorative approach provides distinct advantages over the retributive method since it is likely to be more effective in fostering the moral and social rehabilitation of individuals and groups. The restorative strategy, I suggest, is powerfully and compellingly set forth by President Abraham Lincoln, who argued that rehabilitation and political reconciliation were more important than punishment in confronting and overcoming the psychological wounds and physical destruction of the Civil War. In the chapter's third section, I review key dimensions of a theory of political forgiveness, focusing on the nature and potential of this ethic. In the final section, I develop some preliminary conclusions about the healing of nations and the promise of political forgiveness based on the four case studies of this book.

TWO TRADITIONS OF POLITICAL COMMUNITY

Political liberalism has been the dominant global ideology, providing the conceptual foundation for modern democracies and their criminal justice systems. According to liberalism, political society is a community of autonomous persons, each entitled to basic human rights. The task of governmental institutions is to secure and protect those rights—a goal that is achieved through the strict and impartial enforcement of the law. When crimes occur, the state is responsible for prosecuting and punishing those who have violated the rights of others. Since liberal theory demands strict legal accountability, this approach is opposed to conflict resolution procedures that weaken the rule of law, and therefore views the role of political forgiveness with skepticism.

The alternative perspective, communitarianism, conceives a political society as a rightly ordered society based on shared values and habits. While communitarianism is not opposed to individual rights or to holding persons account-able for their actions, it emphasizes traditions and shared norms to advance the common good. As a result, this perspective gives priority to social habits that help maintain political solidarity and moral values that help sustain civic society. Since communitarianism gives priority to the maintenance of domestic order and to the restoration of social bonds, this approach is open to the potential role of collective forgiveness in confronting political wrongdoing.

Political Liberalism

The central claim of Enlightenment liberalism, from John Locke to John Rawls, is that political justice is achieved by securing people's rights. These rights do not derive from a general conception of the common good but from principles of justice derived from a hypothetical social contract. For liberals, rights have precedence over the pursuit of the community's political and social well-being. According to liberal theory, governments are instituted to secure and protect individual rights and derive their legitimacy through consent, expressed in free, periodic elections. Since individual rights are paramount in Enlightenment thought, states have an obligation to prosecute and punish people who commit crimes and violate the individual rights of others. Indeed, prosecution and punishment of criminal behavior is imperative not only to secure justice but also to sustain a legitimate constitutional order.

Since political liberalism demands legal accountability, it assumes that political justice is promoted through the rule of law, or what might be termed legalism. According to legalism, human rights are best protected when laws are applied strictly and impartially, resulting in the prosecution and punishment of culpable offenders. Besides retribution, legal accountability also calls for the return of property or goods that were unjustly confiscated (restitution) and for the material compensation for property and goods that cannot be returned (reparations).[4]

According to Gary J. Bass, the establishment of international war crimes tribunals in the twentieth century has been chiefly inspired by the ideas of political liberalism.[5] In his view, the creation of international tribunals—such as the Nuremberg and Tokyo military tribunals[6] and the more recent UN war crimes tribunals in The Hague and Arusha[7]—is a direct by-product of the effort to extend constitutional legal procedures from domestic society to the international system. Liberals claim that constitutional practices of domestic society, especially due process, should be extended across state borders both because it is morally just to do so and also because such practices are essential to the ordering of political life and the creation of a just, peaceful society. Since liberal theory holds that a primary task of government is to protect individual rights by prosecuting and punishing individuals who violate state laws, it assumes peace can be created and sustained only when legal accountability is enforced. Liberalism's motto is best summarized as "no justice, no peace." As U.S. Secretary of State Madeleine Albright observed in 1999 after NATO had forced the withdrawal of Serb armed forces from Kosovo, "justice is a parent of peace."[8]

Liberals claim that legal accountability for past regime offenses is necessary for a variety of reasons. First, legalism helps to purge former leaders who might impair the consolidation of democratic government and disrupt future peace. If a humane, constitutional system is to be institutionalized, past human rights abusers must be isolated and their influence reduced, if not eliminated. Purging leaders from the former government provides a way to consolidate the power of a new government and to isolate those who bear responsibility for past collective wrongdoing.

A second legalist claim is that prosecution and punishment are desirable because they act to deter future criminal behavior, thereby fostering long-term peace. This argument is based on the widely accepted belief that swift and certain punishment deters crime and thereby contributes to communal peace and justice. Geoffrey Robertson, a British human rights lawyer, writes that "crimes against humanity will only be deterred when their would-be perpetrators . . . are given pause by the prospect that they will henceforth have no hiding place."[9] Accordingly, he and other liberals advocate "universal jurisdiction," giving international tribunals or states themselves the legal right to prosecute individuals who have committed crimes against humanity regardless of where such offenses may have been committed. The effort to extend legal accountability from domestic society to the international system has been expressed most recently by the establishment of the International Criminal Court (ICC) in The Hague in 2003. The ICC is evidence that the principle of "universal jurisdiction" has been widely accepted in the international community.[10]

Liberals also argue that trials and reparations help to establish and restore constitutional government. According to liberal theory, legalism helps to rehabilitate states by promoting the rule of law and by strengthening legal structures and governmental practices that are conducive to a humane government. When regime perpetrators are prosecuted, the power of former leaders is challenged, and their actions are judged in terms of the law. Susan Jacoby observes that legalism, for all its weaknesses and limitations, is likely to contribute far more to the creation of a humane political community than the restoration of human relationships rooted in forgiveness.[11]

A fourth justification for legalism is that trials establish individual accountability. Legalism emphasizes the individualization of guilt because liberalism is a political theory based on individual rights. As President Clinton and other senior government officials emphasized repeatedly during the 1990s, America's quarrel with Iraq and Yugoslavia was not with their people; rather, the conflict was with the governments of these states and more particularly with the public policies of their leaders, Saddam Hussein and Slobodan Milosevic.

Speaking of the war crimes perpetrated in the Bosnian war, Albright noted that since responsibility for the human rights abuses rested with the political and military leaders who had devised and implemented policies resulting in atrocities, it was imperative to hold them accountable for their actions. "The wounds opened by this war," said Albright, "will heal much faster if collective guilt for atrocities is expunged and individual responsibility is assigned."[12]

Finally, trials are considered important because they are thought to contribute to the discovery and disclosure of truth about past collective offenses. While truth commissions can provide a powerful instrument for discovering and disclosing truth, trials can help corroborate their findings and conclusions through specific court testimony. For example, while Argentina's 1984 truth commission report provided a general account of the armed forces' responsibility for abducting and killing nearly ten thousand people, the 1985 trials of the country's top military leaders provided specific information about regime crimes, thereby reinforcing the general conclusions of the truth commission. Moreover, the widespread media coverage of the court proceedings helped to capture the nation's consciousness in ways that the general commission report could not.

While each of these five claims is plausible, none is unambiguously self-evident, and none has been fully corroborated by twentieth century history. Bass argues that based on the historical record of international war crimes tribunals, only the truth telling claim is fully convincing.[13] Still, each of these arguments provides some justification for the legalist argument that regime wrongdoing should be subject to the law. Liberal theory does not specify whether domestic courts or international tribunals should carry out the retributive task. All that is demanded is that those who have committed war crimes and human rights abuses should be held legally accountable and that reparations and restitution should be carried out wherever possible. In sum, only when the law is supreme can a just political regime be developed.

Since most human rights abuses explored in previous chapters were a by-product of political violence committed by groups or the state as part of an effort to undermine, replace, or defend government authority, the legalist liberal paradigm is not well suited to reckon with past collective offenses. A preferable paradigm is restorative justice because it balances a backward-looking accountability with forward-looking political reconstruction. This alternative approach is especially appropriate in confronting past regime offenses because it seeks to restore social and political relationships through truth telling, political forgiveness, and the renewal of political morality. Since political liberalism is uncompromising in its defense of individual rights, it is largely opposed to the notion of forgiveness in public life. Victims may individually forgive their offenders, but the state has no authority to limit or minimize the responsibility for collective wrongdoing. Forgiveness and repentance of regime wrongdoing are therefore not morally permissible within the confines of strict liberalism.

Communitarianism

A number of theorists have challenged liberalism's claim that it is possible to develop a coherent theory of political community from an atomistic, individualistic foundation. For them, the common good is not simply the sum of the individual wants and rights of people but rather the shared well-being of community members. A shared interest entails both wide support from the community as well as the affirmation of the inherent dignity of people in their common life.[14] Communitarian scholars emphasize two distinct approaches.

The first, represented by such theorists as Amitai Etzioni, Charles Taylor, and Michael Walzer, has emphasized the need to balance individual rights with communal bonds, freedom with order. According to this strand, a rights-based theory provides an inadequate account of political community and of the common good because people are not solitary, independent, unencumbered selves, but human beings whose very identity is dependent on the societies of which they are a part. Thus, the communitarian perspective emphasizes the cultivation of social and political relationships and of moral values and traditions that help to sustain the common life. Because of the important role of communal bonds, communitarians, unlike liberals, refuse to give precedence to individual rights over social solidarity and harmonious relationships.

The second strand of communitarianism, represented by Michael Sandel and others, emphasizes the capacity to choose rightly. According to Sandel, the ability to pursue the common good does not depend only on individual choice or the respect of others' right to choose; rather, it requires "a knowledge of public affairs and also a sense of belonging, a concern for the whole, a moral bond with the community whose fate is at stake."[15] Whereas political liberalism emphasizes a procedural democracy that makes no presuppositions about human choices, the republican conception of freedom that Sandel and others celebrate asserts that politics should not be neutral toward the values its citizens espouse. Instead, it should pursue "rightly ordered" social and political relationships. From this perspective, the essential requirement of communities is not liberty or personal choice per se, but the capacity to make "right" choices based on moral habits and values developed through communal traditions. As George Weigel has noted, the tradition of Catholic social thought has historically defined the common good as rightly ordered communal relationships, or the tranquillity of a just order (*tranquillitas ordinis*).[16] For him, the common good is a peaceful and just moral order that affirms human dignity and communal harmony.

Communitarians believe that peace is not an automatic by-product of the quest for justice. As a result, they tend to emphasize the maintenance of a just public order by balancing the ideals of peace with those of justice. Indeed, communitarians tend to give precedence to the restoration of political order as a precondition for justice.[17] Thus, when civil strife and war erupt, leading to widespread violence, communitarians assume that the primary task in public life is to restore a just peace rooted in the pursuit of national unity and reconciliation. Since some regime offenses cannot be repaired through legal retribution, the communitarian perspective promotes the renewal and healing of divided societies through the moral rehabilitation of social and political relationships. While qualifying but not negating the need for legal accountability, the communitarian perspective encourages the healing of deeply fragmented and alienated communities through truth telling, apologies, and empathy. For the communitarian, then, political forgiveness provides a means by which communities can begin to restore those social and political relationships that will ultimately lead to a just and legitimate political order.

In light of the contrasting perspectives of political liberalism and communitarianism, two divergent strategies are available to emerging democratic regimes for confronting the wrongs and injustices of the past: an individualistic strategy of legal retribution and a communal strategy of social and political rehabilitation. The first presupposes the existence of a community and seeks to address past wrongs by identifying individual victims and holding offenders personally accountable for criminal wrongdoing regardless of the context in which the offenses were committed. It assumes that the pursuit of individual justice will lead to the rehabilitation and restoration of political community. The most effective way to cure the legacy of destruction and injustice from civil strife, terror, and war is through the application of the rule of law. The second strategy, by contrast, assumes that since individual accountability is only possible within a stable legal order, the healing of fragmented, alienated communities is a prerequisite for individual justice. Accordingly, the communitarian perspective emphasizes the healing of political communities through the moral and political rehabilitation of collective relationships, guided by a shared conception of the community's common good.

THE RESTORATION OF COMMUNITY

The liberal and communitarian traditions offer two distinct models of justice—retributive justice and restorative justice. As noted earlier, retributive justice involves giving everyone his or her legal due. As a result, it seeks to provide an impartial system to which individuals are accountable. Since political liberalism is a paradigm grounded in individual rights and responsibilities, regime wrongdoing can be addressed only by focusing on the culpability of individual offenders.

As I argued in chapter 4, the retributive paradigm is appropriate when confronting personal crimes, but it is much less effective in addressing political

violence. Since domestic political conflict is undertaken to contest the existing structure of political society, it challenges the legitimacy of domestic laws.
Not surprisingly, in waging domestic war insurgents rarely regard existing
laws as binding, nor do they consider the codified laws of war applicable to
their collective violence. For their part, regimes that seek to protect the state
from covert terror may resort to counterinsurgency strategies that cannot be
easily reconciled with the widely accepted norms of warfare. Thus, when
groups resort to collective violence in the pursuit of political objectives, either
by toppling a regime or by undermining its authority, the violence is not,
strictly speaking, a crime or war. Rather, it is a form of "low-intensity conflict,"
falling into an intermediary zone between stable peace and unstable war.
Since such domestic political violence is difficult to classify legally and
morally, the domestic model of legal retribution is difficult to apply and not
always appropriate in confronting past collective violence.

The alternative model of restorative justice confronts wrongdoing by fostering the healing of individuals and groups and the renewal of community
relationships. Whereas liberal retribution seeks to deter criminal wrongdoing
by ensuring an effective and credible legal order, restorative justice is a forward-looking model that emphasizes the healing and moral rehabilitation of
victims and the renewal of social and political relationships. According to the
restorative model, healing the individual and collective injuries is best realized not through legal or political processes but rather through social and
moral actions that involve both victims and offenders. In particular, restorative justice calls on offenders to confront and publicly acknowledge offenses
and to offer appropriate reparations as an expression of authentic remorse.

Victims, for their part, must be empathetic toward offenders, be willing to
acknowledge perpetrators' repentance, and, where circumstances justify it,
to offer forgiveness by reducing or eliminating deserved penalties. To be
sure, moral rehabilitation cannot fully undo the damage and destruction
from political wrongdoing, but it can provide a basis for personal healing
and the restoration of communal solidarity. In short, since individuals are not
autonomous, isolated agents but people whose humanity is rooted in communal bonds, the renewal and restoration of human relationships is an essential dimension of the good life and a key element of justice.

Lincoln's Strategy

President Abraham Lincoln powerfully demonstrates the idea of restorative justice in his approach toward the national healing and reconstruction of
the United States in the aftermath of the Civil War. For Lincoln, the great challenge in confronting the evils of slavery and the resulting destruction from
the bitter and costly war was to pursue a forward-looking strategy that would
heal the nation's wounds. The goal was not to pursue retribution but to pro-

mote political reconciliation and national unity. Lincoln's forward-looking strategy emerged with his famous Gettysburg Address in November 1863 and his subsequent Proclamation of Amnesty and Reconstruction.

At the battlefield at Gettysburg, Lincoln, after paying tribute to those who had given their lives so that "the nation might live," rededicated the country to the ongoing task of advancing a free and equal society based on a government "of the people, by the people, for the people." He sought to honor the dead, but he did so by calling on citizens to dedicate themselves to the forward-looking task of building a free society, so that "these dead shall not have died in vain." A month later, Lincoln announced the Amnesty Proclamation that pardoned citizens and soldiers who had participated in the war against the Union, provided they had not served as senior military or political leaders of the Confederacy or perpetrated crimes against prisoners of war. To receive the pardon, people needed to sign an oath of loyalty to the United States, agree to abide by all wartime acts of Congress, and accept all government proclamations regarding slavery. A major aim of this action was to stress the priority of promoting political unity over legal retribution. The impact of this forward-looking strategy is evidenced by the fact that only one military officer was tried in the aftermath of the Civil War.[18]

Perhaps the most compelling expression of the Lincolnian restorative justice strategy is the president's second inaugural on March 4, 1865, given thirty-seven days before the end of the Civil War and shortly before his own death. According to William Safire, Lincoln used this address "to preach a sermon looking past the war's bitterness to a time of what he felt had to be reconciliation and reconstruction."[19] In the inaugural, Lincoln acknowledged that both parties to the war had asked for God's aid, but he suggests that the path forward is through nonjudgmentalism, calling on his listeners to "judge not, that we be not judged." The way toward national healing is to be found not in righteous indignation, recrimination, or retribution but in the quest for political unity through an all-embracing communitarianism rooted in charity. This call for national reconciliation and moral restoration is movingly expressed in the inaugural's conclusion:

> With malice toward none, with charity for all, with firmness in the right as God gives us to see the right, let us strive on to finish the work we are in, to bind the nation's wounds, to care for him who shall have borne the battle and for his widow and his orphan, to do all which may achieve and cherish a just and lasting peace among ourselves and with all nations.

It is significant that the peace to be cherished is not *between* former antagonists but *among* all people. Rather than viewing society as divided between unionists and secessionists or those who affirmed the political equality of people and those who did not, Lincoln's postwar strategy focused on the quest for political reconciliation and communal restoration by emphasizing the (re)construction of a shared political identity. Instead of seeking to punish those who had opposed the Union, Lincoln pursued the healing of the nation, believing that the pursuit of national unity needed to take precedence over claims of retribution.

According to Robert Meister, Lincoln's strategy of postwar reconciliation was based on the assumption that all Americans were victims of the evils of slavery and of the suffering caused by the Civil War.[20] Whereas political antagonists are typically classified as victims or offenders, the innocent or the guilty, Meister argues that Lincoln approached political healing and national reconciliation by regarding all political antagonists as survivors. For Meister, Lincoln's "survivorship" ethic had three elements: First, it assumed that communal healing comes through identification with a shared political vision rather than through representation. As a result, victims and perpetrators must not view themselves as different peoples—North or South, black or white—but as one nation seeking to overcome distrust, animosity, and division.

Second, the survivorship ethic assumed that antagonists were morally equal. Meister observes that "to break the cycle of victimization, the historical victims of abuse are morally expected to dedicate themselves to the 'proposition' that peace is victory enough."[21] Finally, the moral logic of survivorship emphasized a new beginning between political antagonists. Although the strategy was rooted in memory of past suffering, the goal of remembrance was not to exact justice but to prevent the repetition of evil. In effect, the ethic of survivorship was a forward-looking strategy rooted in memory.[22]

The Lincolnian strategy stands in stark contrast to the model of Jeffersonian political liberalism. While liberalism provides a useful system for fostering accountability and maintaining a credible legal order in conditions of relative political stability, it is wholly inadequate in addressing the suffering and destruction arising from intractable political disputes, as was the case in the Civil War. In such circumstances, where culpability for political violence is likely to be broadly shared among antagonists, the pursuit of strict justice based on a distinction of offender and victim is likely to be inappropriate. What is needed in the aftermath of such widespread violence is a strategy that balances a backward-looking concern with memory and accountability with a forward-looking focus on healing and reconciliation. Thus, the Lincolnian strategy of communal restoration based on memory and hope is an important alternative in confronting past regime wrongdoing.

Ideally, transitional regimes seeking to address former wrongdoing should rely on both restorative and retributive justice. If societies fail to identify and condemn evil, the consolidation of constitutional rule and civil society will be impaired. At the same time, a regime that focuses solely on retribution will necessarily neglect the renewal of interpersonal relationships and the restoration of communal bonds that are indispensable to the healing of alienated and deeply divided communities. Although both legal retribution and moral reconstruction can contribute to the social and political healing of fragmented societies, fragile transitional societies have much to gain by pursuing a forward-looking strategy that encourages renewal and restoration through truth telling and individual and collective forgiveness.

The Limits of Legalism in Healing Collective Violence

How should a transitional regime confront the wrongdoing of a former government? Should it attempt to prosecute the abuses of the leaders and government agents of the former regime or should it devote its scarce political resources to the consolidation of democracy? If it does the former, what laws should it use to prosecute wrongdoing—the laws that were in existence at the time the abuses were committed, the constitutional rules that have emerged under the new regime, or the widely accepted legal principles of international human rights? If, on the other hand, a regime seeks to establish a clear break with the past and concentrate its resources on the consolidation of democratic rule, it is likely that it will pursue few trials. If evidence and political pressures warrant prosecution, the transitional regime may carry out trials of a few senior political and military officials. Even limited judicial actions, however, may be deemed problematic since many of the crimes and abuses were carried out as part of an antigovernment subversion campaign, a deeply contested domestic political contest, or even a civil war.

In peaceful times, courts provide a means for holding individuals accountable for individual criminal action. On the other hand, when domestic order is broken down and violence and human rights abuses are perpetrated as part of a political contest, judicial procedures lose much of their credibility and effectiveness. Domestic courts are constructed to prosecute individual crimes, but their authority is diminished when attempting to prosecute war crimes committed during a civil war.

As noted earlier, domestic political violence constitutes an intermediary category between the zone of peace and the zone of international war. In peacetime, a state's legal system provides rules and institutions to ensure individual compliance with the law. When people violate a state's legal rules, the state will hold individuals accountable for wrongdoing by prosecuting and punishing the guilty. And when war breaks out among states, the codified laws of war provide rules for regulating and judging wartime violence. Although there is no international legal system comparable to a domestic criminal justice system, the enforcement of the laws of war is carried out chiefly by states themselves.[23]

When revolutionary groups resort to domestic political violence in order to topple an existing regime, judging domestic political violence is a much more ambiguous task. This is especially the case if revolutionary groups adopt unconventional strategies involving terror, rural insurgency, and urban guerrilla operations. When such strategies are utilized—as was the case by ANC guerrillas (MK) in South Africa or the IRA in Northern Ireland—defining what constitutes legally and morally acceptable political violence is a difficult task. Moreover, ascertaining what constitutes a legitimate counterinsurgency strategy by the state is similarly a challenging and morally problematic undertaking.

Personal crimes are of course a different type of offense from politically motivated offenses in domestic disputes or international wars. Although violence can be perpetrated for personal gain as part of domestic or international political conflicts, it is important not to conflate crime with domestic or international violence.[24] While personal offenses and public coercion can result in human suffering and destruction, the two categories of violence are not morally symmetrical. Domestic crime involves individual wrongdoing committed for private gain during times of relative stability. Domestic political violence or international war crimes, by contrast, are abuses committed as part of a political contest. Murder and wartime killing are both evil, but while the first is always unacceptable, the latter may be morally and legally justified if appropriate moral preconditions are fulfilled. Moreover, it is important to differentiate between conventional war and terrorism perpetrated by revolutionary groups.

In recent years there has been an increasing transnational effort to regard gross human rights violations as a threat to the international community itself. This trend has been expressed in the growing acceptance of universal jurisdiction, which provides that any state or international organization may prosecute crimes against humanity regardless of where the crimes take place. As a result of the growing acceptance of this claim, the UN Security Council authorized the creation of an international war crimes tribunal in The Hague in order to prosecute Serb leaders responsible for ethnic cleansing, rape, torture, and widespread killing in Bosnia. The most dramatic illustration of universal jurisdiction was the effort by a Spanish prosecutor to extradite Augusto Pinochet, Chile's former head of government, from the United Kingdom to Spain in order to stand trial for the death of some eighty Spanish citizens.[25]

Despite the global eagerness to identify and prosecute wrongdoing, criminal prosecution of politically motivated violence is problematic, whether pursued domestically by an emerging constitutional regime or by an international tribunal. When domestic societies are deeply divided and the political conflicts lead to deep and widespread violence, individual legal accountability is unlikely to satisfactorily address past wrongdoing. More significant, trials are unlikely to contribute to the restoration of communal bonds.

Indeed, the application of legal accountability by the emerging constitutional regime is likely to be regarded not as a quest for political justice but as an instrument of political domination or even victor's justice. Indeed, when the notion of community is itself contested—when citizens dispute who the "we" is and which people's rules are authoritative—the quest for retributive justice is unlikely to heal the divisions and mistrust within society. The prosecution of human rights abuses by international tribunals is also problematic since such action may impair rather than facilitate reconciliation. It may do so by undermining domestic initiatives and reforms that are necessary to ensure a limited just peace.[26] For example, the UN war crimes trials in The Hague and in Arusha for crimes perpetrated in the Bosnian War and in the 1994 Rwandan genocide, respectively, have been inefficient and costly and have received limited public support in either country.

If the institutionalization of democracy is to succeed in deeply polarized societies, transitional regimes must not disregard the quest for national unity and the restoration of relationships. Ideally, countries emerging from civil war or unjust authoritarian rule should pursue justice and political reconciliation, the rule of law, and the restoration of national unity. As a general rule, however, emerging democratic societies have often given priority to justice and legal retribution and to de-emphasizing social and political reconciliation.

Regardless of whether domestic or international courts prosecute leaders and agents who committed human rights crimes, the restoration of deeply divided societies will necessitate more than legal prosecution. If the deep political cleavages of society are to be healed and if enemies are to move toward reconciliation, the injuries, crimes, and injustices of the past will have to be confronted through truth telling and acknowledgment. It will also require the moral reformation of society and the reconstruction of a society's legal and political institutions. In particular, the healing and renewal of social relationships will demand different attitudes and values. If the ethic of political forgiveness is to be incorporated into the public life of nations, former enemies will have to publicly confront their own shortcomings. This means that perpetrators and their agents must be willing to acknowledge wrongdoing and express contrition for the suffering they have inflicted. For their part, victims and their agents must be willing to respond with empathy toward offenders, give up the desire for retaliation, and be willing to lift some or all the offenders' deserved penalty. If leaders of political communities can carry out these actions, the ethic of forgiveness can contribute to the healing of nations by fostering peace, moral order, and the promotion of national reconciliation.

FORGIVENESS IN PUBLIC LIFE

Historically, forgiveness has been regarded as an element of interpersonal ethics, relevant solely to individual wrongdoing. According to conventional wisdom, forgiveness is an idea rooted in religion, especially the Judeo-Christian belief in a gracious and merciful God who forgives people who acknowledge their sin, express contrition for their wrongdoing, and promise not to repeat moral offenses. In the Judeo-Christian conception of forgiveness, divine pardon results in the lifting of moral guilt and deserved punishment and in the renewal of a person's moral standing and the restoration of human-divine relationships. Unlike divine forgiveness, which is an unmerited gift, individual human forgiveness is an interpersonal process between an offender and victim and is conditional on the voluntary action of the victim. Ordinarily such forgiveness entails an acknowledgment of culpability, remorse for the offense, empathy by both victims and offenders, and the lifting of some or the entire offender's deserved penalty. It is important to stress that the mitigation or abolition of a deserved penalty generally presupposes repentance, which may be authenticated through acts of reparation or restitution and the promise to not commit further wrongs.

The Idea of Political Forgiveness

Political forgiveness is a public response to a collective offense. Unlike individual crimes, collective wrongdoing involves offenses and human rights abuses that are carried out for political purposes and are perpetrated by state agents or representatives of political groups. Like private forgiveness, however, political forgiveness is a process in which offenders and victims move toward reconciliation in the aftermath of a serious moral offense. As noted in chapter 3, political forgiveness depends on certain preconditions, including truth, public acknowledgment of collective offenses, avoidance of revenge, mutual empathy and compassion, and the reduction or cancellation of a debt or deserved punishment.

The ultimate goal of forgiveness is reconciliation. Although partial forgiveness is realized when enemies stop hating each other and victims overcome their inward resentment and anger, the forgiveness process culminates only when victims and offenders are reconciled and when enemies begin to recognize each other's humanity. The goal of forgiveness is to provide an alternative response to wrongdoing so that the moral reconstruction of communal relationships can occur.

Political forgiveness represents an extension of interpersonal forgiveness to the actions of collectives. Such forgiveness is possible because groups and communities, like individuals, commit moral offenses that result in anger, distrust, and ruptured communal relationships. If collective forgiveness is to occur, legitimate leaders must acknowledge their members' collective offenses, publicly apologize for them, and authenticate remorse through symbolic or tangible reparations. In turn, leaders of victim communities must acknowledge the contrition, refrain from retaliation, and express empathy and compassion toward former enemies.

Of course, some atrocities and injustices may be so serious that healing can only occur with time. To the extent that political communities can confront and overcome the legacy of egregious systemic violence, however, it is far more likely that they will do so through a restorative justice model than through legal retribution. Indeed, overcoming enmity, distrust, and anger is likely to be facilitated only through moral actions in which offenders acknowledge offenses and express contrition and victims refrain from vengeance and reply to offenders' remorse with empathy and a willingness to restore communal bonds. To the extent that public officials fulfill these preconditions, their mutual and interdependent action will permit groups and communities to both receive and offer collective forgiveness, thereby restoring offenders' human dignity and relieving victims of their compulsion to retaliate. In effect, collective forgiveness helps to undo the past by fostering individual healing and communal reconstruction.

The application of forgiveness to the political realm can be viewed as the extension of "thick" interpersonal morality to the "thin" morality of social groups and political communities.[27] Thick morality is expressed in specific moral obligations that govern interpersonal behavior. Such "maximal" morality applies to those near and dear—parent, friend, or fellow citizen—and is embodied in such norms as the Ten Commandments and the moral precedence given to family and friends over strangers. Because thick morality is distinguished by its limited, narrow scope coupled with a high level of depth, the memory associated with such morality is robust and richly textured. In the words of philosopher Avishai Margalit, it is a "shared" memory in which community members have a deep, integrated view of the past.[28]

Thin morality, by contrast, is abstract, universal, and impersonal, providing norms for all human beings. Moreover, since such morality is broad in scope but limited in specificity, it is associated with a limited collective memory—one composed of the aggregate of people's individual conceptions of the past.[29] Because thin morality is expressed individually in human rights concepts such as liberty and equality and collectively through communal rights notions such as self-determination and political autonomy, it calls for caring and love to be expressed uniformly and impartially to family and strangers alike. Moral minimalism is a thin morality not because it is unimportant or makes few claims on individuals but because its claims are general and diffuse.[30]

According to conventional wisdom, forgiveness is a form of thick morality, applicable only to individuals. But the claim that forgiveness cannot be a part of the thin collective morality of groups and nations is unpersuasive. Since communities can act as moral agents and are capable of independent moral action, it is conceivable that leaders can offer and receive forgiveness on behalf of their members, just as they can impose financial and other regulatory obligations on them.[31] As a result, when governments enact policies the lead to moral offenses, such actions impose responsibility not only on the agents that carried out such actions but also on the entire community itself. Thus, in confronting past regime wrongdoing, legitimate governments are legally and morally entitled to offer or receive collective forgiveness by acknowledging collective wrongdoing, expressing remorse, offering reparations, or granting amnesty.

The Promise of Political Forgiveness

Whether forgiveness is possible within and among political communities will depend largely on leaders' capacity to fulfill the ethic's preconditions. At a minimum, communities must be capable of defining collective wrongdoing, identifying individuals and groups responsible for and victims of the offenses, as well as atoning for the wrongdoing. If groups and communities are to participate successfully in the forgiveness process, those who have committed crimes and injustices must acknowledge wrongdoing, express remorse to victims, and treat their former enemies with dignity and respect. Victims, in turn, must be prepared to acknowledge offenders' remorse, renounce claims of retribution, and be willing to reduce or eliminate offenders' deserved punishment.

The primary challenge to incorporating forgiveness into public life is not conceptual or philosophical. Instead, the main obstacle to implementation is practical and moral, requiring wisdom and courage of leaders and citizens. As in interpersonal relationships, the major impediment to the successful application of political forgiveness may be the demanding nature of this ethic. Indeed, forgiveness may be more elusive than justice in political society, not because it provides easy reconciliation, but because of the unwillingness or inability of leaders to fulfill the ethic's demands. In particular, offenders may be unprepared to recognize their injustice and communicate their culpability to victims, while victims may be reluctant to give up their quest for retribution and to view offenders not as inhuman monsters but as individuals entitled to dignity.

Since politics inevitably compounds human moral frailties by increasing national selfishness and pride,[32] the expression of collective contrition and repentance is a rare occurrence. For example, despite their attack on Pearl Harbor, the Japanese government has never officially expressed contrition to the American people for this heinous offense. At the same time, the United States has always regarded the nuclear bombing of Hiroshima and Nagasaki as a necessary evil and has refused to apologize for the widespread civilian casualties resulting from this act. From time to time, however, leaders take the courageous step of acknowledging culpability and expressing remorse. This was the case when Argentina's Army chief expressed contrition for the offenses committed by the armed forces during the 1970s dirty war.[33] This was also the case when Pope John Paul II asked for forgiveness for the collective injustices committed by the Roman Catholic Church.

The theory of political forgiveness does not offer a formula or fixed set of norms by which to resolve collective injustices. Rather, it provides a moral process by which offenders—whether individual or collective, public or private—accept moral responsibility for wrongdoing. The admission of culpability is essential because without consensus about the nature of, and responsibility for, the offenses, no moral restoration of relationships can take place. This does not mean that agents must be classified as victims or perpetrators; rather, the restoration of communal solidarity insists that decision makers and state agents take responsibility for collective wrongdoing, acknowledging and apologizing for individual and collective offenses. If repentance is truly authentic, leaders must not only express remorse publicly but also offer reparations and restitution. Indeed, they must be prepared to participate in the process of legal justice to the extent that it is feasible within domestic society.

While repentance may entail criminal prosecution, the core requirement of political forgiveness is not legal retribution but public acknowledgment of wrongdoing and repentance for collective offenses. The theory of forgiveness assumes that if a community is to pursue the common good and restore its social relationships, the truth about past collective offenses must be made known. The prosecution and punishment of some leaders and agents may be necessary to maintain the authority of the rule of law and to authenticate repentance. While forgiveness may result in trials and reparations, however, the theory of political forgiveness does not demand criminal prosecution. Rather, it focuses chiefly on truth telling, acknowledgment of culpability, remorse, and compassion by the victims in response to the offenders' contrition.

The concept of political forgiveness sketched here is grounded in the need for communal well-being coupled with accountability based on truth. Unlike political liberalism, which privileges individual rights over the general community welfare, a theory of political forgiveness acknowledges the priority of rights but as a complement to the common good. Moreover, communitarianism gives precedence to communal well-being by emphasizing the healing of victims and the restoration of social relationships. In addition, it assumes that the quest for the common good is not achieved through an adversarial legal trial or through the punishment of offenders. While such developments may facilitate the restoration of legal order, they will not contribute to the moral and cultural reconstruction of society and the renewal of social trust. A theory of political forgiveness thus seeks the healing of individuals, the reconstruction of communal relationships, and the pursuit of a just political order.

THE HEALING OF NATIONS

Can nations overcome the destructive legacy of regime violence? Can fragile and deeply divided political communities that have experienced widespread abuse of human rights reduce political polarization and distrust and foster reconciliation through forgiveness? Our examination of collective violence in

Argentina, Chile, Northern Ireland, and South Africa suggests that the process of political healing and communal restoration is difficult and elusive and that fulfilling the preconditions for collective forgiveness is morally challenging. In none of the four cases has political forgiveness played a prominent role in fostering political reconciliation—in great part because major political actors have been unable or unwilling to fulfill the prerequisites for forgiveness. For example, despite their professed commitment to the truth, political antagonists have remained deeply divided over the nature of, and culpability for, past wrongdoing.

Although some antagonists have been able to achieve consensus about factual truth, the quest for narrative or explanatory truth has been far more difficult since the parties to the conflict remain divided over the causes and justification of past offenses. Moreover, although some leaders have admitted using inappropriate force in fighting enemies, most organizations and political groups have refused to acknowledge human rights abuses, even when substantial evidence exists of widespread terrorism, torture, abductions, and secret killings. Even when political groups and state institutions have admitted using excessive or indiscriminate violence, they have often continued to justify their tactics as necessary in the pursuit of legitimate political objectives. Not surprisingly, political antagonists have been reluctant to acknowledge and apologize for civilian atrocities and mass cruelties, while victims have refused to admit culpability for antistate violence, demanding instead full legal accountability for the government's excesses.

The failure to fully implement political forgiveness does not mean, however, that this ethic has been completely absent from the states' processes of transitional justice. As noted earlier, the process of forgiveness entails a number of steps, including truth telling, avoidance of vengeance, remorse, empathy, and lifting of debts or deserved punishment. Thus, to the extent that political actors fulfill any of these conditions, they create the potential for political healing through the ethic of collective forgiveness.

Of the four countries examined in previous chapters, the one that appears to have achieved the most success in confronting, acknowledging, and overcoming past collective offenses is South Africa. Although the nation was deeply polarized politically and on the verge of civil war in the late 1980s, political leaders—guided by the extraordinary statesmanship of President F. W. de Klerk and ANC leader Nelson Mandela—were able to craft a process of democratic transition rooted in truth telling. Because of the public nature of the truth commission and the promise of amnesty to perpetrators who fully disclosed their politically motivated crimes, a significant level of truth telling was achieved throughout the society. While significant racial, economic, and political fragmentation remains, South Africa's "truth and reconciliation" process is a landmark achievement in promoting national unity and reconciliation based on the public disclosure and acknowledgment of truth.

At the opposite end of the continuum, Northern Ireland appears to have achieved the least success in confronting and overcoming the legacy of political violence. Because the conflict between Catholic Republicans and Protestant Unionists centers on the issue of political identity, the dispute remains seemingly intractable. Indeed, the animosity and distrust between Unionists and Republicans is so profound that the immediate political objective has been the creation of an acceptable power-sharing government to inhibit political violence. The absence of political violence, not national healing or reconciliation, has been the primary objective of the peace process.[34] Accordingly, the Good Friday Agreement (GFA) of 1998 did not seek to reckon with past wrongdoing but simply attempted to establish a power-sharing framework to maintain domestic order and prevent further killing. To a significant degree, the forward-looking GFA has helped to contain violence and restore peace, but the underlying political dispute over the constitutional fate of Northern Ireland remains unresolved.

Unlike Northern Ireland, Argentina attempted to directly confront past collective violence in the early 1980s. After assuming office in 1983, President Raúl Alfonsín sought to come to terms with past regime offenses by identifying and disclosing them and then holding senior leaders legally responsible as a strategic means of political reconciliation. Although the "truth plus trials" approach was widely supported within the society, the prosecution of military officials ultimately led to political instability that undermined the accountability process itself, forcing Alfonsín to relinquish power early and President Carlos Menem to pardon convicted guerrillas and state officials. Most important, rather than promoting justice and consolidating democracy, the Argentine strategy resulted in some truth, little justice, and no reconciliation. Because major political actors remain deeply divided over culpability for past offenses and distrustful of each other's interests, society is fragmented and political order is fragile.

Seeking to avoid some of Argentina's difficulties, Chile's democratic government focused its transitional justice strategy on the discovery, disclosure, and acknowledgment of truth, in the hope that truth telling would contribute to national reconciliation. Unlike Argentina's democratic transition, which involved the immediate repeal of the military's self-amnesty decree, the restoration of democracy in Chile was predicated on the reality that the amnesty law would not be repealed and that military personnel would continue to be protected by this decree.[35] Since Chilean courts have been reluctant to prosecute senior military leaders and elected leaders have been unwilling to repeal the military's amnesty decree, civil-military relations have remained stable and less strained than in Argentina. Nevertheless, military officials have refused to acknowledge their offenses and have been reluctant to provide information about the fate of victims, lest such disclosure provide prosecutors with incriminating evidence.

While victims' families have received financial reparations, few perpetrators have been prosecuted. Moreover, while the quest for national reconciliation based on truth has borne little fruit to date, the major achievement of Chile's transitional justice strategy has been the rehabilitation and consolidation of constitutional government. This significant achievement has provided the foundation for the continued social and political rehabilitation of Chilean society.

In light of the four case studies examined in previous chapters, several preliminary findings emerge about the process of transitional justice and the quest for reconciliation through political forgiveness. These include the following:

- If fragmented and alienated communities are to be restored and renewed in the aftermath of regime atrocities, the truth about past collective wrongdoing must be discovered, disclosed, and acknowledged. Without the acknowledgment of past collective offenses, no moral accountability is possible, and without moral accountability, there can be no restoration of interpersonal relationships and communal bonds.
- While truth commissions can contribute to the discovery and disclosure of factual truth, they are unlikely to generate consensus about the causes and justification for regime violence. In other words, commissions can uncover information about the nature and scope of regime violence, but they are unlikely to generate an authoritative, widely accepted explanation of the factors that precipitated government actions.
- One of most important contributions that truth commissions can make is to provide victims with an opportunity to "tell their story." Such disclosure can contribute to a nation's collective awareness about past regime offenses and injustices.
- Leaders can contribute to the moral rehabilitation of communities through the public expression of collective remorse. The official acknowledgment of past regime offenses can contribute to national healing and political reconciliation.
- Although apologies can contribute to the restoration of truth between antagonists, leaders rarely acknowledge collective contrition—in great part because groups are rarely willing to admit culpability, preferring instead to continue justifying collective violence as politically and morally necessary.
- Groups responsible for collective offenses can authenticate their remorse through reparations. Whether or not financial or symbolic, reparations provide victims with a tangible acknowledgment of a regime's responsibility for past collective offenses.
- Individual and collective forgiveness is a difficult and demanding process, but one that is greatly facilitated when culpable offenders acknowledge their offenses and offer public repentance.

- While morally problematic, the decision to pardon offenders can facilitate the peace process.
- Since self-amnesty decrees are enacted to protect rulers from future prosecution, they are of dubious constitutional legitimacy. Though self-amnesty laws impair the quest for retributive justice, they may nonetheless contribute to political stability and facilitate the consolidation of democratic institutions.
- When regime offenses are a by-product of domestic political conflict, focusing solely on individual culpability for collective wrongdoing will result in dubious justice and impede political reconciliation.
- While trials of former regime officials may foster justice and help consolidate the rule of law, they can also undermine political order and inhibit the consolidation of democratic institutions. This is especially the case where the authoritarian government has voluntarily relinquished power and remained an influential political actor in society.
- Finally, since governmental resources are limited, the decision of whether to pursue trials, truth commissions, comprehensive reparations, or some other transitional justice strategy will depend on the availability of political and economic resources.

CONCLUSION

Despite the expansion of democracy in the international system, political actors continue to commit atrocities and human rights abuses as they pursue such political objectives as self-determination, regime replacement, or ethnic cleansing. In the post–Cold War millions of innocent civilians have died in wars of national liberation, civil wars, and terrorist campaigns as political groups have competed for political control. In some cases the absence of governmental authority has resulted in virtual anarchy, allowing armed groups to perpetrate widespread atrocities for ethnic, economic, or even criminal reasons.[36]

While it is important to hold offenders accountable for gross human rights violations, the far more pressing task is to restore a humane public order and thereby prevent the recurrence of atrocities, ethnic violence, and genocide. The major challenge in weak or failed states is not to hold trials but to constitute legitimate political authority and strengthen democratic norms and institutions in order to foster a more accountable, tolerant, and humane political culture. Since most models of transitional justice are rooted in a backward-looking legalism, political forgiveness offers a promising forward-looking alternative. Rather than seeking to repair past wrongdoing through legal retribution, political forgiveness pursues the healing of victims and the restoration of relationships through the moral reformation of individuals and groups based on accountability rooted in truth.

Fundamentally, political forgiveness seeks to create the preconditions that will prevent the repetition of offenses while simultaneously fostering the renewal of a community's moral and political order and the restoration of social and political bonds. Since forgiveness requires mutually constructive and conciliatory actions between victims and offenders, it helps to establish a moral foundation for the restoration of social and political relationships. Because history cannot be undone, political forgiveness calls on antagonists to redeem the past by acknowledging that which cannot be changed (the suffering and destruction) and reforming that which can be changed (the dispositions, moral values, commitments, and future actions). It is important to stress that political forgiveness is not a means of achieving cheap reconciliation but a demanding moral process among offenders and victims based on a balancing of retribution and restoration, accountability and healing. Its aim is not to minimize past wrongdoing but to heal injuries and to prevent the repetition of wrongdoing.

Of course, political actors may not wish to pursue collective healing and national reconciliation. To the extent that antagonists' political and social identities are rooted in their seemingly irreconcilable beliefs and memories, they may prefer continued political fragmentation and distrust to the promotion of national unity and social reconciliation. They may prefer to persist in self-righteous indignation even if such a condition contributes to low national cohesion, political instability, and economic stagnation. Since perpetrators' ideological values and commitments influenced their collective actions, they are undoubtedly reluctant to modify their worldviews in exchange for greater national unity. More likely, political antagonists will continue to defend resorting to political violence. For example, Pinochet and his staunch supporters have continued to defend and justify political repression used during the era of military rule, while ANC guerrillas and the IRA have similarly justified their military operations as necessary in pursuit of political liberation.

People and relatives who have suffered loss from political violence may also be unwilling to give up their status as victims, especially since it has served as a basis of social identity and political influence. Since political forgiveness would bring an end to victimhood, victims have remained adamantly committed to legal accountability and opposed to political reconciliation. In Argentina, for example, the two leading human rights organizations—the Mothers and Grandmothers of the Plaza de Mayo—have continued to demand information on the fate of missing victims and to search for the true families of "stolen" children. At the same time, however, they continue to oppose political accommodation, to demand retribution for those responsible for the crimes of the dirty war, and to maintain a prominent posture as a major human rights lobby.

If political forgiveness is to become a part of national healing, antagonists must be willing to confront the truth about past politically motivated offenses and to assume responsibility for their individual and collective role in such wrongdoing. This means, as Alexander Solzhenitsyn has pointed out, that antagonists must be prepared to acknowledge mutual responsibility for past violence, thereby making possible the "path of mutual repentance."[37] But as suggested in the four case studies, major political actors in each of the countries have been reluctant to acknowledge responsibility or to express remorse for widespread killings, kidnappings, and torture. Instead, they have continued to deny culpability or to justify the use of unconventional force as a necessary national security strategy. Thus, if political healing is to occur, the endless cycle of self-righteousness and self-justification must be halted. As Solzhenitsyn has noted, "at some point the endless account must be closed, we must stop discussing whose crimes are more recent, are more serious, and affect most victims. It is useless for even the closest neighbors to compare the duration and gravity of their grievances against each other."[38]

Although truth is the basis for both retributive and restorative justice, the healing of social and political relationships is possible only when antagonists view each other as human beings and are willing to express empathy and compassion toward each other. It is not enough to ascertain culpability and to impose retributive punishment on perpetrators. Indeed, the healing of individuals, either from paralyzing guilt or from the compulsion toward revenge, coupled with the renewal of social solidarity, is possible only when individuals and groups begin to regard their opponents as people entitled to respect and dignity. The promise of political forgiveness is that it provides a moral process by which political healing and social solidarity can emerge out of the ashes of cruelty and destruction. Given the immense suffering from past collective offenses, it would be a pity if political groups failed to explore the potential of collective forgiveness in confronting and overcoming past evil. Whether or not forgiveness is applied to the legacy of past wrongdoing, one thing is clear: the road to communal safety, prosperity, and peace can only come through the acknowledgment of truth and the healing of memories, which alone provide a foundation for harmonious, productive relationships.

Notes

1. The phrase "purification of memory" was central to the Mass of Reconciliation celebrated by Pope John Paul II in March 2000. In that mass, the Pope confessed the church's most important faults in the hope of purifying the church's collective memory and thereby modeling and promoting reconciliation. The mass was rooted in the work of the International Theological Commission, which issued a study titled "Memory and Reconciliation: The Church and the Faults of the Past" several months beforehand. For the full study, www.vatican.va/roman _curia/congregations/cfaith/cti_documents/rc_con_cfaith_doc_20000307_memory-reconc-itc _en.html [accessed February 27, 2004].

INTRODUCTION

1. Adam Michnik and Václav Havel, "Confronting the Past: Justice or Revenge?" *Journal of Democracy* 4 (January 1993), p. 22.

2. "Speech by Richard von Weizsäcker, President of the Federal Republic of Germany, in the Bundestag during the Ceremony Commemorating the 40th Anniversary of the End of the War in Europe and of National Socialist Tyranny, May 8, 1985," in *Bitburg in Moral and Political Perspective,* ed. Geoffrey H. Hartman (Bloomington: Indiana University Press, 1986), p. 265.

3. Quoted in "Address by Helmut Kohl, Chancellor of the Federal Republic of Germany, during the Ceremony Marking the 40th Anniversary of the Liberation of the Concentration Camps at the Site of the Former Bergen-Belsen Concentration Camp, April 21, 1985," in *Bitburg,* p. 250.

4. Interview with Alicia Juica in Santiago on March 29, 2000.

5. Alicia tells me that when her father failed to return home, he was assumed to have been abducted, tortured, and then killed by military intelligence agents.

6. This discussion with senior retired military officers, which took place on March 29, 2000, with fourteen officers, was carried out with the understanding that the meeting would be kept confidential.

7. The National Commission on Truth and Reconciliation, an investigatory body established by presidential decree, issued its report in March 1991—a year after democracy had been restored in Chile.

8. General Augusto Pinochet first expressed this perspective immediately after the truth commission report was made public. President Pinochet said of the report: "Its content reveals an unpardonable refusal to recognize the real causes that motivated the action to rescue the nation on September 11, 1973." He went on to suggest that Chile's Army "sees no reason to ask pardon for having fulfilled its patriotic duty." *New York Times*, March 28, 1991, A1.

9. For a brief overview of the ethical dimensions of this case, see Mark Amstutz, *International Ethics: Concepts, Theories, Cases* (Lanham, MD: Rowman & Littlefield Publishers, 1999), pp. 21–24.

10. "Remarks of Elie Wiesel at Ceremony for Jewish Heritage Week and Presentation of Congressional Gold Medal, White House, April 19, 1985," in *Bitburg*, p. 243.

11. "Remarks of Elie Wiesel," *Bitburg*, p. 243.

12. "Remarks of Elie Wiesel," *Bitburg*, p. 243.

13. "Interview of President Reagan by Representatives of Foreign Radio and Television," in *Bitburg*, pp. 250–51.

14. See Elazar Barkan, *The Guilt of Nations: Restitution and Negotiating Historical Injustices* (New York: Norton, 2000).

15. "Speech by Richard von Weizsäcker," in *Bitburg*, p. 265.

16. Zalaquett, "Balancing Ethical Imperatives and Political Constraints: The Dilemma of New Democracies Confronting Past Human Rights Violations," in *Transitional Justice: How Emerging Democracies Reckon with Former Regimes: Country Studies*, vol. 2, ed. Neil J. Kritz (Washington, DC: United States Institute of Peace Press, 1995), p. 496.

17. Timothy Garton Ash, "The Truth about Dictatorship," *The New York Review of Books* 45 (February 19, 1998): 35.

18. Jean Hampton, "Forgiveness, Resentment and Hatred" in *Forgiveness and Mercy*, ed. Jeffrie G. Murphy and Jean Hampton (Cambridge: Cambridge University Press, 1988), pp. 36–43.

19. Beginning in the mid-1990s, a number of thinkers began to consider the potential of this ethic. Perhaps the most significant early study was Donald Shriver Jr., *An Ethic for Enemies: Forgiveness in Politics* (New York: Oxford University Press, 1995). Other important studies on the social and political dimensions of forgiveness include R. Scott Appleby, *The Ambivalence of the Sacred: Religion, Violence, and Reconciliation* (Lanham, MD: Rowman & Littlefield, 2000); P. E. Digeser, *Political Forgiveness* (Ithaca, NY: Cornell University Press, 1991); Miroslav Volf, *Exclusion & Embrace: A Theological Exploration of Identity, Otherness, and Reconciliation* (Nashville, TN: Abingdon Press, 1996).

20. Hannah Arendt, *The Human Condition* (Chicago: University of Chicago Press, 1958), p. 237.

21. Desmond Tutu, *No Future without Forgiveness* (New York: Doubleday, 1999).

22. Simon Wiesenthal, *The Sunflower: On the Possibilities and Limits of Forgiveness*, rev. and exp. ed. (New York: Schocken Books, 1998), p. 27.

23. Wiesenthal, *Sunflower* (1998), p. 54.

24. Wiesenthal, *Sunflower* (1998), p. 97.

25. Nicholas Tavuchis, *Mea Culpa: A Sociology of Apology and Reconciliation* (Stanford, CA: Stanford University Press, 1991), pp. 69–89.

26. Simon Wiesenthal, *The Sunflower* (New York: Schocken Books, 1976), p. 160. Konvitz' reflections appear in the first edition of the book but not in its revised 1998 edition.

27. Wiesenthal, *Sunflower* (1998), p. 220.

28. Wiesenthal, *Sunflower* (1998), p. 169.

29. Wiesenthal, *Sunflower* (1998), p. 211.

30. For a brief description of Lincoln's strategy, see chapter 9, pp. 218–21.

31. Miroslav Volf, *Exclusion & Embrace: A Theological Exploration of Identity, Otherness, and Reconciliation* (Nashville, TN: Abingdon Press, 1996), chap. 3.

CHAPTER 1: CONFRONTING HUMAN RIGHTS ABUSES: APPROACHES TO TRANSITIONAL JUSTICE

1. Simon Wiesenthal, *The Sunflower: On the Possibilities and Limits of Forgiveness* (New York: Schoken Books, 1998), p. 211.

2. Quoted in Stanley Cohen, "State Crimes of Previous Regimes: Knowledge, Accountability, and the Policing of the Past," *Law and Social Inquiry*, 20, no. 1 (1995): 7.

3. Samuel P. Huntington, *The Third Wave: Democratization in the Late Twentieth Century* (Norman: University of Oklahoma Press, 1991), p. 231.

4. Juan E. Méndez, "In Defense of Transitional Justice" in *Transitional Justice and the Rule of Law in New Democracies*, ed. A. James McAdams (Great Bend, IN: University of Notre Dame Press, 1997), p. 8.

5. The inquiry into this topic has spawned an extensive scholarly literature. The best general introduction to this subject is the three-volume study titled *Transitional Justice: How Emerging Democracies Reckon with Former Regimes*, edited by Neil J. Kritz and published by the United States Institute of Peace Press. Vol. 1 deals with general considerations, vol. 2 concerns country studies, and vol. 3 covers relevant laws, rulings, and reports.

6. Michael Ignatieff, *The Warrior's Honor: Ethnic War and the Modern Conscience* (New York: Henry Holt, 1997), p. 171.

7. Adam Michnik and Václav Havel, "Confronting the Past: Justice or Revenge?" *Journal of Democracy* 4 (January 1993), p. 24.

8. Timothy Garton Ash, "The Truth about Dictatorship," *The New York Review of Books* 45 (February 19, 1998), p. 35.

9. Ash, "Truth about Dictatorship," p.35.

10. For an excellent brief account of Turkey's continued denial of the Armenian genocide of 1915, see Gary Jonathan Bass, *Stay the Hand of Vengeance: The Politics of War Crimes Tribunals* (Princeton, NJ: Princeton University Press, 2000), pp. 106–146. See also Samantha Power, *A Problem from Hell: America and the Age of Genocide* (New York: Basic Books, 2002), pp. 1–16.

11. Ian Buruma, *The Wages of Guilt: Memories of War in Germany and Japan* (New York: Meridian Books, 1995), p. 294.

12. In developed constitutional systems, executives have the authority to pardon people who have been judged guilty by a court of law. Since a pardon frees an offender from his legal sentence, it is similar to amnesty. But whereas amnesties are granted to anyone, only a criminally guilty offender may be pardoned by the state.

13. Since passage of the amnesty measure resulted in significant public opposition, human rights groups immediately began demanding a referendum to overturn the new measure. Because a referendum needed 550,000 signatures (out of a population of less than 3 million!), a massive campaign was mounted to gather the necessary popular support. Through extensive political action, the pro-referendum campaign succeeded in collecting more than enough signatures to review the amnesty law. Accordingly, a hotly contested referendum was carried out in 1989, with the supporters for amnesty surprisingly winning 58 percent of the vote.

14. The amnesty decreed by the Pinochet government provided that all politically motivated crimes committed during the state of siege—that is, from the coup d'etat in 1973 until 1978—were exempt from prosecution. This act led to the release of several hundred government opponents from prison, but it also provided the basis for protecting state agents from prosecution, the major aim of the decree.

15. Kritz, *Transitional Justice*, vol. 3, p. 591.

16. Bruce Ackerman, *The Future of Liberal Revolution* (New Haven, CT: Yale University Press, 1992), p. 73.

17. According to this claim, crimes against humanity are so heinous and evil that any state or international organization may prosecute such offenses. In other words, state sovereignty cannot protect egregious criminal action.

18. International law does not provide a simple, coherent perspective on amnesties. Indeed, the relevant conventions and judicial interpretations provide a complex, contested interpretation. For a discussion of some of the major international legal issues relevant to amnesty, see Naomi Roht-Arriaza and Lauren Gibson, "The Developing Jurisprudence on Amnesty," *Human Rights Quarterly* 20 (November 1998): 843–85.

19. José Zalaquett, "Truth, Justice, and Reconciliation: Lessons for the International Community," in *Comparative Peace Processes in Latin America*, ed. Cynthia J. Arnson (Stanford, CA: Stanford University Press, 1999), p. 348.

20. For a brief discussion of this point, see Ignatieff, *Warrior's Honor*, p. 168.

21. Quoted in Donald W. Shriver, Jr., *An Ethic for Enemies: Forgiveness in Politics* (New York: Oxford University Press, 1995), p. 110.

22. For an illuminating account of a review of his personal file, see Timothy Garton Ash, *The File: A Personal History* (New York: Random House, 1997).

22. For an overview of the nature and role of truth commissions, see Pricilla B. Hayner, *Unspeakable Truths: Confronting State Terror and Atrocity* (New York: Routledge, 2001). See also Hayner's, "Fifteen Truth Commissions—1974 to 1994: A Comparative Study," *Human Rights Quarterly* 16 (August 1994): 600–55.

24. Some commissions, such as those of El Salvador, Guatemala, and Paraguay, were broad in scope, providing a historical account of the origins and manifestations of statewide violence; other reports, such as those from Honduras and Uruguay, were more limited in scope, focusing only on killings and abductions. Commissions have also differed in their origins and political authority. For example, the commissions of Argentina, Chile, and South Africa were governmental, while those of Brazil and Uruguay were unofficial and undertaken by nongovernmental actors. In addition, some commissions, such as those of Argentina and Chile, undertook investigations confidentially, disclosing their findings only when the final report had been completed. The South Africa truth commission, by contrast, carried out its investigations publicly. Finally, some commissions, such as those of Guatemala and El Salvador, sought to identify officials and institutions responsible for human rights violations, while others, such as the commissions in Chile and South Africa, declined to name individuals on the grounds that evidence had not been gathered through cross-examination.

25. According to Osiel, three types of facts are generally missing from truth commission reports: 1) no effort is made to challenge perpetrators' claims that the victims of the military's repression were associated with antigovernment guerrillas; 2) no effort is made to examine the failure of political and legal institutions to respond to terrorism; and 3) truth commissions, unlike courts, cannot compel testimony and thereby refute their "official story." See Mark J. Osiel, "Why Prosecute? Critics of Punishment for Mass Atrocity," *Human Rights Quarterly* 20, no. 1 (2000): 118–47.

26. Mahmood Mamdani, *When Victims Become Killers: Colonialism, Nativism, and the Genocide in Rwanda* (Princeton, NJ: Princeton University Press, 2001), pp. 266–67.

27. See especially David Mankovsky, *Making Peace with the PLO: The Rabin Government's Road to the Oslo Accord* (Boulder, CO: Westview Press, 1996), p. 22.

28. Ignatieff, *Warrior's Honor*, p. 173.

29. "Chile: Statement by President Aylwin on the Report of the National Commission on Truth and Reconciliation," in *Transitional Justice*, vol. 3, p. 171.

30. Nicholas Tavuchis, *Mea Culpa: A Sociology of Apology and Reconciliation* (Stanford, CA: Stanford University Press, 1991), p. 48.

31. Tavuchis, *Mea Culpa*, p. 109.

32. Trudy Govier and Wilhelm Verwoerd, "The Promise and Pitfalls of Apology," *Journal of Social Philosophy* 33 (Spring 2002), pp. 67–82.

33. Govier and Verwoerd, "Promise and Pitfalls of Apology," p. 74.

34. For a discussion of the recent practice of public apologies, see Michael Cunningham, "Saying Sorry: The Politics of Apology," *Political Quarterly* 70 (July/September 1999): 285–93.

35. *Washington Post*, December 30, 1996, pp. 1 and 14.

36. The statement is titled "Memory and Reconciliation: The Church and the Mistakes of the Past," www.vatican.va/roman_curia/congregations/cfaith/cti_documents/rc_con_cfaith _doc_20000307_memory-reconc-itc_en.html [accessed February 27, 2004].

37. "Address by Helmut Kohl, Chancellor of the Federal Republic of Germany, during the Ceremony Marking the 40th Anniversary of the Liberation of the Concentration Camps at the Site of the Former Bergen-Belsen Concentration Camp, April 21, 1985," in *Bitburg in Moral and Political Perspective*, ed. Geoffrey H. Hartman (Bloomington: Indiana University Press, 1986), p. 249.

38. For an illuminating study of how nations have sought to respond to national guilt through restitution and reparations, see Elazar Barkan, *The Guilt of Nations: Restitution and Negotiating Historical Injustices* (New York: Norton, 2000).

39. Martha Minow, *Between Vengeance and Forgiveness: Facing History after Genocide and Mass Violence* (Boston, MA: Beacon Press, 1998), p. 104.

40. Kritz, *Transitional Justice*, vol. 2, p. 48.

41. Shriver, Jr., *An Ethic for Enemies*, p. 89.

42. Japanese Americans were not the only ethnic group singled out for internment. Other national groups, including Germans and Italians, were considered potential security threats and classified as "enemy aliens." It is estimated, for example, that about sixteen hundred Italian Americans were placed in detention camps, while another ten thousand were forced to move from their homes in the West Coast. *New York Times*, August 11, 1997, p. 8.

43. Shriver, Jr., *An Ethic for Enemies*, p. 166.

44. Barkan, *Guilt of Nations*, p. 31.

45. Jeremy Waldron, "Superseding Historic Injustice," *Ethics* 103 (October 1992), p. 25.

46. This idea is briefly explored by Martha Minow. See Minow, *Between Vengeance and Forgiveness*, pp. 108–9.

47. Ironically, this initiative also resulted in growing criticism of Switzerland's negligence of Jews during World War II. To quell this criticism, the government established a fund to offer symbolic reparations to Jewish victims who were refused refuge and a historical commission to examine the government's role during the war. See *New York Times*, May 5, 2002.

48. *New York Times*, December 7, 1999, 13. For an overview of how the Swiss bankers were forced to confront unclaimed Jewish deposits, see Barkan, *Guilt of Nations*, chap. 5. For a more recent and comprehensive treatment of this subject, see Stuart E. Eizenstat, *Imperfect Justice: Looted Assets, Slave Labor, and the Unfinished Business of World War II* (New York: Public Affairs, 2003).

49. In the late 1940s Catholic Church properties included more than eight hundred churches, parishes, and monasteries and 6 percent of the country's agricultural land.

50. One of these measures was a statute calling for the return of church properties. As a result of this legislation, 74 properties were immediately returned to the church and another 176 properties were set aside for future consideration. The church, for its part, gave up its claim to some 550 remaining structures because of poor condition or destruction. See Kritz, *Transitional Justice*, vol. 3, p. 576.

51. In retribution for the suffering inflicted by Nazis against Czechoslovakia, Czechs forced some 3 million Germans to flee the Sudentenland in 1945 and 1946, even though German families had lived in the region for more than five centuries.

52. According to the act, the Communist regime was "responsible for . . . the systematic destruction of the traditional values of European civilization, for the conscious violation of human rights and freedoms, for the moral and economic ruin combined with judicial crimes and terror against advocates of different opinions, the replacement of a prospering market economy with command management, the destruction of the traditional principles of ownership, the abuse of training, education, science, and culture for political and ideological purposes, and the careless destruction of nature."

53. Funding for therapy was provided in the early 1990s, but by the end of the Eduardo Frei administration, the state had stopped its assistance program. See *New York Times*, January 3, 2000, 1 and 10.

54. The term lustration, which is derived from the Latin *lustratio*, refers to sacrificial purification, or the rite of cleansing.

55. Although citizens themselves can carry out purges unofficially, our concern here is with the official actions taken by successor regimes to cleanse society from the values, institutions, and leaders associated with the former regime. The informal or unofficial process of purging is illustrated by the efforts of French liberation forces in 1944 to isolate citizens who had supported the Vichy regime. After France was liberated, resistance forces embarked on a campaign to identify men and women who had collaborated with the Nazis. For example, although there was no public directive to do so, women who had collaborated with the Vichy regime or German forces were shorn of their hair so that they could be easily identified.

56. Quoted in Peter Novick, *The Resistance versus Vichy: The Purge of Collaborators in Liberated France* (New York: Columbia University Press, 1968), p. 158.

57. Kritz, *Transitional Justice*, vol. 2, p. 604.

58. The American denazification program, which was formally established with the 1946 Act for Liberation from National Socialism and Militarism, was carried out in several stages. In the first phase, a mandatory screening was instituted to identify different levels of collaboration. German boards were then given the responsibility of classifying individuals in terms of four categories, ranging from "major offender" to "follower." By the time the denazification program was halted in 1948, local boards had processed some 3.5 million cases, of which 2.5 million were granted immediate amnesty. Of the remaining million cases, boards issued the following judgments: 370,000 were exonerated, 510,000 were judged followers, 107,000 were judged lesser offenders, 22,000 were classified as offenders, and 1,600 were classified as major offenders. See John H. Herz, "Denazification and Related Policies," in *From Dictatorship to Democracy: Coping with the Legacies of Authoritarianism and Totalitarianism* (Westport, CT: Greenwood Publishing Group, 1982).

59. Using secret files from the Communist secret police (StB), the commission determined that twelve deputies, thirty-three employees of the prime minister's office, and twenty-five employees of the Federal Assembly were former Communist collaborators.

60. As a result, President Václav Havel submitted a bill to the Czechoslovak Federal Assembly that would ban from government Communists or informers who had committed human rights violations. The parliament, however, rejected this initiative.

61. Ironically, those most in favor of lustration were generally people who had remained inconspicuous during the suffering under Communist rule. Journalist Lawrence Weschler writes: "Go through Amnesty International's old Czechoslovak files, and you'd find that the more severely persecuted an oppositionist had been under the old regime, the less adamant he was likely to be today about lustration." See Lawrence Weschler, "The Velvet Purge: The Jan Kavan Case," *The New Yorker*, October 19, 1992, 66–96.

62. For example, the Czech and Slovak lustration process used files of the secret police to determine guilt. However, rather than placing responsibility on the state for proving guilt, lustration presumed the culpability of people identified as informers or collaborators by the Ministry of the Interior.

63. Tina Rosenberg, "Overcoming the Legacies of Dictatorship," *Foreign Affairs* (May/June 1995): 136.

64. Václav Havel, *The Art of the Impossible: Politics as Morality in Practice* (New York: Fromm International, 1997), pp. 4–5.

65. Quoted in Bass, *Stay the Hand of Vengeance*, p. 284.

66. *New York Times*, October 19, 1999.

67. Bass, *Stay the Hand of Vengeance*, p. 295.

68. Jaime Malamud-Goti, "Trying Violators of Human Rights: The Dilemma of Transitional Democratic Governments," in *State Crimes: Punishment or Pardon* (Washington, DC: Aspen Institute, 1989), p. 81.

69. For example, Erich Mielke, the head of the Ministry of State Security (Stasi), was prosecuted not for infringing on people's liberties and basic human rights but rather for his alleged role in the murder of two policemen in 1931. Mielke's trial is further noteworthy because the prosecution was based on evidence secured by Nazis allegedly through torture. Moreover, Markus Wolf, the head of foreign espionage for the Stasi and arguably the worst East German human rights offender, was sentenced to six years for bribery and treason. See Tina Rosenberg, *The Haunted Land: Facing Europe's Ghosts after Communism* (New York: Vintage Books, 1995), pp. 333–35.

70. Individuals are criminally liable only for actions that violate laws that are in effect at the time a crime is committed.

71. Of course, leaders can also be prosecuted in terms of international human rights law. The growing body of international humanitarian law and the creation of the International Criminal Court have greatly strengthened the capacity of governments and international tribunals to enforce international human rights laws, regardless of the existing domestic legislation.

72. In former Communist states, only Bulgaria and former East Germany carried out significant trials. Hungary, Poland, the Czech Republic, Slovakia, and Russia avoided not only trials but truth telling as well.

73. Huntington, *Third Wave*, p. 231.

74. Huntington, *Third Wave*, p. 231.

75. This phrase is taken from the Vatican's March 2002 study of memory and reconciliation. See International Theological Commission, "Memory and Reconciliation: The Church and the Faults of the Past," www.vatican.va/roman_curia/congregations/cfaith/cti_documents/rc_con_cfaith_doc_20000307_memory-reconc-itc_en.html, [accessed February 27, 2004].

CHAPTER 2: THE NATURE AND PURPOSE OF FORGIVENESS

1. Hannah Arendt, *The Human Condition* (Chicago: University of Chicago Press, 1958), p. 241.

2. Quoted in Jeffrie G. Murphy, "Repentance, Punishment, and Mercy," in *Repentance: A Comparative Perspective*, ed. Amitai Etzioni and David E. Carney (Lanham, MD: Rowman & Littlefield, 1997), p. 150.

3. Simon Wiesenthal, *The Sunflower: On the Possibilities and Limits of Forgiveness* (New York: Schoken Books, 1998), p. 216.

4. Arendt, *Human Condition*, p. 237.

5. Nicholas Wolterstorff, "The Place of Forgiveness in the Actions of the State." (Research Group on Political Reconciliation and Forgiveness, Erasmus Institute, University of Notre Dame, 2001.)

6. Avishai Margalit, *The Ethics of Memory* (Cambridge, MA: Harvard University Press, 2003), p. 202.

7. Miroslav Volf, *Exclusion and Embrace: A Theological Exploration of Identity, Otherness, and Reconciliation* (Nashville, TN: Abingdon Press, 1996), p. 132.

8. Margalit defines these two types or models of dealing with past offenses as "covering up" and "blotting out." See Margalit, *Ethics of Memory*, p. 204.

9. Lewis B. Smedes, "Stations on the Journey from Forgiveness to Hope," in *Dimensions of Forgiveness: Psychological Research and Theological Perspectives*, ed. by Everett L. Worthington, Jr. (Philadelphia, PA: Templeton Foundation Press, 1998), p. 352.

10. Volf, *Exclusion and Embrace*, p. 135.

11. Lewis B. Smedes, *Forgive and Forget: Healing the Hurts We Don't Deserve* (New York: Harper & Row, 1984), p. 136.

12. Smedes, *Forgive and Forget*, p. 136.

13. Elliot N. Dorff, "The Elements of Forgiveness: A Jewish Approach" in *Dimensions of Forgiveness: Psychological Research and Theological Perspectives*, ed. Everett L. Worthington, Jr. (Philadelphia, PA: Templeton Foundation Press, 1998), p. 46

14. Catholic theologians believe that since Christ would not always be visibly present with the Church, he transferred the authority to forgive sins to his apostles, commanding them to forgive in his name (Matt. 18:18). As a result, the Catholic Church developed the sacrament of penitence that called believers to confess their sins to a priest ("auricular confession") and to carry out acts of restitution and charity so that absolution could be pronounced on their wrongdoing. The Reformation claimed that temporal intermediaries were unnecessary for forgiveness, since authentic penitence was based only on the contrition of the sinner and belief in the grace of Christ. Although the Reformation helped to restore the biblical teaching of the unqualified and unmediated love and mercy of God, the emphasis on forgiveness as a private, spiritual affair between God and sinner encouraged the privatization of forgiveness.

15. Some theologians argue that divine forgiveness is not conditional on human repentance. Walter Wink, for example, argues that God, through the atonement of Christ, has already forgiven humans, whether they ask for it or not. People can repent, he suggests, precisely because God has already forgiven them. See Walter Wink, *When the Powers Fall: Reconciliation in the Healing of Nations* (Minneapolis, MN: Fortress Press, 1998), p. 18. Smedes similarly suggests that repentance is not a necessary condition for divine forgiveness. But while God does not demand repentance as a condition for forgiveness, he believes that it is important for people to repent because it is the only way by which they will feel forgiven in their heart and mind. See Smedes, *Forgive and Forget*, p. 69.

16. Because of the unqualified scope of Christian forgiveness, some critics have suggested that Christianity leads to the minimization of wrongdoing by providing offenders with a release from guilt without repaying debts or fulfilling a deserved punishment.

17. Geiko Müller-Fahrenholz, *The Art of Forgiveness: Theological Reflections on Healing and Reconciliation* (Geneva, Switzerland: WCC Publications, 1996), pp. 4–5.

18. Reinhold Niebuhr, *An Interpretation of Christian Ethics* (New York: Harper & Brothers, 1935), p. 223.

19. Niebuhr, *Interpretation of Christian Ethics*, p. 226.

20. Niebuhr, *Interpretation of Christian Ethics*, pp. 43–44.

21. This is expressed most emphatically in the Lord's Prayer: "Forgive us our debts, as we forgive our debtors" (Matt. 6:12), but the Apostle Paul also exhorts believers to be humble, meek, and long-suffering, "forebearing one another, and forgiving one another," for "even as Christ forgave you, so also do ye" (Col. 3:12–13).

22. Volf, *Exclusion and Embrace*, p. 223.

23. Rabbi Meir Soloveichik argues that forgiveness is inappropriate for dealing with people who are "hopelessly wicked," such as Hitler, Stalin, or Osama bin Laden. In such cases, he thinks that hate can be virtuous. See "Meir Y. Soloveichik, "The Virtue of Hate," *First Things* (February 2003): 41–46. See also the discussion precipitated by this article in *First Things* (May 2003): 2–9.

24. The prophet Jeremiah captures this idea when he writes: "For I will forgive their wrongdoing and remember their sin no more" (31:34). The contrast between these two conceptions is based on Margalit, *The Politics of Memory*, pp. 188–206.

25. The lingering effects of moral offense are illustrated in the biblical account of Cain and Abel. (Gen. 4:2–10) When Cain repents of his sin (the killing of his brother), God partially forgives him but does not erase the sin completely. As a sign of past wrongdoing, God places a mark on Cain, leaving a reminder that sins can be covered up but not forgotten.

26. Of course, the brothers had not stolen the funds. Rather, without their knowing it, Joseph had ordered the money returned in order to display his power as well as to manipulate his brothers' mistrust and fear.

27. Robert Burt argues that the parable is mistitled. He argues that the parable is not about reconciliation between the younger son and his father, as is commonly claimed. Rather, the parable, he suggests, is fundamentally about the father's relationship to his older son as well as the relationship between the two brothers. "The basic question posed by the parable," writes Burt, "is whether the elder son would forgive his father and whether the two brothers in turn would be reconciled with one another." Robert A. Burt, "Reconciling with Injustice" in

Transgression, Punishment, Responsibility, Forgiveness: Graven Images (Graven Images: Culture, Law, and the Sacred, vol. 4), ed. Andrew D. Weiner and Leonard V. Kaplan, 4 (1998): 106–22.

28. Volf, *Exclusion and Embrace,* p. 159.

29. Just as the shepherd goes after the lost sheep (Luke 15:4–7), so too the father awaits the return of his lost son. For an excellent discussion of the unconditional nature of love, see Henri J. J. Nouwen, *The Return of the Prodigal Son: A Story of Homecoming* (New York: Doubleday, 1992).

30. Volf, *Exclusion and Embrace* p. 165.

31. Smedes, *Forgive and Forget,* p. 81.

32. According to the story, a ruler was owed a large sum of money by one of his servants. The king commanded that the servant and his family be sold in order to repay the debt. The servant, however, pleaded with his master to have patience with him, promising to repay the debt in full. After being moved with compassion, the king forgave the servant's debt. The servant then went out and found one of his workers who owed him a small amount of money and demanded immediate repayment. When the worker asked for patience to repay the debt, the servant had him placed in prison. When the king found out what his servant had done, he became angry and "turned him over to the jailers to be tortured, until he should pay back all he owed." Jesus draws this conclusion: the heavenly Father will treat us in this manner if we do not forgive others.

33. Donald W. Shriver, Jr., *An Ethic for Enemies: Forgiveness in Politics* (New York: Oxford University Press, 1995), p. 7.

34. As I note in the following discussion of therapeutic forgiveness, victims may forgive offenders and thereby become free from justified anger and resentment. Since such forgiveness occurs unilaterally, it does not require offenders' remorse or public repentance.

35. Smedes, "Stations on the Journey from Forgiveness to Hope," p. 345.

36. Shriver's model has the following elements: agreement about past wrongdoing, resistance to revenge, empathy toward offenders, and the restoration of human relationships. Shriver, *An Ethic for Enemies.*

37. Lewis B. Smedes, *The Art of Forgiving* (Nashville, TN: Morrings Publications, 1996), p. 124.

38. Smedes, *Forgive and Forget,* p. 20.

39. Smedes, *Art of Forgiving,* pp. 6–11.

40. Smedes, *Forgive and Forget,* p. 118.

41. Quoted in Johann Christoph Arnold, *Why Forgive?* (Farmington, PA: Plough Publishing House, 2000), p. 140.

42. Quoted in Geraldine Smyth, "Brokeness, Forgiveness, Healing," in *Forgiveness and Reconciliation: Religion, Public Policy and Conflict Transformation,* ed. Raymond G. Helmick and Rodney L. Petersen (Philadelphia, PA: Templeton Foundation Press, 2001), p. 332.

43. Some Christian thinkers argue that forgiveness is a religious duty. For them, the need to forgive is based on Christ's atonement, which calls on forgiven believers to express divine forgiveness to others. See Paul Lauritzen, "Forgiveness: Moral Prerogative or Religious Duty," *Journal of Religious Ethics* 15 (1987).

44. A fuller account of forgiveness is as follows: "Forgiveness is a change of heart toward the wrongdoer in which one drops any emotions of hatred or resentment toward him and his deed, takes a pro-attitude toward him and is disposed (under most conditions) to make the offer of reconciliation." Jean Hampton, "The Retributive Idea," in *Forgiveness and Mercy,* ed. Jeffrie G. Murphy and Jean Hampton (Cambridge: Cambridge University Press, 1988), p. 157.

45. Hampton, "Retributive Idea," p. 150.

46. Hampton, "Retributive Idea," p. 149.

47. Hampton, "Retributive Idea," p. 155.

48. Quoted in Arnold, *Why Forgive?* p. 15.

49. Hampton, "Retributive Idea," p. 156.

50. L. Gregory Jones, *Embodying Forgiveness: A Theological Analysis* (Grand Rapids, MI: Eerdmans, 1995), p. xii.

51. Although Jones's study is rooted in the Christian religion, his analysis is potentially applicable to other religions or traditions as well.

52. Jones, *Embodying Forgiveness*, p. xii.

53. Jones, *Embodying Forgiveness*, p. 233.

54. Jones, *Embodying Forgiveness*, p. 226.

55. Jones identifies two types of sources that can foster learning the craft of forgiveness. First, observers can learn about the craft of forgiveness by assessing traditions, perspectives, and habits that contribute to the success or failure of the embodiment of forgiveness. Second, observers can develop the moral abilities and practices of forgiveness by being attentive to people in our surroundings who excel in forgiveness. Jones, *Embodying Forgiveness*, p. 228.

56. Jean Hampton, "Forgiveness, Resentment and Hatred," *Forgiveness and Mercy*, p. 42.

57. Kathleen Dean Moore, *Pardons: Justice, Mercy, and the Public Interest* (New York: Oxford University Press, 1989), pp. 184–86.

58. Jeffrie Murphy, "Forgiveness and Resentment," in *Forgiveness and Mercy*, p. 15.

59. Beverly Flanigan, *Forgiving the Unforgivable* (New York: Macmillan, 1992), p. 11.

60. Robert C. Roberts, "Forgivingness," *American Philosophical Quarterly* 33 (October 1995): 289–93.

61. See, for example, Susan Jacoby, *Wild Justice* (New York: Harper & Row, 1982), pp. 334–36. She argues that forgiveness is essentially a private moral virtue that allows victims to release offenders from the guilt of their moral offenses.

62. President Clinton, for example, had no difficulty in apologizing for the failure of the international community to rescue Rwandans from genocide in 1994, but was incapable of admitting the truth about his sexual misconduct with Miss Monica Lewinsky and apologizing for his actions.

63. Vincent Brummer, *The Model of Love: A Study in Philosophical Theology* (Cambridge: Cambridge University Press, 1993), p. 185.

64. Arnold, *Why Forgive?* p. v.

65. Jürgen Moltmann, "Political Reconciliation," in *Religion, Politics and Peace*, ed. Leroy S. Rouner (Notre Dame, IN: University of Notre Dame Press, 1998), p. 30.

66. Robert J. Schreiter, a Catholic theologian, argues that this view is applicable only to social reconciliation, not interpersonal reconciliation. Using a biblical perspective, Schreiter argues that a more likely path of reconciliation is for victims to accept the healing power of God, which leads them, in turn, to forgive their offenders. Thus, the biblical, interpersonal model of reconciliation begins with reconciliation with God, followed by interpersonal forgiveness, and culminating with repentance. See Robert J. Schreiter, *The Ministry of Reconciliation: Spirituality and Strategies* (Maryknoll, NY: Orbis Books, 1992), p. 64. Theologian Walter Wink, who similarly shares this perspective on repentance and reconciliation, claims that divine forgiveness makes possible human repentance. See Wink, *When the Powers Fall*, p. 18.

67. Brummer, *Model of Love*, p. 186.

68. Supreme Pontiff John Paul II, "Dives in Misericordia," November 30, 1980, sec. 14. See www.cin.org/jp2ency/dives.html, 1996 [accessed January 25, 2004].

CHAPTER 3: THE POSSIBILITY AND
PROMISE OF POLITICAL FORGIVENESS

1. Walter Wink, *When the Powers Fall: Reconciliation in the Healing of Nations* (Minneapolis, MN: Fortress Press, 1998), p. 54

2. David Martin, *Does Christianity Cause War?* (Oxford: Clarendon Press, 1997), p. 175.

3. Quoted in Timothy Garton Ash, "The Truth about Dictatorship," *The New York Review of Books*, February 19, 1998, 36.

4. Pope John Paul II, "Offer Forgiveness and Receive Peace," Message for World Day of Peace, January 1, 1997.

5. R. J. Rummel has estimated that in the twentieth century domestic killings by authoritarian and totalitarian regimes—a phenomenon he has termed *democide*, to contrast it with genocide—has claimed the lives of 169 million persons, more than four times the rate of wartime deaths. The two most destructive regimes have been the Soviet Union and Communist China, which together account for the murder of 97 million people. R. J. Rummel, *Death by Government* (New Brunswick, NJ: Transaction Publishers, 1994), pp. 4 and 15.

6. The challenge of identifying culpability for collective evils is graphically illustrated by the difficulty of ascertaining responsibility for the structural and institutional injustices and suffering inflicted by South Africa's apartheid government and East Germany's Communist regime. In both cases, responsibility was so widespread that identifying individual or group responsibility was virtually impossible.

7. See especially Reinhold Niebuhr, *Moral Man and Immoral Society* (New York: Scribner, 1960).

8. Andrew Schapp, "Guilty Subjects and Political Responsibility: Arendt, Jaspers and the Resonance of the 'German Question' in Politics of Reconciliation," *Political Studies* 49 (September 2001): 749–51.

9. Alexander Solzhenitzyn, "Repentance and Self-Limitation in the Life of Nations," in *From Under the Rubble*, ed. Alexander Solzhenitzyn et al. (Boston, MA: Little, Brown, 1974), p. 129.

10. Solzhenitzyn, "Repentance and Self-Limitation in the Life of Nations," p. 134.

11. Interestingly, fifty years after the defeat of Nazism, historian Daniel Goldhagen has written a provocative and widely debated book claiming that responsibility for the Holocaust was with the German people themselves. As the title of his book suggests, ordinary Germans were "Hitler's willing executioners." See Daniel Jonah Goldhagen, *Hitler's Willing Executioners: Ordinary Germans and the Holocaust* (New York: Random House, 1996).

12. Joseph W. Koterski, SJ, new introduction to *The Question of German Guilt* by Karl Jaspers (New York: Fordham University Press, 2000), p. 27.

13. Jaspers, *Question of German Guilt*, p. 26.

14. Avishai Margalit, *The Ethics of Memory* (Cambridge, MA: Harvard University Press, 2003), p. 200.

15. Miroslav Volf, "Forgiveness, Reconciliation, and Justice: A Theological Contribution to a More Peaceful Social Environment," *Millennium* 29, no. 3 (2000): 874.

16. Jaspers, *Question of German Guilt*, p. 26.

17. Volf, "Forgiveness, Reconciliation, and Justice," p. 875.

18. Of course, legislatures may enact laws that grant amnesty to offenders (for example, the Chilean amnesty of politically related crimes carried out from 1973 through 1978), and executives may pardon the offenses of specific officials charged with crimes (for example, President Ford's pardon of former President Nixon).

19. For example, while F. W. de Klerk, the former president of South Africa, has claimed responsibility for implementing apartheid policies, he has denied that senior government leaders ever authorized state-sponsored violence, such as torture and genocide, against antigovernment activists. According to de Klerk, state crimes committed during the apartheid era were an unintended result of the government's internal security strategy in responding to antigovernment actions, especially covert ANC attacks. Former Chilean president Augusto Pinochet has similarly claimed that although force was used to protect the state from subversive threats, the regime used only necessary security measures to defend the nation—a claim vigorously contested by human rights groups.

20. Hannah Arendt, *The Human Condition* (Chicago: University of Chicago Press, 1958), p. 241.

21. George Kateb, *The Inner Ocean: Individualism and Democratic Culture* (Ithaca, NY: Cornell University Press, 1992), p. 220.

22. The public apology was preceded by the release of a carefully worded study by a Vatican-appointed international theological commission created to study the subject of collective repentance and forgiveness. The report, which was titled "Memory and Reconciliation: The Church and the Faults of the Past," served as a foundation for the Pope's homily. See www.vatican.va/roman_curia/congregations/cfaith/cti_documents/rc_con_cfaith_doc_20000 307_memory-reconc-itc_en.html [accessed February 28, 2004].

23. It is significant that in expressing repentance for the church's errors and failings, the Pope distinguished between the Church—the mystical body of Christ, which is blameless and without sin—and its individual members who as human beings commit sins and errors.

24. *New York Times*, March 13, 2000, A10.

25. Richard John Neuhaus, "Forgive Us Our Trespasses . . . " *First Things* (June/July 2000): 83.

26. Neuhaus, "Forgive Us Our Trespasses . . . ," 81.

27. For example, this view is expressed by theologians Vincent Brummer and Dietrich Bonhoeffer. See Vincent Brummer, *The Model of Love: A Study in Philosophical Theology* (Cambridge: Cambridge University Press, 1993), p. 184; and Dietrich Bonhoeffer, *Ethics* (New York: Macmillan, 1965), p. 117.

28. This view is expressed by author Susan Jacoby, who claims that forgiveness is a part of private morality and should not be applied to politics. She claims that legalism "affords a far more hospitable environment for the spread of liberty and decency than does hopeful reliance on the loving potential of the human heart." Susan Jacoby, *Wild Justice* (New York: Harper & Row, 1982), p. 345.

29. Donald W. Shriver, Jr., *An Ethic for Enemies: Forgiveness in Politics* (New York: Oxford University Press, 1995).

30. These three elements can be translated as 1) acknowledgment of guilt, 2) authentic remorse and a change of heart, and 3) reparations.

31. Jürgen Moltmann, "Political Reconciliation" in *Religion, Politics, and Peace*, ed. Leroy S. Rouner (Notre Dame, IN: University of Notre Dame Press, 1998), p. 28.

32. Arendt, *Human Condition*, pp. 236–43.

33. Shriver, *Ethic for Enemies: Forgiveness in Politics*, pp. 6–8, 30–32.

34. Webster's Dictionary, for example, defines forgiveness as a) the giving up of resentment, b) the giving up of a claim to requital, and c) the granting of relief from payment.

35. P. E. Digeser, *Political Forgiveness* (Ithaca, NY: Cornell University Press, 2001), pp. 20, 35. In addition to these three elements, Digeser's model of forgiveness includes four other features: 4) forgiveness must be conveyed explicitly and directly to debtors by persons competent to offer it; 5) motives and feelings must be disregarded in the act of forgiveness; 6) since receiving one's due is important, moral reasons must be given for not pursuing "just deserts"; and 7) forgiveness may contribute to the restoration of relationships among antagonists.

36. Digeser, *Political Forgiveness*, pp. 67–68.

37. Digeser, *Political Forgiveness*, pp. 20–21.

38. Digeser, *Political Forgiveness*, p. 38.

39. José Zalaquett, "Truth, Justice, and Reconciliation: Lessons for the International Community," in *Comparative Peace Processes in Latin America*, ed. Cynthia J. Arnson (Stanford, CA: Stanford University Press, 1999), p. 348.

40. Shriver, *Ethic for Enemies: Forgiveness in Politics*, p. 7.

41. Apologies can play an important role in communicating both moral culpability and remorse for past offenses. But the increasing use of apologies by public officials has perhaps cheapened their impact, especially since tangible reparations rarely support such declarations. If apologies are to serve as instruments of public repentance, the public expressions of contrition must be reinforced by acts of restitution and promises that future wrongdoing will not be repeated.

42. Scholars disagree on the priority of repentance in forgiveness. David Little, for example, argues that a key element of forgiveness is repentance. His forgiveness model, derived from Jesus' Parable of the Unforgiving Servant, involves five elements: 1) transaction between two or more persons; 2) shared acknowledgment between the offender and victim about a) culpability for wrongdoing and b) a fitting punishment; 3) contrition and repentance on the part of the offender; 4) merciful response by the victim, including the annulment of 2b; and 5) obligation of the forgiven offender to forgive others. See David Little, "A Different Kind of Justice: Dealing with Human Rights Violations in Transitional Societies," *Ethics & International Affairs*, 13 (1999): 71. Other conceptions of forgiveness, such as Digeser's and Shriver's, do not require repentance. Theologian Alan Torrance similarly claims that a Christian conception of forgiveness does not require prior repentance. He claims that evangelical repentance (*metanoia*), which involves the "transformation of the orientation of our minds," is not carried out to condition forgiveness but to express love. Thus, the Christian faith calls on believers to forgive unconditionally.

43. Solzhenitzyn, "Repentance and Self-Limitation in the Life of Nations," pp. 133–34.

44. Václav Havel, *The Art of the Impossible: Politics as Morality in Practice* (New York: Fromm International, 1997), p. 4.

45. Although forgiveness normally qualifies the norms of retributive justice, it does not fully override a state's obligation to prosecute wrongdoing. Still, when enemies seek to overcome past collective injuries through forgiveness, criminal justice procedures may be partially circumvented.

46. Nicholas Wolterstorff, "The Place of Forgiveness in the Actions of the State." (Research Group on Political Reconciliation and Forgiveness, Erasmus Institute, University of Notre Dame, 2001.)

47. Miroslav Volf, following Nicolai Hartmann, argues that human forgiveness, unlike divine forgiveness, does not remove moral guilt. See Volf, "Forgiveness, Reconciliation, and Justice," p. 875.

48. Brandt had initiated the policy of *Ostpolitik* shortly after becoming chancellor in 1969 in order to foster political reconciliation between West Germany and the German Democratic Republic as well as other Eastern European nations under Soviet domination.

49. Geiko Müller-Fahrenholz, *The Art of Forgiveness: Theological Reflections on Healing and Reconciliation* (Geneva, Switzerland: WCC Publications, 1996), p. 62.

50. Pricilla Hayner, "In Pursuit of Justice and Reconciliation: Contributions of Truth Telling," in *Comparative Peace Processes in Latin America*, ed. Cynthia J. Arnson (Stanford, CA: Stanford University Press, 1999), p. 375.

51. Reinhold Niebuhr held this perspective, believing that a radical chasm existed between the moral nature of individuals and that of collectives. In *Moral Man and Immoral Society*, he argues that contrary to prevalent views of modern moralists, self-interest and egoism are greatly exacerbated in groups and nations, making the behavior of collectives ethically intractable. Niebuhr argues that since individual and group behaviors differ significantly, a radical dichotomy exists between the selfless, disinterested behavior possible among individuals and the pronounced egoism of groups. He concludes his study by arguing that it is preferable to accept the "frank dualism" of individual and group moralities than to seek to harmonize them. Since a "morality of pure disinterestedness" is impossible within collectives, he claims that "the conflict between the purest individual morality and an adequate political policy must therefore remain." Reinhold Niebuhr, *Moral Man and Immoral Society: A Study in Ethics and Politics* (New York: Scribner, 1960), p. 271.

52. L. Gregory Jones, *Embodying Forgiveness: A Theological Analysis* (Grand Rapids, MI: Eerdmanns Publishing, 1995), p. 267.

53. Quoted in Alex Boraine, *A Country Unmasked: Inside South Africa's Truth and Reconciliation Commission* (Oxford: Oxford University Press, 2000), p. 41.

54. Charles Villa-Vicencio, "Getting on with Life: A Move Towards Reconciliation," in *Looking Back, Reaching Forward: Reflections on the Truth and Reconciliation Commission of South Africa*, ed. Charles Villa-Vicencio and Wilhelm Verwoerd (London, UK: Zed Books, 2000), p. 209.

55. Adam Michnik and Václav Havel, "Confronting the Past: Justice or Revenge?" *Journal of Democracy* 4 (January 1993): 26.

56. Paul Lauritzen, "Forgiveness: Moral Prerogative or Religious Duty?" *Journal of Religious Ethics* 15 (Fall 1987): 143.

57. Some of the reasons for the victims' prerogative to forgive include the following: first, because victims have suffered from offenders' wrongdoing, they have the primary moral right to lift any deserved punishment; second, since wrongdoing leads to victims' anger and resentment, such feelings can be transformed only by the voluntary action of victims themselves; forgiveness cannot be imposed by external parties; and third, since forgiveness entails a transformation of relationships between victims and offenders, such changes can only occur if victims participate in the reformation process.

58. Trudy Govier and Wilhelm Verwoerd, "Forgiveness: The Victim's Prerogative," *South African Journal of Philosophy* 21 (2002): 97–111.

59. Piers Benn, "Forgiveness and Loyalty," *Philosophy* 71 (1996): 369–84.

60. According to political theorist Peter French, communities can be distinguished by whether they are simply a collection of people who are joined by chance through some shared feature or whether they are purposive organizations that have a shared purpose and common decision-making structure. Examples of the first type of organization ("aggregates") include the families of victims of an air crash or the members of an ethnic or religious group. Examples of the second type ("conglomerates") include purposive well-structured organizations like General Motors Corporation, the International Red Cross, the U.S. Supreme Court, the Palestinian Authority, and the state of Cost Rica. Peter A. French, *Collective and Corporate Responsibility* (New York: Columbia University Press, 1984), pp. 5–18.

61. This does not mean, however, that a community is incapable of communicating shared beliefs or moral dispositions toward other communities, but only that it is incapable of independent moral action. For example, if most members of nation A distrust citizens of nation B, it would be valid to claim that nation A distrusts nation B based on the distribution of people's perceptions.

62. These fallacies are discussed in Trudy Govier and Wilhelm Verwoerd, "Trust and the Problem of National Reconciliation," *Philosophy of Social Sciences* 32 (June 2002).

63. For a philosophical assessment of the requirements for collective moral responsibility, see J. Angelo Corlett, "Collective Moral Responsibility," *Journal of Social Philosophy* 32 (Winter 2001): 573–84.

64. Elazar Barkan, *The Guilt of Nations: Restitution and Negotiating Historical Injustices* (New York: Norton, 2000).

65. See Miroslav Volf, *Exclusion and Embrace: A Theological Exploration of Identity, Otherness, and Reconciliation* (Nashville, TN: Abingdon Press, 1996).

66. Lewis Smedes, *Forgive and Forget: Healing the Hurts We Don't Deserve* (New York: Harper and Row, 1984) p. 124.

67. Arendt, *Human Condition*, p. 237.

68. In an important study of religion, memory, and political identity, Donald Harman Akenson shows how religious peoples in Northern Ireland, South Africa, and Israel have used a biblical interpretation to define and justify their special relationship between land and people using a "covenant" paradigm. See Donald Harman Akenson, *God's Peoples: Covenant and Land in South Africa, Israel, and Ulster* (Ithaca, NY: Cornell University Press, 1992.

69. International Theological Commission, "Memory and Reconciliation: The Church and the Faults of the Past," Sec. 5.1. www.vatican.va/roman_curia/congregations/cfaith/cti_documents/rc_con_cfaith_doc_20000307_memory-reconc-itc_en.html [accessed February 28, 2004].

70. Amos Elon, "The Politics of Memory," *The New York Review of Books*, October 7, 1993, 5.

71. R. Scott Appleby, *The Ambivalence of the Sacred: Religion, Violence, and Reconciliation* (Lanham, MD: Rowman & Littlefield, 2000), p. 195.

72. Solzhenitzyn, "Repentance and Self-Limitation in the Life of Nations," pp. 134–35.

73. Arendt, *Human Condition*, p. 237.

74. Jean Bethke Elshtain, "Fear, Forgiveness, and the New World Disorder," *Religion and Values in Public Life* (Fall 1994): 7.

CHAPTER 4: JUSTICE, RECONCILIATION, AND POLITICAL FORGIVENESS

1. John de Gruchy, "The TRC and the Building of a Moral Culture," in *After the TRC: Reflections on Truth and Reconciliation in South Africa*, ed. Wilmont James and Linda van de Vijver (Athens: Ohio University Press, 2001), p. 170.

2. Miroslav Volf, "Forgiveness, Reconciliation, and Justice: A Theological Contribution to a More Peaceful Social Environment," *Millennium: Journal of International Studies* 29, no. 3 (2000): 874.

3. Quoted in Miroslav Volf, *Exclusion and Embrace: A Theological Exploration of Identity, Otherness, and Reconciliation* (Nashville, TN: Abingdon Press, 1996), p. 122.

4. Martha Minow, *Between Vengeance and Forgiveness: Facing History after Genocide and Mass Violence* (Boston, MA: Beacon Press, 1998), p. 10.

5. Quoted in Lawrence Weschler, "A Reporter at Large," *The New Yorker*, December 10, 1990, 127.

6. Minow, *Between Vengeance and Forgiveness*, p. 11.

7. Jeffrie Murphy, "Forgiveness and Resentment," in *Forgiveness and Mercy*, ed. Jeffrie G. Murphy and Jean Hampton (Cambridge: Cambridge University Press, 1988), p. 16.

8. Jean Hampton, "The Retributive Idea," in *Forgiveness and Mercy*, p. 147.

9. Lawrence Crocker, "The Upper Limits of Punishment," *Emory Law Journal* 41 (1992): 1060–63.

10. Robert Nozick, *Philosophical Explanations* (Cambridge, MA: Belknap Press of Harvard University Press, 1981), pp. 366–74.

11. Minow, *Between Vengeance and Forgiveness*, p. 12.

12. Raúl Alfonsín, "'Never Again' in Argentina," *Journal of Democracy* 4, no. 1 (1993): 16.

13. Hampton, "Retributive Idea," p. 143.

14. Writing about interpersonal forgiveness, theologian Lewis Smedes expresses the injustice of forgiveness as follows: "Love makes forgiving a creative violation of all the rules for keeping score." Lewis B. Smedes, *Forgive and Forget: Healing the Hurts We Don't Deserve* (New York: Harper & Row, 1984), p. 81.

15. For a discussion of how retribution can be reconciled with forgiveness, see Hampton, "Retributive Idea," p. 157.

16. For a discussion of this point, see Miroslav Volf, "The Social Meaning of Reconciliation," *Interpretation* 54 (April 2000): 158–68.

17. Tristan Anne Borer, for example, argues that in the South African context the use of the idea of reconciliation was problematic because it resulted in conceptual confusion about the tasks of the TRC. See her article "Reconciliation in South Africa: Defining Success" (University of Notre Dame, Kroc Institute Occasional Paper 20:OP:1, March 2001), p 5.

18. Trudy Govier and Wilhelm Verwoerd, "Trust and the Problem of National Reconciliation," *Philosophy of the Social Sciences* 32 (June 2002).

19. Francis Fukuyama, *Trust: the Social Virtues and the Creation of Prosperity* (New York: The Free Press, 1995).

20. This classification is based on a classification developed by David A. Crocker, "Retribution and Reconciliation," *Report from the Institute for Philosophy & Public Policy* 20 (Winter/Spring 2000): 6.

21. For a discussion of different levels of toleration, see Michael Walzer, *On Toleration* (New Haven, CT: Yale University Press, 1997).

22. Rajeev Bhargava, "Restoring Decency to Barbaric Societies," in *Truth v. Justice: The Morality of Truth Commissions*, ed. Robert I. Rotberg and Dennis Thompson (Princeton, NJ: Princeton University Press, 2000), pp. 45–48.

23. For an overview of Desmond Tutu's *ubuntu* vision, see Michael Battle, "A Theology of Community: The Ubuntu Theology of Desmond Tutu," *Interpretation* 54 (April 2000): 173–85.

24. For a superb overview of these policies, see John W. Dower, *Embracing Defeat: Japan in the Wake of World War II* (New York: Norton, 1999).

25. Bhargava, "Restoring Decency to Barbaric Societies," p. 60.

26. Crocker, "Retribution and Reconciliation," p. 6.

27. Timothy Garton Ash, "True Confessions," *The New York Review of Books*, July 17, 1997, 37.

28. Amy Gutmann and Dennis Thompson, "The Moral Foundations of Truth Commissions," in *Truth v. Justice: The Morality of Truth Commissions*, ed. Robert I. Rotberg and Dennis Thompson (Princeton, NJ: Princeton University Press, 2000), pp. 35–36.

29. Gutmann and Thompson, "Moral Foundations of Truth Commissions," pp. 22–23.

30. Elizabeth Kiss, "Moral Ambition Within and Beyond Political Constraints: Reflections on Restorative Justice," *Truth v. Justice*, p. 80.

31. Michael Feher, "Terms of Reconciliation," in *Human Rights in Political Transitions: Gettysburg to Bosnia*, ed. Carla Hesse and Robert Post (New York: Zone Books, 1999), pp. 325–28.

32. Abraham Lincoln, "Second Inaugural," in *Lend Me Your Ears: Great Speeches in History*, ed. William Safire (New York: Norton, 1992), p. 441.

33. The Kairos Document, a 1985 antiapartheid declaration by South African theologians, illustrates the "justice first, then reconciliation" approach. According to the statement, authentic reconciliation can only be pursued if oppression is first addressed and eliminated. To pursue peace without confronting injustice is to engage in "cheap" or counterfeit reconciliation. The Document declares: "No reconciliation is possible in South Africa without justice." *The Kairos Document. Challenge to the Church: A Theological Comment on the Political Crisis in South Africa* (Grand Rapids, MI: Eerdmanns Publishing, 1986), Art. 3.1.

34. See Miroslav Volf, "The Social Meaning of Reconciliation," *Interpretation* 54 (April 2000): 160–64.

35. According to Volf, since God's love is unconditional and unlimited, "the will to embrace the other is the most fundamental obligation of Christians." Volf, "Forgiveness, Reconciliation, and Justice," p. 872. See also Volf, *Exclusion and Embrace*, chap. 3.

36. This truth was illustrated in the Czech Republic's 1991 Lustration Law, which barred leaders and citizens associated with the former Communist regime from serving in government. Although the law was designed to "cleanse" the Czech political regime of the political influence of Communist leaders, it resulted in new injustices since the decision of whether someone had "worked" with the Communist authorities was itself a deeply flawed process, not based on "due process" procedures. For a discussion of this law and its applications, see Neil J. Kritz, ed., *Transitional Justice*, vol. 3, pp. 307–74.

37. George Weigel, *Tranquillitas Ordinis: The Present Failure and Future Promise of American Catholic Thought on War and Peace* (New York: Oxford University Press, 1987).

38. Diane F. Orentlicher, "Settling Accounts: The Duty to Prosecute Human Rights Violations of a Prior Regime," *Yale Law Journal* 100 (1991): 2542–44.

39. Carlos Santiago Nino, *Radical Evil on Trial* (New Haven, CT: Yale University Press, 1996), p. 188.

40. When Communists took control of Czechoslovakia after World War II, they carried out widespread human rights crimes, imprisoning about 100,000 persons, sentencing 232 to death, and deporting some 22,000 to labor camps without trial. John Borneman, *Settling Accounts: Violence, Justice, and Accountability in Postsocialist Europe* (Princeton, NJ: Princeton University Press, 1997), p. 153.

41. The primary initiative by the Czechoslovakian regime to reckon with the past Communist offenses was by keeping Communist collaborators from participating in politics or government.

But this effort—known as lustration—was not a serious initiative to reckon with the past, according to many observers. The Czech journalist Jan Urban wrote: "The silence was what mattered. . . . And all the current noise surrounding lustration is simply a way of keeping silent about the silence. . . . We are not looking for facts but hunting for ghosts." Lawrence Weschler, "The Velvet Purge: The Trials of Jan Kavan," *New Yorker*, October 19, 1992, 82.

42. The rebel fighters were led by the Farabundo Martí para la Liberación Nacional (FMLN).

43. "Argentina: Presidential Pardons" in *Transitional Justice*, vol. 3, pp.528–32.

44. Kiss, "Moral Ambition Within and Beyond Political Constraints," p. 79.

45. Robert Meister, "Forgiving and Forgetting: Lincoln and the Politics of National Recovery," in *Human Rights in Political Transitions: Gettysburg to Bosnia*, ed. Carla Hesse and Robert Post (New York: Zone Books, 1999). For a further discussion of the Lincolnian strategy, please see chapter 9.

46. Mahmood Mamdani, *When Victims Become Killers: Colonialism, Nativism, and the Genocide in Rwanda* (Princeton, NJ: Princeton University Press, 2001), pp. 272–73.

47. "Argentina: Nunca Más—Report of the Argentine Commission on the Disappeared," in *Transitional Justice*, vol. 3, p. 6.

48. Desmond Tutu, *No Future without Forgiveness* (New York: Doubleday, 1999), p. 19.

49. Tutu, *No Future without Forgiveness*, p. 23.

50. As conceptualized by the TRC, the approach of restorative justice involves a number of distinctive features. First, it calls for a redefinition of crime that focuses on personal injuries and human suffering rather than on impersonal rule breaking. Second, it emphasizes reparations for victims in order to facilitate their restoration into the fabric of communal life while also emphasizing the rehabilitation of perpetrators based on full accountability for past offenses. Third, it encourages direct conflict resolution among victims, offenders, and the community. And finally, it calls for "a spirit of understanding" between victims and offenders, without mitigating or undermining offenders' accountability for wrongdoing. Such accountability is not only legal and political but also moral. Truth and Reconciliation Commission, *Truth and Reconciliation Commission of South Africa Report*, vol. 1 (London: Macmillan Reference Limited, 1999), pp. 126–31.

CHAPTER 5: RETRIBUTIVE JUSTICE AND THE LIMITS OF FORGIVENESS IN ARGENTINA

1. HIJOS is the name of a human rights group called Children for Identification and Justice against Forgetting and Silence—"*Hijos por la Identidad y la Justicia contra el Olvido y el Silencio.*"

2. Quoted in Mark Osiel, "The Making of Human Rights Policy in Argentina: The Impact of Ideas and Interests on a Legal Conflict," *Journal of Latin American Studies* 18 (1986): 172.

3. Juan Méndez, "Afterword," in Horacio Verbitsky, *The Flight: Confessions of an Argentine Dirty Warrior* (New York: The New Press, 1996), p. 162.

4. Noga Tarnopolsky, "The Family That Disappeared," *The New Yorker*, November 15, 1999, 48–57.

5. The name Montonero was taken from the name given to irregular fighters in Argentina's war of independence from Spain in the early nineteenth century.

6. Prior to 1973 the major armed groups included the moderate Peronista Armed Forces (Fuerzas Armadas Peronistas [FAP]) and two radical groups—the Revolutionary Armed Forces (Fuerzas Armadas Revolucionarias [FAR]) and the Armed Forces of Liberation (Fuerzas Armadas de Liberación [FAL]). In time these were consolidated, with the FAR joining the more moderate Montoneros and the FAP and FAL being absorbed into the ERP.

7. It was widely assumed that Aramburu, who had participated in the overthrow of Perón's government in 1955 and had authorized the removal and shipping of his wife's (Evita) corpse out of the country, was executed by revolutionary forces in 1970 as an act of revenge.

8. The Peronista party slogan—"Cámpora al gobierno, Perón al poder" (Cámpora to the government, Perón to power)—aptly captures the political reality that Perón was the real source of power in the Peronista movement.

9. The so-called Ezeiza Massacre resulted in the death of some twenty-five people and injuries to more than four hundred.

10. Richard Gillespie, *Soldiers of Perón: Argentina's Montoneros* (Oxford: Oxford University Press, 1982), pp. 134–44.

11. For example, the government of Isabel Perón sought to reduce leftist influence in university campuses by seeking to eliminate administrators, professors, and students who were regarded as a threat to the nation. In August 1974, Isabel appointed a fascist minister of education who helped to bring about radical change in university life. It is estimated that by July 1975 some four thousand lecturers had been fired and sixteen hundred students had been imprisoned.

12. Gillespie, *Soldiers of Perón: Argentina's Montoneros*, pp. 153–56.

13. Gillespie, *Soldiers of Perón: Argentina's Montoneros*, p. 216.

14. Tina Rosenberg, *Children of Cain: Violence and the Violent in Latin America* (New York: Penguin Books, 1991), p. 121.

15. Luis Moreno Ocampo, "Beyond Punishment: Justice in the Wake of Massive Crimes in Argentina," *Journal of International Affairs*, 52, no. 2 (Spring 1999): 673.

16. Gillespie, for example, estimates the size of Montoneros at the height of the terror campaign in 1975 at 5,000, while leading journalists claim the number ranged from 7,000 to 10,000 persons. Gillespie, *Soldiers of Perón: Argentina's Montoneros*, p. 178–79. The Argentine armed forces estimated the number of subversives who were "technically able and ideologically trained to kill" at 15,000. See Neil J. Kritz, ed., *Transitional Justice: How Emerging Democracies Reckon with Former Regimes*, vol. 3 (Washington, DC: U.S. Peace Institute Press, 1995), p. 46.

17. The military government's loss of authority and credibility was due to Argentina's military defeat by Britain in the 1982 Falklands/Malvinas War and also the government's failure to devise a viable economic strategy to overcome inflation and recession.

18. According to Jaime Malamud-Goti, Alfonsín's commitment to trials and punishment for those responsible for gross human rights violations had a decisive effect on the election. Jaime Malamud-Goti, *Game without End: State Terror and the Politics of Justice* (Norman: University of Oklahoma Press, 1996), pp. 57–59.

19. Osiel, "Making of Human Rights Policy in Argentina," p. 147.

20. Osiel, "Making of Human Rights Policy in Argentina," p. 149.

21. Carlos Santiago Nino, *Radical Evil on Trial* (New Haven, CT: Yale University Press, 1996), p. 69.

22. Michael Ignatieff, *The Warrior's Honor: Ethnic War and the Modern Conscience* (New York: Henry Holt, 1997), p. 174.

23. Ignatieff, *Warrior's Honor*, p. 175.

24. Ronald Dworkin, "Report from Hell," *The New York Review of Books*, July 17, 1986, 11.

25. For a succinct description of the system of repression imposed by the military government, see Ocampo, "Beyond Punishment," pp. 675–81.

26. The commission report states: "Among the victims are thousands who never had any links with such [terrorist] activity but were nevertheless subjected to horrific torture because they opposed the military dictatorship, took part in union or student activities, were well-known intellectuals who questioned state terrorism, or simply because they were relatives, friends, or names included in the address book of someone considered subversive." *Transitional Justice*, vol. 3, p. 46.

27. *Nunca Más—The Report of the Argentine Commission on the Disappeared* (New York: Farrar Straus Giroux, 1986), p. 1.

28. Nino, *Radical Evil on Trial*, p. 68.

29. Although military officers were to be prosecuted initially in military tribunals, civilian courts could review the former's decisions or could themselves begin trials if military courts

failed to institute legal proceedings against an alleged criminal or to complete a trial within a specified period of time.

30. During the trial, some 833 witnesses testified.

31. The court found General Videla guilty of the following crimes: 83 homicides, 504 illegal deprivations of freedom, 254 acts of torture, 94 robberies, 180 counts of falsifying public documents, 4 acts of stealing, 23 acts of forced labor, one count of extortion, 2 kidnappings, 7 counts of child stealing, and 7 counts of torture resulting in death. Admiral Massera was held legally responsible for the following crimes: 83 homicides, 523 illegal deprivations of freedom, 267 counts of torture, 102 robberies, 201 counts of falsifying public documents, 4 acts of stealing, 23 counts of forced labor, 2 kidnappings, 11 cases of child stealing, and 7 counts of torture resulting in death. Marguerite Feitlowitz, *A Lexicon of Terror: Argentina and the Legacies of Torture* (New York: Oxford University Press, 1999), p. 14.

32. Mark J. Osiel, "Why Prosecute? Critics of Punishment for Mass Atrocity," *Human Rights Quarterly* 22, no. 1 (2000): 134.

33. It is significant that at the same time that the government was pursuing criminal trials against state officials, some citizens commenced civil proceedings against the state. One of these was begun by Daniel Tarnopolsky in 1987 against two former military leaders—Admiral Emilio Massera and Admiral Armando Lambruschini—for the abduction and wrongful deaths of his parents and siblings. Seven years later, in November 1994, a Buenos Aires federal judge issued an unexpected and unprecedented judgment against the state and two military defendants, granting Tarnopolsky $1 million in symbolic reparations. Although the government appealed the decision, in 1999 the Supreme Court upheld most of the original judgment, awarding Tarnopolsky $1.25 million, the cost to be paid equally by each of the defendants and the state.

34. Ragnar Hagelin, a Swedish citizen, initiated one of the first and most important civil suits brought against the state for crimes committed during the era of the dirty war. Mr. Hagelin's young daughter was mistakenly identified as a subversive and shot in 1981 by Alfredo Astiz, a flamboyant naval officer, when she tried to run away. Severely injured by the attack, she was taken to a military detention center. Because she was too handicapped to be released, she was presumed to have been killed.

35. These rebellions were led by army commandos, known as *carapintadas* because their faces were painted, to force the government to halt trials against their army comrades. The two most important rebel leaders were Lieutenant Colonel Aldo Rico and Colonel Mohamed Alí Seineldín.

36. Ocampo, "Beyond Punishment," p. 686.

37. "Argentina: Presidential Pardons," *Transitional Justice*, vol. 3, p. 529.

38. See, for example, Malamud-Goti, *Game without End: State Terror and the Politics of Justice* (Norman: University of Oklahoma, 1996).

39. Anna Husarska, "Third Person," *The New Republic*, March 11, 1996, 12.

40. Horacio Verbitsky, *The Flight: Confessions of an Argentine Dirty Warrior* (New York: The New Press, 1996). For an assessment of the impact of the Scilingo disclosures—the so-called Scilingo effect—see Feitlowitz, *Lexicon of Terror*, pp. 193–206.

41. The Mothers of the Plaza de Mayo, the most influential Argentinean human rights organization concerned with regime human rights abuses, came into being in the late 1970s as mothers began parading every week at this famous Buenos Aires plaza to dramatize their demand for information about their missing children.

42. Using data from a national genetic data bank, scientists and government officials have been able to identify the true families of about seventy-one young adults. Some of these have decided to leave their adoptive parents and return to their blood families, while others have preferred to remain with their current families.

43. In 1998 two judges concluded that stealing babies had been planned by top military commanders. As a result, General Jorge Videla and Admiral Emilio Massera, two junta leaders

who had been convicted in 1985 of human rights crimes but later pardoned by President Menem, were again charged with human rights crimes and placed under house arrest. Subsequently, several other senior military leaders were charged with participation in this crime.

44. For a description of the development of "truth trials," see Human Rights Watch, "Reluctant Partner: The Argentine Government's Failure to Back Trials of Human Rights Violators," December 12, 2001. See www.hrw.org, 2004 [accessed January 29, 2004].

45. *Nunca Más*, p. 5.

46. "*No olvidamos, no perdonamos, y no nos reconciliamos.*"

47. Samuel P. Huntington, *The Third Wave: Democratization in the Late Twentieth Century* (Norman: University of Oklahoma Press, 1991), p. 224.

48. Osiel, "The Making of Human Rights Policy in Argentina," pp. 161–62.

49. Malamud-Goti, *Game without End*, p. 8.

50. Malamud-Goti, *Game without End*, p. 9.

51. Malamud-Goti, *Game without End*, p. 184.

52. Malamud-Goti, *Game without End*, p. 187.

53. This type of case is illustrated by the civil suits brought by Daniel Tarnopolsky, a case noted at the outset of the chapter, and by the Hagelin family, alluded to in the earlier text. In the former case Tarnopolsky sued the state for the disappearance of his mother, father, brother, and sister, and in the latter case, the Hagelins sued for the disappearance of their daughter. In both cases, significant out-of-court settlements were reached.

54. Ocampo, "Beyond Punishment," p. 687.

55. It can be argued that such culpability extended to the mass public as well since it failed to confront and condemn widespread atrocities and to sustain a civic culture that respected human rights and affirmed political tolerance.

56. *The New York Times*, March 13, 1995, 1.

57. Feitlowitz, *Lexicon of Terror*, p. 223.

58. Husarska, "Third Person," p. 14.

59. Enrique Molina Pico, "Mensaje a la Armada en Relación con la Guerra Subversiva," May 3, 1995. Statement provided to the author in 2000 by the retired admiral from Buenos Aires, Argentina.

60. *The New York Times*, March 13, 1995, 1.

61. Feitlowitz, *Lexicon of Terror*, p. 197.

62. For a critical analysis of the Catholic Church's role during military repression, see Emilio F. Mignone, *Witness to the Truth: The Complicity of Church and Dictatorship in Argentina* (Maryknoll, NY: Orbis Books, 1986).

63. In 1990 a French court sentenced Mr. Astiz in absentia to life in prison for the kidnapping and death of the two French nuns.

64. *Nunca Más*, "Prologue," p. 5.

65. Personal interview, April 3, 2000. According to the administrator of the "Círculo Militar," guerrillas were responsible for killing more than eighty-five army soldiers and officers during the 1970–1975 period.

66. "Bishops Repent Role in 'Dirty War,'" *Christian Century*, May 10, 1995, 505.

67. Reuter Information Service, April 27, 1996.

68. Tarnopolsky, "Family That Disappeared," p. 57.

69. *New York Times*, April 5, 1995, 1.

70. Ragnar Hagelin, a Swedish citizen, filed civil suits for the death of his daughter Dagmar. After exhausting legal remedies in Argentina, Hagelin filed a petition with the Inter-American Commission on Human Rights, and in 1999 the Commission initiated discussions to facilitate a settlement between Hagelin and the Argentine government. A friendly settlement was reached on March 17, 2000.

71. *La Nación*, March 21, 2000.

CHAPTER 6: THE QUEST FOR RECONCILIATION
THROUGH TRUTH TELLING IN CHILE

1. "Statement by President Aylwin on the Report of the National Commission on Truth and Reconciliation," (March 4, 1991) in *Transitional Justice: How Emerging Democracies Reckon with Former Regimes*, vol. 3, ed. Neil J. Kritz (Washington, DC: U.S. Institute of Peace Press, 1995), pp. 171–72.

2. *La Tercera*, May 16, 2000.

3. "Human Rights in Chile—Then and Now," www.chipsites.com/derechos/index_eng .html [accessed March 1, 2004].

4. Elizabeth Farnsworth, "Confronting the Past," PBS's *NewsHour with Jim Lehrer*, PBS, March 13, 2000.

5. In the 1970 election, Allende's Popular Unity coalition won with a 36.2 percent of the vote; the two other candidates—Jorge Alessandri, leader of the conservatives, and Rodomiro Tomic, head of the centrist Christian Democratic Party, received 34.9 and 27.8 percent of the vote, respectively. According to Chilean law, when no candidate receives an absolute majority of the vote—as had been the case frequently from the 1930s through the 1960s—Congress must select the president between the top two candidates. Thus in October 1970, one month after the election, the Congress selected Allende as president by a substantial majority (153 votes for, 35 votes against, and 7 abstentions).

6. Paul E. Sigmund, *The Overthrow of Allende and the Politics of Chile, 1964–1976* (Pittsburgh, PA: University of Pittsburgh Press, 1977), p. 131.

7. After expropriating the copper mines, the Allende government ruled that it did not owe compensation to the United States companies because they had paid insufficient taxes in previous years. The Allende government decision was contested by the companies, which instituted legal proceedings in various European ports where Chilean copper was being delivered.

8. Lois Hecht Oppenheim, *Politics in Chile: Democracy, Authoritarianism, and the Search for Development*, 2nd ed. (Boulder, CO: Westview Press, 1999), p. 56.

9. Sigmund, *Overthrow of Allende and the Politics of Chile*, p. 140.

10. Tina Rosenberg, *Children of Cain: Violence and the Violent in Latin America* (New York: Penguin, 1991), p. 341.

11. Sigmund, *Overthrow of Allende and the Politics of Chile*, p. 173.

12. Sigmund, *Overthrow of Allende and the Politics of Chile*, p. 215.

13. The major parties of the (*Confederación para la Democracia*) CODE coalition were the National Party and the Christian Democratic Party.

14. For example, the ENU program defined its goals as "the construction of a new socialist society based on the development of productive forces, the overcoming of economic, technological, and cultural dependence, the establishment of a new property relations, and authentic democracy and social justice guaranteed by the effective exercise of the power of the people." Sigmund, *Overthrow of Allende and the Politics of Chile*, pp. 202–6.

15. Pamela Constable and Arturo Valenzuela, *A Nation of Enemies: Chile under Pinochet* (New York: Norton, 1993), p. 29.

16. Rosenberg, *Children of Cain*, p. 343.

17. Rosenberg, *Children of Cain*, p. 344.

18. Sigmund, *Overthrow of Allende and the Politics of Chile*, p. 249.

19. The two major armed groups supporting Allende were the Manuel Rodriguez Patriotic Front, an offshoot of the Communist Party, and the larger and more dangerous Movement of the Revolutionary Left (MIR).

20. *Report of the Chilean National Commission on Truth and Reconciliation*, vol. 2, trans. Phillip E. Berryman (Notre Dame, IN: University of Notre Dame Press, 1993), p. 900.

21. Edgardo Boeninger, "The Chilean Road to Democracy," *Foreign Affairs* (Spring 1986): 813.

22. Sigmund, *Overthrow of Allende and the Politics of Chile*, p. 250.

23. Of the 2,279 people killed during the era of military rule, 18 percent were Socialists, 17 percent were MIR, and 16 percent were Communists. Oppenheim, *Politics in Chile*, p. 119.

24. Subsequently, the U.S. government requested the extradition of Colonel Manuel Contreras, the head of DINA when Letelier was killed. Chile's Supreme Court, however, refused the request on technical grounds. After democracy returned in 1990, courts were allowed to proceed with the trials of both Contreras and his DINA deputy, Pedro Espinoza, for ordering the killing of Letelier and a co-worker. This trial was ultimately possible because it was specifically exempted from the 1978 Amnesty Law. It is also important that in response to U.S. pressures, the Chilean government agreed to make financial reparations to the Letelier family, which an Organization of American States tribunal set at $2.6 million in 1992. A year later Contreras and Espinoza were found guilty and sentenced to prison terms of seven and six years, respectively. They entered prison in 1995 after the Supreme Court upheld these judgments.

25. For an overview of the important human rights work of these two organizations, see Pamela Lowden, *Moral Opposition to Authoritarian Rule in Chile, 1973–1990* (Oxford, UK: St. Martin's Press, 1996).

26. It has been estimated that of the nearly five thousand cases that were presented to the courts by the Peace Committee and the Vicariate during the military era, sentences were issued in only twelve cases. Arturo Valenzuela, "Judging the General: Pinochet's Past and Chile's Future," *Current History* (March 1999): 101.

27. Although voluntarily relinquishing the presidency would no doubt be difficult, Pinochet knew that he would nevertheless retain enormous political influence since he was constitutionally able to serve another eight years as the chief of the army and to serve as a member of the Chilean Senate for life.

28. This decree was greatly criticized subsequently by human rights advocates. It is important to stress, however, that soon after the law was enacted several hundred leftist militants were released from prison. For a description of the Amnesty Law, see Neil J. Kritz, ed., *Transitional Justice: How Emerging Democracies Reckon with Former Regimes*, vol. 2 (Washington, DC: United States Institute of Peace Press, 1995), pp. 500–502.

29. José Zalaquett, "Introduction to the English Edition," in *Report of the Chilean National Commission*, vol. 1, p. xxxi.

30. Zalaquett, "Introduction to the English Edition," p. xxx.

31. Zalaquett, "Introduction to the English Edition."

32. Kritz, *Transitional Justice*, vol. 2, p. 460.

33. Since the Peace Committee and Vicariate of the Catholic Church had served as the principal organizations that defended victims and their families, its human rights records provided indispensable data to the commission.

34. Naomi Roht-Arriaza, "The Need for Moral Reconstruction in the Wake of Past Human Rights Violations: An Interview with José Zalaquett," in *Human Rights in Political Transitions: Gettysburg to Bosnia*, ed. Carla Hesse and Robert Post (New York: Zone Books, 1999), p. 209.

35. Of this total, 1,322 people were killed and 957 disappeared after their arrest. Of those killed in political violence, 132 were members of the armed forces. See *Report of the Chilean National Commission*, vol. 2, pp. 899–904.

36. *Report of the Chilean National Commission*, p. 837.

37. The Corporation, which was given three years to complete its work, identified 899 additional human rights crimes, including 766 extrajudicial killings and 123 "disappeared" persons. This raised the total number of official human rights cases to 3,197—2,095 killings and 1,102 disappearances.

38. To be eligible for reparations, people needed to be classified as victims by either the Commission or the Corporation.

39. This pension was to be distributed as follows: 40 percent to the surviving spouse, 30 percent to the victim's mother (or father in the mother's absence), 15 percent to the mother or father of the natural children of the victim, and 15 percent to each of the victim's children under the age of 25.

40. Although state agents tortured thousands of people, victims of torture were not considered eligible for state assistance. The government's position on torture has continued to fester in Chilean society, however. For a discussion of the ongoing political debate by victims of torture, see *New York Times*, January 3, 2000, A1 and A10.

41. Interview with Jorge Correa, Santiago, Chile, March 23, 2000.

42. *Report of the Chilean National Commission*, p. 892.

43. Kritz, *Transitional Justice*, vol. 3, p. 170.

44. Kritz, *Transitional Justice*, vol. 3, p. 171.

45. Kritz, *Transitional Justice*, vol. 3, p. 171.

46. Kritz, *Transitional Justice*, vol. 2, p. 493.

47. Kritz, *Transitional Justice*, vol. 2, p. 477.

48. In answer to the question, "In your view, does the Rettig Report contribute to reconciliation?" the response was as follows: 42.5 percent of the respondents answer yes and 39.5 percent answer no. Quoted in Americas Watch, *Human Rights and the "Politics of Agreements": Chile during President Aylwin's First Year* (Human Rights Watch, 1991), p. 30.

49. The major chronology of events in the legal saga of Pinochet's detention is as follows: 1) on October 16, 1998, the British state places Pinochet under house arrest; 2) on October 28, a three-judge High Court rules that Pinochet has immunity from arrest in either criminal or civil cases originating while he was president; 3) on November 25, the Judicial Committee of the House of Lords overrules the High Court, stating that Pinochet can be extradited to Spain; 4) on December 9, Jack Straw, the home secretary, rules that the extradition can proceed; 5) on December 17, the Lords of Appeal, in an unprecedented decision, vacate their previous ruling because one of the five judges failed to disclose his ties to a human rights organization; 6) on March 24, 1999, the Law Lords confirm the earlier judgment, ruling that Pinochet did not have immunity from prosecution and could be extradited, although it reduced the number of charges; 7) on April 15, Straw again confirms his decision to extradite Pinochet to Spain; 8) on October 8, a court orders the extradition of Pinochet to Spain; 9) the Republic of Chile calls into question this order, suggesting that the president's health has seriously deteriorated; 10) on January, 5, 2000, a panel of doctors appointed by the home secretary examines Pinochet; 11) on January 11, Straw notifies the governments of Spain, Belgium, Switzerland, and France—the four states requesting extradition—that the medical report has concluded that Pinochet is not fit to stand trial; 12) on February 15, the High Court orders the home secretary to disclose the medical report to the four states seeking Pinochet's extradition; and 13) on March 2, Straw rules that Pinochet can leave for Chile. Pinochet immediately flies to Chile where he is given an emotional welcome by the Chilean armed forces.

50. Kritz, *Transitional Justice*, vol. 3, p. 170.

51. Undoubtedly, the two most important developments honoring regime victims have been the reburial of President Allende in Santiago's Central Cemetery in President Aylwin's first year in office and the subsequent construction of a large Memorial Wall for all known victims, whether dead or missing.

52. Pamela Constable and Arturo Valenzuela, *A Nation of Enemies: Chile under Pinochet* (New York: Norton, 1991).

53. Alexander Wilde, "Irruptions of Memory: Expressive Politics in Chile's Transition to Democracy," *Journal of Latin American Studies*, 31 (May 1999): 475.

54. Alexander Solzhenitzyn, "Repentance and Self-Limitation in the Life of Nations," in *From Under the Rubble*, ed. Alexander Solzhenitzyn et al. (Boston: Little, Brown, 1974), pp. 133–34.

55. *New York Times*, March 28, 1991, A3.

56. For a discussion of the nature and role of state terrorism in combating leftist insurgency, see José Zalaquett, "From Dictatorship to Democracy," *The New Republic* (December 16, 1985): 18–19.

57. It is significant that the United States and the Soviet Union relied heavily on unconventional war-fighting strategies in pursuing insurgency and counterinsurgency in proxy wars. Although these Cold War tactics raised few public concerns when used in international conflicts,

their application in domestic political disputes has precipitated an ongoing debate about the morality and legality of such operations.

58. To ensure fairness, the amnesty also applied to radical militants who had been imprisoned for acts of political violence. As a result, hundreds of activists were released from prison after 1978.

59. Kritz, ed., *Transitional Justice*, vol. 3, p. 170.

60. Kritz, ed., *Transitional Justice*, vol. 3, p. 171.

CHAPTER 7: INTRACTABLE POLITICS WITHOUT TRUTH OR FORGIVENESS: THE CASE OF NORTHERN IRELAND

1. Steve Bruce, *The Edge of Union: The Ulster Loyalist Political Vision* (Oxford: Oxford University Press, 1994), p. 128.

2. The Faith and Politics Group, *Forgive Us Our Trespasses . . . ? Reconciliation and Political Healing in Northern Ireland* (Belfast: The Faith and Politics Group, 1996), p. 8.

3. Woodstock Theological Center, *Forgiveness in Conflict Resolution: Reality and Utility, the Northern Ireland Experience* (Washington, DC: Georgetown University, June 18, 1997), p. 12.

4. To be sure, it is possible to conceive of several nations comprising one state, as has been the case with many contemporary multinational states. It is also conceivable for citizens to have dual nationality and split their political allegiance between two communities. But as the experience of the late twentieth century suggests, political identity is a divisive issue, and the resolution of nationalist claims among competing groups is not easily reconciled.

5. For a discussion of the role of the covenantal culture of the Ulster-Scots, see Donald Harman Akenson, *God's Peoples: Covenant and Land in South Africa, Israel, and Ulster* (Ithaca, NY: Cornell University Press, 1992), pp. 183–89.

6. Historically, Ulster comprised nine counties. When the partition was made, however, Protestants in Ulster decided they were only interested in those six counties where they were a majority. Whereas the original nine counties of Ulster had 900,000 Protestants and 700,000 Catholics, the six counties of Northern Ireland had 820,000 Protestants and 430,000 Catholics—a much larger ratio of Protestants to Catholics.

7. A. T. Q. Stewart, *The Narrow Ground: Aspects of Ulster, 1609–1969* (London: Faber & Faber, 1977), p. 157.

8. The classic case of gerrymandering was in Derry (Londonderry), where Protestants regularly controlled the city council throughout much of the twentieth century even though they were greatly outnumbered.

9. In 1931, for example, Protestants won eleven of the thirteen seats to the United Kingdom Parliament.

10. Akenson, *God's People*, p. 201.

11. Akenson, *God's People*, p. 200.

12. Reforms included appointment of a permanent ombudsman to protect citizens with a valid grievance, dissolution of the hated "B-Specials" police force, adoption of "one man, one vote" electoral principle, and creation of a new housing agency to ensure the distribution of housing on a nondiscriminatory basis.

13. In taking this step, the British government issued a communiqué emphasizing the following principles: 1) Northern Ireland would remain a part of the United Kingdom as long as that was the will of the people and government; 2) the conflict was a domestic political issue, not an international dispute; 3) the introduction of British soldiers was solely a temporary measure; and 4) domestic reforms should be carried out to further advance equality, freedom, and justice for all. Paul Dixon, *Northern Ireland: The Politics of War and Peace* (New York: Palgrave, 2001), p. 108.

14. Throughout the 1970s and 1980s, IRA and paramilitary groups carried out a low-intensity war that resulted in much violence and destruction. From 1969 to 1989, political violence claimed the lives of 2,761 people, of whom 31 percent were members of security forces, 13 percent were paramilitaries, and the remaining 55 percent were civilians.

15. The most important of these was the hunger strike of IRA leader Bobby Sands, who was serving a criminal sentence for firearms violations. Sands saw himself as a political prisoner, not a criminal. He claimed: "I am a political prisoner because I am a casualty of a perennial war that is being fought between the oppressed Irish people and an alien, oppressive, unwarranted regime that refuses to withdraw from our land." To dramatize this claim, he and other Republican prisoners refused to wash, leave their cells, or use their toilets. Soon thereafter Sands began a hunger strike that resulted in his death.

16. From Clem McCartney, introduction in *Accord: Striking a Balance. The Northern Ireland Peace Process*, www.c-r.org/accord/ireland/accord8/intro.shtml [accessed February 1, 2004].

17. As John Hume, former head of the Social Democratic and Labour Party (SDLP), has noted, Republicans have killed six times more people than the British Army, the RUC, and the Ulster Defense Regiment (UDR) together. Although the aim of IRA violence has been to inflict suffering on the British and the Protestant Unionists, more than two-thirds of all victims were Roman Catholic. Furthermore, the IRA has killed more of its own members (149) than British army and police (115). Moreover, while the British army was responsible for killing 138 Catholic civilians, the IRA killed an even greater number of its own people (198). Fintan O'Toole, "Are the Troubles Over?" *The New York Review of Books*, October 5, 2000, 12.

18. Paul Arthur, "The Anglo-Irish Process: Obstacles to Reconciliation," in *After the Peace: Resistance and Reconciliation*, ed. Robert L. Rothstein (Boulder, CO: Lynne Rienner Publishers, 1999), p. 96.

19. Akenson, *God's Peoples*, pp. 264–65. Akenson notes that from 1969 to 1989, the average annual rate of political deaths per 100,000 people was 12.4, which was lower than the 1970 homicide rate in Cleveland (36.1), Detroit (32.7), Dallas (28.7), and Chicago (24.1).

20. This section is based largely on Steve Bruce, *The Edge of the Union: The Ulster Loyalist Vision* (Oxford: Oxford University Press, 1994), pp. 129–46.

21. Ironically, since assuming control of the affairs of Northern Ireland, a major goal of British policy has been to ensure fair distribution of resources and the protection of human rights.

22. Bruce, *Edge of the Union*, p. 132.

23. Bruce, *Edge of the Union*, p. 133.

24. In defining ethnic identity, it is not important that groups fulfill clear, objective criteria. Rather, what is important is that its members affirm shared beliefs, historical memories, and myths and pursue national ideals through collective action.

25. Steve Bruce, *God Save Ulster: Religion and Politics of Paisleyism* (Oxford: Clarendon Press, 1986), p. 249.

26. Indeed, a number of observers argue that the intractability of the conflict is not due to politics, religion, or even sectarianism but to paramilitary violence. Peter O'Toole, for example, writes that sectarian prejudice has not been the cause of political violence but rather, violence itself has been the cause of "the prejudice." O'Toole, "Are the Troubles Over?" p. 10.

27. John Hickey, *Religion and the Northern Ireland Problem* (Totowa, NJ: Barnes & Noble Books, 1984), pp. 89–90.

28. Sinn Fein is the name of the political party that seceded from the British parliament and demanded a separate government. The goal of the party is to establish a unitary government over all thirty-two counties of Ireland.

29. This truth is captured in the official title of the UK—the "United Kingdom of Great Britain and Northern Ireland."

30. The Provisional IRA had been created in 1970 after the Official IRA had declared a cease-fire. The Provisionals—the more militant wing composed of some three hundred to four hundred IRA soldiers—believed that continued violence was necessary in order to force the British to withdraw from Northern Ireland and to allow Ireland to become united.

31. Sinn Fein was adamantly opposed to disarmament as a precondition for negotiations. Gerry Adams, Sinn Fein's leader, argued that decommissioning could occur only in the context of an overall peace settlement that involved the withdrawal of British troops.

32. For a discussion of how the decommissioning conflict was resolved, see George J. Mitchell, *Making Peace* (New York: Alfred A. Knopf, 1999), pp. 31–36.

33. The negotiations would involve three separate dimensions or "strands." Strand One would focus on the internal political dynamics within Northern Ireland. Strand Two would focus on North–South relations within the island of Ireland. And Strand Three would be concerned with bilateral ties between Britain and Ireland.

34. The people of Northern Ireland and the Irish Republic endorsed the GFA by a majority vote of 71 percent and 96 percent, respectively. Interestingly, in Northern Ireland 95 percent of Catholics approved of the accord, while only 55 percent of Protestants did so. Dixon, *Northern Ireland*, pp. 273–74.

35. Terence McCaughey, "Northern Ireland: Burying the Hatchet, Not the Past," in *Burying the Past: Making Peace and Doing Justice after Civil Conflict*, ed. Nigel Biggar (Washington, DC: Georgetown University Press, 2001), p. 256.

36. Arthur, *After the Peace*, p. 107.

37. In the immediate aftermath of the GFA, some 433 prisoners were released from prison. As a result of this action, the authorities permanently closed Northern Ireland's notorious high-security prison, known as " the Maze."

38. Faith and Politics Group, *Transitions* (Belfast: Faith and Politics Group, 2001).

39. McCaughey, "Northern Ireland," p. 266.

40. The major exception to this has been the British Government's inquiry into "Bloody Sunday," discussed elsewhere in this chapter.

41. Woodstock Theological Center, *Forgiveness in Conflict Resolution*, p. 35.

42. Woodstock Theological Center, *Forgiveness in Conflict Resolution*, p. 5.

43. Woodstock Theological Center, *Forgiveness in Conflict Resolution*, p. 6.

44. Woodstock Theological Center, *Forgiveness in Conflict Resolution*, pp. 6–7.

45. "The IRA says Sorry (Sort of)," *The Economist*, July 20, 2002, 50.

46. Woodstock Theological Center, *Forgiveness in Conflict Resolution*, p. 12.

47. Mark Noll, "Belfast: Tense with Peace," *Books & Culture* (November/December 1995), p. 12.

48. Kenneth Bloomfield, "We Will Remember Them: The Report of the Northern Ireland Victims Commissioner, Sir Kenneth Bloomfield" (Belfast, The Stationary Office, 1998), p. 14.

49. Quoted in Arthur, *After the Peace*, p. 97.

50. Quoted in Arthur, *After the Peace*, p. 97.

51. Faith and Politics Group, *Forgive Us our Trespasses . . . ?* p. 8.

52. Faith and Politics Group, *Forgive Us our Trespasses . . . ?* p. 17.

CHAPTER 8: THE PROMISE OF RECONCILIATION THROUGH TRUTH AND SOME FORGIVENESS IN SOUTH AFRICA

1. Desmond Tutu, *No Future without Forgiveness* (New York: Doubleday, 1999), pp. 278–79.

2. John de Gruchy, "The TRC and the Building of a Moral Culture," in *After the TRC: Reflections on Truth and Reconciliation in South Africa*, ed. Wilmont James and Linda Van de Vijver (Athens: Ohio University Press, 2000), p. 171.

3. Antjie Krog, *Country of My Skull: Guilt, Sorrow, and the Limits of Forgiveness in the New South Africa* (New York: Times Books, 1999), p. 142.

4. Leonard Thompson, *A History of South Africa*, 3rd ed. (New Haven, CT: Yale University Press, 2000), p. 190.

5. Some of the most important legislation fostering racial segregation in the early twentieth century included a 1913 law defining where blacks and whites could live and work, the 1913

Pass Laws that regulated the movement of blacks, and the 1923 Native (Urban Areas) Act that extended the principle of racial segregation to urban areas. For a comprehensive overview of all major South African statutes enacted from 1910 through the early 1980s that institutionalized racial segregation, see Truth and Reconciliation Commission, *Truth and Reconciliation Commission of South Africa Report*, vol. 1 (London: Macmillan Reference Limited, 1999), pp. 450–66.

6. Truth and Reconciliation Commission, *Commission Report*, vol. 1, p. 195.

7. One of the most important of these was the creation of a of tricameral parliament, giving Indians and Coloureds, but not Africans, their own legislature along with some participation in executive power sharing.

8. Piet Meiring, *Chronicle of the Truth Commission: A Journey through the Past and Present—into the Future of South Africa* (Vanderbijlpark, S.A.: 1999), p. 146.

9. Alex Boraine, "Truth and Reconciliation in South Africa: The Third Way," in *Truth v. Justice: The Morality of Truth Commissions*, ed. Robert I. Rotberg and Dennis Thompson (Princeton, NJ: Princeton University Press, 2000), p. 143.

10. According to the TRC Report, *ubuntu* is generally translated as "humaneness," and expresses itself in the phrase "people are people through other people."

11. The commission's specific tasks were 1) to uncover the truth about gross human rights violations perpetrated from March 1, 1960 to May 10, 1994; 2) to establish the fate or whereabouts of victims; 3) to assist in restoring the dignity of victims by giving them an opportunity to testify about their suffering; 4) to recommend a set of measures of reparation that would help restore the human dignity of victims; 5) to grant amnesty to those who confessed their crimes; 6) to prepare and disseminate a comprehensive report on the commission's findings; and 7) to make recommendations that contribute to the establishment of a humane society and prevent the future violations of human rights. Truth and Reconciliation Commission, *Commission Report*, vol. 1, p. 55.

12. Truth and Reconciliation Commission, *Commission Report*, vol. 1, pp. 110–14. The Commission distinguishes between four types of truth: factual, narrative, social, and restorative. Narrative truth is based on the testimonies and personal written submissions of victims; social or "dialogical" truth is based on an understanding about past events discovered through discussion and debate; and healing or restorative truth is based on an awareness and recognition of objective information that results in a deep moral understanding and public acceptance of past events. My category of moral truth is based on these three types of truth, but especially the last.

13. Truth and Reconciliation Commission, *Commission Report*, vol. 1, p. 114.

14. The members represented a broad cross section of South African society and included seven women, ten men, seven Africans, two Indians, two Coloureds, six whites, six lawyers, and four church ministers. Most had been strongly identified as opponents of the apartheid regime.

15. Krog, *Country of My Skull*, p. 201.

16. The TRC officially began its work in December 1995 and concluded most of its operations in July 1998, when three of its four offices (Johannesburg, East London, and Durban) were closed. After the TRC's final report was published in October 1998, the Cape Town office continued to function with a small staff to support the ongoing amnesty hearings and the drafting of a supplementary report, released in early 2003.

17. Since victims' testimony was not subject to cross-examination, a South African court ruled that the TRC could not arbitrarily identify alleged offenders without first warning them of the charge and allowing sufficient time to contest it in court.

18. Ironically, judges refused to participate in these hearings, claiming that such participation would compromise their judicial independence.

19. The full report and supporting documents are at www.truth.org.za, April 10, 2003 [accessed February 1, 2004].

20. According to the TRC process, amnesty depended solely on three conditions: 1) full confession of crimes; 2) crimes had to be a part of the political struggle over apartheid; and 3) the crimes must have been carried out during the legally prescribed time frame specified by Parliament (March 1960 to May 1994).

21. More than one-third of these applications were rejected because they failed to fulfill the objective criteria necessary for eligibility.

22. Some victims who faced urgent medical needs or were living in destitution were given immediate financial assistance.

23. A person was legally considered a victim if he or she had been classified as such by the human rights committee. The only people eligible for reparations were those who had been mentioned in victim statements before December 15, 1997. Wendy Orr, "Reparation Delayed Is Healing Retarded," in *Looking Back, Reaching Forward*, ed. Charles Villa-Vicencio and Wilhelm Verwoerd (London: Zed Books, 2000), p. 243.

24. The committee recommended that eligible victims receive from 17,000 to 23,000 Rands per year for six years.

25. Nomfundo Walaza, "Insufficient Healing and Reparation," *Looking Back*, p. 254.

26. *New York Times*, April 16, 2003, A5.

27. Tutu, *No Future without Forgiveness*, p. 19.

28. Tutu, *No Future without Forgiveness*, p. 23.

29. Tutu, *No Future without Forgiveness*, pp. 54–55.

30. Truth and Reconciliation Commission, foreword by Chairperson, *Commission Report*, vol. 1, p. 15.

31. Gregory Jones, "Truth and Consequences in South Africa," *Christianity Today*, April 15, 1999, 63.

32. Truth and Reconciliation Commission, *Commission Report*, vol. 1, pp. 126–31.

33. Truth and Reconciliation Commission, foreword by Chairperson, *Commission Report*, vol. 1, pp. 18–19.

34. Wynand Malan, "Minority Position," Truth and Reconciliation Commission, *Commission Report*, vol. 5, p. 442.

35. Truth and Reconciliation Commission, *Commission Report*, vol. 5, p. 351.

36. De Gruchy, "The TRC and the Building of a Moral Culture," p. 171.

37. In the TRC's final report, reconciliation was viewed as a healing process at five levels: 1) acceptance and adjustment to the crimes and injustices of the past, 2) reconciliation between victims and offenders, 3) reconciliation at the community level, 4) promotion of national unity, and 5) reconciliation and redistribution. See TRC, *Commission Report*, vol. 1 (Oxford: Macmillan Reference Limited, 1998), p. 107.

38. Quoted in Boraine, "Truth and Reconciliation in South Africa," in *Truth v. Justice*, p. 143.

39. See, for example, Amy Gutman and Dennis Thompson, "The Moral Foundations of Truth Commissions," in *Truth v. Justice*, pp. 22–44.

40. David A. Crocker, "Retribution and Reconciliation," *Report from the Institute for Philosophy & Public Policy* 20 (Winter/Spring 2000): 6.

41. Timothy Garton Ash, "True Confessions," *The New York Review of Books*, July 17, 1997, 37.

42. Elizabeth Kiss, "Moral Ambition within and beyond Political Constraints: Reflections on Restorative Justice," in *Truth v. Justice*, p. 80.

43. Only about 250 police and security officers applied for amnesty, and only two senior government leaders—law and order minister Adriaan Vlok and police commissioner Johan van der Merwe—did so.

44. P. W. Botha's refusal to testify publicly led the TRC to a court subpoena, which he refused to fulfill. As a result, a trial was held where he was found guilty of obstruction of justice. On appeal, the judgment was reversed because the statute of limitations had run out.

45. John Dugard, "Retrospective Justice: International Law and the South African Model," in *Transitional Justice and the Rule of Law in New Democracies*, ed. A. James McAdams (South Bend, IN: University of Notre Dame Press, 1997), pp. 284–86.

46. Tutu, *No Future without Forgiveness*, p. 23.

47. Rajeev Bhargava, "Restoring Decency to Barbaric Societies," in *Truth v. Justice: The Morality of Truth Commissions*, ed. Robert I. Rotberg and Dennis Thompson (Princeton, NJ: Princeton University Press, 2000), p. 60.

48. Crocker, "Retribution and Reconciliation," p. 6.

49. Fareed Zakaria, *The Future of Freedom: Liberal Democracy at Home and Abroad* (New York: Norton, 2003).

50. D. A. Rustow has observed that the first step in establishing a democratic regime is the development of national unity. He argues that communal solidarity must precede the other three phases of democratization—namely, the acceptance of political conflict, the institutionalization of rules governing political conflict, and the habituation of political struggle. See D. A. Rustow, "How Does a Democracy Come into Existence?" in *The Practice of Comparative Politics: A Reader*, ed. Paul G. Lewis and David C. Potter (Bristol, UK: The Open University Press, 1973), pp. 120–30.

51. Kiss, "Moral Ambition within and beyond Political Constraints," p. 83.

52. Michael Ignatieff, *The Warrior's Honor: Ethnic War and the Modern Conscience* (New York: Henry Holt, 1997), p. 168.

53. The name of the revolutionary group means "spear of the nation."

54. Following the just war doctrine, the laws of war comprise two dimensions—the principles of going to war (justice of war) and the rules of war (justice in war). A war may be morally legitimate but prosecuted in a criminal manner. Similarly, an unjust war can be carried out legally and justly by, for example, targeting only military personnel or using only the minimum force to achieve military objectives. Thus, the ANC's military purposes (the destruction of the apartheid regime) may have been just but the resort to terror, the indiscriminate bombings, and the killing or torture of informants was contrary to the laws of war.

55. Alex Boraine, *A Country Unmasked* (Oxford: Oxford University Press, 2000), p. 326.

56. Kader Asmal, Louise Asmal, and Ronald Suresh Roberts, *Reconciliation through Truth: A Reckoning of Apartheid's Criminal Governance*, 2nd ed. (New York: St. Martin's, 1997).

57. Antjie Krog, *Country of My Skull*, 76.

58. Quoted in Boraine, *A Country Unmasked*, p. 317.

59. Quoted in Boraine, *A Country Unmasked*, pp. 320–21.

60. The court justified its ruling based on the postamble of the Interim Constitution, which set forth the argument for the political and moral reconstruction of the nation. The court argued that amnesty for civil and criminal liability was justified by the postamble's claim that amnesty would encourage truth telling and by the promise of reparations to victims. In addition, the court found that the amnesty provision was not inconsistent with international law, nor did it violate the country's treaty obligations. For a further discussion of the court's ruling, see Boraine, *A Country Unmasked*, pp. 118–21.

61. This report is available at www.gov.za/reports/2003/trc, March 21, 2003 [accessed February 1, 2004].

62. Tutu's emphasis on confession is illuminated by Antjie Krog's moving account of the Winnie Madikizela-Mandela hearings. Winnie, the former wife of ANC leader Nelson Mandela and her small cadre of loyal aides (known as the Mandela United Football Club) had committed human rights abuses, but she had refused to acknowledge culpability. After some witnesses implicated Winnie in the death of a little boy, she refused to accept responsibility for any wrongdoing. Tutu pleaded with her to tell the truth. According to Krog, Tutu said to Winnie: "There are people out there who want to embrace you. . . . If you are able to bring yourself to be able to say: 'Something went wrong . . .' and say 'I'm sorry, I'm sorry for my part in what went wrong.' I beg you. I beg you." After a long silence, Winnie finally accepted responsibility, saying: "I am saying it is true: things went horribly wrong and we were aware that there were factors that led to that. For that I am deeply sorry." See Krog, *Country of My Skull*, pp. 338–39.

63. For a discussion of the role of the TRC in promoting reconciliation, see Charles Villa-Vicencio, "Getting on with Life: A Move Towards Reconciliation," in *Looking Back, Reaching Forward: Reflections on the Truth and Reconciliation Commission in South Africa*, ed. Charles Villa-Vicencio and Wilhelm Verwoerd (London: Zed Books, 2000), pp 200–207.

64. R. W. Johnson, for example, wrote on the release of the commission's final report that the TRC "appeared to have done something for truth but very little for reconciliation." *New York Times*, November 3, 1998, 1.

65. Boraine, *A Country Unmasked*, p. 341.

66. *New York Times*, November 1, 1998, p. 14.

CHAPTER 9: CONCLUSION: TOWARD A THEORY OF POLITICAL FORGIVENESS

1. Lewis Smedes, *The Art of Forgiving* (Nashville, TN: Moorings Publishing, 1996), p. 556

2. Patrick Glynn, "Toward a New Peace: Forgiveness as Politics," *Current* (March/April 1995): 19.

3. Carlos Santiago Nino, *Radical Evil on Trial* (New Haven, CT: Yale University Press, 1996), pp. 186–87.

4. Elazar Barkan, *The Guilt of Nations: Restitution and Negotiating Historical Injustices* (New York: Norton, 1999), p. xix.

5. Gary Jonathan Bass, *Stay the Hand of Vengeance: The Politics of War Crimes Tribunals* (Princeton, NJ: Princeton University Press, 2000), pp. 20–36.

6. These tribunals were established by the victorious allied powers to hold German and Japanese military and political leaders responsible for "crimes of aggression," "war crimes," and "crimes against humanity." The development of this latter category of crimes was a major contribution of the World War II military tribunals to the development of international humanitarian law.

7. In 1993, the Security Council, at the encouragement of the United States, established the International Criminal Court for the Former Yugoslavia in order to prosecute political leaders and military officers responsible for war crimes and crimes against humanity committed during the Bosnian War. A year later the Security Council added an ancillary court to the Hague Tribunal to deal with the 1994 Rwanda genocide. Although the United Nations International Criminal Court for Rwanda is headquartered in Arusha, Tanzania, its work is directed from The Hague.

8. Bass, *Stay the Hand of Vengeance*, p. 284.

9. Geoffrey Robertson, *Crimes against Humanity: The Struggle for Global Justice* (New York: The New Press, 2000), p. 237.

10. The legal basis for the International Criminal Court (ICC) was established with the signing of the Rome Treaty of 1998 and the subsequent ratification of that convention by sixty states. The court formally came into being in July 2002 and became functional in 2003 with the creation of an institutional structure and staff.

11. Susan Jacoby, *Wild Justice* (New York: Harper & Row, 1982), p. 345.

12. Bass, *Stay the Hand of Vengeance*, p. 297.

13. Bass, *Stay the Hand of Vengeance*, p. 287.

14. These two emphases—popular support and inherent goodness—have given rise to different perspectives. For some communitarians, such as Michael Walzer, justice derives from the widely shared values and habits within each political community. The common good does not derive from some ideal conception of justice but from the shared understandings and traditions that inform the political life of each society. Thus, communal norms of the common good are morally legitimate because they are widely affirmed by society. For other communitarians, such as Michael Sandel, however, the common good derives not from the widespread belief in a tradition but from the moral worth or intrinsic good of the goals themselves. For a discussion of these two perspectives see Michael J. Sandel, *Liberalism and the Limits of Justice*, 2nd ed. (Cambridge: Cambridge University Press, 1998), pp. x–xi.

15. Michael J. Sandel, *Democracy's Discontent: America in Search of a Public Philosophy* (Cambridge, MA: Harvard University Press, 1996), p. 5.

16. George Weigel, *Tranquillitas Ordinis: The Present Failure and Future Promise of American Catholic Thought on War and Peace* (New York: Oxford University Press, 1987). Weigel borrows the concept of *tranquillitas ordinis* from St. Augustine's *The City of God*.

17. In her book *The Need for Roots*, Simone Weil argues that the fundamental need in society is for public order, which she defines as "the first need of all." Simone Weil, *The Need for Roots: Prelude to a Declaration of Duties toward Mankind*, trans. Arthur Wills (Boston, MA: Beacon Press, 1952), p. 11. As a result, when social and political order is threatened, whether or not from internal threats or external aggression, the first moral duty of the state is to protect society. The German poet Goethe similarly held that peace and political order were indispensable to human dignity. He once observed: "If I had to choose between justice and disorder, on the one hand, and injustice and order on the other, I would always choose the latter." Quoted in John G. Stoessinger, *Henry Kissinger: The Anguish of Power* (New York: Norton, 1976), p. 14.

18. Robert Meister, "Forgiving and Forgetting: Lincoln and the Politics of National Recovery," in *Human Rights in Political Transitions: Gettysburg to Bosnia*, ed. Carla Hesse and Robert Post (New York: Zone Books, 1999), p. 144.

19. William Safire, *Lend Me Your Ears: Great Speeches in History* (New York: Norton, 1992), p. 439.

20. Meister, "Forgiving and Forgetting," p. 139.

21. Meister, "Forgiving and Forgetting," p. 140.

22. Meister, "Forgiving and Forgetting," pp. 139–41.

23. In special circumstances—such as the Nuremberg and Tokyo Military Tribunals and more recently the creation of the United Nations Criminal Tribunals in The Hague—courts may attempt to prosecute leaders for war crimes and crimes against humanity. The establishment of the International Criminal Court (ICC) created a judicial body that could in the future prosecute leaders for war crimes if their own states refuse to do so.

24. For a discussion of this point, see David Rieff, "A New Age of Imperialism?" *World Policy Journal* (Summer 1999): 5–6.

25. Soon after Pinochet was declared medically unfit to stand trial in March 1990, he was allowed to return to Chile. A Chilean court sought to prosecute Pinochet, but the Chilean Supreme Court ultimately ruled that he was not medically fit to stand trial.

26. For a critique of the notion of universal jurisdiction, see Henry Kissinger, *Does America Need a Foreign Policy? Toward a Diplomacy for the 21st Century* (New York: Simon & Schuster, 2001), pp. 273–82. For a penetrating moral critique of the concept of crimes against humanity and its related notion of universal jurisdiction, see John D. Carlson, "Trials, Tribunals, and Tribulations of Sovereignty: Crimes against Humanity and the Imago Dei," in *The Sacred and the Sovereign: Religion and International Politics*, ed. John D. Carlson and Erik C. Owens (Washington, DC: Georgetown University Press, 2003), pp. 196–232.

27. This discussion of "thick" and "thin" moralities is based in part on Michael Walzer, *Thick and Thin: Moral Argument at Home and Abroad* (Notre Dame, IN: University of Notre Dame Press, 1994), pp. 1–19.

28. Avishai Margalit, *The Ethics of Memory* (Cambridge, MA: Harvard University Press, 2003), pp. 50–51.

29. Margalit calls this limited collective memory "common," to differentiate it from "shared" memory, pp 50–51. Margalit, *Ethics of Memory*.

30. Michael Walzer observes that because of this "thin" universal morality people from different societies "can acknowledge each other's different ways, respond to each other's cries for help, learn from each other and march (sometimes) in each other's parades." Walzer, *Thick and Thin*, p. 8.

31. A war, for example, is not simply the aggregation of violent acts of its soldiers but the result of collective action by the state, forcing duties and obligations on its members. Thus a state's antiterrorist campaign against rebel insurgents is a public act resulting in collective responsibility.

32. Reinhold Niebuhr, *Moral Man and Immoral Society: A Study in Ethics and Politics* (New York: Scribner), 1960.

33. For General Balza's admission of collective guilt, however, he was criticized by the country's president and senior military leaders and subsequently removed from the prestigious army officers' club in Buenos Aires.

34. A peacekeeping force of the Economic Community of the West African States (ECOWAS), led by Nigeria and backed by the United States, eventually intervened in Liberia after its president, Charles Taylor, agreed to give up power. The aim of the peacekeeping force was not to resolve the dispute or even to seek justice but simply to halt the politically motivated killing that had claimed tens of thousands of innocent civilians and resulted in widespread suffering throughout the region. Since Taylor was allegedly responsible for widespread human rights crimes, a UN criminal tribunal indicted him in the Ivory Coast in 2003, but he is now under the protection of the Nigerian government.

35. Politically it was impossible to challenge the constitutionality of the amnesty decree because the Chilean armed forces remained politically powerful until 1990, when they voluntarily relinquished power.

36. This had been the situation in the 1990s in several West African states, including Liberia, Ivory Coast, and Sierra Leone, and was the situation in Rwanda in 1994 when Hutu militia perpetrated one of the deadliest genocides in history against Tutsis.

37. Alexander Solzhenitzyn, "Repentance and Self-Limitation in the Life of Nations," in *From Under the Rubble,* ed. Alexander Solzhenitzyn et al. (Boston, MA: Little, Brown, 1974), pp. 133–34.

38. Solzhenitzyn, "Repentance and Self-Limitation," p. 134

Index

Hiroshima and Nagasaki in Japan by, 226; racial discrimination in, 19; reparations for Japanese American detainees during World War II, 32–33
Uruguay: amnesty law *(Ley de Caducidad)* of, 22, 236n13; prosecution of former regime offenses in, 39

vengeance: as form of accountability, 8; motives and destructiveness of, 55, 78, 92–97
Verbitsky, Horacio, 127
Verwoerd, Wilhelm, 30, 83, 97
victims: ambiguous nature of memory in forgiveness by, viii–ix, 44–45, 88; independent role in forgiveness for, 57–58; inward restoration of, 56–58; opportunity to "tell their story," 230; personal rehabilitation as reparation, 33–34; prerogative to forgive of, 81–83; primary, 82–83; secondary, 82–83; tertiary, 82–83
Videla, Jorge, 124, 252n31
Villa-Vicencio, Charles, 82
Viola, Robert, 114, 124–25
violence: state-supported forms of, 23; theories of political violence, 172–74
Volf, Miroslav, 15, 44, 48, 52, 70, 72, 87, 91, 104
von Weizsäcker, Richard F., 1, 7, 25, 234n1

Waldron, Jeremy, 32
Walzer, Michael, 216

Weigel, George, 105, 216
West Germany, partnership with the U.S., 5, 100
"We Will Remember Them" (Bloomfield), 185
Widgery, Lord, 184
Wiesel, Elie, 6, 41
Wiesenthal, Simon, 13–15, 66
Wilde, Alexander, 159
William of Orange, 167
Wilson, Gordon, 182–83
Wilson, Marie, 182–83
Wink, Walter, 66
Wolterstorff, Nicholas, 43, 78
World Trade Center, terrorist attacks of, 83
World War II: funds and lands confiscated during, 33, 89, 238n47–48, 238n51; internment of Japanese-Americans in the U.S. during, 32–33; Japanese policy of denial of atrocities committed during, 20; myth of a unified French resistance during, 20; suppressed Nazi memory after, 20; U.S. policies of reconstruction after, 100
wrong doings: effects of, 43, 56 moral inequality resulting from, 43–44, 54, 56

Yugoslavia, 214

Zakaria, Fareed, 205
Zalaquett, José, 9, 24, 77, 15

About the Author

Mark R. Amstutz is professor of political science at Wheaton College in Illinois.